The Wines of Canada

The Wines of Canada

by John Schreiner

MITCHELL BEAZLEY

To Marlene, a wonderful wine touring companion,
who contributes her support and sound judgment to all of my wine books.

First published in Great Britain in 2005
by Mitchell Beazley, an imprint of
Octopus Publishing Group Limited,
2–4 Heron Quays, London E14 4JP.

A CIP catalogue record for this book is available from the British Library.

ISBN: 1 84533 007 2

The author and publishers will be grateful for any information which will assist them in keeping future editions up-to-date. Although all reasonable care has been taken in the preparation of this book, neither the publishers nor the author can accept any liability for any consequences arising from the use thereof, or the information contained therein.

Printed and bound in England by Mackays, Chatham.

Contents

Acknowledgments

I would like to salute Mitchell Beazley for commissioning this book. This is very likely the first international publisher to discover that the wines of Canada are to be taken seriously. I acknowledge the generosity of the wine producers across Canada who, as a group, provided the time, the information, and the extensive tastings necessary for this book. Too many to list here, they are all named in the text.

For additional valuable insights into the Ontario wine industry, I thank Dr. Helen Fisher, Dr. Linda Bramble, and Dr. Andy Reynolds of Brock University and Steve Gill, Dan Peterson, and Jim Warren of Niagara College; Linda Watts of the Wine Council of Ontario; Debbie Zimmerman, chief executive of The Grape Growers of Ontario, Donald Triggs of Vincor International; John Peller of Peller Estates; wine consultant Peter Gamble; vintner Donald Ziraldo; Dan Taylor, the economic development officer of Prince Edward County; Geoff Heinricks, a wine-grower in the county.

I also acknowledge the help of Penny Athans and her colleagues at the British Columbia Wine Institute; and of C William Ross, president of the Canadian Vintners Association; and of L'Association des Vignerons du Québec. In the Atlantic provinces, Hans Christian Jost provided guidance in addition to welcoming me at his two properties. Valuable guidance on viticulture was provided by Lloyd Schmidt of International Viticultural Services; Richard Cleave, the Okanagan's most seasoned vineyard manager; Alain Breault, a vineyard consultant in Québec; and John Warner, a leading Nova Scotia grape-grower.

Key to star ratings

*****   Leading producer
****   Highly recommended
***   Range includes wines of special interest
**   Average quality
*   Everyday wines

1

Introduction

A Canadian businessman found himself hosting a small dinner at a hotel in Britain's Yorkshire Dales in 2003. He was astonished to find that the wine list included a Chardonnay from British Columbia's Mission Hill Family Estate winery. When he ordered it, the sommelier complimented him on his choice and volunteered that the Mission Hill red was even better. A decade earlier, it is inconceivable that any Canadian wine would have been available, much less praised, in rural Yorkshire, nor in many other places outside Canada. Aside from Icewine, not many good wines were being grown in Canada before 1990. However, fifteen years later, Canada has a wine industry for the world to discover and take seriously. "There is every reason to believe that we can challenge countries like New Zealand and Australia, and areas such as Oregon and Washington," believes John Peller, the chief executive of the country's second-largest winery, Andrés Wines.

It is a small industry, more on the scale of that of New Zealand, which is the viticultural model for a number of Canadian wineries. Only a few regions in Canada are suitable for premium wine grapes. The limits for viticulture are being tested in other regions, notably Québec and eastern Ontario, where remarkably daring grape-growers are establishing the world's only wine region based on hybrid vines bred in Minnesota for extreme winter hardiness.

New wineries are being established at a rapid rate across the country. As an example of this pace, British Columbia, the second largest wine region, had thirteen wineries in 1984 and thirty-five in 1994; currently, around 135 are open or under development. Ontario's expansion is comparable. The majority of wineries have been started either by small growers or by passionate newcomers to wine-growing. Significantly, the newcomers include professionals and investors from outside wine-growing who are investing capital in an industry that is still not well financed. In a handful of recent examples, seasoned French wine producers have invested in ultra-premium wine projects, the beginning, perhaps, of the Old World's validation of Canada's potential.

In contrast to the Old World's rigid rules of appellations, Canada is a viticultural kaleidoscope where little is fixed. Grape varieties that grow thousands of miles apart in Europe might easily be found in adjoining rows in Canadian vineyards. Canada has not had to time to sort out the ideal terroirs for the many varieties being grown. John Peller, among others, cautions against rushing toward what he sees as Europe's confining rules.

THE REGIONS

There is much to distinguish Canada's wine regions, which are spread across four time zones, from each other. The largest area of vineyards, 7,100 hectares, is in Ontario and encompasses three quite distinct regions. Most of those vines grow in the Niagara region around the southwestern shore of Lake Ontario, only an hour's drive from Toronto. The grape-growing area is about 43° North, roughly the same latitude as Tuscany. The growers consider this a cool climate region but, because of the hot-water bottle effect of Lake Ontario, there is abundant heat to ripen most vinifera varieties. On average, the maximum summer temperature reaches 24°C (75°F), with short periods when the heat and humidity spike above that. Autumn is generally dry and prolonged, with a temperature range of 6–16°C (43–60°F). Including snowfall, there is enough annual precipitation (an average of seventy-two centimetres/twenty-eight inches) for irrigation not to be required. Consequently, vineyards succeed with such varieties as Chardonnay, Riesling, Syrah, Pinot Noir, Gamay, and even the Bordeaux reds, including Cabernet Sauvignon. The risk around Lake Ontario arises from winters that are occasionally cold enough to kill vines; and from late spring frosts, should a mild March wake up the vines. Such weather events in the winters of 2001–2 and again in 2002–3 reduced the Niagara crop to about half of its potential.

Ontario's second largest winegrowing region, now about 400 hectares, is on the flat farmland of southwestern Ontario, beside Lake Erie, and thirty to forty-five minutes from Windsor and its US twin across the St Claire River, Detroit. This includes Pelee Island, one of several agricultural islands in the lake between Canada and the USA. These vineyards grow in the southernmost extension of Canada; it lies as far south as the wine regions of northern California and enjoys comparable heat units. The mean daily temperature in July is 22°C (72°F), with daytime spikes approaching 30°C (86°F) accompanied by clammy humidity. The growing season arrives about two weeks earlier than in the Niagara Peninsula, giving vineyards more than 200 frost-free days a year. Growers can mature the major vinifera varieties, including the Bordeaux reds. Again, there is a winter risk. Lake Erie, which is much shallower than Lake Ontario, captures enough heat to extend the autumn, but freezes in winter and does nothing then to moderate the climate. In compensation, the region's heavy snowfalls often provide insulation for the vines.

The smallest wine region is Prince Edward County, about 200 hectares, a peninsula on the northwestern shore of Lake Ontario, about two and a half hours east of Toronto. The county has some of Ontario's finest Burgundy-type limestone soils and the majority of the vineyards grow Pinot Noir and Chardonnay. But the winter risk is greater here than elsewhere in Ontario because the lake freezes around the peninsula. There is nothing to temper the cold winter winds that sweep off the lake and over the vineyards. Here, most growers bury the lower portion of the vines each fall to bring them through the winters. As arduous as this is, the promising quality of the wines from this new region make it worth the effort.

In British Columbia, most of the 2,200 hectares of vineyards are in the Okanagan and Similkameen Valleys. These neighbouring valleys are about five hours east of Vancouver by highways that snake spectacularly through two mountain ranges. In addition to providing scenery, the mountains block nearly all of the coastal storms, giving the valleys a hot, dry climate where the vineyards must be irrigated. Average precipitation in the Okanagan is about thirty centimetres (twelve inches) a year. Most of the vineyards of the Okanagan, a valley that stretches 160 kilometres (100 miles) from north to south, are in the southern half of the valley, part of which is true desert with sage brush and rattlesnakes. In the Similkameen, to the west of the Okanagan and separated from it only by a moderate band of mountains, the climate is similar. The daytime temperatures in July and August usually exceed 30°C (86°F) and occasionally reach a blistering 40°C (104°F). Because the sky is typically cloudless in summer, the heat of the day is not retained at night (unlike in Ontario), resulting in a diurnal swing in temperature. The comparatively cool nights benefit the wines by retaining flavours and acidity that would otherwise be burned from the grapes. Most of the vineyards are planted on benches that tip gently toward one of the Okanagan's four major lakes or toward the valley bottom between the lakes.[1] This geography creates superb conditions for growing nearly all of the major varieties from Auxerrois to Zinfandel. There is little disease in the dry growing season; long days with intense sunlight promote growth and ripening while the cool nights preserve fruit flavours in the grapes. The risk comes from frost in late spring or early autumn; vulnerable vineyards rely on wind machines to drive the frigid air into the bottom of the valley, where no one grows grapes successfully. Historically, there have been periods of vine-killing winter temperatures about once in a decade. There is some speculation that global warming is making these less severe.

The vineyards in the Okanagan and the Similkameen Valleys have more in common with those of eastern Washington State than with other Canadian regions. The same grape varieties flourish on both sides of the border, showing comparable profiles in the wines, notably peppery Syrah, juicy Merlot, elegant Cabernet Sauvignon, and citrus Chardonnay. The average age of Washington vineyards now is twenty to twenty-five years, about double that of the more recently replanted Okanagan. There is every reason to agree with John Peller of Andrés that British Columbia's wines can be as distinguished as those of Washington State.

The coolest Canadian regions are those on the two coasts. Vancouver Island gets its long, cool, and occasionally wet season from the influence of the Pacific Ocean; Nova Scotia and Prince Edward Island's somewhat comparable seasons are influenced by the Atlantic Ocean. In both regions, the vineyard microclimates (which, between the two regions, comprise perhaps 400 hectares) are found in the protective lee of modest mountain regions that deflect inclement weather but trap the heat of the summer sun. Only certain grape varieties – often not the mainstream ones – will succeed. That does not stop the determined from planting varieties such as Pinot Noir and Chardonnay. In Nova Scotia's Annapolis Valley, where most vines are grown, the daily July temperatures average

---

1. Bench is a geological term used to describe a terrace on the side of a river or lake which at one time formed its bank.

about 19°C (66°F) and some vineyards host Burgundy varieties, though most grow hybrids developed for cooler climates. The most reliable white in Nova Scotia is L'Acadie Blanc, a grape that was developed in Ontario but did not succeed there. In the Annapolis Valley, the variety yields crisp, fruity whites with a grapefruit zestiness sometimes recalling Sauvignon Blanc or an unoaked Chardonnay. The most reliable red varieties are French hybrids, notably the full-bodied Maréchal Foch with its smoky, cherry flavours.

Excellent wines can be produced from the Burgundy varieties if grape growers go to extraordinary lengths in the vineyards, including cropping for very low yields. Several vineyards in coastal British Columbia, as an example, jump-start the vines in the spring by covering them for a week or two with plastic tents, creating a greenhouse effect to accelerate growth. With July high temperatures averaging only 24°C (74°F) in the Cowichan Valley (where most vineyards are), growers need to grab all the heat they can. The technique works: British Columbia's most expensive Pinot Noir, made by Venturi-Schulze Vineyards of Cobble Hill, is started under tents each spring on Vancouver Island. The bread-and-butter wines on both coasts are from less familiar varieties. The most reliable white on Vancouver Island is Ortega, a German crossing of Müller-Thurgau and Siegerrebe. It ripens early, producing wines that range from dry to slightly sweet, but invariably tasting of spice and apricots.

The most challenging region for viticulture is Québec. The growing season is hot enough to mature grapes: maximum high in the townships east of Montréal averages 25°C (77°F) in July. However, the season is too short for late-ripening varieties. The continental winters can be cold enough to kill both *Vitis vinifera* and French hybrid vines. Few of Québec's vineyards try to grow vinifera; many of the growers bury the lower portions of their vines each autumn under protective layers of earth, which are removed each spring when risk of frost has passed. An increasing number of Québec vineyards are growing the so-called Minnesota hybrids, varieties developed under the direction of the University of Minnesota. A few vineyards grow other hybrids developed in Québec, which, like the Minnesota, are so resistant to severe cold that the vines need not be buried. Needless to say, the wines of Québec are distinct. The white wines – the workhorse grape is Seyval Blanc, a French hybrid – are crisply refreshing, sometimes with bracing citrus acidity but with moderate alcohol. The red wines – and there are exceptions to this generalization – are lean and bright with flavours sometimes recalling cranberries, and with more than enough acidity. The personality of the wines sometimes recalls young Beaujolais. As more than one Québec vintner will say, perhaps in a defensive tone that is not necessary, these are "honest" wines.

Signature wines are found in each region. Ontario makes remarkable Rieslings in a style rivalling Australia or Alsace and Cabernet Francs that could grace tables in the Loire. British Columbia's Okanagan Valley is succeeding with red Bordeaux varieties, but also with Gewürztraminer and Pinot Gris. Both regions produce Chardonnay and, more recently, Pinot Noir wines of internationally competitive quality. Elsewhere, varieties that are not well-known internationally are producing credible table wines. Examples include Nova Scotia's crisply fruity L'Acadie Blanc whites and Vancouver Island's refreshing Ortegas. Québec, meanwhile, has become a proving ground where the new hybrid vines from Minnesota will live or die. In nearly all regions, superb Icewine is being made.

In addition to grape wineries, a large number of fruit wineries, cider-makers and even mead houses have opened. While most of the fruit wineries serve local markets, often with sales only from the cellar door, a handful have begun to export. Perhaps the most significant fruit product to emerge in Canada in the past decade is ice cider. Developed in Québec and now made across the country, ice cider vies for a place of prestige beside Icewine. Ice cider is virtually exclusive to Canada because apples need an even harder freeze than grapes.

2

From whisky to wine

Some wineries in Canada have made wine good enough to be taken seriously for fewer than twenty-five years. Canada arrived so late among the world's wine producers for several reasons but, most fundamentally, because for a long time Canadians preferred beer and spirits.

The French, who were the first Europeans to settle in Canada, found native grape vines. However, these *Vitis labrusca* and *Vitis riparia* vines yielded wine so poor that even the Jesuit missionaries disdained to use them for sacramental wines. Instead, breweries and distilleries sprang up. A rum distillery was established in 1769 in what is now Québec. In Ontario, extensive grain farming supported the production of whisky. In the 1840s, at the same time as James Busby was planting vinifera vines in Australia, there were about 200 distilleries in Lower and Upper Canada (as Québec and Ontario were formerly called). On the Canadian frontier, whisky was the tonic that fortified individuals during great exertion and against brutally cold winters. By all accounts, including the rabid writings of nineteenth-century temperance advocates, consumption was heavy. Even Canada's founding prime minister, Sir John A Macdonald, indulged in what his biographer called "gargantuan" drinking bouts. On such barren ground, a wine culture scrabbled in futility.

The first winery was created by Johann Schiller, a mercenary from the Rhine who settled around 1811 near modern-day Toronto on land he had been granted for his military service. Finding native vines on his property, he developed a small vineyard. He sold wine to his neighbours but the venture was dubious. "Wine simply could not compete in popularity with the plentiful and cheap whisky and beer that were consumed in large amounts," wrote William F Rannie, the author in the 1970s of books on Ontario wineries and Canadian distilleries.[1]

The passion that drives wine-growing surfaced again in 1864 when Count Justin M de Courtenay assembled a consortium of Toronto's social bluebloods to form the Vine Growers Association. The count, who wrote two pamphlets on vineyards and winemaking, established Château Clair. He appears to have been the first Canadian vintner to show off his wines in France. The wines, made with North American grapes, got surprisingly good comments ("pure and of excellent quality"). However, the Vine Growers Association, despite operating under a twelve-year tax holiday, did not succeed either.

Vineyards continued to be planted in both the Niagara region and near Windsor, the major vineyard areas today in Ontario. The varieties were primarily *Vitis labrusca*, since *Vitis vinifera* plantings failed when the European vines came up against phylloxera and mildew, to which they had no resistance. The most successful grape was the Concord. Bred in the USA in 1843, it was quickly adopted by Ontario growers. "In terms of vigor, hardiness, disease resistance, productivity, and beauty of fruit, it outshone anything else then in cultivation," wrote Philip M Wagner, an American viticultural authority.[2] Concord and its labrusca relatives, while woefully unsuited for dry table wines, continued to be planted in Ontario and in British Columbia through to the early 1970s.

Gradually, a wine industry arose, based on Concord and similar grapes. Invariably, the wines were sweet, similar to ports and sherries, because that was what Canadians drank – when they drank wine at all. George Barnes established a winery bearing his name in 1873 near St Catharines. One of his most successful wines was Golden Diana, a sweet, fortified sherry-style wine made with labrusca whites. The brand survived until 1982. (The winery itself closed a decade later.)

During the 1920s, Ontario wineries even imported a substantial tonnage of Concord grapes from New York State to meet an unexpected demand for their wines, caused by the Canadian experiment with Prohibition. Canada's two-fisted whisky drinking spawned a vigorous

1. Rannie, William F, *Wines of Ontario, An Industry Comes of Age*, WF Rannie, Lincoln, Ontario, 1978, p.48.

2. Wagner, Philip M, *Grapes into Wine*, Alfred A Knopf, New York, 1976, p.39.

temperance movement. In 1916 the federal government, in conjunction with the provinces, was persuaded to impose temperance nationally, ostensibly so that the distillers could produce industrial alcohol for the war effort. Prohibition was not lifted in Ontario until 1927.

SURVIVING PROHIBITION

Ontario's grape-growers, however, had a friend in the province's United Farmers party, which was in government and which agreed to exempt wine from Prohibition, under the condition that wineries sold only at the cellar door, in five-gallon minimum quantities or sold wine as tonic on prescription. Since there were few other legal alcoholic beverages, wine sales increased 100-fold and the number of licensed wineries increased to fifty-one from twelve. Ontario wine (along with whisky and beer) was also being smuggled into the dry USA, since Canada had not banned the production of alcoholic beverages, but only their sale. Export was permitted to markets where drinking was allowed. In reality, most Canadian spirits consigned to the Caribbean were shipped to the USA.

It would be charitable to describe the quality of the wines being made in Ontario during this period as variable. After the Ontario government established its liquor retailing monopoly in 1927, its ministry of health provided training in making wine. For the most part, Canadians returned to beer and spirits as Prohibition ended and the wineries consolidated. T G Bright of Niagara Falls, formed in 1874, bought fourteen other winery licenses and set out to raise wine quality. The company hired a French technical director named Adhémar de Chaunac. Not happy with wine from labrusca grapes, he arranged in 1938 to import winter-hardy French hybrid vines with much better winemaking properties. The war delayed shipment, but in 1945 de Chaunac secured thirty-five hybrids and four vinifera varieties, including Chardonnay. Over the next few years, vineyard and winemaking trials identified the successful ones. Beginning in the 1960s, Canadian vineyards were converted to varieties such as Maréchal Foch, Seyval Blanc, Verdelet, and Vidal. The most widely planted of the reds was Seibel 9549, which was renamed De Chaunac. Unfortunately De Chaunac grapes yield wines that are serviceable at best: the variety remains only in Canadian vineyards where vinifera do not ripen.

Efforts to grow vinifera grapes were haphazard. The trial plantings done at government research vineyards in Ontario and in British

Columbia's Okanagan Valley invariably failed. The researchers, to a man, did not think that European grapes could survive Canadian winters. Paradoxically, European varieties now dominate the vineyards while most of the hybrids are gone. There are two explanations for this. The growers in the 1950s, including the government researchers, did not understand how to grow vinifera successfully; today's growers do. Secondly, winters have become warmer.

BABY DUCK AND LOCAL "LIEBFRAUMILCH"

Even with no better raw materials than hybrid and labrusca grapes, the Canadian wine industry began expanding in the 1960s. A new generation of consumers – including European immigrants and war veterans who had acquired the taste during World War II – started drinking wine as well as beer and spirits. The wines seldom bore any resemblance to those of Europe. Cyril Ray, the noted British wine critic, advised his readers after tasting Canadian wines in 1965 that almost any cheap vinifera wine from Europe or South America was better. The best-selling wines in British Columbia were fruit-flavoured, while those in Ontario were gin-flavoured. The single largest selling wine in the 1960s was Baby Duck, a low-alcohol sparkling wine made with a Concord base.

Increasingly, Canadian wine consumers showed a preference for imported wines, even when these were more expensive than domestic wines. To preserve market share, Canadian wineries restyled their table wines in the European mould, right down to the brand names. Wines appeared such as Canadian Liebfraumilch, which became Rhine Castle to avoid a suit from the German wine industry; or Schloss Laderheim, an off-dry white in a hock bottle with Germanic script on the label. Dozens of other pseudo-labels appeared: Sommet Blanc, Toscano, Alpenweiss, Schloss Weinberg, Capistro, Tollercranz, La Rienha, Nietzscheim, and many more, none of them Canadian place-names. The quality of the wines seldom rose to international standards.

Canadian wine began turning the corner in about 1975. That year, Ontario awarded the first new winery licence in fifty years to Inniskillin, a winery with vineyards of its own. At the time, it was rare for any Canadian producer to own its own vineyard or even to exercise much control over the quality of fruit grown by independent growers. After Inninskillin, estate wineries emerged in Ontario as well as in British

Columbia, Nova Scotia, and Québec. Not all succeeded but those that did, often with wine made from newly planted European vines, showed the first genuine promise of decent wines.

KICK-STARTING THE NEW

In the end, the catalyst for overhauling Canadian wine quality was the shock of the 1989 Free Trade Agreement with the USA. That agreement, along with an overlapping world trade agreement, stripped away the protected status, such as preferred listings and lower prices in provincial liquor stores, enjoyed so long by mediocre Canadian wines. In a free trade environment, wine made with De Chaunac or Verdelet simply could not compete with imported Cabernet Sauvignon or Chardonnay. Many hybrid vines were pulled up from vineyards in Ontario and British Columbia, and some wineries closed.

Since then, vineyards have been replanted with mainstream grape varieties, often with vines originating in European nurseries. The signature vines of Bordeaux, Burgundy, Alsace, the Rhône, and Germany are all growing now in Canadian vineyards. Lesser-known *Vitis vinifera*, like Bacchus, Ortega, and Madeleine Angevine, have been planted in more marginal climates. A few hybrid varieties have survived, notably Vidal for Icewine and Maréchal Foch, a variety that makes big, bold reds when grown correctly. In Québec, Canada's most marginal wine-growing province, valiant efforts are being made with various winter-hardy hybrids. Along with planting appropriate wine grapes, Canadian wineries hired well-trained vineyard managers and winemakers, giving them modern winemaking tools. To cite a simple but crucial example, new French and American oak barrels have replaced the used bourbon barrels once found in so many Canadian wineries.

The impact on quality has been huge. In 2002, for example, the Okanagan's CedarCreek Estate Winery entered two Chardonnays in the Los Angeles Country Fair, the oldest wine competition in the USA. In the heart of the New World's Chardonnay country, gold medals were given to six Chardonnays – including both the CedarCreek wines.

The profile of Canadian wine is muddied, however, by the way many wineries are allowed to blend imported wines with domestic wines that then go to market masquerading as Canadian. The practice has been embedded in Canadian wine production since at least the 1960s, justified then by the lack of good wine grapes. Concord was the most widely grown grape in Ontario while Bath, another labrusca hybrid variety, was grown extensively in British Columbia's Okanagan Valley. But vinifera grapes such as Mission and Zinfandel were available by the carload from California and made the sort of table wines that consumers had begun to demand. Wineries found it more economic to import grapes rather than make the major investment required to improve domestic viticulture. Governments allowed this, provided accommodations were reached with domestic growers. Consequently, wineries both in Ontario and British Columbia agreed to process the majority of the domestic wine grapes in exchange for the right to use imported grapes or imported bulk wine.

The 1970s was a decade when grape-growers prospered. Wineries fought to retain domestic market share with a plethora of blends; and the foreign-sounding pseudo-labels, as the industry called them, were disdained by connoisseurs but kept Canadian wineries alive.

"CELLARED IN CANADA"

The major wineries renewed the argument for continued imports of bulk wine (few still import fresh grapes) when there was a massive uprooting of labrusca and hybrids in Ontario and British Columbia between 1988 and 1992. Growers were encouraged by payments from the government to rid vineyards of varieties unsuited to making premium wines. This created a shortage of wine grapes which would not be remedied until replanted vineyards were in production. The large wineries began importing bulk wines from Chile, South Africa, California, and Australia. To take advantage of an emerging demand among consumers for Canadian wine, the imported bulk wines were labelled either "Product of Canada" or "Cellared in Canada".

Some discipline was imposed by the Wine Content and Labelling Act in Ontario, which took effect in 2001. It requires that wineries importing bulk wine put at least thirty per cent domestic wines into "Cellared in Canada" blends (this was lowered temporarily in 2003 to ten per cent after severe frost reduced the harvest by half). "Product of Canada" blends must contain a minimum of seventy-five per cent domestic wine. A similar rule has not been imposed in British Columbia, where some wineries sell wines as "Bottled in British Columbia" while indicating the country of origin. In both provinces, these wines are sold in government and private liquor stores as Canadian wine, although British Columbia places wines made entirely from domestic grapes in dedicated displays in its liquor stores.

The confusion for both consumers and uninformed restaurateurs has been compounded by the use of colour-coded labels. An example is Vincor's successful Jackson-Triggs brand: a black or gold label adorns many of the grown-in-Canada wines but a white label is used if imported wines constitute most of the blend. The success of the white label wines, often value-priced, benefits significantly from the award-winning quality of the black and gold label wines.

THE VQA PROGRAMME

The most reliable guide for consumers is that the majority of wines made exclusively from Canadian grapes bear the VQA decal of the Vintners Quality Alliance. The VQA programme was launched in 1989 in Ontario and adopted shortly thereafter in British Columbia. The VQA regulations embody winemaking standards and appellation rules similar to those found in any mature wine-growing region. All wines seeking the VQA decal are screened by professional tasting panels so that substandard wines do not reach the market. In Ontario, the VQA standards are now enforced by legislation. In British Columbia, membership of VQA has been voluntary. Some of the leading wineries in British Columbia (such as Blue Mountain, Venturi-Schulze and Kettle Valley) do not apply for the VQA seal even though all make wines only with British Columbia grapes and use appropriate appellations on their labels.

This anomaly is the result of an unfortunate rift between the wineries, a rift which has frustrated efforts to develop a national wine standard for Canada. In 2005, the British Columbia government imposed a provincial wine authority on the fractured industry. Neither Québec nor Nova Scotia have been brought under the VQA umbrella as yet, primarily because both regions grow many varieties not yet accepted for VQA production. Most wineries, however, use the appropriate geographic indicators. These may not be legally enshrined appellations but they provide the necessary reassurance that the wines are made from Canadian grapes.

All Meritage wines in Canada must also be VQA certified. The term "Meritage" was created in 1988 by a group of California wineries who wanted a premium wine name that was better than "Red Table Wine" and that did not infringe on French appellation language. Only Bordeaux grape varieties can be used in Meritage wines. Primary permitted varieties for Red Meritage are Cabernet Sauvignon, Cabernet Franc, Merlot, Malbec, and Petit Verdot. Primary varieties for white Meritage are Sauvignon Blanc, Sémillon, and Sauvignon Vert. In 1993 Harry McWatters of Sumac Ridge winery secured permission for Canadian use of the Meritage term for blends from Bordeaux grape varieties. Non-VQA wines that are Bordeaux blends may be released under various proprietary labels.

It is the VQA wines and the other wines made from Canadian grapes that drive the rising reputation of Canadian wines. Ironically, they constitute perhaps twenty per cent of the wine produced or bottled by Canadian wineries. Because it is profitable and even critical to the well-being of large wineries, it will be a very long time before some producers stop processing imported bulk wine.

3

Vincor: global wine group

On an Air Canada flight from Toronto to Vancouver in the early 1980s, Edward Arnold, then president of TG Bright, spotted a competitor on the aircraft and offered to buy him a glass of wine. Because Bright's wines were on board, he refused the French wine that the flight attendant wanted to serve. A few minutes later, the attendant returned with six small bottles of Bright's wines, saying: "You may as well have them all – nobody else wants them." The demand for domestic wines on Canada's flag-carrier was so lukewarm at the time that cabin crew referred to the wines as "million milers" because the bottles seldom left their carts.

That was then. This is now: TG Bright is one of the constituents of Vincor International, the first company in the history of Canadian wine to become an international success. Vincor dominates the Canadian wine scene. It is the fourth largest wine group in North America. It owns wineries in the USA, Australia, and New Zealand, as well as having interests in South Africa. Some of Vincor's premium Canadian wines are made by joint ventures with two leading French producers; one makes burgundy-style wines in Ontario and the other makes a bordeaux-style red in British Columbia. Because Vincor operates globally, the company has begun selling significant volumes of Canadian wines to sophisticated markets in the USA, Europe, and Asia. Vincor's success powerfully validates the Canadian wine industry. The company would never have taken its place among the world's leading wine producers if Canadian wines had remained at the quality of the million-milers.

Vincor was established in 1994 but its family tree begins in 1874 with the Niagara Falls Wine Company, established by Thomas Bright, who in 1911 changed the name to TG Bright & Co. In 1933 a wealthy distiller named

Harry Hatch took over the company. Foreshadowing what Vincor did sixty years later, he began consolidating the fragmented industry, gradually taking over a quarter of Ontario's wineries, most of which were struggling. Each winery licence included the right to operate a retail store, allowing Brights to create a critically important network of its own wine stores.

Hatch recognized that there were almost no qualified professionals then working in the Ontario wine industry. He hired a Virginian food chemist, Dr John Ravenscroft Eoff, as winemaker, and Adhémar de Chaunac, a French-born microbiologist, as his assistant. De Chaunac took over when Eoff died in 1940. De Chaunac recognized that he needed to replace the labrusca-based wine grapes in the vineyards that Brights owned or controlled if he was going to make decent table wines. He asked for, and got, a substantial research budget that enabled him in 1947 to import thirty-five French hybrid varieties and four vinifera: Chardonnay, Pinot Noir, Riesling, and Perle of Csaba.[1] He was joined in this venture by the Horticultural Research Institute of Ontario. The trials they undertook identified the varieties on which the Canadian wine industry based itself for the next forty years. One of the red hybrid varieties was named for de Chaunac in 1972, just before he died. Brights may well have done more research and development than any other Canadian winery. A subsequent research director estimated in the early 1980s that the company had spent $3m on research, including the evaluation of 600 grape varieties, in the previous half century.

The Vincor family tree also includes two other Ontario wine producers that were once significant in their own right. One was Jordan, established in 1920 in the village of that name between the Niagara Escarpment and the western end of Lake Ontario. Jordan had a succession of owners, including the Seagram distilling family, until 1972 when it was purchased by the Rothmans tobacco group of South Africa and the UK. The following year, Jordan took over the Growers' winery in Victoria and called the new national company Jordan & Ste-Michelle Cellars. Brights acquired this company in 1986, closing all of the wineries to consolidate production in Brights facilities. The heritage buildings in the village of Jordan, some dating from 1870, are now occupied by Cave Spring Cellars, an independent boutique winery founded in 1986.

1. Perle of Casaba is a white cross with Muscat flavours, thought to have originated in Hungary. Because it ripens early, it was widely used in Canadian grape breeding programmes from the early to mid-twentieth century.

The other important Ontario winery in the Vincor history was Canadian Wineries, later known as Château-Gaï, formed in 1928 by the merger of several small wineries. Château-Gai was run from 1936 until 1964 by a former newspaper advertising salesman named Alexander Sampson, who took to travelling to Europe after the war. "The great weakness of Canadians in relation to wines and spirits is that too many of us never learned to consume them while eating," he opined in 1950, in an assessment with which no one would argue. In 1955 Sampson hired a shop window in Paris for what was undoubtedly the first display of Canadian "Champagne" in France. The publicity photographs, snapped up by newspapers in Canada, lifted Château-Gai's sales in Canada, if not in France. The French, having just won a court case in Britain to protect the name of Champagne, promptly sued Château-Gai in Canadian courts. The Canadian wine industry finally agreed in the 1990s to respect French appellations because, without that agreement, Canadian table wines and Icewine could never be sold in Europe.

Several years after Sampson died in 1964, the winery was taken over by John Labatt, a major brewer making a big plunge into the wine business. By the mid-1970s, Labatt controlled both Château-Gai and the Casabello winery in British Columbia. In 1976, Labatt had taken over a struggling winery in California called Lamont Cellars and sent Donald Triggs, one of its rising vice-presidents, to turn it around. Born in 1945, Triggs grew up on a Manitoba farm. With degrees in agriculture and business administration, he joined the Labatt wine division after acquiring marketing skills at Colgate-Palmolive. At Lamont, he ran a winery crushing more grapes than the entire Canadian industry crushed at the time. "It was a fabulous experience," he recalls. "I got to understand the California industry from a different per-spective." With Lamont profitable by 1982, Triggs accepted an offer to run the Vancouver-based North American operations of Fisons, a UK fertilizer company. The job appealed to him but he also was drawn back to Canada by his innate nationalism. As a university student he had circulated petitions supporting the creation of a Canadian flag. "The water ran deep when it came to my sense of Canada," he says.

The water also ran deep when it came to the wine business, even after Fisons promoted him to the UK, where he became a director and ran one of its divisions. "I've always had this yearning to be in my own business," Triggs says. "And I really had a twinge in my bones for the wine business." In 1989 Labatt decided to exit from the turbulent wine industry. Triggs returned from the UK and set his sights on Cartier Wines (the remaned Château-Gai group). It had major wineries in Niagara Falls and in the Okanagan Valley, annual sales of $50 million and just enough profit to convince Triggs and his associates – twenty-four Cartier managers and about twenty employees – that they could make it work. They did it on a shoestring, with a $22.5 million bank loan and only $2.25 million in equity. "It was a stretch," he admits. Triggs raised the money by selling his ski chalet and re-mortgaging his home. "The first year, and going into the second year, was all about survival."

Many told him, he recalls, that he was nuts to take such a risk. Conventional wisdom had concluded that the Canadian wine industry was doomed to be crushed by imported wines following the free trade agreement with the USA. "I saw competition as a blessing," Triggs says. He believed that the desire for survival would spur growers to plant better grape varieties. He calculated that the government would have to fund the transition because it had created the industry crisis by negotiating a trade agreement that removed historic protections. Like Harry Hatch in 1933, Triggs saw there would be a chance to consolidate the industry. And as a savvy wine marketer, he calculated that wine consumption was set to rise in key New World markets. The baby boomers – the term that describes people born in the decade after World War II – were getting ready to indulge their well-travelled tastes and their disposable incomes in wine. By the new millennium, it has become clear that he was correct. "Per capita consumption is growing," he notes. "That's the rising tide that makes all of us look good."

Cartier merged with Inniskillin Wines in 1992 and then with Brights in 1993. The company, already Canada's largest wine producer, was renamed Vincor International. Consumers, however, know it by its various brands, notably Jackson-Triggs, named for Triggs and one of his partners, Allan Jackson, a winemaker who had started in Labatt's research department in 1977. The new Vincor, soon a well financed company with stock exchange listings, has acquired additional wineries since then. Some, like the now-closed London Winery, were purchased for the retail store licenses, echoing the Hatch strategy. To give a national reach to the iconic Inniskillin brand, Vincor acquired struggling Okanagan Vineyards at Oliver in 1996 and transformed it into Inniskillin Okanagan. Fours years later, in 2000, Vincor purchased Sumac Ridge Estate Winery and Hawthorne Mountain Vineyards, two of the Okanagan's best mid-sized wineries.

GOING INTERNATIONAL

With the Canadian elements in place, Vincor moved towards a series of international acquisitions: RH Phillips of California in 2000; Hogue Cellars in Washington in 2001; Goundrey in Australia in 2002; Kim Crawford Wines of New Zealand and Amberley Estate of Australia in 2003; and, in 2004, Western Wines, the UK wine merchant that owns South Africa's Kumala brand. "We have a strategy of developing a New World wine portfolio," Triggs says. There is obvious synergy between these wineries and Vincor's Canadian wineries. "We can give better attention to our whole portfolio than if we were just selling Canadian wine." There also is a useful exchange of knowledge among the wineries. For example, Tom Seaver, senior winemaker at the Jackson-Triggs winery in Ontario, has spent at least one crush at Goundrey in Australia.

Vincor has invested heavily in its Canadian wineries and vineyards. The Jackson-Triggs winery, a modern structure of gleaming glass and stainless steel, opened in 2001 near Niagara-on-the-Lake, either replacing or supplementing the old Brights and Château-Gai wineries. In British Columbia, the winery that Brights built in 1981 near Oliver has been almost entirely rebuilt and more than quadrupled in size since 2001. More fundamental to making good wine are the vineyards that Vincor developed in the Okanagan since 1997, when it began planting the hot, sandy benches near Osoyoos. Vincor now controls about 400 hectares in the Okanagan, most of it on long-term lease from the Osoyoos Indian Band. The grapes grown are entirely vinifera, including red and white Bordeaux varieties, Syrah, Viognier, Chardonnay, and one of Canada's first plots of Zinfandel.

All of this has born fruit in awards and recognition. Jackson-Triggs was named the best Canadian winery competing at both the 1999 and 2000 International Wine and Spirits Competitions in London. It won similar awards at Vinitaly in 2002 and 2003, and at the San Francisco International Wine Competition in 2001, 2002, and 2004.

For all the attention these awards bring to Canadian wines (which are still often for Icewine), two of Vincor's most important moves to get Canada noticed are joint ventures that have involved French producers in making top-notch Canadian wine. In Ontario, Le Clos Jordanne is being developed near Jordan by Vincor and the Boisset family of Burgundy, with Chardonnay and Pinot Noir wines due to be released in 2005. In the Okanagan, the

Osoyoos Larose winery, a joint venture winery with Bordeaux's Groupe Taillan, released its first wine in 2004 to considerable acclaim.

Vincor initiated both of these ventures. "We sat down strategically and we said we believed we could benefit from their technical expertise," Triggs explains. "We started in Burgundy because we believe that Pinot Noir and Chardonnay are the varieties that in the long term are going to be the best in Ontario. We went knocking on doors. We went to see three or four people." Boisset responded favourably. Its Jaffelin subsidiary had already made wine in Ontario jointly with Inniskillin. The Bordeaux group was enticed to the Okanagan because the vineyards there are best suited to Bordeaux varieties.

In both ventures, Vincor has allowed its French partners to call the technical shots, from buying and planting vineyards to equipping and staffing wineries. Vincor's initial expertise lies in marketing the wines. "And we are going to school," Triggs says. "It has been fabulous for us." The entire Canadian wine industry benefits as Vincor's efforts bring notice to what Canada can achieve today.

4

Viticulture today

The dramatic improvement in the quality of Canadian wine reflects the upheaval in viticulture that began when meaningful plantings of *Vitis vinifera* began to replace French hybrid and *Vitis labrusca* vines in Ontario and British Columbia. Formerly, many growers cropped the vines heavily because both hybrids and the labrusca gave prodigious yields. Growers had little incentive to reduce yields because they were represented by marketing boards empowered to require wineries to buy what was being grown. Even when wineries began negotiating grape quality standards, those standards had no teeth until the early 1990s. Until then, grape-growing was not very different from growing other crops where the objective is to maximize yields.

One of British Columbia's most experienced growers, Richard Cleave, began managing vineyards for absentee owners on the Okanagan's Black Sage Road in 1975, before any vinifera was planted there. The hybrid varieties under his care produced up to eighteen kilograms (forty pounds) of grapes from each vine. "High quantity, low quality," Cleave says now. The wines from those grapes were so mediocre that Cleave seldom drank them. In the early 1990s, when he planted vinifera in his own Phantom Creek Vineyard, he showed he could grow good wine. The vines, carefully selected clones, are planted on vigour-reducing rootstock, with much denser spacing in the vineyard, to produce only 1.3 kilograms (three pounds) of grapes from each vine. Sandhill Wines, which participates with him in making critical vineyard decisions, makes powerful wines from the grapes. Cleave signs each bottle and now maintains a personal wine cellar. His story is the microcosm of the transformation in grape-growing.

ARRIVAL OF THE CLONES

The first recognized clone of a *Vitis vinifera* grape in Canada was the Weis 21B Riesling which had been selected and fostered in a Mosel nursery. It began to be planted in 1976, both in Ontario and in British Columbia, and remains the dominant Riesling clone in Canada. Once 21B began proving itself in Canadian vineyards, some growers began searching for other good vinifera clones.

The world's best clonal selection programme was (and still is) at Montpellier in the south of France, at the Etablissement National Technique pour l'Amélioration de la Viticulture, or ENTAV. Set up in 1962, it collects and propagates superior cultivars in a precise scientific environment. It has generated many good clones which are released to nurseries only when the plants are free of viruses. In 1987, in response to a growing Canadian interest in planting vinifera, a group of French nurseries sent a large selection of clonal material to be grown under quarantine in Canada. By 1991, when Canadian vineyards began a major conversion to vinifera, a good stock of virus-free vines had been certified by Canadian authorities.

Cautiously, the Canadian government keeps a tight lid on its approvals. For example, there are more than fifty clones of Pinot Noir available through ENTAV but only ten have approval to be imported into Canada. However, the French clones – the most widely planted in Canada is Dijon Clone 115, capable of producing rich, full-bodied wine – are proving to be superior to earlier clones that came to Canada from California and Germany. Quails' Gate Estate Winery in the Okanagan, one of Canada's top Pinot Noir producers, first turned to California in 1987 to obtain Davis clones 1 and 2. Late ripeners, they now "serve their purpose in the blend," as winemaker Grant Stanley puts it. In 1990, Quails' Gate added early ripening German clones, 91R and 93R, which bring power and chunky tannins to the blends. But the Dijon clones that Quails' Gate planted in 1996 – 667 and 777 as well as 115 – have proven a significant step forward. "These are the real deal," Stanley says. "Low vigour, small berries and bunches, great tannin structure and elegance." There is another reason that growers favour clone 115: it is reliably hardy in winter.

While there is a limit to the number of available clones, those that are available are, for the most part, superior performers. Nine clones of Merlot are approved for Canadian vineyards, the most widely planted of which, in both Ontario and British Columbia, are 181 and 347. These were specifically chosen for the Osoyoos Larose vineyard in British Columbia, the joint venture with Vincor that is directed technically by the French partners. Pascal Madevon, the winemaker at Osoyoos Larose, contends that those are the best Merlot clones in Bordeaux and they are not disappointing anyone in Canada. The same is true of Cabernet Sauvignon: of the four French clones so far approved for Canada, the most successful, 169 and 191, are also strong in Bordeaux. Of the seven authorized Cabernet Franc clones, the most widely planted are 214 and 327. Only one clone each has been approved for Malbec (598) and Petit Verdot (400), but both are making good wine. Madevon, who spent fifteen years making wine in Bordeaux before coming to British Columbia, believes that the Petit Verdot he made in 2004 is the best he has ever tasted.

The selection of French clones currently approved for import to Canada has supported the massive conversion of the major Canadian vineyards to better vines. However, the nurseries have recently applied for additional approvals to address needs that have become apparent. For example, most believe that the selection of Syrah, plantings of which are expanding rapidly, is too limited and does not include the best clones. Only French clones 99 and 100 are approved. ENTAV's catalogue of French clones dismisses both as producing "weakly structured wines". Also available is what growers call clone 7. This is believed to have arrived in California from Australia. After being propagated at a Washington State research station, some clone 7 vines were brought into British Columbia in 1992 by vineyard consultant Lloyd Schmidt, who now thinks it may just be another version of clone 100.

An adequate selection of clones in the vineyard gives the winemaker a richer palette of flavours. "It is almost unanimous that the best wines are made from a blend of all the clones," contends Schmidt. Now based in Ontario, Schmidt has imported French clones for growers in every region of Canada since setting up his company in 1988 in Niagara. When a vineyard grows several clones, they are seldom, if ever, inter-planted in Canadian vineyards as field blends. "The wineries plant them separately, harvest them separately, and ferment them separately," Schmidt explains. "Then barrel selections of all the clones are taken, especially for making reserve blends."

Invariably, Pinot Noir is the variety with the greatest mix of clones in vineyards, followed by Chardonnay. Ten French clones of Chardonnay are approved for Canadian vineyards, with the most widely planted being 76, 95, 96, and 548. ENTAV's catalogue speaks well of them all: 76 makes "well-balanced aromatic fine wines" while 95 makes "full, rich and balanced wines." Clone 96 yields "nervous, balanced and aromatic wines" and 548 makes "meaty wines with complex aromas." Some Ontario and British Columbia vineyards also have substantial plantings of 809, more frequently called Chardonnay Musqué because the resulting wines may show a fruitiness that recalls Muscat grapes. Some Canadian vineyards also grow Chardonnay that was sourced in the USA and may be the low-yielding Wente clone. However, the clonal identification of vines sourced from the USA is not as reliable as ENTAV identification. "I don't know what we were getting from California," admits Schmidt, who began importing vines into British Columbia in 1981. "It was all screwed up."

ROOTSTOCKS
When the growers in Canada began replacing hybrid vines with vinifera, they also had to make decisions regarding rootstock and vine density. Vinifera vines are planted on their own roots only where the risk of killing winter frosts seems greater than the phylloxera risk. Ungrafted vines that freeze to the ground can perhaps be regenerated from their roots to bear fruit again; but when grafted vines freeze to the ground, regeneration is from rootstock which bears no fruit.

Currently, fifteen rootstocks are approved for Canada. The choices depend on the vineyard sites and on the productivity demanded of the vines. The SO4 rootstock (Selection Oppenheim 4, named because it emerged from Germany's Oppenheim research station) promotes vigorous yields. In Ontario, most Vidal vines are grafted onto SO4 since the variety needs to be vigorous to stand up to the stress of producing Icewine grapes. When grafted onto other varieties, SO4 is chosen for the least fertile soils. In the Osoyoos Larose vineyard, for example, the only block of vines on SO4 is on poor, stony soil. In the light, sandy vineyards of Black Sage Road, across the Okanagan Valley from Osoyoos Larose, SO4 is the rootstock of choice because it best survives nematode damage, caused by tiny worms that chew on hair roots. "You need a fairly vigorous rootstock to compensate for the damage that the nematodes do," says vineyard manager Richard Cleave.

In the more fertile soils elsewhere in the Okanagan and in Ontario, growers often plant vines grafted to such vigour-reducing rootstocks as 3309 Couderc, 101-14, and Riparia Gloire. Each has disadvantages as well as advantages. For example, 3309 Couderc has no resistance to nematodes while 101-14 tolerates nematodes but does not handle drought well. Drought tolerance is not a concern in the arid British Columbia interior because all vineyards are irrigated, of necessity. Pascal Madevon, the Osoyoos Larose manager, suggests that a south Okanagan vineyard without water would be dead within a week. Elsewhere in Canada, where there is more rain, irrigation is the exception.

GETTING CLOSER

To keep vinifera vines from over-abundant production, growers are planting more densely than in the hybrid days. Prior to 1990, it was common to find three to four metres (ten to twelve feet) between rows, along with an ample 1.5 to two metres (five to six feet) between each vine. The hybrids still yielded prodigiously at less than 2,400 vines per hectare, and it was easy to manoeuvre machinery through the rows. Densities like this are still found in many Nova Scotia vineyards, the majority of which still grow hybrids.

To yield more full-flavoured wines, vinifera must be cropped less heavily, which can be achieved by green harvesting. If only to save costs, growers also control production by using appropriate rootstocks and planting more vines per hectare. The most common density in Ontario and British Columbia vineyards is about 3,300 vines per hectare. Rows are spaced 2.4 metres (eight feet) apart, with 1.2 metres (four feet) between each vine.

There is, however, a trend towards higher densities, sometimes much higher. One new vineyard in Ontario, with perhaps the highest density in Canada, has nearly 7,000 vines per hectare. "The jury is still out over whether it is going to work," says consultant Schmidt, warning that it is challenging to cultivate vines in such close quarters and to deal with disease. The more typical close density is that chosen by the Bordeaux consultants for Osoyoos Larose in British Columbia: at 2.1 metres (seven feet) between rows, it is growing close to 4,000 vines per hectare. Quails' Gate's more recent Pinot Noir vines are grown at about 5,200 vines per hectare. A similar density can be found in Québec vineyards, but for a practical reason: high density compensates for the inevitable winter kill.

5

Icewine: Canada's calling card

Most wine regions have signature wines: Sauvignon Blanc in New Zealand, for example, or Shiraz in Australia, Riesling in Germany, and Grüner Veltliner in Austria. For Canada, it is Icewine, a tour-de-force wine that has won more international awards for more Canadian wineries than any other style. "We think it is the flagship for Canadian wine internationally, as well as in Canada," says Donald Triggs, chief executive of Vincor International. Canadian wine struggled to be taken seriously until Icewine impressed informed palates. Reif Estate Winery's 1987 Vidal Eiswein (as it was labelled at the time) is believed to have been the first Canadian wine to be reviewed favourably by the influential American critic Robert Parker. After tasting an unsolicited sample from the winery, he added it to his list of best wines tasted in 1989. Then Reif's neighbouring winery, Inniskillin, astonished the trade when its 1989 Vidal Icewine took the Grand Prix d'Honneur, the top award, in competition at the 1991 Vinexpo in Bordeaux.

In earlier years, Canadian wineries had boasted of awards from dubious competitions or engaged in stunts meant to impress a gullible home market. In one of the most brazen, the Château-Gai winery of Niagara Falls put its "Champagne" and its "Sauternes" on display in a Paris shop window in 1955. Photographs and a press release about this "coals to Newcastle" effort were circulated to the media in Canada. A subsequent profile of winery owner Alexander Sampson in the magazine of the Toronto *Globe and Mail* newspaper was headlined: "He sells Ontario's wines in the very heart of France". In fact, all Sampson did was infuriate the French, who spent the next generation litigating to ban French appellation terms from Canadian wines. Indeed, Canadian wine began selling in Europe without restriction only after 2001, when Canada signed an agreement to respect European appellation names. What facilitated that agreement was the mutual desire of European and Canadian wineries to enforce each other's Icewine standards.

Knowledge of Icewine was brought to Canada by Europeans. The first person credited with making an Icewine in Canada was Walter Hainle. A German textile salesman who had grown up near Stuttgart, he took up hobby winemaking after emigrating to British Columbia. In 1973, he made Icewine opportunistically when an early winter froze the Okanagan vineyard from which he bought grapes. He began making it regularly, once even using a commercial freezer. (Hainle judged the result unsatisfactory and never repeated this method.) His hobby turned into a profession when he planted a vineyard near Peachland, in the North Okanagan, and sent his son, Tilman, to a wine school in Germany. When they opened Hainle Vineyards in 1988, the wine shop offered the first commercial Canadian Icewine, from the 1978 vintage. The winery continues to make Riesling Icewine, invariably in quantities of a few hundred litres each vintage. Even if Canada's winters enable commodity-scale production of Icewine, Tilman Hainle believes that it is an "oxymoron" to make this rare wine in quantity.

Annual production of Icewine in Canada averages 500,000 to 900,000 litres, primarily from Ontario. "Our major strategy in Icewine is Ontario-based because Ontario has a much more reliable freeze," explains Vincor's Triggs, whose wineries make the largest volume of Canadian Icewine, and some of the best. He is referring to the legal requirement that the grapes must be frozen naturally at −8°C (18°F) or lower before being picked. "Ontario gets two or three such freezes each winter. The Okanagan gets one freeze and usually it is quite short."

The predominant Icewine grape in Canada is Vidal and most of it grows in Ontario. The variety has fallen out of favour for table wines (the wine is good, but Chardonnay is better and sells for twice the price). However it makes superb Icewines, rich and aromatic, with luxurious tropical fruit favours. "Vidal is in that magical area of not making a really great table wine but a phenomenal Icewine," Triggs says. "I did the maths once. If you took all of the Vidal in Ontario and did not use any of it for table wine, converted all of it to Icewine, you would have 100,000 nine-litre cases. That is without planting a grape." He calculates that the current quantity of Vidal Icewine (other varieties are also used) is about 35,000 cases. In some of Ontario's better vineyard sites, Vidal has been replaced with premium vinifera varieties for table wine. That is not a threat to Icewine, however. "Vidal will thrive in a lot of secondary sites," Triggs points out. "This is a grape that can produce an enormous profit for the grower on sites that are unsuitable for vinifera. The margins are still good for the grower and the winery. So we think it has a great future."

IN THE BEGINNING

The first efforts at making Icewine in Ontario were comic. TG Bright, a Niagara Falls winery now absorbed by Vincor (*see* page 15), had a research scientist named John Paroschy who studied at Geisenheim in the 1970s and picked up knowledge of Eiswein. On his return to Brights, he made an experimental lot of Vidal Icewine in 1979. However, the winery forfeited the chance of releasing Ontario's first Icewine, when, as Paroschy recalls, "the owners took it all home". Brights was a few years behind its competitors; its first commercial release was the 1986 vintage. In an era when so many Canadian wines sported European names, it was labelled Eiswein.

While Paroschy's employers were savouring his experiment, the real work of launching Canadian Icewine emerged in 1983 from the circle of German-speaking winemakers around Austrian Karl Kaiser, co-founder of Inniskillin. Grapes were left on the vines into the winter at Inniskillin. They were also left at three other locations: the neighbouring vineyard operated by Ewald Reif; at Hillebrand Estate Winery, where the consultant was a German winemaker, the late Bernhard Breuer; and at Pelee Island in south-western Ontario, where the general manager was Austrian Walter Strehn.

Strehn was the only one to net his grapes against birds, since Pelee Island in Lake Erie is situated not far from an important bird sanctuary. All of the Inniskillin and Reif grapes were eaten by birds before they could be picked. Hillebrand picked quickly, before all of its Vidal was lost, and placed the grapes in cold storage. When the weather turned cold enough in mid-December, the grapes were brought out to freeze naturally. Hillebrand pressed a small quantity, making the first Niagara Eiswein in 1983. In the following year, Inniskillin, Hillebrand, and Reif all had nets.

Strehn, meanwhile, had netted eight rows of grapes in 1983. Predictably, birds became entangled. The government's conservation officers dismantled the nets and charged Strehn with trapping out of season. However, he salvaged enough grapes to make some Icewine. He also got the charges dropped and, the following year, bought netting with a tighter mesh so that fewer birds would be ensnared.

A market for Icewine now had to be developed. The Liquor Control Board of Ontario returned a shipment of Pelee Island's 1983 Vidal Icewine after finding almost no buyers at $12.50 a bottle. The winery, a few miles across the river from Detroit, turned to markets in the USA, setting a pattern for the industry: acclaim in export markets established the credibility and the viability of Icewine, since the domestic market is small.

EASTERN PROMISE

The single biggest market is Asia, where the sales breakthrough followed the 1991 Vinexpo award to Inniskillin. Icewine is tailor-made for Asia. It is a luxury wine, beautifully packaged, that appeals to Asia's gift-giving cultures, and to palates still attuned to sweet wines. Inniskillin's Donald Ziraldo, an indefatigable salesman, soon had his Icewine in Hong Kong and Singapore boutiques and in duty-free stores. Other producers quickly followed. Charles Pillitteri, whose Niagara winery became a major Icewine producer, opened a huge market in Taiwan, with sales briefly touching $1 million a year in the late 1990s before local entrepreneurs rushed in with cheap, simulated products that mimicked real Icewine right down to fake Canadian labels. Stamping out fraudulent Icewine remains an unresolved problem in Taiwan and China. Fortunately for Canadians (and also for European Eiswein exporters), Japan, Singapore and Korea police the authenticity of wines in their markets.

Canada's rising popularity with Asian tourists has also translated into Icewine sales. Two of the most visited destinations are Banff in the Rockies and Niagara Falls in Ontario. In both instances, tour buses pass through or near wine regions en route to the resorts. Large wineries go to considerable lengths to make purchasing easy, from having tasting room staff who speak Mandarin, Cantonese, and Japanese, to delivering purchases from stock warehoused in Asia so that tourists need not carry it home themselves.

Asian buyers have often sought out Canadian wineries, as was the case with Vineland Estates, one of Ontario's best Icewine producers. In 1992 Allan and Brian Schmidt, the adventurous brothers who run Vineland, organized an expedition to the North Pole by dog sled. At a wine writer's suggestion, they took a case of Icewine with them. At their destination they toasted success with one bottle and brought the rest back for comparative tastings against similar wines that had not travelled from Vineland's cellar. (The tastings were entertaining but the results were inconclusive.) An account of the Schmidt expedition in a wine magazine was read by a Japanese wine buyer, who promptly placed the first of many continuing Asian orders for Vineland's Icewine.

GRAPES AND GROWING

While Vidal is the dominant Icewine grape in Canada, other varieties are also used. In the Okanagan, where almost no Vidal remains in the vineyards, Riesling is the variety of choice. Several wineries make Icewine with Ehrenfelser or Kerner – two German white varieties with Riesling antecedents yielding flavours recalling ripe pineapples – or with Pinot Blanc or Chardonnay, with flavours running from ripe melon to peach. In Nova Scotia, Icewine is made both with Vidal and with an American hybrid called New York Muscat. The latter gives a somewhat theatrical Icewine, that rises to a crescendo of exotic spice flavours and aromas. Red Icewine is made, typically, with Cabernet Franc, which has tough-skinned grapes that will stay on the vines when other varieties have fallen to the ground. Other reds used occasionally for Icewine are Pinot Noir, Merlot, Cabernet Sauvignon, and Zweigelt. In 2003, Pillitteri made Icewine for the first time with Chambourcin, a dark-coloured French hybrid. Red Icewines typically display the tastes and aromas of such red fruits as cherries and currants in the case of Cabernet Franc and strawberries in the case of Pinot Noir. The wines have a slightly firmer, more tannic, impression than white Icewines.

Québec wineries making Icewine (called *vin de glace* in French) – usually with Vidal – face unusual challenges. On the one hand, there is no doubt that it will get cold enough in December to freeze the grapes, perhaps even too hard. On the other hand, the severe cold might also kill the vines unless the bottom canes, bearing next year's buds, are placed on the ground and covered with an insulating layer of earth. Several winries, such as Vignoble du Marathonien, have solved this problem by training the vines so that there are fruiting canes on both upper and lower wires (*see* page 234). The upper zone is tightly enclosed in netting, protecting the grapes from the birds. Grape clusters on the lower cane are cut off and also placed inside the net, and the lower cane is buried. The upper canes are sacrificed to winter but all of the grapes are frozen naturally, allowing Québec wineries to make Icewine in conformity to Canadian and European rules. Because the technique is so laborious, no Québec producer makes much Icewine.

In style, Canadian Icewine is quite distinct from German Eiswein. This goes beyond the difference in the major varieties used (Vidal in Canada; Scheurebe, Silvaner, and Riesling in Germany). Canadian wines have more alcohol (eleven degrees compared with eight to nine degrees in Germany) and at times they can have more residual sugar. The explanation lies in the climate. Higher summer temperatures in Canadian vineyards produce grapes with more sugar while the colder freezes, on average, allow winemakers to extract sweeter musts. One of the first vintners to discover that was Klaus Reif, who came from Germany in 1987 to help his uncle, Ewald, establish Reif Estate Winery. Five years earlier, he made his first Eiswein while still an apprentice winemaker in Germany. The must had a sugar concentration of thirty-six degrees Brix. In Ontario, he could get much sweeter must – as high as fifty-one degrees Brix – by freezing riper grapes at lower temperatures. It determined his style. "I just believe in a heavy Icewine," he says. "I love German Eiswein. It is very elegant and a very pleasant wine to drink. But you drink a Canadian Icewine and you say 'Wow!' It is like a powerhouse."

There is a trade-off. Canadian Icewines, especially those made with Vidal, are unlikely to have the racy acidity of German Eiswein, which is still held by connoisseurs as the benchmark for this style of wine. Generally Canadian Icewines have enough acidity to ensure that they are pleasantly balanced, but not enough for prolonged ageing. German vintners speak of laying down Eiswein at the birth of a child, to be opened at the child's twenty-first birthday. Canadian Icewine is best in its exuberant youth, when the flavours and aromas are bursting with fruit, and should be consumed within seven to ten years of vintage. Old Icewine appeals to those who like sherry.

OTHER CANADIAN DESSERT WINES

Other dessert wines struggle to be noticed under the long shadow of Icewine. Not infrequently, the late harvest wines are a corollary, made from grapes not frozen hard enough to make Icewine or made from second pressings of Icewine grapes. Even after the extraction of Icewine must, a surprising amount of juice remains in the blocks of frozen grapes. Vintners permit these to thaw partially before pressing them again and drawing off juice of an adequate quality for simple late-harvest wines. On rare occasions, a third pressing occurs but the quality of the juice is marginal.

A number of producers, such as British Columbia's CedarCreek, have chosen to make late harvest wine rather than Icewine. Such vintners have decided it is not worth risking a plot of grapes on the uncertain arrival of an

Icewine freeze, when the grapes can be picked in November, with the certainty of making a marketable wine. Late harvest wines sell for half the price of Icewine, however, the unfrozen vineyards will yield at least twice as much late harvest wine. Some winemakers, not all of whom enjoy making Icewine, like the convenience of finishing every vintage before Christmas.

Botrytized dessert wines are also produced, more often in Ontario where the nearby lakes provide the misty mornings in which *Botrytis cinerea* – a fungus which dehydrates grapes and concentrates flavours by drawing off water through the skins – thrives. The grape varieties most commonly used are Riesling and Gewürztraminer. Vidal grapes are so thick-skinned that they are seldom attacked successfully by botrytis. In the much drier climate of the Okanagan Valley, botrytis is rare, with the exceptions of a handful of vineyards overlooking Okanagan Lake near Kelowna. In particular, Quails' Gate is well-regarded for a botryized dessert wine made with Optima grapes.

The varieties for late harvest wines are usually the same as those used for Icewine. However, some producers have access to, or are growing, Muscat varieties dedicated for dessert wines. Jeff Martin of British Columbia's La Frenz winery, took his inspiration from Australia's Rutherglen Muscats when he planted Muscat varieties for a wine he calls Alexandria.

Wineries in every region of Canada make port-style wines (and occasionally counterparts of sherry or madeira), either by fortifying them as the Portuguese do, or by pushing alcoholic fermentation as far as possible. (Most wine yeasts die when the alcohol reaches sixteen degrees but it is possible to nurse a few more degrees from the yeast by gradually adding sugar during fermentation. Recently, new yeasts tolerant of high alcohol have also been developed.) Since Portuguese grape varieties are almost never grown in Canada, wineries use varieties at hand. The most common port varieties are the French hybrids, such as Maréchal Foch and Baco Noir, because they ripen to high sugars, are full-flavoured, and dark in colour. In recognition of European rights to geographic indicators, Canadian producers have had to be creative in naming these wines. For example, Sumac Ridge's port-style wine (originally made with Chancellor grapes but now made with red vinifera) is called Pipe. Hainle's version is called Fathom and Andrés has made a comparable wine called Dune. Because the market for these wines is limited, only small volumes are made, typically for cellar-door sales only.

6

Niagara: Ontario's largest wine region

In 1970, there were only eight wineries in Ontario, and the province (unlike the community of Ontario, California) did not even rate a mention in Hugh Johnson's *World Atlas of Wine*. Today, there are fifty-one Ontario producers making wine from local grapes, another thirty-nine are licensed to make fruit wines and additional wineries are under development. The majority are in the Niagara region, a suburbia-interrupted terroir with rare grape-growing qualities wrapped around the southeastern end of Lake Ontario. Only an hour's drive from Toronto, Canada's largest city, the Niagara region now offers compelling wine tourism. "In the future, Niagara Falls will become a secondary tourist attraction to wine," predicts Norman Beal, whose Peninsula Ridge winery at Beamsville is one of the growing number of destination wineries. "People will know Niagara for great wines just as Niagara Falls is known now as the seventh wonder of the world."

The Ontario wine industry has become globally competitive in a remarkably short period of time. Beginning in the 1980s and especially since 1990, Ontario wineries have done what was needed to be taken seriously. "A world-class wine region needs world-class infrastructure," says Dan Pederson, principal of Niagara College. In 1997 Ontario began to train its own winemakers at Brock University's Cool Climate Oenology and Viticulture Institute in St Catharines, and in 2000 started to offer similar training at nearby Niagara College. According to one estimate, seventeen per cent of Ontario winemakers now are Brock graduates.

Well-equipped new wineries have opened, often as destinations like Peninsula Ridge, with restaurants to showcase the wines. The only one of the 1970 wineries still in its original (totally renovated) building is

i. Ontario

Andrés Wines – but the company presents its consumer face with two destination wineries near Niagara-on-the-Lake, Peller Estates and Hillebrand.

Equally important, the Ontario wine industry has mapped out where it wants to be in 2020. The wineries are shooting for fifty-six per cent of the Ontario market, targeting wine sales of $1.5 billion, or five times what they sold in 2000. "Every day more and more Canadians are discovering the quality of Canadian wines," asserts Donald Triggs, chief executive of Vincor. "Why shouldn't we have half the market? I would think that is a bare minimum position. It is not going to happen overnight but it will happen if we continue to produce great products."

LABRUSCA OUT, VINIFERA IN

The change in what is growing in Ontario's 7,100 hectares of vineyards has made the most fundamental difference. Niagara vineyard owners have invested more than $100 million since 1990. In 2002, according to a vine census by the Grape Growers of Ontario, 8.9 million of the 15.3 million vines were *Vitis vinifera*. French hybrids had fallen to 3.2 million vines, a third of which was Vidal. There were still 2.4 million *Vitis labrusca* vines in 2002. No longer allowed for table wines, labrusca grapes are sustained only by the declining demand from juice processors and by the sale of fresh table grapes.

Previously, it had been the practice in Ontario to publish a vine census every five years. The first census in which vinifera varieties showed up separately was 1976. In that year, the leading vinifera in Ontario was Chardonnay, accounting for just 69,797 of the fourteen million vines then growing. Concord, grown for juice and jam as well as wine, accounted for 4,720,000 vines; the most important of the French hybrids was De Chaunac, at 1,275,000 vines. Tracking those three varieties through several vine counts provides a snapshot of how much Ontario's vineyards have changed since 1976 (*see* table on page 36). The decline in the number of vines in 1991 resulted from a $50 million programme by the government of Ontario to eliminate a surplus of largely mediocre grapes by removing about 3,500 hectares of vines.

Removal of the remaining labrusca grapes in Ontario will not necessarily add a lot of vinifera plantings, since labrusca is grown on the coolest sites in a region that is already considered cool. A person who stands in a Niagara area vineyard with a compass in hand discovers that, unusually

Trends in Ontario vineyards: annual vine census

Variety	1976	1981	1986	1991	1996	2001
MAJOR VINIFERA VINES						
Cabernet Franc	*	*	*	150,328	484,437	1,299,612
Cabernet Sauvignon	*	*	*	93,612	205,095	1,113,523
Chardonnay	69,797	165,111	2 56,673	716,421	1,156,986	1,927,563
Gamay	57,608	62,885	72,158	142,225	334,050	525,659
Gewürztraminer	*	*	18,487	76,924	111,995	227,027
Merlot	*	*	*	72,145	226,540	857,392
Pinot Gris	*	*	*	45,031	135,942	207,276
Pinot Noir	NA	NA	43,120	109,976	216,342	549,329
Riesling	36, 395	306,163	564,305	453,783	742,501	1,057,871
Sauvignon Blanc	*	*	*	7,002	67,001	269,613
MAJOR HYBRID VINES						
Baco Noir	29,488	104,782	143,140	134,860	432,358	710,379
De Chaunac	1,274,715	1,283,287	1,116,315	277,131	148,862	147,248
Maréchal Foch	523,231	583,229	504,724	183,790	159,709	188,139
Seyval Blanc	58,506	670,149	929,637	916,664	782,833	317,092
Vidal	14,225	168,943	800,626	993,534	1,255,424	1,325,879
MAJOR LABRUSCA VINES						
Catawba	479,077	524,178	495,429	NA	NA	NA
Concord	4,720,090	3,593,097	3,095,132	2,770,681	1,963,943	1,534,267
Elvira	914,024	1,020,753	1,179,166	178,830	120,806	107,371
Niagara	1,599,105	1,019,521	844,879	751,464	732,635	724,338
Total	**14,034,256**	**13,591,892**	**14,205,074**	**9,683,468**	**10,944,455**	**14,883,494**

Source: Grape Growers of Ontario

for the northern hemisphere, the vineyard exposure is frequently north. Vinifera grapes mature here because the vineyards are seldom more than a few miles from Lake Ontario. Brock University geographer Tony Shaw, who has written a ground-breaking paper defining sub-appellations in Niagara, summed up the lake effect in his description of one proposed sub-appellation west of St Catharines:

> The moderating effect of the lake keeps the diurnal temperature range between 10 and 12°C (50 and 53.6°F). In spring, the cooler lake surface lowers air temperature over the area until the threat of frost has

diminished. In the warmer summer months, cooler air from the lake replaces the rising unstable air over the land, helping to lower the day time maximum temperature. In the fall, the process is reversed; the ambient air with higher than normal temperatures moves inland and prolongs the growing season ..."

The defining feature is the Niagara Escarpment, above which vinifera is not cultivated. The escarpment is a ridge rising thirty to fifty metres (ninety-eight to 164 feet) above the bench on which the vines are planted. In the spring, this ridge shelters vineyards from cold prevailing winds which blow strongly from the southwest. In conjunction with the lake, the escarpment creates air-flow patterns that help disperse frost and generally create micro-climates that make the Niagara region work for viticulture.

It is surprising to see where the Niagara vineyards are situated in comparison with other northern-hemisphere regions: on the forty-third latitude, the same latitude as Northern California and further to the south than Burgundy. Commercial vineyards have been established here at least since the late nineteenth century, but it took a long time to unlock the potential for quality.

ONTARIO PIONEERS

Early Canadian winemaking occurred in an environment of knowledge so different from that of today that it could have happened on another planet. Chronicling Ontario winemaking in a 1979 book, Georges Masson, a writer and grape-grower at Niagara-on-the-Lake, observed: "With some exceptions, most of the winemakers had no experience and no tradition to rely upon, and even the new immigrants from wine-producing countries had to contend with varieties of grapes very different from those they previously had known."[1] An amateur winemaker of some renown was a Toronto lawyer named John Hoskin who, according to Masson, had learned sophisticated European techniques. Consequently, his wines often won awards in local competitions. Hoskin used the new North American hybrids with the least foxy flavours, such as Delaware and Iona. Masson quotes him as saying: "I know that Clinton and Concord are grown extensively for winemaking, and that has given the

1. Masson, Georges, *Wine from Ontario Grapes*, G Masson, Niagara-on-the-Lake, Ontario, 1979, p.50.

wines of Canada a very bad name. I condemn Concord for winemaking." The quote is undated but is likely to have been made in the 1880s. It is a remarkable diagnosis of a situation which lasted for the next 100 years.

The history of Ontario wine-growing generally starts with one Johann Schiller who planted vines in about 1800 at Cooksville (today's Mississauga), and in 1811 made wine for sale. But since this venture lasted only a few years, it hardly counts as the beginning. Justin M de Courtenay, a Frenchman who first sought government support for grape-growing in what is now Québec, moved to Cooksville in around 1860, and is said to have developed a sixteen-hectare vineyard on Johann Schiller's homestead.[2] He was ambitious, according to Georges Masson. In 1865 Clair House Vineyards, de Courtenay's winery, constructed cellars with a capacity of 20,000 gallons. "Besides dry white and red wines, the winery made champagne and dry sherry," Masson wrote. A Clair House red wine was shown at the Paris Exposition in 1867 and was compared favourably with Beaujolais. De Courtenay is reported to have operated Clair House for fourteen years, after which the winery went through several ownership changes and finally vanished from the scene.

COMMERCIAL BEGINNINGS

Serious development of commercial wineries in the Niagara region began in 1873 when George Barnes started the Ontario Grape-Growing & Wine Manufacturing Company in St Catharines; it changed its name in 1934 to Barnes Wines and closed in the 1980s when the land was worth more as an industrial park than as a winery. Throughout its history it was successful primarily with port- and sherry-styles, the most appropriate wines that could be made from labrusca grapes and the most appealing to consumers of the day. One of the longest-lived brands in Canadian wine was Barnes Golden Diana (see page 8), a sherry-type that was made for about 100 years until it was retired in 1982.

A second important Ontario winery was opened in 1874 by Thomas Bright, initially as the Niagara Falls Wine Company and later as TG Bright & Co (see page 15). Throughout much of its history it was Canada's largest winery and, in its day, the most innovative. Brights sponsored the importation of hybrid and vinifera vines from France after World War II.

2. Rannie, William F, *Wines of Ontario: An Industry Comes of Age*, WF Rannie, Lincoln, Ontario, 1978, p.49.

Research in its vineyards and at its Niagara Falls winery proved the viability of many varieties, including Vidal, Maréchal Foch, and Baco Noir (a particular Brights speciality). In 1951, Brights planted 2.4 hectares of Chardonnay, believed by the winery to have been North America's first successful commercial block of vinifera east of the Mississippi. In 1956, the company released Canada's first varietal Chardonnay. The lustre of that achievement was dimmed because the early vintages, reflecting inadequate viticulture, tasted more of green asparagus than ripe grapes.

In response to the rising interest in viticulture, in 1905 the Ontario government established a horticultural research institute near Vineland, on the shore of Lake Ontario. The grape trials and grape breeding programmes here, while not always at the cutting edge, contributed significantly to the industry. (When the institute closed recently, its viticulture programmes were divided among several universities.)

By 1916 there were, depending on the source, ten or twelve wineries in Ontario, most in the Niagara region. Then Canada entered into Prohibition, with an unforeseen consequence. The grape-growers in Ontario managed to have winemaking exempted, providing the wine was sold as medicinal tonic or in very large containers (*see* page 9). This ludicrous regulation, rather than discouraging consumption, triggered a major boom in wineries. The requirement that some wines had to be sold as tonics conveniently allowed inept winemakers to hide flaws with flavourings.

AFTER PROHIBITION

By the end of Prohibition in 1927, there were forty-three wineries in Ontario (some sources show numbers as high as fifty-one). Winemaking facilities were rudimentary; typical was the converted hog barn at Beamsville where Dominic Depietro's reds sold for fifty cents a gallon. He had previously run a fruit store in Toronto. At least thirteen licences were issued to individuals with Italian names, such as Franco Cerra, Badaloto, Antonio de Conza, Antonio Nero, Giovanni Paproni, Nicola Pataracchia, and Caesar Abow. Many of the vintners were Italian immigrants recruited to build the Welland ship canal, which began in 1913, or the major hydroelectric projects at Niagara Falls. None of these vintners remained long in the wine business, typically selling their licences, usually their only valuable asset. Leonard Pennachetti, one of the founders of Cave Spring Cellars, is the grandson of an Italian stonemason who worked on the canal and cultivated a hobby vineyard in his retirement. By coincidence, the wave of Italian immigration after World War II led to a new round of wineries with an Italian heritage, such as Magnotta, Colio, Cilento, Pillitteri, Milano, and Vinoteca.

Wine production grew so rapidly during Prohibition that grapes were imported from New York State. Ontario farmers planted as fast as they could, with a heavy bias towards Concord. A variety developed in Massachusetts in 1843, Concord quickly dominated vineyards because it is easy to grow and is hugely productive. By 1933, seventy-three per cent of the vines in Ontario were Concord. It was only in 1963 that it was removed from the list of recommended vines for commercial planting. The labrusca varieties made serviceable "ports" and "sherries" but recently planted hybrids, such as De Chaunac, Seyval Blanc, and Maréchal Foch made much more palatable dry table wines. Ironically, labrusca varieties got a new lease of life in 1971 when Andrés developed its wildly successful Baby Duck sparkling wine, using Concord or comparable grapes (*see* page 10). This brand, which is still made, was Canada's biggest selling wine for several years; it was even exported to the UK. Most domestic wineries copied the idea. There was not much incentive, therefore, for growers to convert their vineyards to less productive and more risky varieties. Wineries coped as best they could. Brights and Jordan Wines both installed expensive machinery to scrub the "foxy" flavour and aroma from the labrusca-based wine they had to make.

POST-WAR REBUILDING

After 1927, there was major consolidation of wineries. The Ontario government offered winemaking courses to improve the sorry quality of the wines but most operators just sold their licences. After World War II the half-dozen survivors set about rebuilding the business. There was a general recognition that better grape varieties were needed and other wineries followed Brights' lead, encouraging their growers to plant something better. It was the Parkdale winery, for example, that helped Bill Lenko import the vines for his Beamsville vineyard, now one of Ontario's best Chardonnay sites. When Rothmans, the South African tobacco company, bought Jordan, German winemakers were sent to run the wineries. Very shortly, they were convincing growers in Ontario (and British Columbia) to plant Riesling. Soon after French-trained Paul

Bosc became Château-Gai's winemaker in 1964, he had his employer supporting the planting of better grapes.

In 1970, eight wineries were operating in Ontario: Barnes, Brights, Jordan, Château-Gai, Parkdale, Turner, Beau Chatel, and London. Most had their niches. Brights claimed credit for having introduced bottled-fermented sparkling wine, marketed for years as Brights President Champagne. Château-Gai also was a substantial sparkling wine producer, having acquired in 1928 the licence to use the Charmat prcess, a French-developed technique in which the wine is fermented in large pressure tanks. Barnes had a strong line of "ports" and "sherries". Turner, besides making cherry wine, had enjoyed some success with what was called Invalid Tonic. Jordan had been hugely successful with gin-flavoured wines, launched in 1962 and copied by most competitors. One of London's specialities was honey wine, because London had taken over the assets of Strawa Honey Wines of Sarnia.

Strawa was licensed in 1960, the first new winery in Ontario since 1931. The provincial government's Wine Standards Committee had, in 1933, been so appalled at the proliferation of incompetent wineries during Prohibition that it recommended against new licences. For a generation, few tried to open wineries and those that did encountered barriers from the regulators. Before establishing the Andrés winery in British Columbia in 1961, Andrew Peller, a former brewer, "pestered" the Liquor Control Board of Ontario (LCBO) for a winery licence. He related the response in his autobiography: "Finally the Liquor Control Board called me into their office and said, 'We're not giving out any more general licences because we feel that there are enough wineries for Ontario's needs. If you can produce a good Rhine wine, we'll give you a licence to make good Rhine wine only'."[3] He turned that down because it would exclude him from the bulk of the market. "Eighty per cent of the wine sold in Ontario was sherry, with the balance being table wine," he observed. He got into the Ontario industry in 1970 by buying Beau Chatel. (Six of the 1970 group of eight merged into Vincor during the 1990s, see page 18. Turner, the seventh, closed in 1977.)

New blood was finally allowed in by the LCBO, beginning in 1974. Major General George Kitching, its chairman since 1970, had riled the

3. Peller, Andrew, *The Winemaker: the autobiography of Andrew Peller*, Andrés Wines Ltd, Winona, 1982, p104.

grape-growers by expressing his taste for European wine. A worldly former chief of staff of the Canadian military, he had been born in China, educated at Sandhurst and had served in the British Army before joining the Canadian army. Kitching concluded that Ontario would emerge more quickly from its labrusca past if he licensed wineries which, in the European way, were based on vineyards of their own. In 1975 Ontario licensed Inniskillin, Podamer Champagne Cellars, and Charal Winery and Vineyards, followed by Château des Charmes (1978), and Newark, which later became Hillebrand (1979). While neither Podamer nor Charal succeeded, the others made wines that justified Kitching's faith in them. The Ontario rejuvenation had begun.

The grape-growers and those wineries slow to change tried to hold off the rising tide of imported wines by insisting on protections. These included lower mark-ups and preferential listings in the LCBO stores. However, the quality of Ontario wine was generally not competitive. The domestic industry's share of wine sales in Ontario, once as high as ninety-five per cent, had dropped to forty-five per cent. A provincial government task force that reported in 1986 suggested the reason: "The bulk of Ontario table wine today contains some modified labrusca juice, stretched with water and sugar for additional flavour modification and is, in many cases, blended with imported vinifera wine."

The task force, chaired by Dr. JW Tanner, a former dean of the University of Guelph, offered many useful ideas (such as a ban, quickly implemented, against using labrusca grapes for wine). But the tone of the report was that dismal wine was good enough and protections should remain. "For a significant portion of Ontario wine consumers, these wines [the stretched wines], properly priced, have proven to be quite acceptable," the report stated. In fact, the report argued that the LCBO, with 730 wines on its list, had quite enough. It asked rhetorically: "Do Ontario wine consumers, who are less sophisticated in their tastes than are the consumers in most developed countries, demand or require such a selection?" And the report recommended that no more wineries be licensed "until the climate improves for the sale of Ontario wine".[4]

The Ontario wine industry was saved from these petrifying views two years later when Canada signed a free trade agreement with the USA. The

4. *Ontario Wine and Grape Industry Task Force*, Ontario Ministry of Agriculture, 1986.

Americans negotiated better access for California wines, to be done by eliminating the Ontario industry's historic protections over several years. But the industry survived because the growers and wineries bargained for major government assistance. They received $100 million under the Grape and Wine Assistance Programme, half of it for pulling out vines. Over the next six years, nearly 3,500 hectares were pulled out, about forty per cent of Ontario's vineyards. This adjustment programme also paid the wineries $45 million in forgivable loans for rebuilding or upgrading their facilities.

Contrary to what Dr. Tanner had feared, the climate for the sale of Ontario wine began to improve. The mediocre stretched wines vanished from the market. Meanwhile, the industry drew attention to its quality wines by launching the Vintners Quality Alliance in 1989 (*see* page 13). Wines that qualified for the VQA sticker had to be made with vinifera grapes grown exclusively in Ontario. Exceptions were made only for the best hybrid varieties, such as Vidal, Baco Noir, and Maréchal Foch.

The consolidation that reduced the number of commercial wineries to a few powerful producers (such as Vincor) reduced, or threatened to reduce, grape sales by independent vineyards. Some opened wineries of their own; others sold to individuals who also wanted to open wineries. To the surprise of those who thought free trade would be the death knell of the industry, wineries began opening after 1989 and, as success breeds success, continue to open.

THE LIQUOR CONTROL BOARD

The growth of wineries was not as rapid in Ontario during the 1990s as in British Columbia, however. The major reason was access to markets. Until 1999, Ontario wineries were not permitted to sell wines directly to restaurants and keep the profits, but were required to route those wines through the Liquor Control Board of Ontario. Established wineries with volume production, or those, such as Cave Spring Cellars, whose wines bowled over the wine writers, did well in such a system. Cave Spring has become a 60,000-case producer since opening in 1986. "We have been riding that horse," Cave Spring president Leonard Pennachetti says. "It has to do with the fact that we have this juggernaut of a liquor board. We have access to the largest retail chain in the world, run by the government."

However, it was not a model that worked well for small new entrants to the business. The LCBO kept most of the profit realized from such sales – and the sales to restaurants were not robust. Untroubled by winery sales people, many restaurants were content to keep ordering imported wines from their one big supplier. Ontario wines were under-represented on wine lists, if they were included at all. Wineries in British Columbia, however, could sell directly to licencees, keeping the profits and generating enthusiastic restaurant support. In such environments, it was much easier to open new wineries in British Columbia than in Ontario. The Ontario Grape Growers' Marketing Board lobbied hard for the change until the province finally allowed direct winery sales to restaurants in May 1999. That created the opportunity for the most recent wave of new wineries. "We are seeing a proliferation of small wineries," Pennachetti says.

The Grape Growers of Ontario (as it is now called) has also lobbied, so far without success, for the opening of wine stores in Ontario that would sell only VQA wines. British Columbia's VQA stores – there are twenty-one – are one reason why west coast consumers are more aware of their wines than is the case in Ontario.

The soft support in Ontario seems to be a hangover from decades of mediocre wine and from an unwillingness to explore the vastly improved wines now available. "We have to contend with the Toronto resistance to Ontario wine," observes Linda Bramble, an Ontario wine writer and teacher at Brock University. Market research has shown that consumers will buy Ontario wine to drink at home but still order imported wines in restaurants where status matters. "It is just Canadian psychology to ignore Canadian products," suggests Inniskillin's Donald Ziraldo. His wines are on the lists of six Michelin three-star restaurants in Paris and he has more than 5,000 accounts in the USA. "I used to think that Canadians would get over it. I feel like a rock star when I visit my accounts in the USA. Here, I feel like I am begging. I don't really care – I will sell my wine around the world."

However, acceptance is rising, especially as marketing programmes kick in. "I remember trying to sell high-end VQA wines fifteen years ago and it was a really tough sell," says Paul Speck, president of Henry of Pelham Family Estate Winery. "But now we have sommeliers in the restaurants who have never heard of Baby Duck and who grew up with VQA quality wine."

7

Wineries of Niagara

ANGELS GATE WINERY ****
4260 Mountainview Road, Beamsville, ON, L0R 1B2.
Tel: 905 563 3942; Website: www.angelsgatewinery.com
Angels Gate is situated on 9.3 peaceful hectares just below the Niagara
Escarpment, the site many years ago of a small convent, hence the name.
The winery's thirteen owners are primarily Toronto business-people, and
the winery opened in 2002. There are two vineyards, both on the
Beamsville Bench. The original four-hectare estate vineyard is planted to
Cabernet Franc, Cabernet Sauvignon, Chardonnay, and Gewürztraminer.
A second ten-hectare vineyard nearby grows the two Cabernets and more
Chardonnay as well as Merlot, Pinot Noir, Riesling, and Shiraz.

Winemaker Natalie Spytkowsky is a fast-rising star. Born in Niagara
Falls in 1970 of Ukrainian parents, she married into a vineyard-owning
family. Spytkowsky has developed some definite ideas in her journey
through the industry. She does not believe in messing around with her
wines. They are often unfiltered and unfined. She summed up her
approach in one magazine profile: "The less there is done to the wine, the
more there is. The characteristics are fuller, there's more body, more
mouthfeel, more aroma, better structure."

The winery has the capacity to produce 20,000 cases, and was halfway
there by 2004. The current portfolio of fourteen wines includes Old
Vines Chardonnay, from thirty-five-year-old vines, intensely spicy
Gewürztraminer, concentrated Cabernet Sauvignon, and a charming
Gamay Noir. One of Spytkowsky's best 2002s was a Pinot Noir identified
as Barrel 56; that particular barrel in the cellar yielded a voluptuously
silky wine. The tasting room staff found out where this superlative barrel

was and only stopped dipping into it when general manager Darryl Field hid it. Enough was salvaged to release twenty-two cases.

BIRCHWOOD ESTATE WINES *

4679 Cherry Ave, Beamsville, ON, L0R 1B1.

Tel: 905 562 8463; Website: www.diamonwines.com

Established in 2000, Birchwood is one of three wineries operated by the Diamond Estates group. The anchor winery in the group is Lakeview Cellars, and winemaker Thomas Green makes the wines for Birchwood there. (The third winery is Salmon River Cellars.) Birchwood's production ranges between 3,000 and 5,000 cases a year. The vineyard includes vines that are more than fifteen years old. The value-priced wines include Gewürztraminer, Chardonnay, Pinot Gris, Auxerrois, Pinot Noir, Cabernet Franc, and Cabernet/Merlot. The winery also offers a selection of Icewines.

CAROLINE CELLARS WINERY **

1028 Line 2, Niagara-on-the-Lake, ON, L0S 1J0.

Tel: 905 468 8814; Website: www.lakeitfarms.com

The Lakeit family has operated a vineyard in the Niagara peninsula since 1978 but opened the winery only in 2002 after one of Rick Lakeit's daughters said to him, "Uncle Fred [Fred Hernder, one of Ontario's largest growers and the owner of the Hernder winery near St Catharines] has grapes and he has a winery. We have grapes. Why don't we have a winery?" Justine, Jacqueline's older sister, adds her own theory as to why the winery was launched. "He built it for us kids," she explains, referring to herself and her three siblings. "He probably figured we wouldn't keep the farm."

The farm consists of two neighbouring properties totalling sixteen hectares and growing a dozen different grape varieties, including Sauvignon Blanc, Pinot Gris, Vidal, the Bordeaux reds, Maréchal Foch, and Zweigelt. Chardonnay is made in three styles, including an off-dry version in which a dash of Icewine is used to add sweetness. The winery also makes a selection of fruit wines, including plum, peach, blackberry, and a blend of Pinot Noir and cherry. One of the more creative is Cranberry Winter Harvest, a tasty blend of late-harvest Riesling and fresh cranberry fermented together. While the fruit wines only comprise a tiny portion of the annual production of 3,000 cases, they satisfy those consumers who prefer sweeter wines.

Riesling and Baco Noir are the best-selling white and red wines here. "Everybody loves Riesling now," Justine marvels. The appeal of the Baco Noir lies in aromas and flavours of cherries and chocolate; it is like drinking a Black Forest cake.

CAVE SPRING CELLARS *****
3836 Main Street, Jordan, ON, L0R 1S0.
Tel: 905 562 3581; Website: www.cavespringcellars.com

Founded in 1986 by Leonard Pennachetti and Angelo Pavan, Cave Spring Cellars is one of Canada's best Riesling producers. Today Riesling comprises a third of the winery's annual production of 60,000 cases. "We've made a decision to let Riesling be our calling card," Pennachetti says. "We have a northern climate here and get this great fruit character. We should play to our strengths." Much is estate-grown: Pennachetti owns twelve hectares of Riesling and his younger brother, Thomas, has a similar-sized planting. There is room for more on their sixty-nine hectares, not all of which is yet under vine. When California winemaker Randall Grahm tasted at Cave Spring a decade ago, he bluntly advised them to replant with Riesling.

Leonard Pennachetti, born in 1954, set out to teach Italian Renaissance history until, as he puts it, "Vino won out over Vico" (referring to the eighteenth-century philosopher Giambattista Vico). The farm is on the Beamsville Bench, a narrow ribbon of clay just below the Niagara Escarpment. It is one of the best sites in Ontario for grapes, protected from the cooler winds by the escarpment and warmed by Lake Ontario, only three kilometres (1.9 miles) away.

After a false start with De Chaunac, in 1978 the Pennachettis planted about 2.5 hectares each of Riesling and Chardonnay, one of the Bench's first vineyards dedicated to vinifera. They persisted even after a sudden cold snap at Christmas 1980, when the temperature plunged to −26°C (14.8°F), damaging many vines. But Pennachetti argued that the damage could be managed, and rejected advice to grow hardy hybrids. "The Europeans have long since learned to live with the risks associated with growing the noblest grape varieties," he wrote in *Canadian Fruitgrower*, "because they saw that the pay-off in the marketplace far outweighed any of the risks associated with production." Nor did he change his mind after the killing winters of 2002 and 2003, even while admitting that "we got a reality check in this region in the last two years." Riesling was among the varieties that withstood the cold. "That is a grape that you can bet your farm on," he has found.

To launch Cave Spring, he put aside his doctoral thesis and teamed up with Angelo Pavan, another doctoral student in philosophy who had become obsessed with wine. Besides the winery, the buildings (which used to be home to the Jordan winery) house On The Twenty, one of Ontario's first winery restaurants, open since 1993. Pennachetti also developed a luxury hotel in an old building across the street from the winery.

The wines include several disciplined Rieslings. "These are serious wines," Pennachetti asserts. "You can't just grab them and gulp them." A number of Chardonnays are made, including one from the floral Musqué clone that is almost as spicy as a Gewürztraminer. The reds include a fleshy Pinot Noir, a full-bodied Cabernet Franc and a pair of generous, peppery Gamay Noir wines, another variety that Pennachetti espouses. "My argument is that Gamay is the red equivalent of Riesling, in terms of market acceptability," he maintains. "We make a beautiful wine – better than Pinot Noir – but the customer does not want to hear of it. It is such a marketing challenge."

CHATEAU DES CHARMES *****
1025 York Road, Niagara-on-the-Lake, ON, L0S 1P0.
Tel: 905 262 4219; Website: www.chateaudescharmes.com

Paul-André Bosc experienced an emotional rush a few years ago when he saw a display of Château des Charmes 1999 Vidal Icewine in Fauchon, the gourmet shop in Paris's Place de la Madeleine. It symbolized acceptance in the land that his father, also named Paul, had left in 1963 because he "felt like a stranger in my own country". Born in 1935 in Algeria, the elder Bosc was managing a cooperative winery there until the French colonists were sent packing. Finding a cold welcome in France, he moved his family to Canada. Bosc worked briefly in the Québec liquor board's cellar until he offered unsolicited quality-control advice to the Château-Gai winery at Niagara Falls. On learning that Bosc had a winemaking degree from the University of Dijon and generations of experience behind him, Château-Gai promptly hired him.

Bosc's career has been among the most influential in Canadian wine. In 1978, the year in which Château des Charmes opened, he planted what was then Canada's largest vinifera vineyard near the Niagara village of St

David's. Almost twenty-four hectares in size, it helped to establish the viability of premium European varieties (including the first Viognier and the first Aligoté grown in Canada). In 1981 Bosc's vineyard accounted for twenty per cent of all the vinifera in Ontario. Some thought he was taking an enormous risk. He figured that the soil and the climate were comparable to those of Burgundy, where the Bosc family had grown wine before they went to Algeria. Château des Charmes began, and continues to be, a strong producer of Pinot Noir and Chardonnay.

The fundamental research in Bosc's vineyard, especially in identifying good clones, benefited both his winery and the Ontario industry in general. His alert vineyard work led to the internationally-recognized discovery of a new clone of Gamay. In the summer of 1982, Bosc spotted one vine in his Gamay block that stretched several feet above all the others. Other plants tended to flop into the rows; this one had powerful tendrils which pulled it erect on the trellis, making it easier to manage. Bosc propagated 225 cuttings. When the wines proved to be full-bodied and attractively peppery, he gradually expanded the planting; today he has four hectares. The clone is called Gamay Droit, because it grows remarkably erect, and since the family rarely part with cuttings, it remains exclusive to Château des Charmes. "I think the future for small wineries and family wineries is distinctive wines," says Paul-André Bosc, a law school graduate who now directs sales. "You could build a name for yourself with Chardonnay but there is nothing to stop the next guy from doing the same."

Their peers would say that, aside from well-made wines, the Bosc family set itself apart in Niagara in 1994 by opening a $6 million winery in the style of a Loire château. "We wanted people to know that we were European wine growers,"says Paul-André. "While we practise New World excellence, ours is still an Old World tradition." It is a long way from what his father found when he arrived in Niagara Falls. In that era, Château-Gai still made "claret" with Concord grapes. Bosc had little patience with labrusca-based wines (once saying that he had never been able to swallow wine made from Niagara, the white version of Concord). In his fifteen years as winemaker at Château-Gai, Bosc orchestrated a switch to French hybrid and vinifera wines.

Château des Charmes's early bread-and-butter wines were made with hybrids. Over the years the portfolio has been converted almost entirely to vinifera as additional vineyards have been developed. The winery now has

113 hectares in four properties, all near St David's, and is about eighty-five per cent self-sufficient. The only hybrid among the fourteen varieties grown here is Vidal, which gives about 20,000 litres of Icewine each year.

In addition to Chardonnay and Pinot, the winery has also established a reputation for its Rieslings and for reds from Bordeaux varieties. The Boscs acknowledge the apparent paradox of growing vines side by side that, in France, would be in separate regions. But the planting decisions have been thought out, and effectively so, judging from the soundness of the wines. "This area is diverse in terms of the land and microclimates," says Bosc.

One of the flagship wines is a Bordeaux blend, Equuleus. "We used to call the wine Cabernet Paul Bosc Estate Vineyard," explains Bosc. With an acute sense of marketing, he thought it a folly to sell a premium-priced red under a generic name that can be found even on $8 wines. He chose a name with an equestrian ring to it because his father has a horse-breeding stable on one of the vineyards. Equuleus, or "the little horse", is a small constellation best viewed, appropriately, only in those months that encompass the grape harvest in the Bosc vineyards.

CILENTO WINES **
672 Chrislea Road, Woodbridge, ON, L4L 8K9.
Tel: 905 264 9463; Email: cilento@ica.net

South African winemaker Terence van Rooyen's experience showed when he made his very first vintage at Cilento in 1999. Among his wines was a bold, ripe, reserve Cabernet Sauvignon with the structure to age for at least a decade. The wine won gold at the 2004 All-Canadian Wine Competition. Since then, he has shown a mastery of varieties ranging from Chardonnay to Shiraz. "We haven't been recognized for our Pinot Noir yet," he grumbled early in 2004. A few weeks later, his peppery 2000 Pinot Noir was judged the red wine of the year at the All-Canadian. Later that year, having stamped a South African style on Cilento's wines, van Rooyen, an oenology graduate from the University of Stellenbosch, moved from Cilento to Stonechurch Vineyards at Niagara-on-the-Lake. As it happens, he was following grapes he knew well, for Stonechurch also purchased a vineyard from Cilento.

Cilento is one of a cluster of wineries at Woodbridge, just north of Toronto, that have an Italian heritage (Magnotta and Vinoteca are neighbours). Managing director Grace Locilento's family came from southern Italy in 1952. Grace and her husband Angelo bought a Toronto company selling grapes and juice to home winemakers. This was built into a substantial business before they established Cilento in 1995.

The winery, with a capacity of 25,000 cases a year, opened two years later, housed in a building whose design has more in common with California missions than southern Italy. Most of the grapes come from Niagara-on-the-Lake vineyards. Varieties include Sauvignon Blanc, a particular favourite with van Rooyen: in South Africa he made a white Sauvignon/Chardonnay blend which became the country's second-largest-selling wine.

He considered the Cilento flagship wines to be the reserves with Chardonnay and Merlot, wines that are made in the best barrels available: "Merlot gets most of the new barrels." Among the reds, van Rooyen developed a personal preference for Shiraz when he was in South Africa. He made a similar style at Cilento, ageing the wine in American oak to produce a wine distinctively different from the Syrah style (aged in French oak) emerging from some other Ontario wineries.

COYOTE'S RUN ESTATE WINERY ★★★★
Concession Road 5, St David's, ON, L0S 1P0.
Tel: 905 682 8310; Website: www.coyotesrunwinery.com

David Sheppard's passion for winemaking was ignited while backpacking in Europe, when he replenished his cash by finding casual work at Weingut Fritz Bastian at Bacharach on the Rhine. "I ended up staying for a year and a half," says Sheppard, now one of four partners who opened Coyote's Run in the spring of 2004. On his return to Canada he approached Inniskillin, and began working in the cellar there in 1982. He stayed for twenty-one years. "I got to do everything," he says. "Karl Kaiser [Inniskillin co-founder] was a great mentor. We spent hours in the tank cellar. I don't think I could ever absorb all his knowledge."

Judging from the quality of the 2003 wines with which Coyote's Run opened, Sheppard absorbed quite a lot. The strengths here include Chardonnay, Pinot Noir, Cabernet Franc, and Merlot. The winery is based on a twenty-three-hectare property, about half of which is now under vines. It is managed by Steven Murdza, another Inniskillin alumnus. The Murdza family, who once owned Inniskillin's Montague Vineyard, were among the Niagara's earliest growers to convert to vinifera varieties.

Consequently, Coyote's Run has Chardonnay and Riesling in its vineyards that are more than twenty years old. "We are not at the mercy of buying someone else's grapes," Sheppard points out.

The vineyard is an historic property once known as Crysler's Farm, after an early settler. It is one of the warmest sites on St David's Bench and has complex soils. Half the vineyard consists of the dark brown clay common to many vineyards; the other half consists of a somewhat rare light red clay reminiscent of Coonawarra soil. Pinot Noir responds quite differently in each soil, allowing Sheppard to make exquisite blends. "I think we have great potential here for Pinot Noir," he says. Coyote's Run now also divides plantings of other varieties between the two soils, with the emphasis on reds, including Syrah and Malbec. "This will end up being a red wine area," Murdza believes.

The other two partners at Coyote's Run are Jeff Aubry (president) and his father Gerald, who initiated the partnership. "I am a high technology refugee," Jeff says. Born in Thunder Bay in 1971, he has postgraduate degrees in both engineering and business. But he became disillusioned with technology after being the victim of staff reductions at two major companies in succession. Coyote's Run has a growth plan that Jeff believes he can control. The winery made 2,500 cases in 2003 and doubled
production in 2004. "We plan to level off at 10,000 to 15,000 cases," Aubry says. "We plan to focus on small batches."

CREEKSIDE ESTATE WINERY ****
2170 Fourth Avenue, Jordan Station, ON, L0R 1S0.
Tel: 1 877 262 9463; Website: www.creeksideestatewinery.com

Creekside's wines mirror the mainstream varieties of Ontario, and all are made well. Laura's Blend, a robust red incorporating the three main Bordeaux grapes, is its top-selling wine. The Pinot Gris is voluptuous in style and the Signature Series Cabernet Sauvignon shows a meaty intensity. However, Creekside's star is hitched particularly to its Shiraz and Sauvignon Blanc, and there are stories behind each variety's prominence here.

The commitment to Shiraz – Creekside grows or controls one of Niagara's most extensive acreages of Shiraz – is the stamp put on the winery by winemaker Marcus Ansems. A young Australian whose family operate Shiraz producer Mount Langhi-Ghiran, Ansems arrived at

Creekside in 1999 with a contract to do three vintages (he did four), to build a new winery, and to develop the vineyards. He convinced Peter Jensen and Laura McCain, Creekside's owners, to make a big bet on Shiraz at a time when others still were planting trial plots. Through connections in Australia, Ansems imported two clones: a big-berried Shiraz that produces richly fruity wine and a small-berried Shiraz that makes a peppery Rhône style. The winery has nine hectares of Shiraz in its own vineyards or in grower vineyards. Ansems' choice appears to have been successful. The vines are more winter-hardy than Merlot. And the 2002 Shiraz was judged Ontario's best Shiraz in an industry competition.

The Sauvignon Blanc story is about the generous welcome that Jensen and McCain got from their peers in the Ontario wine industry. Jensen entered the business in 1992 by developing a modest chain of Toronto stores making small lots of wine, usually with concentrates, for budget-conscious consumers. "It has an important and practical place in getting people to drink cheap wine early on, because eventually they go to the premium stuff," Jensen maintains.

When Jensen and McCain married a few years later, they honeymooned in California's Napa Valley, which inspired them to open their own winery. Their first, now called Blomidon Estate, was established in 1996 in Nova Scotia's Annapolis Valley. It was originally called Habitant, and was Nova Scotia's third winery; Jensen and McCain had been encouraged by the provincial liquor commission, which told them that a good opportunity existed for a winery. It was a learning experience. "We made mistakes" – such as making wine from concentrate – "that would never have been forgiven in Ontario," Jensen reflects. Since 2000 Blomidon Estate has entirely refocused, making good wines with estate-grown grapes.

Meanwhile, Jensen and McCain got into Ontario by purchasing VP Cellars, a small, struggling winery near Jordan. "I was wet behind the ears when I arrived here in September 1998," Jensen admits. "We had taken over this little cottage winery and I had no grapes." He took his problem to Charles Pillitteri, who offered Jensen enough grapes for that first vintage. "He said, 'I'll take care of you. I'll get you some Pinot Noir. And I have some Sauvignon Blanc growing in one of our vineyards and we've never had any particular success in it, so why don't you take that too?'" Creekside's 1998 Sauvignon Blanc, made by consulting winemaker Ann Sperling, launched the winery's stellar reputation with this variety.

Personally well-financed, Jensen and McCain built a new winery with a capacity of 30,000 cases a year. The winery's 400 French oak barrels are in an underground cellar with an Old-World ambience. Seven hectares of grapes have been planted at the estate and a further seventeen hectares have been planted near the village of St Davids.

Before Ansems left – first to consult in Australia and then to join the Blasted Church winery in British Columbia – he recruited a winemaking team that, Jensen quips, is "joined at the hip." Craig McDonald, another Australian, has made wine in numerous regions around the world. Rob Power, born in Peterborough in 1961, is a University of Toronto arts graduate whose interest in wine was fired by twelve years as a sommelier. He was in the first graduating class of Brock University's wine programme and honed his practical skills as winemaker at Blomidon.

"My relationship with Craig is a rare friendship," Power says. "Neither one of us brings any ego to the table. If someone has a better idea, we go with the better idea. We came up with a goofy marketing slogan: two heads are better than one, two noses are better than one. I don't think it would always work. But with us, our skill sets are very complementary."

CROWN BENCH ESTATES WINERY ***
3850 Aberdeen Road, Beamsville, ON, L0R 1B7.
Tel: 905 563 3959; Website: www.crownbenchestates.com

This winery, opened late in 1999 by Livia Sipos and her husband, Peter Kocsis, takes its name from the crowning position it occupies on the Beamsville Bench, with a view of Lake Ontario and the Toronto skyline from the vineyard. The surrounding area is well-forested and home to abundant wildlife. Peter Kocsis had sold grapes to other winemakers for several years. After seeing prizewinning wines made from his grapes, he established Crown Bench to make his own winning wines, initially with advice from Deborah Paskus, who is one of Ontario's best consulting winemakers. The vineyard includes a block of Chardonnay more than thirty years old. Kocsis also has Pinot Noir and the Bordeaux red varieties. Crown Bench has a production target of 5,000 cases of table wines a year.

The owners use Icewine as a base for remarkable confections. "Every winery makes Icewine; we want to do something different," Livia explains. "The winery's best seller is Hot Ice, an apéritif produced by infusing

Icewine with five different Jalapeño peppers. In spite of the name, the wine is warmly spiced, not sharp. Beamsville Bench Ambrosia is an appealing blend of Icewine and good quality chocolate. There are also fruit-infused Icewines with raspberries, cranberries and blueberries. Ginger Ice is an Oriental bazaar of a wine, made with wild ginger root and Icewine. One of the newest products is an Icewine delicately flavoured with Madagascar vanilla beans. Controversial, perhaps, with Icewine purists, these are well made wines and enjoy a deservedly solid following.

DANIEL LENKO ESTATE WINERY *****
5246 Regional Road 81, Beamsville, ON, L0R 1B3.
Tel: 905 563 7756; Website: www.daniellenko.com

In 2003 Daniel Lenko decided that he would only sell his Old Vines Merlot (the vines were planted in 1975) by the case. When his customers tolerated this, he began selling his Riesling and some of his other whites the same way. At midsummer in 2004 he announced that "The tasting room is closed for the season until February 2005". His object is to sell his production (of about 4,000 cases) quickly, in order to have time for the vineyard. The supremely self-confident Lenko gets away with it because the winery, which opened in 2000, has a simple marketing strategy: it wins awards. The winery's début Chardonnay, from the 1999 vintage, was judged to be Ontario's best Chardonnay at the industry's major annual competition in early 2001. Lenko won Ontario's best Merlot in 2002, Ontario's best aromatic white in 2003 (with Viognier), and Ontario's best Pinot Noir in 2004.

While there clearly is good winemaking going on here, the secret is the thirteen-hectare Lenko vineyard on the Beamsville Bench. In 1947 Bill Lenko, Daniel's father, began growing grapes here, mostly Concord. But in 1960, through the Parkdale winery to which he sold grapes, he imported 2,000 Chardonnay vines from France. One of the earliest Chardonnay plantings in Ontario, it has now grown to 2.4 hectares, achieving something of a "grand cru" reputation. Several producers have made award-winning wines with Lenko's Chardonnay. Bill replaced all of his Concord in 1975, even though it still was in demand, with four hectares of Merlot at the request of Château-Gai, the winery then buying grapes from him. Those vines – not all made it through the bitter winter of 1980 – now permit Lenko to make intensely concentrated wine.

When Lenko, who was born in 1967, took over the family farm, he concluded that he could wring more value from the vineyard's superior grapes with his own winery. His mentor for the early vintages was Jim Warren, who had made stunning Chardonnay elsewhere from Lenko grapes. "His style is very good," Lenko says of Warren's wines. "And we want to remain true to that style." Today Lenko handles winemaking with the assistance of Winnipeg-born Ilya Senchuk. The winery makes three different Chardonnays, including one without oak, along with Riesling and Viognier. Occasionally, it also releases eccentric whites from Merlot and Cabernet Sauvignon. The reds include Cabernet Franc, Merlot, a Bordeaux blend, and Pinot Noir. Here the style has changed slightly: Lenko and Senchuk opt for extended skin contact, and wines structured for ageing. "As our pedigree grows, the customers are demanding wines that can be put down for eight or ten years," Lenko explains. "They drink them in a week, but they still want to buy them in that style."

DE SOUSA WINE CELLARS **

3753 Quarry Road, Beamsville ON, L0R 1B0.

Tel: 905 563 7269; Website: www.desousawines.com

802 Dundas Street West, Toronto, ON, M6J 1V3. Tel: 416 603 0202.

The winery's bread-and-butter wines are called Dois Amigos, the Portuguese phrase for "two friends". The wines are honest and everyday, and are sold in containers as large as four litres. The brand is a memorial to the friendship of two winemakers who worked here during the initial vintages for founder John De Sousa, who had come to Canada from Portugal in 1961. In 1979 he acquired a nine-hectare vineyard near Beamsville and replaced the labrusca grapes with premium hybrids and vinifera, including Touriga Nacional. The De Sousa family subsequently purchased the adjoining twenty-seven hectares.

The elder De Sousa died in 1997 and the winery is now under the direction of his son, also John, who has carried on Portuguese traditions, including serving wines in clay cups (which are also sold in the shop). Most notably, he produces dessert-style wine and sells it under the name of "port", because the wine is made in the traditional Portuguese way. Making it in Canada presents its own challenge: the tender Touriga Nacional must be buried over winter to protect the vines. De Sousa makes about 1,800 litres of port-style wine a year. The winery also makes several Icewines but John says he prefers making port styles.

The winery's reserve wines – Chardonnay, Merlot, Cabernet Franc, and a Cabernet/Merlot blend – are made by consulting winemaker Andrzej Lipinski. A rising star among Ontario winemakers, he has worked with De Sousa since the 2001 vintage. De Sousa also operates a second winery, opened in 1998, 112 kilometres (seventy miles) away in Toronto, strategically located for selling wine. "This is the only winery located in the heart of Toronto," he says.

DOMAINE VAGNERS **
1973 Four Mile Creek Rd, Niagara-on-the-Lake, L0S 1J0.
Tel: 905 468 7296; Email: mvagners@scottlabsltd.com

Martin Vagners, an agent for winery supply company Scott Laboratories, operates this tiny winery so quietly that it has Niagara's lowest profile. "I make wine as I see fit," he says. He began planting two hectares of vines, mostly Bordeaux varieties, in 1990. His first release was 100 cases of 1993 Cabernet Franc and he is proud of his Meritage. Since then, winter kill and vine disease have forced him to replant Merlot and Cabernet Franc twice. Recently, he has added Pinot Noir to his range. Vagners is of Latvian origin and has a strong following in that community; his fans can find him on the weekends when the wine shop may be open.

EASTDELL ESTATES *
4041 Locust Lane, Beamsville ON, L0R 1B2.
Tel: 905 563 9463; Website: www.eastdell.com

Susan O'Dell and partner Michael East have both had long careers in the corporate fast lane, and bring their skills to what they call "not your average winery". East was also an amateur winemaker before purchasing a small vineyard in 1996 near Beamsville. Three years later they bought the nearby Walters Estates, renamed it EastDell, and quadrupled the vineyard base. A new winery was completed for the 2003 crush.

As befits the business background of the owners, EastDell's well-wooded twenty-five hectares have been developed to attract corporate clients looking for business retreats with a difference. "A business think-tank in the vineyard," the winery proclaims. The wines include a sparkler, whites from Chardonnay, Riesling, and Gewürztraminer, reds from Cabernet and Merlot, Icewine, and even several iced fruit wines.

FEATHERSTONE ESTATE WINERY ***

3678 Victoria Ave, Vineland, ON, L0R 2C0.

Tel: 905 562 1949; Website: www.featherstonewinery.ca

Producing the wine required to make white wine gravy provided the seed for this winery. Before David Johnson and Louise Engel opened Featherstone in 2002, they operated The Guelph Poultry Gourmet Market. Their prepared gravy, popular among customers buying turkeys, consumed a substantial volume of commercial wine. Engel suggested that Johnson could reduce costs by making his own wine. Even though the initial lot, made with a wine kit, was not promising, Johnson was instantly smitten with a passion for winemaking and joined a winemaking club. Soon he was making award-winning wines with fresh Niagara grapes and had become a qualified wine judge.

Their commitment to wine moved to the next level late in 1998 when the couple purchased a nine-hectare producing vineyard near Vineland. Johnson immediately began planning a winery to realize more value from his grapes. "In primary agriculture," he says, "there is no money in growing anything." He began making Featherstone wines in 1999. The Gourmet Market was sold just before the winery opened.

Johnson took to growing grapes as quickly as he took to winemaking. After only his fifth season as a grower, he was recognized by his peers in 2003 as "Grape King" and the Featherstone property was named vineyard of the year. His commitment to growing without using insecticides is one reason that he won the award. He decided not to spray for pests in his first year of growing grapes. "It isn't that we are Mr and Mrs Organic," he says; "we live in the middle of the vineyard." He did once bring home two bags of chemical insecticide, but when he saw that the instructions warned, very sternly, that no one was to go into the vineyard for seven days after it had been applied, he never used them. He relies primarily on natural predators to protect his vines from insects. Featherstone's method of bird control also relies on nature. Engel has taken up falconry and keeps a Harris hawk, indigenous to South America, in a large enclosure in the back of the winery. The hawk's territorial habit, she believes, will ensure that it keeps returning to the winery after a hunt, if only to be fed. Its very presence frightens the starlings and the robins into other vineyards.

Johnson's winemaking is clean and correct, with a focus on a limited number of varieties. The whites are Riesling, Gewürztraminer, and two styles of oak-aged Chardonnay. One is done traditionally in French oak. The other is one of the several Ontario Chardonnays aged in Canadian oak. Featherstone considers this to be premium oak and the wine is their top-priced table wine. The reds include Cabernet Franc, Pinot Noir, Merlot, Gamay and a quaffable blend, Gemstone Red, based on Baco Noir. The curiosity in his range is a cranberry wine, a zesty, rose-coloured "fun wine", in Johnson's words. "We think it goes great with turkey."

FLAT ROCK CELLARS ***
2727 Seventh Avenue, Jordan, ON, L0R 1S0.
Tel: 905 562 8994; Website: www.flatrockcellars.com

But for a legal barrier to registering the name, this winery would be called Jordan Summit. That name was inspired by this hexagonal winery's spectacular site at the top of the Jordan Bench. The winery's tasting room commands a view over undulating vineyards, and beyond to Lake Ontario and the distant Toronto skyline. When owner Ed Madronich, a Toronto lawyer, found that Jordan Summit was not available, he remembered the unusual flat rocks in a ravine on the property and devised a new name. The winery opened in 2004.

Set into the side of a hill, this is a cleverly designed gravity-flow winery. The six-sided design makes for a compact multi-level processing area where everything can be handled by one or two individuals. The winery is filled with technical innovations, including a geothermal heating and cooling system. At the heart of this are 4,572 metres (15,000 feet) of pipes snaking back and forth at the bottom of a small man-made lake beside the winery. Heat exchangers give the option of cooling or heating, as required. The advantage is a green image and inexpensive climate control.

"I've never started a winery from scratch before," says Darryl Brooker, the lanky Australian who arrived in time to make the winery's debut 1,000 cases in 2003. The winery, planned ultimately for 15,000 cases of wine from its 26-hectare vineyard, is focused on Chardonnay, Pinot Noir, and Riesling. "We would like to make one Chardonnay, one Pinot, and one Riesling," he says. "I won't say no to releasing reserve wines, but the problem with reserves is that you take your best wines for them, and that can affect the quality of the rest."

Born in Canberra in 1973, Brooker studied winemaking at Charles Sturt University. He spent four years at New Zealand's well-regarded Villa

Maria, and brought New Zealand ideas with him: Flat Rock is releasing all its wines, red and white, with screw-cap closures.

FROGPOND FARM *

1385 Larkin Road, RR 6, Niagara-on-the-Lake, ON, L0S 1J0.

Tel: 905 468 1079; Website: www.frogpondfarm.ca

In 1996, when Jens Gemmrich and Heike Koch purchased a small, abandoned orchard near Niagara-on-the-Lake, the decision to grow grapes organically was a simple one. "My wife said that, with small children in our family, we were not going to spray on our farm," the softly-spoken Gemmrich says. He believes that the organic designation also gives the winery an edge. "Anything that makes you a little bit different gives you some advantage."

Born in 1961 near Stuttgart, Gemmrich believes Canada has "a much more open wine industry than Germany".The first vintage at Frogpond Farm was 2001. Before the winery's modest tasting room opened in 2004, Frogpond sold most of its wine directly to restaurants. With that trade in mind, Gemmrich bottles his wines – primarily Riesling and a Cabernet/Merlot blend – exclusively in half-litre bottles.

Gemmrich's use of oak is very conservative. The barrels in the winery are mostly large-capacity ovals, purchased used from another winery and re-coopered by Gemmrich. They impart only a limited oak flavour and that's the way the winemaker wants it. "For a Canadian style of wine, we should back off a little on the oak," he maintains. "Let the fruit and the terroir show."

HARBOUR ESTATES WINERY **

4362 Jordan Road, Jordan Station, ON, L0R 1S0.

Tel: 905 562 6279; Website: www.hewwine.com

In 1997, when peach grower Fraser Mowat turned forty, he decided there was a better future in grapes. Vines soon began replacing fruit trees on his property and the winery opened in August 2000. The winemaker is Ken Mowat, Fraser's son, who took over in 2002 after the original winemaker left. The entry-level 2002 Chardonnay, crisply fresh with a note of cloves on the finish, emerged from a competitive tasting in 2004 as the house wine for the Ontario Legislature's dining room.

Ken has a creative touch with blends, as shown by three value-priced wines: Harbour Sunrise (Vidal and Chardonnay), Harbour Sunset (a vibrantly fruity rosé with Riesling and Merlot), and Harbour Midnight (Cabernet Franc, Cabernet Sauvignon, and Merlot). The flagship red wine here is also a blend, called Premier Vintage, a sophisticated marriage of five red Bordeaux varieties. The winery also blended Gamay with Zweigelt for another of its releases. The Harbour Estates' Icewines, with Vidal as well as Riesling, have won numerous awards.

One of the winery's biggest problems has been selling its wines too quickly. "We are attempting to increase volumes so we can carry a vintage longer," it announced to customers recently. "2003 was a very challenging year as a result of the killer winter last year. As a result, we were unable to move our 2003 volumes upwards. The Niagara Peninsula experienced a fifty per cent crop failure and it was almost impossible to get grapes."

HARVEST ESTATE WINES *
1607 Eighth Avenue, St Catharines, ON, L2R 6P7
Tel: 905 682 0080; Website: www.harvestwines.com

This is a sister property to nearby Hernder Estate Winery, established in 1999 to provide another outlet for the production of Fred Hernder's extensive vineyards. Near the heart of the city, the winery's tasting room shares space with a farm market, many of whose patrons have proven to be impulse wine buyers. The wines are made by Hernder winemaker Ray Cornell, and are often more forward than the bold Hernder wines. One of the most approachable is a red called Autumn, a blend of Cabernet Sauvignon, Cabernet Franc, and Zweigelt. In common with Hernder, Harvest Estate also offers an extensive selection of fruit wines.

HENRY OF PELHAM FAMILY ESTATE WINERY *****
1469 Pelham Road, RR # 1, St Catharines, ON, L2R 6P7.
Tel: 905 684 8423; Website: www.henryofpelham.com

In 1989 Paul Speck was a twenty-two-year-old planning to study law, when his father's illness forced him to help run the winery that the family was just launching. "I had no formal training in this business," he recalls. "The first five years were interesting." But by 1993, when Paul's schoolmaster father died of cancer, the winery had broken even. Since then, Paul and his two younger brothers have grown the winery to 75,000 cases a year and become leaders in Ontario. Paul has been chairman of the Wine Council of Ontario. Matthew Speck, who manages the family's sixty-one hectares of vineyards, won industry acclaim as

Grape King in 2000, the youngest grower ever to win the award. The third brother, Daniel, handles the winery's booming sales.

The Speck family's connection with this property, in the township of Pelham, goes back to 1794. In that year, it was deeded to Nicholas Smith in reward for service to Great Britain during the American War of Independence. In 1842, his son Henry built an inn on it. The property changed ownership several times until 1982 when it was purchased by the father of the Speck brothers, Paul Speck Sr, a descendant of Nicholas Smith. Two years later, after assembling other parcels also owned by his ancestor, he began planting vineyards and planning the winery.

It was a contrary decision; pessimists believed there was no future in Canadian wine. "We're out there planting and next door they're bulldozing their vineyards," Matthew Speck later told one journalist. But the winery was built and the first vintage was made in 1988. When he took over in 1989, Paul Speck Jr dipped into the research cellar at the Brights winery to recruit an experienced winemaker, since none of the brothers had any training. St Catharines native Ron Giesbrecht, from the University of Guelph's oenology programme, has fitted into Henry of Pelham as seamlessly as a fourth brother.

With the maturing of the Speck family's vineyards (the winery also buys half its grapes from independent growers), Henry of Pelham has developed four tiers of wine, crowned in the best vintages only with Speck Family Reserve wines. "We never dreamed that we could make wines like this," Paul says about wines emerging now from low-cropped vineyards yielding perhaps one intensely-flavoured bottle per vine. "They are purist wines. I call them our race cars." This top tier, priced at $25 to $35 a bottle, is limited to Riesling, Chardonnay, Pinot Noir, and Cabernet/Merlot. Overall, the winery's production is evenly divided between red and white wine, with the strongest in each range being Riesling, Chardonnay and Sauvignon Blanc.

Henry of Pelham also has a cult wine, a Baco Noir so well grown and processed that one wine critic called it "Barolo-sized" and others have called it the Zinfandel of Ontario. "My mother and father wanted to produce a bigger, juicier style of red wine," Paul recounts. "We planted Baco and gave it the same respect in our vineyards that we give other varieties." The winery releases both a regular Baco Noir, a chewy wine aged in American oak, and a reserve, a powerful, richly extracted red that could indeed come from northern Italy. Henry of Pelham's Baco Noir, notably the reserve, has done well consistently at competition. "It got a gold medal in the first competition we sent it to," Paul says, "but when the judges learned it was Baco Noir, they reduced the award to silver. Variety snobs don't like it."

HERNDER ESTATE WINES ***
1607 Eighth Avenue, St Catharines, ON, L2R 6P7.
Tel: 905 684 3300; Website: www.hernder.com

Fred Hernder is one of Canada's largest independent grape growers, with about 200 hectares on seven farms in Ontario. These vineyards produce everything from grape juice (exported to the USA) to wine kits. The centrepiece is this 10,000-case winery, opened in 1993, which operates from an 1867 barn.

There is a Hernder Estates wine for virtually every palate. A tasting guide produced by the winery in 2004 listed an astonishing fifty-one grape and fruit wines, from a sparkling Riesling to Icewine-style fruit wines. The presiding winemaker is folksy, moustachioed Ray Cornell, a veteran of Ontario winemaking. Born in 1953 in the little Ontario town of Troy, he went to the nearby University of Guelph to study microbiology and chemistry. He was introduced to wine by one of his professors. After graduating, he tolerated two years doing research with a meat packer until, in 1980, he found a job at T G Bright & Co.'s winery in Niagara Falls. From there, he went on to a start-up winery called Willowbank. Cornell left the wine industry for a couple of years when Willowbank was absorbed by another winery. He found he couldn't stay away and joined Hernder when it was being launched. The extensive Hernder vineyards supply nearly all the grapes the winery needs. "We are well known for our Riesling," Cornell says. The wines are correct expressions of the variety, piquant with fresh citrus flavours and with the potential to age.

Hernder is notable for not hurrying its red wines to market. Cornell ages the premium reds in barrels for about two years, and then holds them back in bottle or in tank for another year or so. Wine is bottled as required; if there is no rush, it is allowed to continue its graceful maturation in tanks. As an example, a portion of the winery's award-winning 1999 Unfiltered Cabernet Franc was not bottled until four years after the vintage. This cellar patience pays off: when a Hernder red is released, it has been polished and rounded by its extra time in the cellar. "Red wines are a lot of fun," Cornell says. "They are more interesting, more complex."

Since 1999, Cornell also has been making an array of fruit wines, including cranberry, rhubarb, blueberry, cherry, blackcurrant and a nectarine-peach blend. There also is a series of iced fruit wines, whose vivid fruit flavours and juicy sweetness are achieved by freezing the juices to concentrate them. Hernder sells most of its wines from its tasting room. The fruit wines, Cornell says, are "quite lucrative."

HIDDEN BENCH VINEYARDS AND WINERY (Range not tasted.)
4152 Locust Lane, Beamsville, ON, L0R 1B2.
Tel: 416 563 8700; Email: hthiel@hiddenbench.com

When Harald Thiel was eighteen, he inherited a wine cellar from his grandfather in Germany. "That was the start of my love of wine," he says. Born in Montreal in 1957, Thiel is a lawyer with a master's degree in business. "I spent the last twenty-five years in business, with the intention of one day owning a winery. I worked with a purpose." His company, which supplied audiovisual products, prospered until he was able to sell it in 2004, giving him the resources to develop the gravity-flow winery of his dreams. When it opens in 2006, he will have wine from three vintages in the cellar. His objective is to produce 5,000 to 8,000 cases of premium wine from Hidden Bench's two vineyards, totalling eighteen hectares. About half the vines are Pinot Noir and a quarter are Chardonnay; the rest are mostly Bordeaux varieties. "I am passionate about Pinot Noirs in general," Thiel says. "And I really love a well-made Meritage, whether that is a New World Meritage or a Bordeaux blend."

One of the vineyards, acquired in 2001, was only planted in 1997. Thiel believes the second vineyard, acquired in 2004, will "jump-start" Hidden Bench's wine quality. The nine-hectare Rosomel Vineyard, as it is called, was planted in 1975. The mature vines there have produced notable Beamsville Bench wines, such as Vineland Estate's $125 Meritage. Rosomel's owner, Roman Prydatkewcysz, is easing into retirement but Thiel has persuaded him to be Hidden Bench's viticultural consultant and work his magic on the winery's other vineyard.

HILLEBRAND ESTATES WINERY *****

1249 Niagara Stone Road (Highway 55), Niagara-on-the-Lake, ON, L0S 1J0.

Tel: 905 468 7123; Website: www.hillebrand.com

Hillebrand is perhaps the only Canadian winery that employs a forager – an individual named John Laidman whose role is finding local produce for the restaurant that the winery opened in 1996. "If someone visits us and only spends an hour and a half, that is not enough," says winery executive Greg Berti. "We want to engage them and make it a memorable experience. We are in the business of wine enjoyment." Berti joined Hillebrand in 1985 as a viticulturist. Today, he is a vice-president for estate wineries with Andrés Wines, the current owner of Hillebrand.

This winery was established in 1979 by Joseph Pohorly, a history buff who called it Newark, the original name of Niagara-on-the-Lake. The winery name was changed after Scholl & Hillebrand, the German wine and spirits group, acquired control in 1982 in collaboration with a Toronto wine merchant named Peter Mielzynski. In a book that he published in 2001, Mielzynski related that he found the Newark name was not well known. "Since we were planning to introduce German-type wines in 1983, we decided to find a name that would convey a sense of tradition and a connection to a European wine heritage." German winemakers and consultants, including the late Bernhard Breuer, reshaped the Hillebrand portfolio, including beginning the production in 1983 of one of Canada's first Icewines. (It was labelled Eiswein.) The winery also acquired modern technology, including the first bladder press to be installed in any Canadian winery.

While the winery succeeded with Germanic wines, including a best-selling white called Schloss Hillebrand, the focus shifted in the mid-1980s when the winery was able to secure Chardonnay and other French vinifera grapes which Ontario growers had begun to plant. Benoit Huchin, a French winemaker, was hired in 1987 and Hillebrand embarked on making single vineyard Chardonnay. Variations on this theme continue to this day. The winery now produces a dozen different Chardonnays, some of which are not only from single vineyards but from single barrels. An example, from a Niagara vineyard that has grown grapes for Hillebrand for twenty years, is Heubel Vineyard Showcase Chardonnay Barrel 4050 Tronçais Oak. Showcase is one of Hillebrand's reserve designations.

Under Huchin (who subsequently returned to France), Hillebrand launched its Trius range, a reserve selection which began with a 1989 Trius Bordeaux Blend. However, the winemaker who really put his stamp on the Hillebrand portfolio was Jean-Laurent Groux, who worked at Hillebrand from 1989 through the 2004 vintage, when he joined Stratus Vineyards in Niagara. Born in the Loire, Groux trained both in Burgundy and Bordeaux. He spent seven years after his 1982 graduation honing his skills both in France and in the New World before coming to Ontario.

With continually improved sources of grapes, Groux has been able to raise standards for all the Hillebrand wines. The winery, which Andrés acquired in 1994, buys from twenty-five growers and has fifty-five hectares of its own vineyards. As the plethora of Chardonnays indicates, Hillebrand is operated very much as a boutique winery even though the annual production is about 300,000 cases a year.

Hillebrand remains a significant Icewine producer. Among other firsts, the winery claims to have exported the first Canadian Icewine to Japan in 1988. Even though he is French, Groux has proved himself adept with Icewine. For example, he was among the first in Ontario to age Icewine in French oak. "The world is our inspiration," he explained. "Château d'Yquem spends three and a half years in barrel."

INNISKILLIN WINES *****
RR 1, Niagara Parkway at Line 3, Niagara-on-the-Lake, ON, L0S 1J0.
Tel: 905 468 2187; Website: www.inniskillin.com

When Philip Dowell arrived from Australia in 1998 to make his first vintage at Inniskillin, he found he had to stop crushing grapes from time to time because hordes of tourists were getting in the way. This consequence of the winery's success would have been hard to anticipate in 1975 when Inniskillin founders Donald Ziraldo and Karl Kaiser got the first winery licence issued by Ontario since 1929. Tenuous at first, Inniskillin has become a cornerstone of Canadian wine, and not just for its superb Icewine. The winery, acquired in 1995 by Vincor International, has an established reputation for Chardonnay, Pinot Noir, and Riesling, as well as an emerging one for Shiraz.

The venture began with a chance encounter in 1971 when Kaiser, who had come to Canada three years earlier, bought some vines for a garden plot from the Ziraldo family's nursery in St Catharines. Born in Austria in

1941, Kaiser had started making his own wine because he found Canadian wine unpalatable. He had picked up winemaking knowledge during a year in an Austrian monastery and, while setting out to be a science teacher in Canada with a chemistry degree from Brock University, gained valuable technical experience. Kaiser shared a bottle of his wine with Ziraldo, who was then only twenty-three. With the optimism of youth, they conceived the idea of applying, against all odds, for a winery licence.

They found an ally in Major General George Kitching (*see* page 41). An urbane Sandhurst-trained officer in the Canadian army who accepted the German surrender in Holland in 1945, he ran the Liquor Control Board of Ontario from 1970 to 1976. He had a low opinion of domestic wines. When a grower criticized Kitching's announced preference for burgundy with roast beef, the general snapped: "Good God, you don't think you make a good burgundy!" Kitching thought that Ziraldo and Kaiser's proposal promised greatly improved wines from the Chardonnay, Riesling and Gamay that Ziraldo planted in 1974. He had the LCBO's accountants help write the business plan, and he committed LCBO stores to sell Inniskillin wines. "I liked the look of Don," the general explained later. "We wanted to make damn sure, if he was going to be the first, that he wouldn't fall down."

The winery opened with wines from the French hybrid varieties, since vinifera fruit from Ziraldo's vineyard was not yet available. At a London tasting of Canadian wines late in 1975, Inniskillin's 1974 Maréchal Foch drew modest praise from well-known British wine critic Hugh Johnson, who was seldom an admirer of Canadian wine. Inniskillin built an excellent reputation with Maréchal Foch, raising production from 500 bottles in 1974 to 20,000 cases in 1980. Ziraldo actually landed a 650-case order for the 1980 vintage from a shipper in Burgundy. The publicity accelerated Inniskillin's sales in Canada even though France, citing Canada's lack of appellations, refused to accept the wine.

By the new millennium, however, the Foch prestige had faded. After Philip Dowell ran into price resistance with a premium Foch, he dropped it entirely. "I wanted to make Inniskillin 100 per cent vinifera," he said. "It was hard to give up on Foch but I didn't think it had a home here anymore, except for nostalgia's sake." Dowell returned to Australia in 2004, having had a major impact on reshaping the style of the wines.

The only hybrid remaining in Inniskillin's production is Vidal for Icewine. Now Inniskillin's winemaker emeritus but intensely involved with Icewine, Kaiser made Inniskillin's first in the 1984 vintage. The Vidal grapes, grown conveniently next to the winery, were picked on a bitterly cold January 8, 1985. The wine was released that December, labelled Eiswein. (All Canadian producers did that at first.) Five vintages later, Kaiser made the Vidal Icewine that won the top trophy at Vinexpo in 1991. In short order, Inniskillin and other Canadian wineries found their wines were being taken seriously.

Vincor's policy when it takes over wineries is to keep the managers (*see* page 18). Kaiser was given the resources to increase Inniskillin's lucrative Icewine production so much that he suggested once he had more Icewine in his cellar than in all of Germany. In addition to Vidal, he also began making Icewine with Riesling and Cabernet Franc; and even with Dornfelder, a dark red variety. He expanded the styles, ageing some in oak and making a sparkling Icewine.

There is controversy over whether Inniskillin or Magnotta made the first sparkling Icewine. "I'm not getting into that," Kaiser growls. Whoever created it, the wine is a brilliant invention. An effervescence moderates the wine's sweetness and gives it a refreshing finish. But perhaps the success of the Icewines overshadowed Kaiser's achievements with Chardonnay and Pinot Noir. Inniskillin's first Chardonnay was made in 1977 from Ziraldo's initial planting. By 1980, Kaiser was one of the first in Canada to begin ageing vineyard-designated Chardonnay in French oak. And while the French had refused his Maréchal Foch, he began making Pinot Noir and Chardonnay in 1993 in a joint venture with Bernard Repolt, the winemaker from Jaffelin. The label for this joint venture is Alliance.

JACKSON-TRIGGS NIAGARA ESTATE *****

2145 Niagara Stone Road (Highway 55), Niagara-on-the-Lake, ON, L0S 1J0.
Tel: 905 468 4637; Website: www.jacksontriggswinery.com

From the road, the Jackson-Triggs winery is deceptively plain: a modern, flat-roofed structure with windows spanning the entire length of the second floor. The winery makes its impact when visitors enter the two-storey Grand Hall. The floor-to-ceiling glass doors on both the north and south entrances open onto vineyards that have been planted almost to the edge of the building. This winery, opened in 2001, is the public face of Vincor's flagship Jackson-Triggs brand. It is one of two Jackson-Triggs wineries and, unlike its counterpart in the Okanagan, offers tours throughout the year. The winery is worth seeing, both for its modern winemaking equipment and the underground cellar with 1,700 barrels.

Jackson-Triggs was launched as a brand in 1993 when Vincor, as the company became known the following year, was rationalizing its brands. The company was named after its founders: Allan Jackson, vice-president for research and development, and Donald Triggs, chief executive. The first wines, from the 1992 vintage, were Chardonnay and Cabernet Sauvignon. Over the next decade, Jackson-Triggs became a national brand. It produces a substantial volume of Proprietors' Selection, blended from imported wines and released with white labels to set them apart from the VQA wines. These are bottled with black and gold labels. The premium Jackson-Triggs wines are made from grapes grown in Canada. The Niagara winery produces about 120,000 cases of wine a year. It is dwarfed by Vincor's winery in Niagara Falls, which is twenty times the size, bottles refreshment beverages as well as wine, and is not open to the public.

The Niagara winery is surrounded by 4.5 hectares planted primarily to Chardonnay and Pinot Noir for sparkling wines. Jackson-Triggs buys grapes from many other vineyards, including the forty-hectare Delaine Vineyard which Triggs and his wife, Elaine, planted in 1999 on the Niagara Parkway, a few kilometres from the winery. In total, ten varieties are grown here, including Syrah and Sauvignon Blanc. Several single-vineyard wines have been released under the Delaine Vineyard designation, including a vibrant Merlot and a complex Cabernet/Merlot blend. The winemaker is Californian Tom Seaver, who helped develop the original Jackson-Triggs wines. His assistant winemaker is Kristine Casey.

The large Jackson-Triggs portfolio of VQA wines is arranged in tiers that begin with Proprietors' Reserve and step up to Delaine Vineyard and Grand Reserve. As vineyards mature, Seaver is planning to add a super-premium level above the Grand Reserve tier. Seaver makes about 15,000 cases annually of Proprietors' Reserve Chardonnay and about 2,000 cases each of Delaine Vineyard and Grand Reserve Chardonnay. All of it is aged in French oak because Seaver believes it to be more subtle than American oak. Interestingly Bruce Nicholson, the Canadian-born winemaker at the Jackson-Triggs winery in the Okanagan, does use some American oak for his Chardonnay. The decision has a lot to do with how differently the grapes mature in the two regions. "Wines from the Okanagan and Ontario are not similar," Seaver observes. He describes Ontario red wines as subtle while Okanagan reds often are "bigger, bolder, and heavier."

Seaver takes particular pride in his red Bordeaux blends, producing as many as 22,000 cases of Proprietors' Reserve Meritage, 3,700 cases of Grand Reserve Meritage and 1,700 cases of Delaine Cabernet-Merlot. "As a winemaker, I really enjoy making the Meritage," he says. "That is the artistic side of winemaking."

JOSEPH'S ESTATE WINES **
1811 Niagara Stone Road (Highway 55), Niagara-on-the-Lake, ON, L0S 1J0.
Tel: 905 468 1259; Website: www.josephsestatewines.com

Joseph Pohorly, the owner of this winery, maintains that he produced Canada's first commercially successful Icewine from Vidal grapes in 1983. At the time he was one of the owners of Newark Wines, which he established in 1979 on his family's farm. After Scholl & Hillebrand took control of Newark in 1982, Pohorly – who had originally trained as a civil engineer – became a developer and hotel owner. But he missed the wine business, so in 1992 he acquired an eight-hectare farm down the road from his original winery and launched Joseph's, which opened in 1996. Pohorly's daughter, Caroline, a banker, joined him as the winery's vice-president in 1998.

With associate winemaker Katherine Reid, Pohorly makes about 30,000 cases annually of table wines and, of course, Icewine from Vidal and Cabernet Franc. The table wines include Petite Sirah, a varietal seldom grown in Canada. This is one of the few wineries still producing Chancellor, including a barrel-aged grand reserve version, from the most harmoniously-flavoured of the red French hybrid grapes.

KACABA VINEYARDS ****
3550 King Street, Vineland, ON, L0R 2C0.
Tel: 905 562 5625; Website: www.kacaba.com

Toronto lawyer Michael Kacaba opened this small, premium winery (production is about 5,000 cases a year, and the goal is double that) after planting red grapes, including Syrah, on undulating terrain high on the Beamsville Bench. Since the first vintage in 1999, the leading wines have been Bordeaux reds, along with one of Ontario's first Syrahs. The winery, using purchased grapes, also produces commendable Chardonnay,

Riesling and Pinot Gris. "I'd like to focus on the reds," said Robert Warren, the winemaker during Kacaba's formative vintages. The winery's 2000 Pinot Noir, a wine that charms with its sweet fruit, was judged the best of its class in the 2003 All Canadian Wine Championships. Warren left for a winery in Virginia in 2004 but Kacaba's winning styles should continue under Beth Mischuk, who was Warren's assistant for three years.

The best wines here are made with the three Bordeaux red varieties, both on their own or blended into elegant, long-lived Meritage. A rising star is the winery's Syrah, a big, leathery wine with concentrated flavours of prunes. Kacaba is notable for not rushing its wines to market, with the result that reds from the 2000 vintage, showing excellent bottle development, were still being sold in 2004. The muscular Cabernet Sauvignon Reserve 2002, one of Niagara's greatest vintages, was still brooding in the barrels. "All of our reserve wines spend sixteen months in oak – twelve months in new oak, four months in older oak," Warren said.

KITTLING RIDGE ESTATE WINES AND SPIRITS **
297 South Service Rd, Grimsby, ON, L3M 1Y6.
Tel: 905 945 9225; Website: www.kittlingridge.com

There are few in the Ontario wine industry with more experience than John Hall. A microbiologist who started thirty-five years ago with the now-vanished Parkdale winery, Hall struck out on his own in 1991, investing in the Rieder Distillery, as it was then called, and expanding the business until Kittling Ridge today is one of Ontario's largest wineries, and the only one with a significant distillery.

The distillery was established in 1971 by Otto Rieder, a talented Swiss eau-de-vie maker. "He made one mistake," Hall says. "Canadians didn't drink eau-de-vie." When Hall took over the company after Rieder's retirement in 1992, he not only secured a winery licence but branched into the production of whisky and other spirits. One of the first wines made under the new licence was Icewine. Hall promptly launched a product made by blending Icewine and brandy. It remains one of Kittling Ridge's flagship beverages. Hall also distilled the Icewine skins, making what is claimed to have been Canada's first Icewine grappa. With a growing line of products, Hall changed the name of the company to Kittling Ridge. The name occurred to him one day as he watched eagles floating – "kittling" – on air currents.

In 1996, Kittling Ridge acquired a small, struggling Ontario winery called Culotta. With six retail wine shops, mostly in the Toronto area, Culotta took the Kittling Ridge products to many more customers than ever were likely to visit the winery.

The product range is enormous, including Ontario-grown wine, imported wine, low-alcohol blends of grape and fruit wines and creative distilled and fortified beverages. In a recent vintage, Hall blended Chardonnay with oak-aged peach spirit, creating something called Chardonnay Angelica. A liqueur made from maple syrup, that iconic Canadian product, is predictably called Oh Canada. One of Hall's most successful spirits is Inferno Pepper Pot Vodka, launched in 1997 and now widely exported. To make it, Hall infuses one or two hot peppers in each bottle of quadruple-distilled vodka. Bartenders all over North America have risen to the challenge of creating fiery cocktails, with Hall obligingly posting the recipes on Kittling Ridge's website.

KONZELMANN ESTATE WINERY ***
1096 Lakeshore Road, Niagara-on-the-Lake, ON, L0S 1J0.
Tel: 905 935 2866; Website: www.konzelmannwines.com

This is one of several top Canadian wineries with a strong German heritage. Herbert Konzelmann's great-grandfather started a winery in Württemberg in 1893. Herbert went to work there in 1958, but he discovered the attraction of Canada in the early 1980s just as the urban sprawl of Stuttgart had begun to overtake the vineyards on which the Konzelmanns depended. They decided to make a fresh start in the New World. After an extensive search, in 1984 Konzelmann purchased a site on the southwestern shore of Lake Ontario, not far from Niagara-on-the-Lake, and planted 30,000 vines. The winery opened in 1986 and production has grown to about 40,000 cases a year.

Now farming thirty-four hectares, Konzelmann is confident that he chose an excellent spot for cool-climate vines. Matthias Boss, the Stuttgart-born winemaker who joined Konzelmann in 2000, agrees. "This area has really good potential for significant white wine production," he says. "I can compare the Riesling to wine from the Rheingau because of its fine fruitiness." (Konzelmann grows all of its reds, except Pinot Noir, at warmer sites farther from the lake.) Like Konzelmann, Boss, who was born in 1965, is a graduate of the Weinsberg wine school; he spent eight years working for Weingut des Grafen Neipperg in Württemberg. "I learned this trade because I wanted to learn something where I will have fun and pleasure for the rest of my life," Boss says. A careful man, he tasted products at numerous Ontario wineries, satisfying himself about the overall quality of Ontario wines, before making the jump from an old and respected German estate to a new one in Canada.

The Konzelmann whites, in addition to Riesling, include an unoaked Chardonnay, one of the most popular and food-friendly wines served in the Konzelmann tasting room. The winery also offers a premium-priced, award-winning grand reserve Chardonnay. Boss describes the wine as "corpulent". A wine that is exclusive to Konzelmann is its Riesling Traminer. This is not a blend but rather is an obscure cross developed at Freiberg in Germany and planted by Konzelmann in Ontario. In the 2002 vintage, Boss produced a strapping late-harvest version. With fourteen degrees of alcohol, it has the weight of an Alsace Gewürztraminer, with concentrated, peppery flavours. The red wines include Pinot Noir, Baco Noir, Cabernet Sauvignon, Merlot, and Zweigelt. Boss argues that Zweigelt has more potential for Ontario than Merlot.

An Icewine producer of note, Konzelmann made its first, a Vidal, in 1987. Since then, the winery has added Icewines from Riesling and Cabernet Sauvignon. The winery also made a superbly concentrated, selected late-harvest Gewürztraminer in 2001 when grapes hanging for Icewine shrivelled too much. The winery's Icewines have won gold medals at many of the leading international competitions, including the 2003 International Wine and Spirits Competition in London. An Icewine made in 1995 with Riesling Traminer captured the top trophy at a subsequent Vinexpo competition in Bordeaux.

LAILEY VINEYARD ****
15940 Niagara Parkway, Niagara-on-the-Lake, ON, L0S 1J0.
Tel: 905 468 0503; Website: www.laileyvineyard.com

The Lailey family's history in Niagara grape-growing began in the 1950s when William Lailey became one of the first to adopt the French hybrid varieties that had just become available in Ontario. His eight-hectare farm was taken over in the 1970s by his son, David, and daughter-in-law, Donna. They replanted with vinifera grapes, becoming such proficient growers that in 1991 Donna was the first woman to win the coveted Grape

King/Queen title recognizing the year's best vineyard. Now, their daughter Tonya has emerged as another of Niagara's most skilled growers. Beginning in 2003, the Laileys stopped using herbicides, probably the first step towards adopting biodynamic viticulture.

The wineries that purchased Lailey fruit included Toronto's Southbrook Winery, whose winemaker, Derek Barnett, made award-winning wines from the grapes. As a result, Barnett formed a partnership with the Lailey family in 1999 to launch a winery. Barnett made 2,500 cases in the 2000 vintage and the winery opened two years later, with the goal of growing to about 8,000 cases a year. "We are just looking at producing small lots of quality wine," he says. "That's all we want to do."

The ruggedly handsome Barnett, who bears a remarkable resemblance to actor Sean Connery, grew up in Scotland and came to Canada in 1973 as a farm manager when Southbrook still had a dairy herd. Transforming himself into a winemaker, he helped launch Southbrook's winery in 1992 and, over the next decade, developed a sure touch for wines both from grapes and fruit.

The winery has been set up as a separate business that buys from the vineyard and generally pays a substantial premium for top quality fruit. "The Chardonnay here is thirty years old and it is producing some intense flavours," Barnett says. This variety emerged early as Lailey's flagship wine, with Barnett exploring the stylistic possibilities of the grape. "We have too many Chardonnays, but that is me," he admits. "I like to do different things with Chardonnay because it is such a winemaker's grape." His Chardonnays often are barrel-fermented, and usually aged in French oak, although he also has trialled Canadian oak. The wines have the rich, creamy fruit of good burgundies, lightened by Niagara's crisp acidity.

Lailey has also expanded its Pinot Noir plantings. "We'd like to think we can make that into a flagship as well," Barnett says. "When you make a good Pinot Noir, you make a good name for yourself." Lailey is already on the way to a reputation for its other reds, including a lively Loire-style Cabernet Franc and a concentrated, age-worthy Cabernet Sauvignon.

LAKEVIEW CELLARS ESTATE WINERY ***
4037 Cherry Avenue, Vineland, ON, LOR 2CO.
Tel: 905 562 5685; Website: www.lakeviewcellars.on.ca
This Beamsville Bench producer has made its mark with robust red wines, a fingerprint of the style of founder Eddy Gurinskas. His peers acclaimed

him in 2003 as Ontario's winemaker of the year. That style is being carried on by winemaker Thomas Green, who was mentored by Gurinskas. At Lakeview, Green's passions include Riesling and Cabernet Sauvignon. However, he makes one of the most extensive portfolios of any Ontario winemaker. The only style that is missing is sparkling wine. This is one of the handful of wineries in Canada to make Kerner. Lakewood's is crisp and fresh, with notes of pear, pineapple, and tangerine.

Lakeview's wines also include the Icewines expected of Ontario wineries: in 2002, one of the best recent Icewine vintages, the winery made four varietal Icewines. Green also makes a dry sherry-style called Amber, and a robust, fortified port-style called Starboard, made with very ripe Cabernet Sauvignon. The wine has the rich tar and baked-plum notes of a genuine port. Green has even promoted the wine's medicinal properties – he finds it an effective treatment for sore throats.

LE CLOS JORDANNE ****
2540 South Service Road, Jordan, ON, L0R 1S0.
Tel: 905 562 9404

It will be at least 2008 before Le Clos Jordanne moves its production into its new Frank Gehry-designed winery. The clamour to tour the building began as soon as the design was unveiled in 2002: the Vancouver Symphony asked for two tickets to the grand opening, as prizes in a fund-raising raffle. Canadian-born Gehry, now based in Los Angeles, was retained precisely because his designs attract attention. "Our biggest concern with Le Clos Jordanne is whether or not we are going to be able to handle all the people who come," confesses Donald Triggs, chief executive of Vincor, an equal partner with Burgundy's Groupe Boisset in this venture.

This winery, with an ultimate capacity of 20,000 to 30,000 cases a year, is one of two joint ventures in Canada involving Vincor and French partners. (The other is the Okanagan's Osoyoos Larose, where the partner is from Bordeaux, see page 181.) With both, Vincor is dipping into the deep well of French wine-growing experience. A Burgundy partner was chosen for Le Clos Jordanne because Vincor believes that Ontario has the potential to grow world-ranked Pinot Noir and Chardonnay. Just in case the world is slow to notice, Gehry's jaw-dropping "Cathedral of Wine" should do the job. The winery's silver roof recalls a billowing cloudscape while the vaulted interior shimmers with glass, warmed by the golden hues of the oak barrels and oak fermenters inside. Gehry's most famous building (so far) is the Guggenheim Museum in Bilbao, Spain. "Tourism in Bilbao rose thirty per cent the year after the Guggenheim was opened," Triggs observes.

The Le Clos partnership was announced in 2000 but Vincor already had its toe in the Burgundy pond through Inniskillin, which in the mid-1990s teamed up with Jaffelin (now owned by Boisset) to produce the Alliance label. Jaffelin selected the wines, a Pinot Noir and a Chardonnay, from some of the best barrels at Inniskillin. Then in 1998, Vincor and Boisset launched two new French brands in Canada. By 2000, Boisset, now comfortable with Canada, agreed to participate in Le Clos. Jean-Claude Boisset, the head of the French company, described the investment in Ontario as "a first for a European wine producer."

Vincor has left the French in charge of vineyard development and winemaking. The four Le Clos vineyards, managed organically, are on the Jordan Bench, within walking distance of each other. Planting began in 2000. The vineyards now total fifty-two hectares, almost three quarters of which is Pinot Noir. Most of the remainder is Chardonnay, with a little bit of Pinot Gris. Curiously, there also is a small block of Riesling, although Icewine would seem an odd fit for a Burgundian project.

The winemakers, Thomas Bachelder (who is also general manager) and Isabelle Roy, are Montréal natives with substantial experience with Pinot Noir and Burgundy. "You have to devote your life to it, to make good Pinot Noir consistently," Bachelder says. Until the Gehry-designed winery is built (in the middle of one of the project's vineyards), the wines are being made in the former warehouse of a plant nursery, a green-painted, functional building with no more charm than a tractor barn. The wines will need to speak for themselves. The first Le Clos vintage was 2003. Bachelder was able to make only 300 cases of wine; the previous winter damaged the young vines, reducing the expected harvest by three-quarters. The first significant volume, a little more than 5,000 cases, was made in 2004.

"I am unabashedly shooting for the Burgundian style or I would not be on the project," Bachelder says. Having worked in Oregon, he believes that many Oregon Pinot Noirs lean toward the big structure and high alcohol that has become the yardstick for California wines. "Pinot Noir for me should be a good mealtime companion that does not fatigue you as you are drinking it, not just a show wine," he believes. "That means a ceiling of about 13.5 degrees of alcohol."

LEGENDS ESTATE WINERY ***

4888 Ontario Street North, Beamsville, ON, L0R 1B3.

Tel: 905 563 6500; Website: www.legendsestates.com

When the Lizak family named this winery, which opened in 2001, they were seeking to remember the legends of an earlier generation. Polish-born John Lizak established a base in the Niagara region in 1946 with four hectares of orchard. That has now grown to eighty-one hectares of fruit trees and seventeen hectares of vineyard at the edge of Lake Ontario. The winery produces both grape and fruit wines.

It was fruit that spawned the winery. Paul Lizak, president, and his father, Ted, were troubled by the waste of discarding fruit that did not meet the picture-perfect requirement of the fresh market. "We began pressing the fruit and using the juice like traditional grape wine," Paul says. It was a short step to hiring a consulting winemaker and vinifying some of their grapes. Ultimately Paul learned to make the wines with consummate enthusiasm. Legends currently makes about 15,000 cases a year, with a target of doubling that as demand grows. Wines at Legends run the gamut of mainstream varietals, including Cabernet Franc. "It is one of the best grapes for red wine in Ontario," Paul says, echoing a widely held view. His Pinot Gris is fresh and delicate while the barrel-fermented Chardonnay Reserve shows a burgundian structure. His Pinot Noir Reserve is like a bowl of cherries. It stands out among Ontario Pinot Noirs because the Lizaks grow what they believe is the only Swiss clone of Pinot Noir in Ontario.

Fruit wines now comprise about a third of production. "They are very versatile," Paul maintains as he launches into a dissertation on their health benefits. The Legends Cherry Riesling is a fruity pink blend in which ten per cent Riesling adds spark to a blend of sour and sweet cherries.

MAGNOTTA WINERY CORPORATION ***

271 Chrislea Road, Vaughan, ON, L4L 8N6.

Tel: 905 738 9463,www.magnotta.com

Few people in Canadian wine are more driven than Gabriel and Rossana Magnotta. They launched their winery on a shoestring in 1989 and have grown it to sales of about $30 million. "We started off with two wines," Rossana recounted early in 2004. "Now we are at 180." Many are easy-drinking value wines of surprising quality, something the winery draws attention to by entering a great many competitions. Now with 1,800 awards, Magnotta can claim to be Canada's most awarded winery.

It also is one of few Canadian wineries fully involved in the international wine business. Since 1996, Magnotta has owned a 142-hectare vineyard in Chile's Maipo Valley. In addition to producing wine under Magnotta's Chile label, the vineyard supplies some of the Canadian Magnotta winery's "international" wines, which are made with wine from around the world. Magnotta is justly proud of its Canadian wines, all of which qualify for Vintners Quality Alliance approval. However, the winery also understands that Canadian consumers are accustomed to buying globally.

"If customers are going to buy Australian or Italian or Chilean wines, they might as well buy our international series because the revenue is being kept here," Rossana reasons. "You are not going to stop people from buying those wines. You give them a choice. Here we are: Canada is our home but the world is our vineyard."

When they decided to open a winery, the couple discovered it might take two years to have the licence approved. Entrepreneurs usually find a way around a problem, and they did. In 1989, they bought Charal Wines and Vineyards, a failed winery in southwestern Ontario that still had a valid licence. The Magnottas moved the licence, which crucially included a retail store, to their suburban location just north of Toronto. Subsequently, they purchased other failed or struggling producers, building a small but efficient distribution network through which most of their table wines are sold.

"Unfortunately, we were not really well versed in the liquor business," Rossana admits. They developed an adversarial relationship with the Liquor Control Board of Ontario. This came to a head in 1999 when Magnotta sued the LCBO for damages of $8 million. The suit alleged that LCBO employees were defaming Magnotta (the statement of claim included a quotation attributed to the LCBO chairman to the effect that he had "more dirt on [Magnotta] than you know what to do with.") The spectacular allegations never came to court because Magnotta and the LCBO, with a mediator's help, reached a confidential settlement in 2001. "We settled our differences with our regulator and [now] we are doing extremely well with them," Rossana says. Magnotta has now emerged as one of the LCBO's leading suppliers of Icewine.

Magnotta has become one of Canada's largest Icewine producers since making its first Vidal version in 1991. Magnotta has often innovated, making the first sparkling Icewine in 1997 and the first Icewine grappa after getting a distillery licence, also in 1997. "We thought the skins were going to waste," Gabriel explains. Thus, after the first pressing of grapes for Icewine, the skins that others discard are fermented, reaching about eight degrees of alcohol, and then double-distilled. Recently Magnotta went further, distilling Icewine itself to produce an eau-de-vie called Primissimo. "It is almost ludicrous to do it," Rossana acknowledges. "It takes more than twenty bottles of Icewine to make one bottle of eau de vie."

Magnotta has made a point of offering wines at popular prices – as low as $6 a bottle. "Even with the cheapest of the wines we sell, Gabe or I have to taste them before an oenologist releases them," Rossana says. "We still have to have the Magnotta acceptance on them." Not many Magnotta wines cost more than the $20, the price of its top Limited Edition range, except for small volume speciality wines. The pricing philosophy extends to Magnotta's Icewines. "Icewine does not have to be $50 to be world class," Gabriel insists. The winery caused a furore in 1998 with an "Icewine celebration" – a sale during which it offered its Vidal Icewine at $19.95 a 375ml bottle, or about half what other wineries were asking. The object was to introduce Icewine to consumers. "We have thirty million people in Canada. Most of them have not tried Icewine." The price moved up after the sale but has always been more modest than that of most other producers.

Another Magnotta innovation was inspired by their Italian heritage: a wine called Enotrium, made in the style of Italy's muscular amarones. It is a blend of three varieties grown in Magnotta's seventy-three hectares of Niagara vineyards: Merlot, Cabernet Sauvignon, and Cabernet Franc. In 2000 and again in 2001, selected bunches of fully ripe grapes were air dried, concentrating the sugar prior to fermentation. The wine then spent twenty-six months in new oak barrels before being released. About 1,600 bottles were made in each vintage, packaged in expensive bottles with paintings by Group of Seven artist AY Jackson on the label.

One of Rossana's passions is to feature Canadian art on Magnotta labels. This has evolved from the substantial art collection which the family has assembled. It includes at least one canvas by Jean-Paul Riopelle, the Québec painter who provided the label for Mouton Rothschild 1978. The Riopelle hangs in Rossana's office but, so far, she has had no success in convincing the painter's estate that it should be on a Magnotta bottle.

MALETA VINEYARDS & ESTATE WINERY ***

450 Queenston Road, Niagara-on-the-Lake, ON, L0S 1J0.

Tel: 905 685 8486; Website: www.maletawinery.com

In a Canadian national wine competition in 2002, the Maleta 1999 Meritage was honoured as the best wine in its category. The victory was especially gratifying to winemaker Stan Maleta, a long-time home winemaker who made his first commercial vintage in 1999. He joined that group of dedicated amateurs who have been a major force in Ontario winemaking. Born in Poland in 1947, Maleta grow up in Canada after his family fled the Communist regime in his homeland. Tall, self-assured, and possessing a salesman's easy charm, he started as a car dealer. His Subaru dealership was one of the largest in Ontario and its success provided the funds to start a winery. In 1998, he and his wife, Marilyn, found a run-down six-hectare acre vineyard on busy Queenston Road, not far from the village of St Davids.

It had mature vinifera vines, including Riesling, Chardonnay, Gamay, and the three Bordeaux reds that went into the prize-winning Meritage. The vines had been planted about 1969. Maleta added Syrah, intending to include it in his red blends until the quality of the first vintage, from 2002, demanded it be released on its own. Early in 2004 Maleta sold the winery, which currently makes about 1,500 cases a year, to Montréal telecommunications engineer Daniel Pambianchi, another keen amateur vintner. "What I am really passionate about is the technology behind winemaking," the new owner says.

Maleta, who has left car sales, has continued as the winemaker. The goal is to increase production to about 3,000 cases, expanding the offerings to include Pinot Noir. In time, Pambianchi is expected to acquire additional property. That would free the winery from a strait-jacket imposed by Niagara-on-the-Lake, where a by-law limits a winery tasting room to a telephone booth-like 18.5 square metres (199 square feet) as long as the supporting vineyard is less than eight hectares. Every time a busload of wine lovers jams into the shop the Maletas envy those of their peers allowed to have tasting rooms at least ten times the size.

MALIVOIRE WINE COMPANY *****

4260 King Street East, Beamsville, ON, L0R 1B0.

Tel: 905 563 9253; Website: www.malivoirewineco.com

Some wineries need a few years to hit their stride. Not Malivoire. It opened in 1999 with first-rate wines, and won a gold medal at that year's International Wine and Spirit Competition for a Gewürztraminer Icewine. The consistent quality of the wines from the very beginning rests on three legs: impeccably managed vineyards, a cutting-edge winery, and sure-footed winemaking.

In 1995, Martin Malivoire, a motion-picture special effects producer, and his partner, Moira Saganski, were seeking a weekend retreat from Toronto when they bought a producing vineyard on the Beamsville Bench. Now called Moira Vineyard, it was then growing a melange of varieties. Malivoire retained its exceptional Gewürztraminer (at least until the hard winter in 2002–3 killed the vines) and replanted the remainder, mostly with Chardonnay and Pinot Noir, before launching the winery. In 1997, Malivoire bought a second property nearby, now called the Estate vineyard, planting more of the varieties in Moira, along with Chardonnay Musqué, Pinot Gris, Gamay, and Melon. The two vineyards total twenty hectares. The winery also manages a third property not far away. Only four hectares in size, this vineyard includes Maréchal Foch vines that were planted in 1975 and now produce Malivoire's cult Old Vines Foch. The vineyards are farmed organically; the Moira Vineyard received its organic designation in 2004.

The winery's unique tubular design undulates over the edge of a ravine like a gigantic Slinky toy. The incline from the crush pad at the back of the winery through seven levels down to the bottling line allows the wines to flow entirely without pumping. At the time of its construction, Malivoire was Ontario's first gravity-flow winery. Since then, at least half a dozen others have adopted the concept.

The vineyards and the winery enabled Ann Sperling, Malivoire's modest and soft-spoken winemaker, to win Ontario's winemaker of the year award in 2004. Born in Kelowna in 1962, Sperling is a member of the Casorso family, pioneering Okanagan grape-growers. She made wine at the Andrés winery in Port Moody and at Kelowna's CedarCreek before moving to Ontario in 1995 as an acclaimed consultant before joining the 15,000-case Malivoire winery. The flagship wines are Chardonnay and Pinot Noir, with the Moira Vineyard Chardonnay always showing concentrated fruit, a full-bodied texture, and a crisp finish. She also makes impressive wines with Gamay, Pinot Gris, Gewürztraminer, Riesling, and a blend of Cabernet and Merlot.

Another of Malivoire's cult wines is its Ladybug Rosé, based on Cabernet Franc and named for the red-shelled beetle that serves as the winery's mascot. Malivoire encourages ladybirds/ladybugs (*Hippodamia convergens*) for natural pest control. It became a marketing challenge when a different species, the yellow-shelled Asian lady beetle (*Harmonia axyridis*), started appearing in Ontario vineyards in 2001. Unlike the *Hippodamia convergens* species at Malivoire, the Asian variety excretes a pungent chemical, which only takes ten to twenty parts per trillion to taint wines. In its tasting room and on its website, Malivoire continues to stand by its mascot. "Nothing has changed our resolve, except to reinforce in our minds that balance, in nature as in everything, is critical," Malivoire states.

MAPLEGROVE VINOTECA ESTATE WINERY

4063 North Service Road, Beamsville, ON.

Tel: 905 856 3200

Second winery of Vinoteca (*see* page 108).

MARYNISSEN ESTATES ***

RR 6, Concession 1, Niagara-on-the-Lake, ON, L0S 1J0.

Tel: 905 468 7270; Website: www.marynissen.com

Born in Holland and fond of Bordeaux reds, John Marynissen took up grape-growing in the Niagara Peninsula the year after coming to Canada in 1952. When he also began making wine at home, he grasped that wine of international quality required vinifera grapes. In 1978, he was one of the first, if not the very first, to plant Cabernet Sauvignon at Niagara. That variety now makes long-lived flagship wines at this family-owned winery.

Sandra Marynissen, one of his daughters, has taken over much of the winemaking. The winery now produces about 12,000 cases a year, selling much of it directly from the farm. While Marynissen produces Chardonnay, Pinot Gris, Sauvignon Blanc, and Riesling, this is a winery where reds predominate. The winemakers aim at a style that is big and full-bodied, achieved by low-tonnage grape production, by extended skin contact during fermentation and by not filtering the reds.

One of his closest friends and mentors is Inniskillin co-founder and Icewine guru Karl Kaiser, and John Marynissen also makes Icewine. His vineyard includes about two hectares of Vidal grapes. On one occasion, Marynissen pushed the envelope to make Icewine from secondary bunches of Gamay grapes. "I'd sooner use it for table wine," he concluded. Gamay Noir is a Marynissen staple.

MOUNTAIN ROAD WINE COMPANY **
4016 Mountain Street, Beamsville, ON, LOR 1B7.
Tel: 905 563 0745; Website: www.mountainroadwine.com

Mountain Road's owner, Steve Kocsis, does not have much patience with bureaucracy after battling five years to licence the winery, which opened in 2003. The town of Lincoln wanted to zone his Beamsville Bench farm for a sub-division. He prevailed and continues to gro grapes and fruit on the property his parents purchased in 1958. Kocsis today operates more than thirty-three hectares of vineyards. Born in Budapest in 1949, he was seven when his family emigrated to Canada. The family had grown fruit for generations. "Back then," Kocsis noted acidly in an interview recently with an industry association, "a farmer could grow grapes, make wine, serve it to a traveller by the glass along with a meal, and he didn't need six permits and a dozen monthly government regulatory filings".

Trained in engineering, Kocsis purchased the family farm in 1981, made his first wine with Ontario Maréchal Foch grapes in 1982, and planted Chardonnay, Gamay, and Vidal in 1983. In subsequent vineyard expansions, he added Cabernet Sauvignon, Cabernet Franc, Riesling, Baco Noir, and Foch. Mountain Road's flagship wines include oak-aged blends of the Cabernets, barrel-fermented Chardonnay, and zesty Riesling.

NIAGARA COLLEGE TEACHING WINERY ****
135 Taylor Road, Niagara-on-the-Lake, ON, LOS 1J0.
Tel: 905 641 2252; Website: http://web.niagarac.on.ca/business/nct_winery.htm

Launched in 2000, the winery at Niagara College is Canada's first and, to date, only teaching winery. Under the eye of veteran winemaker Jim Warren, the students make about 2,500 cases of wines annually, some of it from a nearby student-run vineyard on the flanks of the Niagara Escarpment. The quality of the wine is professional. The Niagara College 2001 Chardonnay was judged the white wine of the year in a national Canadian wine competition in 2002. In the following year, every wine entered by Niagara College that year won a medal, earning it a "winery of the year" nomination.

The wine programme at Niagara College was developed after the college surveyed Ontario's wineries in 1999 and found that while Brock

University had begun to graduate academically-trained winemakers and Guelph University had long turned out microbiologists and other food industry professionals, the wineries also wanted technicians with hands-on experience in vineyards and winemaking. Niagara College provides this with a three-year programme. Every year, more than 100 people apply for twenty-four places. Even foreign students attend. Recently, a young Chinese man was equipping himself to run a winery that his family was developing in China.

Born in 1942, Warren has juggled successful parallel careers as a teacher and a winemaker almost all his life. "Because I am a teacher, if I learn something, I learn it well enough so that I can teach it," he says. Stoney Ridge winery, founded in 1985, was his first professional winery. He consults for numerous Ontario wineries and is a founder and executive director of Fruit Wines of Canada.

Warren and the students at Niagara College make at least ten different wines each year, exploring a variety of styles. With Chardonnay, for example, the students make both a rich barrel-fermented version and a bright unoaked one. Niagara College claims to be the only teaching winery in the world that covers Icewine production. Most of the wines are sold through the campus wine shop.

PALATINE HILLS ESTATE WINERY ***
911 Lakeshore Road, Niagara-on-the-Lake, ON, L0S 1J0.
Tel: 905 646 9617; Website: www.palatinehillsestatewinery.com

John Neufeld's vineyard coerced him into opening Palatine Hills in 2003. He had begun selling Vidal juice for Icewine to other wineries in 1994, developing a market that he still pursues, even selling to wineries in New York State. When the bountiful 1998 vintage yielded more high-quality juice than wineries had ordered, he hired a winemaker to convert his surplus to Icewine. He did the same thing in 2000 after he and a major winery failed to agree on a price for the juice. Then in 2001 he also produced late-harvest and table wines with his excess fruit – still without having a licence to sell the finished wine. Then he entered the 1998 Icewine into a local competition in 2002, won a gold and had consumers banging on his door. He promptly converted a machine shed on his farm into Palatine Hills, a winery that now produces betweeen 5,000 and 7,000 cases of table wines annually, as well as a significant volume of Icewine.

Neufeld began growing grapes in 1972. Born in Niagara-on-the-Lake in 1948, he grew up on his family's fruit farm. After graduating in agriculture from the University of Guelph, he bought his own farm, a property planted largely with labrusca grapes, and in 1975 decided to plant four hectares of Gamay and Gewürztraminer. "Everybody told me that I was nuts spending that much money putting in varieties that were going to get killed," he says. To be on the safe side, he added winter-hardy Seyval Blanc and Vidal, planted peaches, and established a construction business. Everything succeeded.

Neufeld also became a director of the Ontario Grape Growers' Marketing Board and was the chair from 1995 to 2002. From this insider's vantage point, he helped to negotiate government compensation to replace mediocre varieties in many Ontario vineyards. In 1994, he switched entirely to vinifera (except for Vidal, essential for Icewine). Today, he is one of the largest independent growers, with forty-nine hectares of his own vineyard, plus a larger leased vineyard. If all the grapes were vinified at Palatine Hills, the winery could make 100,000 cases to 130,000 cases a year. He prefers to remain diversified, selling grapes and juice to other wineries as well as making wines.

Since 2001, the winemaker at Palatine Hills has been David Hojnoski, a veteran of the Canadian and American wine industries. Making wine at Palatine Hills is quite different from his previous jobs at New York's Gold Seal winery and subsequently at Andrés in Ontario. For the first time in his career, he has built a winery from scratch. "I hadn't really been involved in the hands-on work, building wines with personalities, like I have been here," he says. "Every wine that I am involved with making now has its own personality and style." He likes to build blending options for himself by, for example, using a variety of yeasts and barrels. "I have six different types of oak barrels," he says. "That gives me the flexibility to create something that is complex and with a lot of depth."

Palatine Hills offers four whites (Chardonnay, Sauvignon Blanc, Riesling, and Gewürztraminer), four reds (Merlot, Cabernet Franc, Cabernet Sauvignon, and Meritage) and three Icewines. Hojnoski also crafts a premium Proprietor's Reserve range. Across the board, the wines express the sumptuous fruit that Neufeld gets from his vines. "There are people who have passion for what they do," Hojnoski says. "John's passion is for growing things."

PELLER ESTATES ****

290 John Street East, Niagara-on-the-Lake, ON, L0S 1J0.

Tel: 905 468 4678; Website: www.peller.com

The Peller winery that opened in 2001 just outside Niagara-on-the-Lake is the public face of Canada's second-largest wine company. Known corporately as Andrés Wines, the firm makes or bottles most of its wine in Ontario at a sprawling industrial complex beside a busy highway at Winona, midway between Hamilton and St Catharines. That winery, which Andrés took over in 1969 from a tobacco company, has neither the location nor the appearance to attract many tourists. That was not relevant until the 1990s when Niagara wineries set out to lure Toronto's wine lovers with destination wineries. Andrés rose to the challenge by building a baronial, French-style château set in a ten-hectare vineyard within walking distance of historic Niagara-on-the-Lake. The views from its dining rooms look westward over the vineyards towards the Niagara Escarpment. The winery offers extensive programmes including tastings, food and wine pairings, and tours of cellars where some of Peller's 1,000 barrels and a wine inventory of 60,000 bottles are stored.

The company has been called Andrés since it was founded in 1961 by Hungarian-born Andrew Peller. He came up with the name because it sounded French; the Canadian wine industry in his era was always taking on European wine imagery. The winery's best-known brands under the Andrés label are still Hochtaler and Domaine D'Or. But in 1992, when Andrew's grandson, John, took over as president, the company began releasing its premium wines under the Peller family name.

The super-reserve tier is the Andrew Peller Signature Series, small lots principally of red varietals, first launched in 1998. "Andrew Peller wines are made from our best grapes," says winemaker Robert Summers. Peller now owns fifty-eight hectares of its own Niagara vineyards, including one vineyard surrounding the château, and works closely with about two dozen growers. "We take the ripest grapes from the best vineyards," Summers adds. He applies all of his premium winemaking practices, such as extended maceration, ages the wines in barrels, and then blends only the best barrels before bottling the wines, which are unfiltered.

Summers seems to have a special affinity for Cabernet Franc. His Andrew Peller Signature Cabernet Franc is a big wine with luscious flavours of black cherries and chocolate. His Cabernet Franc Icewine in the same premium series displays a brilliant ruby hue and delivers a bowlful of sweet plum flavours. "When we have the chance to do what we want to do, Cabernet Franc shines for me," Summers says. He notes that in some vintages, processing of this variety is sandwiched uncomfortably between earlier-ripening Merlot and later-ripening Cabernet Sauvignon. "In Ontario, we struggle to get Cabernet Sauvignon to maturity," the winemaker notes. "If I had my own winery and if I had to focus my energies, it would be Cabernet Franc, Riesling, Chardonnay, and Gamay."

Peller also releases wines under its Private Reserve series, primarily barrel-aged and made in a style that emphasises the varietal fruit. Larger volumes of good value wines, also varietals, are released under its Vineyard Series of wines.

PENINSULA RIDGE ESTATES WINERY *****
5600 King Street West, Beamsville, ON, L0R 1B0.
Tel: 905 563 0900; Website: www.peninsularidge.com

Norman Beal spent two decades in the corporate fast lane working as an international oil trader before, in a quality-of-life career change, he built one of Ontario's most ambitious new wineries. Peninsula Ridge opened in 2000, with the objective of growing to 30,000 cases a year. The winery was two-thirds of the way there within four years, surprising even Beal. "We can never enter our best wines in competitions," he says sadly. "They sell out too quickly."

Beal looked at properties in California and New York before taking a closer look at the Beamsville Bench, not far from his birthplace of Hamilton. When he had left Ontario two decades earlier, the wines had been mediocre. The wines that he tasted on coming home showed exciting potential. In 1999, he purchased a thirty-two-hectare former orchard. Since then, he has invested $7 million in building a superbly equipped winery, rehabilitating a turreted mansion (which has been turned into a restaurant); and planting eighteen hectares of vineyard. The view from the tasting room is one of the best in Niagara: vineyards sweep downhill, with the distant Toronto skyline afloat on Lake Ontario.

Beal wanted to hire a winemaker consistent with his goal of making wine that can stand on the world stage. He learned from his barrel supplier in France that Jean-Pierre Colas, then head winemaker at Domaine Laroche in Chablis, might be available. Colas was not a stay-at-home winemaker. He had done numerous crushes in South America and

New Zealand. It took some wooing, however, to recruit him. "Jean-Pierre knew I was going to invest what it took to build a world-class winery," Beal says. "His concern was, can you actually grow grapes in Ontario?" Beal arranged for Colas to spend a week in Ontario, examining vineyards and wineries in detail with viticultural consultant Lloyd Schmidt. He even chartered a helicopter so the two could view the vineyards from above. Colas took the job.

The skill with Chardonnay that Colas honed in Chablis is reflected at Peninsula Ridge. The winery's unoaked Inox Chardonnay has all the freshness and crispness of Chablis, but with more weight. The reserve Chardonnay is as big as any fine burgundy. Chardonnay is one of Peninsula Ridge's flagship whites. The other is Sauvignon Blanc, made in the same remarkably intense style that turned heads when New Zealand began making this variety. "The New Zealanders have nothing on us," Beal says.

Beal is also putting a big wager on reds. The winery's eight-hectare planting of Syrah is one of the single largest in Ontario. The variety was planted over several years, starting with a small planting so that trial lots of wine could be made. The 2002 Syrah proved to be a powerful, peppery wine in the style of the northern Rhône, encouraging Beal to make a major commitment to it. There is a risk that the variety will not take well to Ontario's cold winters. "Given the quality we produced at our experimental stage, it was worth the gamble," Beal believes.

The winery's flagship red wine is a blend called Arcanum, a name that alludes to alchemical efforts to turn lead into gold. The blend includes the red Bordeaux varieties used in Meritage, along with Syrah, in a quest for depth and complexity. There is also a practical reason for taking the blend beyond Meritage. Colas explains: "Meritage has lost its power as being the premium blend for a wine producer because there are now many average wines at all price points on the market."

Beal practises his own style of risk management at Peninsula Ridge. "We are the only winery in Niagara that has a grape surplus," he says. In addition to the eighteen hectares of vines on the winery property, Peninsula Ridge has thirteen hectares across the road and a twenty-year contract on 44.5 hectares. "It goes back to my trading days. I always thought that [grapes] was one of those markets you had to go long in." In the bountiful 2002 harvest, Peninsula Ridge processed so much Cabernet Sauvignon that the winery sold Chardonnay in bulk to free tank space.

Niagara's 2003 harvest was sharply down because of vine damage the previous winter. Many wineries began running out of wine, but not Peninsula Ridge. "We are sitting in the catbird seat," Beal chuckles. "It makes me look a lot smarter than I am."

PILLITTERI ESTATES WINERY ★★★★
1696 Niagara Stone Road (Highway 55), Niagara-on-the-Lake, ON, L0S 1J0.
Tel: 905 468 3147; Website: www.pillitteri.com

Two things happened to Gary Pillitteri in 1988: he failed to win a seat in the Canadian Parliament but he did win a gold medal in a home winemakers' competition for his Icewine. Born in Sicily in 1936, he arrived in Canada in 1948, ultimately buying an orchard near the village of Virgil on the Niagara Peninsula. Over time, the fruit trees were replaced with vines and Gary flourished, both as a grape-grower and as a keen amateur vintner. He began his political career in municipal politics but when he was denied a federal seat in 1988, he poured his prodigious energy into turning his roadside farm market into a winery, which opened in 1993. Ironically, it coincided with his second run at federal politics, when he won a seat. He remained a Member of Parliament until 2004, retiring to return to a thriving 60,000-case winery under the administration of Charles, his son, Connie, his daughter, and Jamie Slingerland, her husband.

Strategically located on a busy regional highway at the edge of Virgil, this winery's unassuming architecture still echoes its farm market origins. Recent renovations, however, have expanded the tasting room to accommodate the rising number of visitors. "A typical Sunday is six busloads of visitors," says Sue-Ann Staff, the winemaker.

Pillitteri Estates considers itself Ontario's largest estate Icewine producer. In 2004, it made an astounding 138,000 litres of Icewine, equal to the average annual Eiswein production of Austria. It accounts for more than a third of the winery's total business. Most of it is exported, virtually hand-sold by Charles Pillitteri. He boasts that he travels 200 days a year, selling Icewine in nineteen different countries.

In 2003, Staff made six different varietal Icewines and two sparkling Icewines. "I can't believe how efficient we have become at doing it," she says of Icewine. Perhaps because she makes so much, Staff finds it hard to wax romantic about it. At Pillitteri's volumes, the Icewine vintage can stretch over many weeks when the temperatures fluctuate, or be compressed when it is quite cold. In one persistent cold period during the 2003 vintage, Pillitteri's crews picked for thirty hours non-stop. The grapes are pressed at temperatures as cold as those in the field, which means the winery can be as uncomfortable as the vineyard. In 2001, when the Pillitteri winery quadrupled its size, Staff had heating installed in the concrete of the new crushing floor. "It is so I can stay warm," she laughs. "That is important for making Icewine. There isn't one part of it that's easy, not one part. The only good thing is drinking it." At the tasting room entrance, the winery displays many of the awards won by Staff's wines. These include a perfect score and a double gold at an American Wine Society competition for a 1998 Riesling Icewine and a recent gold medal, again for Icewine, at Vinitaly. "That one had been eluding me," she says.

For all the emphasis on Icewine, the winery produces a substantial range of other wines, seventy per cent of which are red. "That's what I like to make," says Staff. She sets out to make reds that are big and bold. When the winery was expanded in 2001, so many fermentation tanks were installed that Staff has the luxury of being able to leave more than 200 tons of reds on their skins at once. She has left fermenting Cabernet Sauvignon on its skins, extracting flavour and enriching the structure, for anywhere from two weeks to a month. Cabernet Franc, the winery's flagship red, can spend three weeks on the skins while Merlot gets at least two weeks.

The best reds and whites at Pillitteri are bottled as Family Reserve. They are made in small volumes, only in the best vintages, and usually sell for about $50 a bottle. Fitting this profile is the winery's Bordeaux blend, a concentrated red called Trivalente. However, the winery also offers wines affordably priced for everyday consumption. Some of the successful wines in this range include an unoaked Chardonnay, a fresh and lemony Pinot Grigio, and a fruity, off-dry blend of Gewürztraminer and Riesling.

PUDDICOMBE ESTATE FARMS AND WINERY ***
1468 Highway 8, Winona, ON, L8E 5K9.
Tel: 905 643 1015; Website: www.puddicombefarm.com
This 121-hectare farm in a suburb of Hamilton, growing both fruit trees and grapes, has been owned by the Puddicombe family since 1797. In the property's recent history, two wineries in succession have risen here. In the 1980s, Murray Puddicombe, the current head of the family, became a

fifty per cent partner in Stoney Ridge Cellars when that winery's founder, Jim Warren, expanded it from his barn. Puddicombe sold his share when, under the energetic Warren, the winery, grown to more than sixty labels, went beyond Puddicombe's vision. Stoney Ridge moved further south while the Puddicombes created a smaller winery. "One of the reasons why my Dad got out is that he wanted it to be more of a family environment, more country winery style," says Lindsay, the oldest of Murray's four children. Now the winemaker at Puddicombe Estate, which opened in 2000, she makes only thirty-two labels, including seven fruit wines.

"My first vintage was in 1999 and I made a Pinot Noir," says Lindsay, who was born in 1978 and has both an agriculture business degree and a winemaking diploma. "It is one of my favourite reds to make. It is the most challenging red anyway." The family's sixty-one hectares of vineyard grow almost all the grapes that she needs, except Merlot and Cabernet Sauvignon which are purchased from a warmer site near Niagara-on-the-Lake. The cooler Puddicombe vineyard is farther from the tempering influence of Lake Ontario than many other bench vineyards. However, Murray Puddicombe's careful grape-growing has avoided much of the winter kill that devastated other vineyards. "He doesn't like to stress his vines," Lindsay says of her father. "He wants to be able to get a crop every year. He is a fantastic grower. It is easier to make wine when you have a good guy to fall back on."

The family has been growing grapes since 1940 and, in 1962, was among the earliest to plant vinifera on the bench. As a result, Lindsay has both mature vines and a selection of varieties going beyond the mainstream for Ontario. Viognier has been growing at Puddicombe for a dozen years. The vineyard also has Sauvignon Blanc which Lindsay, who makes fruit-forward wines, turns into a zesty, New Zealand-style white. With a modest amount of Colombard, she produces Ontario's only varietal from a grape known for its electric fruit and its equally electric acidity.

Lindsay also produces a small range of fruit wines, all of which (except the cranberry) are made with fruit grown on the farm. The style is straightforward: the wines must always be a clear expression of the fruit. "They play a huge role in this industry," Lindsay says. "There are a lot of young people that are trying to get interested in wine. They don't have the ability to like 'wine' wines yet, so they'll go to fruit wines." Except for the light, fragrant peach wine, all of the fruit wines finish with notable but well-balanced sweetness. Consequently Puddicombe makes no late-harvest grape-wine except Icewine.

REIF ESTATE WINERY *****
15608 Niagara Parkway, Niagara-on-the-Lake, ON, L0S 1J0.
Tel: 905 468 7738; Website: www.reifwinery.com

Whether it is wine or cars, Klaus Reif likes power. His hobby is racing vintage sports cars. His passion is making big wines. He planted Zinfandel grapes in 1994 "because I wanted to make a big red" and he did in fact produce one powerful Zinfandel in 2001 before a famously cold Ontario winter wiped this tender California variety from the Reif vineyards. Now Reif and associate winemaker Roberto DiDomenico are focused on making intense Bordeaux reds, particularly Cabernet Sauvignon. Other wineries may argue that Cabernet Franc is more suitable for Ontario; not Reif. "Cabernet Sauvignon is the better variety, period," says Reif. "If it were a woman, I would marry her."

The emphasis on reds is a big shift from the winery's initial white offerings when it was opened in 1983 by Ewald Reif, Klaus's uncle. The Reif family has been growing wine near the Rhine in Germany since the sixteenth century. Ewald's interest in Canada was derived from the frontier literature he read as a youth. In 1977 he bought a vineyard on the Niagara Parkway and replaced the labrusca and hybrid vines with primarily white vinifera. He was encouraged to open the winery by his brother in Germany, who sent Klaus to Canada in 1987 to make the wine and to manage the winery.

Born in 1963, Klaus had just graduated from Geisenheim with degrees in viticulture and oenology. In Germany he had made delicate Eisweine; in Ontario, he made Icewines of luxuriant richness. He grasped that he could make "powerhouse" Icewine in Ontario by harvesting grapes when they are frozen more deeply than is usual in Germany. "A lot of people produce Icewine to be served with dessert," he says. "My Icewine, because I produce it in a richer style, is a dessert. I see it more as a liqueur than a wine." The winery now makes about 35,000 cases a year. Most is grown on the winery's fifty-five hectares of vineyard, about a quarter of which is dedicated to red varieties. "We started out as a Riesling producer," Reif recalls. He continues to make good Riesling, along with Chardonnay and an increasing volume of Sauvignon Blanc.

The switch to reds began after Hamilton-born DiDomenico joined in 1989. The winery began releasing wines from the Bordeaux varieties in 1991. As the vines got older, a proprietary blend called Tesoro was released in 1995. Reif raised its own standards again in 2004 with a limited production of reds in the winery's First Growth series – a Merlot, a Cabernet Sauvignon, and a Pinot Noir, all 2001. The grapes for these come from minimally-cropped vines that are at least twelve years old. The wines are fermented in oak and spend at least twenty-six months in barrel. They are richly concentrated, with good ageing potential. Soon after release, the Cabernet Sauvignon was judged Ontario's best example of that variety in a 2004 Niagara competition.

"Our goal is to produce better wines," Reif states, explaining that he is planning to add super-premium Chardonnay and Riesling to the First Growth range. "If I say one day that this is the best I can do, I will stop making wine."

RIDGEPOINT WINES **
3900 Cherry Avenue, Vineland, ON, L0R 2C0.
Tel: 905 562 8853; Website: www.ridgepointwines.com

Mauro Scarsellone was a chartered accountant with one of the major firms until he fell in love with Icewine. That passion led to the creating of Ridgepoint, which began selling wines from its temporary barrel cellar in 2003 while he prodded the contractor to complete the main winery. "If I'd used my accountant's hat, I probably would not be in the wine business," he says with a grin. Rotund and moustachioed, he presides over the tasting room with infectious enthusiasm.

Born in Toronto in 1964, Scarsellone gave little thought to the wine region about an hour's drive down the road until his infatuation with Icewine led him to begin exploring Niagara-area tasting rooms. Ultimately he purchased eight hectares on the Beamsville Bench and plunged into the wine business. Beginning in 1995, he planted the vineyard largely with an eye to making big reds. Most is given over to Pinot Noir, Cabernet Sauvignon and Merlot. In a nod to his Italian heritage, he has small plantings of Sangiovese and Nebbiolo. The first twenty-eight cases of Nebbiolo, made from the 2001 vintage, sold out almost as soon as the winery opened. Naturally, there was also an Icewine in the first vintage, a light and lively Vidal with a refreshing piquancy.

Although he grew up in an Italian household and made wine with his grandparents, Scarsellone employed consultants when Ridgepoint made its initial vintages. His first consulting winemaker was the redoubtable Jim Warren and the bold Warren style is stamped on many 2001 wines from Ridgepoint. Warren was succeeded by Arthur Harder, a former winemaker at Hillebrand and a consultant to many new wineries.

RIVERVIEW CELLARS ESTATE WINERY *
15376 Niagara Parkway, Niagara-on-the-Lake, ON, L0S 1J0.
Tel: 905 262 0636; Website: www.riverviewcellars.com

It pays to be alert to what the customer demands. When Riverview opened in 2000, the portfolio included an off-dry Vidal table wine. Tasting room visitors – especially the Americans – began asking for an off-dry red. Sam Pillitteri made one, calling it Fontana Dolce. A blend of Cabernet Franc, Cabernet Sauvignon, and Baco Noir, it sold in a flash. Now Fontana Dolce is Riverview's best-selling wine, accounting for about twenty per cent of the winery's 10,000-case annual production.

Pillitteri was encouraged to open his own winery by his brother, Gary, the founder of Pillitteri Estates Winery (see page 89), which formerly bought Riverview's grapes. The Pillitteri brothers came to Canada from Italy in the late 1940s. Sam settled for some years in Halifax, operating a pizzeria before moving his family here in 1975. For many years, the ten-hectare farm operated as an orchard, supplying the family's farm market. Beginning with Gewürztraminer in 1990, it has now been converted entirely to grapes. There are eight varieties in the vineyard, including a significant planting of Vidal to support the winery's Icewine programme.

To cope with the winery's growing volume, the Pillitteris went outside the family in 2004, hiring winemaker Fred Di Profio to produce the wines. The flagship wine is Salvatore's Reserve Cabernet Franc, first made in the 2002 vintage.

ROCKWAY GLEN GOLF COURSE & ESTATE WINERY
3290 Ninth Street Louth, St. Catharines, ON, L2R 6P7.
Tel: 905 641 1030; Website: www.rockwayglen.com

On rainy days, the 200 members of Rockway Glen can still find reasons to come to their club. The eighteen-hole golf course, which was developed in 1990 on property that formerly grew grapes, also offers its members a restaurant, a winery that opened in 2001 and even a wine museum with knowledgeable guides. The museum shows wine-growing as it was in the nineteenth century, with tools and garments collected in Europe. From time to time, items from Brock University's massive collection of wine objects are also on display. Portions of the former vineyard were replanted in 2003 to varieties including Cabernet Franc, Gamay, Riesling, and Chardonnay.

ROYAL DEMARIA WINES CO *****
4551 Cherry Avenue, Beamsville, ON, L0R 1B1.
Tel: 905 562 6767; Website: www.royaldemaria.com

According to vintner Joseph DeMaria, Canadian Icewine deserves the same position in the marketplace as Rolex watches or Versace accessories. In the 2002 vintage, he made thirty-three cases (about 400 half-bottles) of red Meritage Icewine. He released it at $395 a bottle. As bottles sold, he raised the price several times. By the time the stock was down to sixty bottles, the price was $5,000 a bottle. "Canadians are producing the greatest Icewines in the world," DeMaria asserts. "If there is a brandy that is selling for $5,000 or $6,000, I can't see why an Icewine can't." Royal DeMaria winery now proclaims itself "Canada's Icewine Specialist" (DeMaria trademarked that in the USA) and is believed to be the sole winery in Canada making only Icewine.

An Ontario native, born in 1961 of Italian parents, DeMaria is a Toronto hairdresser and, recognizing the hazards in his winery's strategy, continues to operate a hair salon. "It is very high risk," DeMaria says. "It is nerve-racking when it comes to the harvest. You become conditioned to it and you learn to accept it for what it is."

DeMaria's Icewine epiphany occurred in 1991 when he tasted it for the first time while touring Niagara-region wineries. "It was fantastic," he remembers. Soon he began making trial lots at his home, started planning a winery and in 1996 purchased a ten-hectare vineyard near Vineland. At first, he sold Icewine juice to other producers. A surplus of 5,000 litres of Vidal juice in the 1998 vintage triggered the decision to bottle the wine under the DeMaria brand. Now, the winery produces about 24,000 half-bottles annually, with premium pricing where quality and scarcity justify it.

DeMaria endeavours to make varietal Icewine from as many as possible of the sixteen varieties in his vineyard. His largest volumes are Vidal and Riesling, the stalwart Icewine varieties in Ontario. In 2000, when he made Icewine from Pinot Gris and Gamay, varieties seldom employed, he discovered a great consumer curiosity about the wines. "That's what started the buzz in the wine world," he recalls. "They lined up at our table to get a taste of those wines. That's when I realized that the wine industry needs a change, and we decided to start producing different varietals." The range now includes Gewürztraminer, Muscat, Chardonnay, Cabernet Sauvignon, Merlot, and Cabernet Franc.

DeMaria claims to have stumbled across a superior, and secret, way to process Icewine. It allows him, he says, to make elegantly balanced Icewines bursting with varietal character and fruit. "Some people like Icewines powerful, sweet and heavy, a little more bold," he says. "But when you get so much sweetness in an Icewine, I believe the sugars mask most of the varietal characters. If we have a Gewürztraminer that has spicy tones to it, ginger notes, whatever, when you taste the Royal DeMaria brand, it is striking. It hits you right away." The effectiveness of DeMaria's little secret can be measured by the results the winery achieves whenever it enters competitions. In 2003, for example, Royal DeMaria wines took five gold medals at the Concours Mondial de Bruxelles, the most ever given to a single winery in just one category. That matched a similar performance the year before at the Vinexpo competition. "We have managed to do quite well internationally," DeMaria says, "and it has raised the bar for Canada."

SOUTHBROOK WINERY ***
1061 Major MacKenzie Drive, Maple, ON, L6A 3P2.
Tel: 905 832 2548; Website: www.southbrook.com

Formerly home to Canada's largest Jersey dairy herd, Southbrook opened its winery in 1992 and now produces about 12,000 cases a year, a third of which are fruit wines. Southbrook is one of several wineries located in Greater Toronto and the only one still on a working farm. The tasting room is in a century-old barn, with stone walls and rough-hewn beams creating the feeling of an old European winery. The winery's barrel cellar is in another former barn built about 1890.

One of Southbrook's attractions is that it has not been swallowed by Toronto's relentless sprawl. This 115-hectare property, in owner Bill Redelmeier's family since 1940, still grows an abundance of berries and vegetables, sold through its compact farm market. Winemaker Colin

Campbell laments that the busiest month is October, when truckloads of Niagara-grown grapes compete for attention with the farm's golden mounds of pumpkins. The patrons of the farm market buy half of Southbrook's wine. That was the strategy when Redelmeier, a passionate wine lover, launched the winery.

This is a disciplined winery, carefully limiting its production to a small number of varietals: Chardonnay, Sauvignon Blanc and Vidal for white wines; and the three major Bordeaux grapes, plus Maréchal Foch, for reds. The winery also makes between 3,000 and 5,000 litres of Icewine each year. Except for the Vidal, Campbell puts most of his wines through some time in barrels, selecting the best for the winery's Triomphe or reserve tier.

Southbrook began making fruit wines in 1992 to use up a surplus from its four-hectare pick-yourself raspberry patch. The winery's Framboise is the flagship of its fruit wines. It is so well made that it was offered for sale in London's Harrods department store in 1996 and won a gold medal the following year at the International Wine and Spirits Competition. All the fruit wines – Cassis, Blueberry, Blackberry and Framboise d'Or, which is made with yellow raspberries – are sweet and slightly fortified to 14.5 degrees of alcohol. It is a style, Campbell points out, that best captures the aromas and tastes of the berries.

STONECHURCH VINEYARDS ***
1242 Irvine Road, Niagara-on-the-Lake, ON, L0S 1J0.
Tel: 905 935 3535; Website: www.stonechurch.com
What sets Stonechurch apart is its practice of holding back some wines each year for subsequent library releases. For example, the Stonechurch 1991 Vidal Icewine, the winery's first, was still available a decade after winning a gold medal at the 1994 Vinitaly competition. Also on sale in the wine shop were Icewines from 1994 and 1997, along with the current release. Collectors of past vintages can find mature reds, such as 1992 Cabernet Franc. The winery's first Cabernet Sauvignon, made in 1991, is sold out but the 1993, 1994, 1995 and 1997 vintages were being offered in 2004 along with the current release, the 2000. It still is rare in the Canadian wine industry to find quality producers that offer library wines.

Stonechurch was opened in 1990, based on vineyards farmed by Lambert and Grace Hunse, who came to Canada from Holland in the 1950s and began growing grapes in 1972. Their son Rick and his wife

Fran took over Stonechurch in 1995. The winery now produces 30,000 cases a year. Hunse positioned it to grow larger in 2004 by purchasing twenty hectares of vineyard, increasing the total to eighty hectares. From the new vineyard, Stonechurch extended its range of wines to include Sauvignon Blanc, a favourite of winemaker Terence van Rooyen. Formerly the winemaker at the Cilento winery in Toronto and KWV in South Africa, van Rooyen promises that "we are going to do super-premium winemaking. We are going to be a winery to take note of."

Stonechurch, which also sells grapes to other wineries, focuses on selected varietals. These include Riesling, Chardonnay, Gamay Noir and the two Cabernets, along with Baco Noir and Vidal (the latter produces easy-drinking table wines, dessert wines and richly flavoured Icewines). It is one of the few Ontario wineries making a table wine from Morio Muscat, a grape developed in Germany. Even though neither of the parents – Pinot Blanc and Sylvaner – are Muscat varieties, this grape yields an exotic wine with the perfume of spice and rose petals. Traditionally, Stonechurch has made the wine in a bone-dry style which, in van Rooyen's judgement, is a little austere. He prefers to leave a touch of natural sweetness, enhancing the wine's charm.

STONEY RIDGE ESTATE WINERY ****
3201 King Street, Vineland, ON, L0R 2C0.
Tel: 905 562 1324; Website: www.stoneyridge.com

Stoney Ridge is a paradox. Over the past two decades, the winery has endured remarkable turbulence, but in most of those years has made some of the best wines in Ontario, both with grapes and with fruit. The common thread through much of the winery's history has been Jim Warren, a self-taught winemaker with so much talent that he now teaches winemakers. He founded this winery in 1985 in the barn of a farmer friend. Stoney Ridge moved twice as the business grew. Warren sold the winery in 1998, quit as winemaker the next year and returned in 2002 to make a range of super-premium wines for the current owners.

Born in 1942, Warren was settled in on a thirty-one-year career (he retired in 1997) as a high-school languages teacher in Hamilton when, in the early 1970s, he made his first wine from grape concentrate. "I almost gave up on my hobby because it turned out so bad," he remembers. On impulse, he added leftover yeast from the wine kit to a thawing mess of strawberries, raspberries and rhubarb he was asked to remove from the family freezer. The resulting rosé was good enough to win several amateur competitions. Winemaking had hooked him. He joined a club and applied himself so intensely that by the time he turned professional he had been Ontario's champion home winemaker three times and Canada's champion three more times. He succeeded, in part, because he sought out the best quality grapes that he could find. In 1975, he began buying Chardonnay from a Beamsville grower named Bill Lenko, one of Ontario's first private growers to plant that and other vinifera varieties. Subsequently, many of Stoney Ridge's award-winning burgundian-style Chardonnays were made with Lenko grapes. In 1999, Warren also helped Daniel Lenko, Bill's son, launch a winery of his own (*see* page 55).

Stoney Ridge was started in 1985 on a farm near Stoney Creek that was owned by Bruce Weylie, a member of the same winemaking club as Warren. Four years later, when the winery grew beyond Weylie's ambition, Warren partnered with Murray Puddicombe to turn a barn on the historic Puddicombe farm into the second Stoney Ridge winery. Here, it seemed that everything Warren touched turned into wine, often highly-acclaimed wine. At the peak, there were sixty-two different wines in the Stoney Ridge portfolio. Puddicombe had a more modest winery in mind and, in 1998, the partnership was ended. A group of businessmen from Ottawa acquired Puddicombe's half interest and moved the winery to a new building near Vineland, right on the wine route. At the same time, two Niagara businessmen bought Warren's interest in Stoney Ridge. Warren became a very busy consulting winemaker, helping launch half a dozen Ontario wineries while installing his successor at Stoney Ridge, a Romanian vintner named Liubomir Popovici.

After another shake-up among the partners in 2002 – the president is now Mark Bonham, a wealthy Toronto financial services entrepreneur – Warren returned, specifically charged with making top-tier wines labelled Founder's Signature Collection. These include a legendary wine called "Charlotte's Chardonnay," a wine that sparkles with vivid fruit flavours. The name is a tribute to Warren's wife, to whom the term "long suffering" might apply. "My wife would be the first to admit that I can be terribly over-focused," he says. "I can be sitting there and she can be talking to me and I don't even hear her. I am just thinking about something else. I am always thinking about wine. There are not many people as focused on wine as me."

The current Stoney Ridge portfolio, while more disciplined than a decade ago, still reflects Warren's unquenchable enthusiasm. Alongside the Meritage and Cabernet Franc and Chardonnay, there is also cranberry wine. "We made the first cranberry wine in British North America," Warren believes. Initially, it was made for a Mohawk band from northern Ontario that owned a cranberry bog and were thinking of developing a winery. The project never materialized but Warren liked the wine so much that it has remained a Stoney Ridge staple.

When the winery's current ownership took over in 2002, an inventory uncovered several thousand bottles of Stoney Ridge from earlier vintages, some as far back as 1985. It speaks well for Warren's winemaking that most of them were sound and have been offered for sale as library wines. The wines available in 2004 included a ten-year-old Chardonnay made from Lenko grapes – the vineyard that launched Warren on his career.

STREWN ESTATE WINERY ****
1339 Lakeshore Road, Niagara-on-the-Lake, ON, L0S 1J0.
Tel: 905 468 1229; Website: www.strewnwinery.com

Strewn is notable, among other things, for being the first Canadian winery with a cooking school attached. Winemaker Joe Will, an Alberta-born former public relations executive with a winemaking degree from Australia's Roseworthy College, opened the winery in 1997 in partnership with Newman Smith, an industry veteran who previously spent nearly three decades as a financial executive at Andrés. The first two vintages for Strewn were made at Pillitteri (see page 89) while Will and Smith converted a former fruit packing house into a 15,000-case winery. The sprawling buildings accommodate a restaurant and the cooking school run by Jane Langdon, Will's wife. "We are as much in the tourism business as we are in the wine business," Will maintains. "The restaurant and the cooking school make Strewn a destination. It never hurts to be unique."

While Strewn makes a familiar range of whites, including Chardonnay and Riesling, production tilts toward reds from the Bordeaux varieties. The flagship is Strewn Three, a blend of Cabernet Sauvignon, Cabernet Franc, and Merlot, selected from the best barrels in the best vintages. In those years when Will makes it – there have been only five vintages between 1995 and 2003 – the quantity ranges from 250 to 750 cases.

"We have kind of defined our territory to basically only the Bordeaux reds," Will says. "There is a lot we can do with those varieties. The biggest challenge is that we have not been able to get enough high-quality grapes." The winery gets only a third of the grapes it needs from its own vineyards. Will is one of those rare winemakers not driven to make Pinot Noir. "When every other challenge is put to bed, we'll look at Pinot Noir," he laughs.

STRATUS VINEYARDS ***
2059 Niagara Stone Road (Highway 55), Niagara-on-the-Lake, ON, L0S 1J0.
Tel: 905 468 1806; Website: www.stratuswines.com

The guiding philosophy of Stratus Vineyards, which opened its wine shop late in 2004, is that the whole is greater than the parts. The flagship wines are not the occasional varietals that will be released but rather Stratus White and Stratus Red, the best blends that the winemaker can put together. "Assemblage is definitely the future way of making great wines," asserts J-L Groux, the French-trained winemaker. "Assemblage with no restriction. If we feel that a Gewürztraminer will fit with a barrel-fermented Chardonnay, that's what we will do. We want to have a lot of freedom in how we blend the wines. In some years, we won't make any. And it is definitely going to be different each year. The objective is to make the best assemblage."

In the varietally-driven Canadian wine industry, this is a radical idea; but Stratus is a winery full of radical ideas. The project was conceived by a group of wine-obsessed Toronto investors headed by David Feldberg, chief executive of Teknion Corp, a major Toronto-based designer and manufacturer of office equipment. Feldberg and his partners bought a vineyard in 2000, close to Niagara-on-the-Lake. Employing an impressive array of consultants, they set out to spend what it takes to produce some of Niagara's best wines.

The vineyard is sixteen hectares in size. About a third – blocks of Cabernet Sauvignon and Chardonnay planted about 1978 – was retained. The remainder is being replanted as quickly as Stratus can acquire the latest clones of the Bordeaux and Rhône red varieties which dominate the production plans (which are for seventy per cent red, thirty per cent white). The winery, completed in 2004, has an industrial appearance. The magic is in the design inside. Stratus sits on flat terrain but is built for gentle, gravity-flow winemaking. When wine needs to be moved, the barrels are emptied (without pumping) into stainless steel tanks that are mounted on elevators in the heart of the winery. By raising these tanks to the top level, the wine can be filtered (if necessary) and bottled by gravity. The wine is accelerated, if needed, only with the pressure of inert gas. "The equipment goes to the wine and the wine does not go to the equipment," explains Groux. "The whole philosophy there is that you respect the wine. We do not pump wine. In our winery, the wine and the grapes have elevators but people have to go by the stairs."

Groux was attracted to Stratus by the opportunity to work in a winery designed from the ground up to make superior wine. Born in the Loire in 1957, he trained in Burgundy and Bordeaux and worked at wineries around the world before coming to Ontario in 1988. After visiting the area twice before and tasting significant improvement in the wines, Groux believed in the Niagara's potential to make great wine. In 1989 he joined Hillebrand Estate Winery where, over the next fourteen years, he achieved a legendary reputation for both his blended table wines and his Icewines (he pioneered barrel-fermented Icewine). "At Hillebrand, there was a very great potential," Groux acknowledges. "But there was a limit in that we did not manage most of our own vineyards and the winery was never designed to make superb premium wines. Everything was retrofitted." Stratus, on the other hand, is primarily an estate producer equipped with the latest winemaking technology. Maximum production will only be 16,000 cases a year. "We can get to different heights," Groux believes.

TAWSE WINERY ***
3955 Cherry Avenue, Vineland, ON, L0R 2C0.
Tel: 905 562 9500; Website: www.tawsewinery.ca
This sand-coloured winery with its bronze-toned roof slopes upward dramatically from a reflecting pond, somewhat like the head-frame of a mine. The rationale for the design becomes clear when you enter and look up from the bottom floor. There is an atrium with a clear view to the top of the winery, twenty-seven metres (ninety feet) above. Each of the six levels steps back from the one below, in a design that proprietor Moray Tawse believes may be "the perfect gravity-flow winery".

The winery rests against a natural hillside, not that Tawse would have hesitated to build a hill if one had not existed. "We intend on cutting no corners." This is not Ontario's first gravity-flow winery but no others approach this bold, even extravagant, design. Tawse, who was born in Toronto in 1957, can afford to finance this winery privately because he owns a very successful mortgage bank. He will not say how much has been spent on the winery, perhaps because his peers in business might ridicule his boyish enthusiasm for the production of landmark Canadian wines. But whatever his business buddies might think, other vintners recognize that this winery, open by appointment only, aims very high and very long term. "I am naming the vineyards after my children," Tawse says. "You can't pass along a lot of businesses but a vineyard is something that survives the ages."

Tawse is especially passionate about French wines, and was thinking of buying a wine-growing property in Burgundy until he happened to taste an Ontario Chardonnay made by Deborah Paskus under the Temkin-Paskus label. Impressed, Tawse bought ten hectares on the Beamsville Bench, including a vineyard planted with mature Chardonnay and Riesling vines. Then he hired Paskus, assumed her grape contracts, and set to planning the winery. "She is fanatical about everything being perfect," Tawse says. Paskus confirms this: "You automatically think of your wish list and what you would do better if you build from scratch," she says. "So things tend to get out of hand."

That explains why the winery is overbuilt for its production target of 3,000 to 5,000 cases a year. For example, there are three barrel cellars, built by burying three vaulted concrete structures, each nearly the size of a tennis court, under six metres (twenty feet) of earth. "The problem in most wineries is that they don't have enough cellar capacity," Tawse explains. This winery has the capacity to give every vintage as much as eighteen months in barrel (premium French oak, of course) without having to move wine to make room for a new vintage. If space gets tight, the third cellar handles the overflow. The winery's focus is Chardonnay, but it also produces a crisp Riesling. The two reds are Pinot Noir and Cabernet Franc. "This is the grape I am most excited about," says Tawse, sampling the winery's remarkably intense Cabernet Franc. "I have always liked the wines of Chinon."

13TH STREET WINERY *****
3983 13th Street, Jordan Station, ON, LOR 1S0.
Tel: 905 562 9463; Website: www.13thstreetwines.com

Canada's best Gamay producer, 13th Street Winery was launched in 1998 by four home winemakers who had become too accomplished for the amateur circuit. "We see ourselves as trying to raise the bar," says Ken Douglas, the winery's president. "We don't actually have to do this. We all have good careers."

Douglas is a lawyer and one of 13th Street's red wine specialists. Irv Willms, whose Sandstone Vineyard in the Niagara peninsula is planted largely to Gamay, is an engineer with a chemical company. Günther Funk, regarded (with his wife Mary) as one of Ontario's best grape-growers, is managing partner of an environmental engineering company. Herb Jacobson, the fourth partner, is a hydraulic engineer with a steel company. Among them, they find time to produce about 2,500 cases of wine a year, including six different sparkling wines. The products sell so quickly that the wine shop opens only on Saturdays. "We don't have any trouble selling our wine," Douglas says. "It just disappears."

All the partners grow grapes except for Douglas, although he takes credit for persuading Willms to do so. The 4.5-hectare Sandstone Vineyard was purchased by Willms in 1981. On the advice of Château des Charmes, which later bought his grapes, he pulled out the labrusca varieties and replanted with Gamay, Riesling, and Chardonnay. When those thrived, Willms added more Gamay. He bought the neighbouring three hectares in 1992 to grow Cabernet Franc, Cabernet Sauvignon and Chardonnay.

Funk, the other grower for 13th Street, has his vineyard, planted in 1976, adjacent to the winery. Funk's grapes include Riesling, Pinot Noir, Nebbiolo, Sauvignon Blanc, and Chardonnay; the latter support the winery's sparkling wines as well as making superb Pinot Noir and Chardonnay in limited volumes. Douglas credits the quality to Funk's "obsessive" dedication to low yields.

13th Street believes it was the first winery in Ontario to plant Syrah, beginning in 1992. The partners admit that they have had only "marginal success" with the variety, which is both tender in winter and prone to over-producing. It was not until the 2002 vintage that the winery released what it called a commercial volume (seventy-five cases) of Syrah. "We can make better wine with Gamay," says Douglas. The 2002 Estate Gamay is meaty and surprisingly dark in colour, with flavours of black cherries and cranberries. The 2002 Syrah seems marginally lighter but, with a whiff of pepper and flavours of leather and prunes, is certainly credible. It would have to be since 13th Street sells lesser wines in bulk or dumps them. As an example, the winery now has products analyzed before being bottled if the partners perceive a need to screen out wines marred by the Asian lady beetle (*see* page 82). "We have decided that life is too short to drink poor wine and we certainly don't want to sell any," Douglas wrote in a recent winery newsletter. "Our winery will not in the future be releasing any wine with measurable quantities of this chemical."

THIRTY BENCH WINES ***

4281 Mountainview Road, Beamsville, ON, L0R 1B0.
Tel: 905 563 1698; Website: www.thirtybench.com

This is a winery where three heads are better than one. Each of the three partners has his own speciality. Physician Dr Thomas Muckle is the master of Riesling: his styles range from barrel-fermented to late harvest. Yorgos Papageorgiou, a retired geography and economics professor, concentrates on premium Chardonnay and red wines. Austrian-born Frank Zeritsch zeroes in on Icewine. They collaborate on the other wines, occasionally with creative results: in 2001 a lady beetle infestation in the twenty-four hectare Thirty Bench vineyard tainted the grapes. The winery covered this in some 2001 wines by turning them into Greek-style resin-flavoured wines. One is even called Retsina.

Muckle has often been the driving force. Born in the UK in 1931, he came to Canada in 1970 to teach in the medical school at McMaster University. Discovering that Canadian wine at the time tasted like "strawberries and glue", he began making his own. After his white 1977 Seyval Blanc swept amateur competitions, Muckle gathered partners to plant vinifera in what they called the French Oak vineyard on the Beamsville Bench.

In 1994 Muckle joined with his current partners at Thirty Bench. (The name reflects a colonial tradition of naming the area's creeks according to their mileage from Niagara Falls.) The landmark wines are the well-regarded, if occasionally eccentric, table wines that often bear vineyard designations. The Chardonnays are invariably big and rich. The late harvest whites absolutely swagger with concentrated fruit and bold alcohol; a typical example is the 2002 Late Harvest Pinot Gris, which has fifteen degrees and could stand in for a Vendange Tardive from Alsace. The premium reds, released under the Benchmark designation, are boldly extracted wines built for long ageing.

THOMAS & VAUGHAN WINEMAKERS **

4245 King Street, Beamsville, ON, L0R 1B1.

Tel: 905 563 7737; Website: www.thomasandvaughan.com

The winery, conveniently located on the busy Beamsville Bench wine route, takes its name from owners Thomas Kocsis and Barbara Vaughan. A second-generation grower with fifteen hectares of vineyard, Kocsis opened the winery in 1999 after noting that his grapes were producing award-winning wines elsewhere. (His cousin, Peter, started the Crown Bench winery nearby for much the same reason.) Kocsis is a Hungarian name which, Thomas asserts, is as common there as Smith in North America. The name became a little less common in Hungary after several members of the family fled Soviet repression in 1956, ending up as grape-growers in Ontario.

At the 5,000-case winery, which made its first commercial vintage in 1997, the flagship wines are the reds, notably the Meritage, the Cabernet Franc, the Baco Noir and a big, plummy Old Vines Foch. Winemaker Jason James likes to make concentrated reds, to the point of bleeding some juice from the Bordeaux reds early in their fermentation. That juice is turned into a full-flavoured rosé. The 1999 Cabernet Franc Reserve, sold at $50 a bottle, had such intense fruit concentration that the wine spent two years in barrels without becoming over-oaked.

TRILLIUM HILL ESTATE WINERY (Range not tasted.)

3420 9th St, Louth, St Catharines, ON, L2R 6P7.

Tel: 905 684 4419

Arlene and Ivan Turek describe their winery as the "Niagara Region's best-kept secret." That may be because the tasting room is not always open at the posted hours. The boutique is in the Turek's sprawling country mansion amid the vineyards of the Jordan Bench and is not hard to find. The winery opened with wines from the fine 2000 vintage, with the flagship products being Cabernet Sauvignon, barrel-fermented Chardonnay, and a Chardonnay Musqué that won gold at the All-Canadian Wine Championship. The speciality wines, in addition to the Vidal Icewine common to Ontario wineries, includes a seldom-seen rosé from the Chambourcin grape.

VINELAND ESTATES WINERY *****

RR 1, 3620 Moyer Road, Vineland, ON, L0R 2C0.

Tel: 905 562 7088; Website: www.vineland.com

Vineland Estates emerged from a demonstration vineyard planted in 1979 just outside the village of Vineland (from which it takes its name) by Hermann Weis, a nurseryman and winemaker from Germany's Mosel region. Ultimately, thirty hectares was planted on the Beamsville Bench. Weis needed to prove that the Riesling vines he was selling would thrive in spite of Canadian winters. By the time Weis sold the winery in 1992, the viability of vinifera was proven.

Vineland, producing an average of about 60,000 cases a year, now has a reputation for top-quality Riesling, excellent Icewine, and a Meritage that, at $125 a bottle, is perhaps the country's most expensive red table wine. The winery has eighty-one hectares acres of vineyard, including Cabernet Sauvignon, Merlot, Cabernet Franc, Pinot Gris, and Pinot Blanc. "The foundation of those vineyards means we can control our own destiny," says winemaker Brian Schmidt. "The consistency we are getting is just remarkable." Riesling will remain the flagship wine, with two other varieties of emerging importance: Cabernet Franc and Sauvignon Blanc. "The industry needs to focus its energies on what we have learned in the last decade," Allan says. "The days of producing ten to fifteen varieties are beginning to wane."

The winery is managed by Brian and his older brother, Allan. Originally from British Columbia, they belong to one of the Canadian wine industry's pioneering families. Their grandfather Frank operated an original Okanagan vineyard (now the site of the St Hubertus winery and vineyard, see page 190). Father Lloyd was a founder of Sumac Ridge Estate Winery in Summerland, where Allan, born in 1963, first worked as a winemaker. Allan moved to Vineland as winemaker and general |manager in 1987. Four years later, he was joined by Brian who trained as a winemaker.

The $125 Vineland Meritage was launched in 1997, with a production of only eighty cases (it never exceeds 150 cases). At the time, people were seldom prepared to pay more than $20 for a bottle of Canadian table wine. "We wanted to break that glass ceiling," Brian explains. When the Meritage began to sell well at the original release price of $60, the winery spread out the sales by increasing the price. Eventually, it reached $125. "If we never sell a bottle of Meritage at $125, it doesn't matter," Brian says. "Having it on our list supports the wines below it." It appears to support the wines of other producers: a number of Niagara wineries now have Bordeaux-style reds selling near $50. "Had nobody stuck his neck out," Brian says, "I think it would be difficult to sell a $49 Cabernet/Merlot."

Vineland began making Icewine in 1989. Allan has found, like so many other Canadian wineries, that Icewine opens doors for the sale of table and sparkling wines. Vineland broke into Japan after a Japanese wine buyer read of a publicity stunt in 1992, when the Schmidt brothers took a dozen bottles along on a trip by dog sled to the magnetic North Pole (*see* page 31). Vineland Vidal and Riesling Icewines have done well in competitions. Most notably, at the 2003 Vinitaly competition, the winery won top honours, taking the Grand Vinitaly Award for the best overall wine. It was a first for a Canadian winery. "The award helped legitimize our potential," Brian says. "And it helps legitimize Canadian wine as a whole because, as an industry, we suffer from an inferiority complex."

VINOTECA *

527 Jevlan Drive, Woodbridge, ON, L4L 8W1.

Tel: 905 856 5700; Website: www.toronto.com/vinoteca

You know that there was a life before wine for Giovanni Follegot when you spot one of his immaculate Ferraris tucked away in a corner of this urban winery. Born in Italy's Veneto, Follegot came to North America in the 1960s to race cars and motorcycles. He settled in Canada after a race meet at Mosport, the original venue for the Canadian Grand Prix, becoming a dealer in Ferraris and other classic European marques. "It's a strange combination, cars and wine, but what can one do?" laughs Follegot.

Vinoteca, which opened in 1989, was the first of a cluster of wineries in this north Toronto suburb. In 1992 Follegot and his wife, Rosanna, began acquiring vineyards near Beamsville. In a clever move, they bought properties from the lake shore to the edge of the Niagara Escarpment. "Having land in many locations minimizes the extremes of climate," he believes. "All the vineyards are also self-sustaining. They could all become estate wineries." In fact, one of the Beamsville vineyards near Lake Ontario now hosts Follegot's tiny Maplegrove Vinoteca Estate Winery. The flagship wine here is Cabernet Sauvignon.

The larger Toronto winery operates with ideas borrowed from Italy, including a brisk trade in simple wines sold in 18-litre buckets or in four-litre bag-in-box containers. Follegot's winemaking knowledge was acquired from his family in Italy, with a bit of mentoring from winemaker Klaus Reif (*see* page 92). Making Icewine was one of the skills picked up from Reif. "I didn't even know what Icewine was," Follegot admits. But he won a silver medal at Vinitaly for his second Icewine, a 1991 Vidal.

WILLOW HEIGHTS ESTATE WINERY ***
3751 King St, Vineland ON, L0R 2C0.
Tel: 905 562 4945; Website: www.willowheightswinery.com

Until his early retirement, Ronald Speranzini spent twenty-nine years at a Hamilton steel company. He took up amateur winemaking, buying grapes from many of Niagara's best growers. Finally Donald Ziraldo, a founder of Inniskillin, challenged Speranzini: "Why not start a winery?" Ready for a second career, it was the push that Speranzini needed.

He launched professionally in the 1992 vintage, making a Chardonnay that has become a signature for Willow Heights, which opened to the public in 1994. The Chardonnay Reserve is made only in top vintages. "It is our best of the best," says Nicole Speranzini, Ronald's daughter. The Chardonnay is made with grapes from older vines, handled gently and, for the most part, fermented in American oak. The outcome is a voluptuously textured wine with flavours of ripe peaches and tangerines. Speranzini also began making Icewine as soon as he started to develop Willow Heights. Depending on the vintage, he now produces between 300 and 500 cases each year. Speranzini's flagship red, a dark, full-bodied wine with an array of tastes from berries to chocolate, is called Tresette after an Italian card game. It is a blend of Cabernet Franc, Cabernet Sauvignon, and Merlot.

Willow Heights relied largely on purchased grapes during its first decade. In 2003, however, Speranzini enlisted some silent partners to acquire about seventy-one hectares near Grimsby, just below the Niagara Escarpment. The varieties planted here include Pinot Gris and Pinot Noir.

WILLOW SPRINGS WINERY **
5572 Bethesda Rd, Stouffville, ON, L4A 7X3.
Tel: 905 642 9463; Website: www.willowspringswinery.ca

The old wine press at Willow Springs, which was opened in 2001 by Mario and Julie Testa, reflects the winery's Italian heritage. It was used in many home vintages by Emilio Testa, Mario's grandfather, and his father Gino, who both left Italy in the 1950s. Testa's main business is two produce and grocery stores in suburban Toronto. He devotes his days off to the winery and the vineyard. Winemaking at Willow Springs, now making 3,500 cases a year, is in the hands of Michael Traynor, a graduate from the viticulture programme at Loyalist College in Belleville. "This is like a hobby to me," Testa demurs. "It's nice to retire to."

Perhaps it was just a hobby at first when, in 1993, he put a test plot of Vidal grapes on the sixty-one-hectare family farm. No one had planted wine grapes near Stouffville, a small town about fifty kilometres (thirty-one miles) northeast of Toronto, far from the moderating influence of Lake Ontario. But Testa believed a vineyard could succeed with early-ripening, winter-hardy grapes. When the Vidal made it through several winters, the hobby took a serious turn and in 1996 he started planting what is now 4.5 hectares of grapes on rich loam. He grows Baco Noir, Kuhlmann, Seyval Blanc, Chardonnay, and one of the white Geisenheim hybrids and has recently added Frontenac and Saverois, tough hybrids grown in Québec and Michigan. Even with these varieties, Testa also hills earth around the base of the vines before winter.

Willow Springs supplements its production with grapes purchased from Niagara vineyards, for the winery's license allows Testa to buy as many tonnes as he grows. Currently the winery's best-selling reds are Baco Noir from the estate vineyard and Cabernet Franc from Niagara; its best-selling whites are Chardonnay and the Riesling-like Geisenheim variety. The most impressive red has been its reserve-grade Meritage, 2002 Testa, a generous, plummy wine with a long finish. Only 600 bottles were made, sold only at the winery and at a price so modest that Testa drew criticism from his winemaker. "You've got to remember that we are a start-up winery," Testa retorts. "We've got to get our name out there.'

8

Lake Erie North Shore and Pelee Island

Wine-growing has had a turbulent history in southwestern Ontario, an appellation now known awkwardly as the Lake Erie North Shore and Pelee Island Viticultural Area. Vin Villa, Canada's first estate winery, opened on Pelee Island in 1866. Within twenty-five years, there were twenty-three wineries in the Pelee Island-Windsor corridor.[1] At the peak of viticulture in 1904, 704 hectares were planted to grapes. Then the farmers switched to more lucrative crops such as soy beans and tobacco. Vineyard hectarage collapsed to eight hectares by 1920. It took a long time to recover, but had reached 400 hectares by the 1980 opening of Colio Estate Winery. Colio and Pelee Island Winery, two of Ontario's larger wineries, now anchor a viticultural area that seems poised for growth. About a dozen wineries are either open or under development.

This is Canada's southernmost grape-growing area, on the same latitude as Mendocino County in California. Topography is relatively flat, particularly on Pelee Island. Some vineyards are on very modest slopes with exposure to the south or southwest toward Lake Erie, which greatly influences the climate. Dr. Tony Shaw, a geographer from Brock University who has written papers on proposed sub-appellations in Ontario, notes that Erie is the warmest of the Great Lakes:

Because the western end of the lake is relatively shallow and located at a southerly latitude, the water warms up rapidly in early spring. In April,

---

1. Tiessen, Ron, *The Vinedressers: A History of Grape Farming & Wineries on Pelee Island*; Pelee Island Heritage Centre, 1996.

strong westerly winds also hasten this warming by driving the ice cover to the east, allowing the open waters to warm while the ice-covered eastern section remains cold. As a result, the growing season for vines usually begins two weeks earlier than in the Niagara Peninsula. Moreover, the expansive surface area of the lake together with its significant summer heat reservoir prolong the growing season into the late fall ... [2]

The growing season, tempered by the lake, is long and warm, with more heat units than Mendocino's Anderson Valley. In addition to abundant growing days, the vineyards get more than enough rain. "The Lake Erie North Shore is located along a major storm track," Shaw notes. Two-thirds of the precipitation, which averages ninety centimetres (thirty-four inches) a year, falls during the growing season and the remainder, which includes heavy snowfalls, comes in the rest of the year. "The soils begin the growing season fully saturated," says Shaw. This means that growers need not irrigate, but they do have to manage the vines attentively to forestall the diseases that can arise during the humid summers. They also cope with occasionally violent hailstorms. The soils, for the most part, are clay and are comparatively fertile. Some grape varieties, such as the Bordeaux reds, thrive in these vineyards while cool-climate varieties such as Riesling produce wines with less finesse than similar varieties in Niagara.

AN ISOLATED BEGINNING

Grape-growing in southwestern Ontario began in the 1850s, primarily with vineyards planted on Pelee Island (or on much smaller Middle Island nearby) by settlers from the United States, where they had learned viticulture. Pelee Island is a flat pancake of 4,000 hectares of fertile land that has lent itself to many different crops over the years. Until the recent inauguration of a fast ferry service, the island's access to the nearest population centres (Windsor in Canada and Detroit in the USA) involved ferry rides of at least ninety minutes. In spite of this comparative isolation, a number of wineries were established on the island – and because of the isolation, many struggled commercially.

The most important winery, which came to be called Vin Villa Vineyards, started in 1866 when Thaddeus Smith and two partners

2. Shaw, Dr. Tony B, *Delimiting Sub-Appellations within the Niagara Peninsula and Lake Erie North Shore Viticultural Area*, prepared for VQA Ontario, 2004.

arrived from Kentucky and planted ten hectares of grapes. The primary varieties are believed to have been Delaware and Catawba. Local historian Ron Tiessen traced the story in his 1996 book, *The Vinedressers*. Smith built a cellar and brought in a German-trained manager. "A portion of the first vintage, in 1871, was sold to wine manufacturers in Sandusky," Tiessen writes, referring to the city on the Ohio shore of Lake Erie.

The search for a Canadian market for the wine led Smith to JS Hamilton, a wine merchant in Brantford. He became the agent for Vin Villa and other Pelee Island wines. In 1888 he formed the Pelee Island Wine and Vineyard company, building facilities both on the island and in Brantford. A hard-driving businessman, Hamilton soon found export markets for the wines and in 1894 brought in a French expert to make sparkling wine. It was sold as L'Empereur Champagne. Tiessen believes that Hamilton was the only sparkling wine manufacturer in Canada at the time. Grape-growing declined on the island in favour of more lucrative crops such as tobacco, which was introduced in 1895. Finally, in 1918, Hamilton moved the Pelee Island Wine and Vineyard Co entirely to Brantford. London Winery bought the assets in 1949 and closed them the following year but kept some of the brands. One of the brands that sustained London until the 1990s, when it was taken over by Vincor International, was St Augustine, a Communion wine sold to Anglican churches.

By the time Hamilton moved his operation off Pelee Island, nearly all the wineries in southwestern Ontario had closed, due either to the weak local markets or to competition. Ontario wineries had begun lobbying the federal government in 1908 to slap tariffs on French wines. A handful of new wineries opened in Essex County in the 1920s when Prohibition in Ontario banned everything but the sale of wine (a concession to Niagara grape-growers). Seldom competent, these wineries were wound up after Prohibition ended in 1927. The surviving producers purchased them for the retail store outlets that went with the licenses. In southwestern Ontario the chief consolidator was the London Winery. The Knowles family who established London in 1925 were well-heeled UK electrical engineers. Unusually among wineries at the time, Joseph Knowles, one of the family members, actually knew how to make wine.

Based in London, Ontario, the Knowles winery remained the only winery in southwestern Ontario until 1977, when a grape-grower named Alan Eastman launched Charal Winery and Vineyards in Blenheim.

Eastman and his father operated a mixed farm, and had turned to grapes – first with test plots in 1968 and then with a large vineyard – not because of romance about wine but because they wanted more profitable crops. "We were looking to increase the acreage of a fruit crop that could be mechanically harvested and treated in a mechanical means," Eastman explained. He sold his grapes until the Liquor Control Board of Ontario ended its fifty-year moratorium on licensing wineries.

His winery was not a success but it renewed interest in the viticultural prospects for southwestern Ontario. By 1977, Ron Moyer, then chair of the Ontario Grape Growers' Marketing Board, predicted a vineyard comeback. One catalyst was that land was cheaper around Lake Erie than in Niagara. That influenced Austrian winemaker Walter Strehn to invest on Pelee Island in 1979. The same economics drew the investors behind Colio Vineyards to Harrow.

Although the Lake Erie and Pelee Island viticultural regions are as far south as northern California, the winters are much colder. Pioneering growers like Eastman played it safe when making planting choices. Eastman, who ultimately planted twenty-four hectares, spread the risk over about thirty varieties, primarily French hybrids but also Chardonnay and Riesling. Strehn was more daring: the thirty-five hectares he planted in 1980, with vines imported from Europe, was then the single largest block of vinifera in Canada. The varieties included Riesling, Kerner, Gewürztraminer, Scheurebe, Zweigelt, and Pinot Noir. He did not plant Vidal until 1984, probably with Icewine in mind. Since the mid-1990s vinifera grapes have come to occupy most of the region's vineyards. Even so, Baco Noir, Maréchal Foch and Vidal remain bread-and-butter wines at the established wineries. Several wineries, in fact, have elevated the red hybrids to premium quality: D'Angelo with Maréchal Foch and Sanson with Baco Noir are examples.

However, premium wines from vinifera grapes are establishing the future of this region. Colio's strongest wines now are its Bordeaux reds, while Pelee Island is an emerging Pinot Noir producer. The white varieties with great promise include Chardonnay, Pinot Gris, and Sauvignon Blanc.

9

Wineries of Lake Erie North Shore and Pelee Island

COLCHESTER RIDGE ESTATE WINERY (Range not tasted.)
108 County Road 50, Harrow, ON, N0R 1G0.
Tel: 519 738 9800

The first significant harvest from Bernard Gorski's five-hectare vineyard, planted in 2002, was four tons of Cabernet Sauvignon. In what was a very difficult season, his were some of the better grapes in Essex County. Gorski knows why: it is his forty-eight years of experience on a farm. "It's all because of the way it's farmed," he says.

The vineyard, a stone's throw from the shore of Lake Erie, is on one of Gorski's family farms. Born in 1954, he worked in the bulk trucking company founded by his father in 1957 and now run by Bernard and his brother, Ted; its customers include some of Ontario's largest wineries. "I was exposed to the industry through my day job," he laughs.

The winery is scheduled to open in the fall of 2005, although the small volume that Bernard made in his initial vintage, about 3,000 litres, may delay the opening. A capable home winemaker for more than a dozen years, he arranged for consulting help in his first commercial vintage from Walter Schmoranz and Martin Janz of nearby Pelee Island Winery. "I guess the next couple of years will let me know whether or not I am going to be a farmer or a winemaker, or both," Bernard says. "My ambition is to be both."

The vineyard should quadruple its production in 2005. In addition to Cabernet Sauvignon, he grows Merlot, Gewürztraminer, and Chardonnay. "I am sitting on a 120-hectare farm," he says. "I can expand as much as I want." He has already drawn up plans for a commodious winery, to be built in five or six years' time with local limestone. It will be modelled on several small French châteaux.

COLIO ESTATE WINES ****
1 Colio Drive, Harrow, ON, N0R 1G0.
Tel: 519 738 9318; Website: www.coliowines.com

As the winemaker at Colio since the winery's first crush in 1980, Carlo Negri has lived the emerging wine industry of southwestern Ontario vintage by vintage. At first, working with the grapes then available, he made Riserva Rosso and Riserva Bianco primarily with hybrids. He even made wine with Concord and Niagara. Since then, the vineyards have been transformed. Today he makes primarily vinifera wines, except for Icewine. "Who would have dreamed, fifteen or twenty years ago, of reaching this level of quality?" he marvels. Colio's flagship wines today include Chardonnay, Cabernet Sauvignon, Merlot, Cabernet Franc, and an exceptional Bordeaux blend called Signature.

Now producing 200,000 cases a year, Colio is one of two wineries – the other being Pelee Island – that anchor Essex County's expanding vineyards. Colio itself owns sixty-five hectares of vines; it also buys from growers. The winery has been enlarged several times to handle a growing number of visitors to what is the primary attraction in the farming town of Harrow. Colio is open every day except Christmas and New Year's Day, offering tours every afternoon and occasional tastings in its grand barrel cellar.

The winery was launched initially by a Toronto food broker, named Enzo DeLuca, along with investors in Italy. Recently, the Italians sold their fifty per cent to Portuguese businessman José Berardo, the owner of JP Vinhos SA, one of Portugal's largest wine producers. While a third of Colio's production is non-VQA blends using imported wine, the resources of Berardo are driving it towards increasing its volume of premium wines. Berardo also funded the complete architectural makeover of the winery in 2002. Formerly plain and functional, it has taken on the appearance of small castle in Normandy.

Negri started his career in 1964 at Collavini in the Friuli region of northern Italy. He moved to Canada because the challenge was appealing. "If I hadn't tried, I would not have known what it is possible to do here," he says. "Now, I have more years of winemaking experience than any other winemaker in Ontario." He has also mastered Icewine, almost a necessity for a winemaker in Canada. He started with Vidal Icewine in 1989, extending the range to include Riesling and Cabernet Franc. However, a commendable touch of Italian style still shows in some of the table wines, notably the refreshing Pinot Grigio.

D'ANGELO ESTATE WINERY ***
5141 Concession 5, RR 4, Amherstburg, ON, N9V 2Y8.
Tel: 519 736 7959; Website: www.dangelowinery.com

D'Angelo was opened in 1989 by Salvatore "Sal" D'Angelo, a former technical school teacher and electrician who was born in Italy in 1953 but grew up in Canada. "Being the oldest son, I had the responsibility to go down to the cellar every night and take out a carafe of wine for the evening meal," he remembers. He learned winemaking from his father but, with his bent for technology, he was soon the more proficient of the two.

In 1979 D'Angelo began looking for his own vineyard, finally buying a farm east of Amherstburg in 1983, where he planted seventeen hectares. Because this farm has proved better for hardy hybrids, D'Angelo has developed a second vineyard of five hectares of vinifera at Colchester, right on the Lake Erie shoreline. He sold this vineyard in 2001 in order to invest in the Okanagan, where he intends to open a winery as early as 2006. The Colchester vineyard is now owned by Viewpointe Estate Winery, which employs D'Angelo as its consulting winemaker. His own winery produces about 5,000 cases, including noteworthy Maréchal Foch and Vidal Icewine.

One of D'Angelo's strengths is his vineyard management. His peers recognized his skill in 1999 by naming him Ontario's Grape King that year. It was the first time since the award was inaugurated in 1956 that it had gone to a grower outside the Niagara region. Another of his strengths is steely determination. At the start of the 1993 vintage, he came down with a debilitating neurological disease called Guillain-Barré Syndrome. Its onset is a creeping paralysis, starting in the feet, which can kill if it proceeds too far up the torso. In "fortunate" victims, like D'Angelo, the paralysis eventually recedes. It was three and a half years before he fully regained the use of his legs. He credits his recovery to a lifelong dedication to fitness. "I was a forty-year-old black belt instructor when the disease struck," he says. He did not give in to his illness, refusing a wheelchair so that he would be forced to use his legs. He employed some help to run the vineyard and winery but continued to make the wines. "The 1993 Maréchal Foch won three gold medals and did very, very well," he remembers.

ERIE SHORE VINEYARD **
410 County Road 50 West, RR 3, Harrow, ON, NOR 1G0.
Tel: 519 738 9858; Website: www.erieshore.ca.

As the name suggests, this winery, which opened in 2002, is close to the northern shore of Lake Erie, on a farm purchased in 1994 by Harvey Hollingshead and his wife, Alma. Two University of Guelph graduates in agriculture, both had long careers in banking. Currently, Alma, whose speciality is crop science, runs the six hectares of vines. About half the production is sold to other wineries and, with a growing demand for grapes, the couple plan to increase the plantings by fifty per cent in 2006.

The varieties being grown include Cabernet Franc, Zweigelt, Baco Noir, Chambourcin, Riesling, Chardonnay, and Vidal for Icewine. "Canadian wineries have to do it, whether or not one is an Icewine fan," Alma says. Her husband is a longtime home winemaker with a penchant for making clean, easy-drinking wines. Now he makes about 2,000 cases a year. It was a big step to move from just growing grapes, but Alma notes that their colleagues in the tightly-knit Essex County wine community have always been helpful. "We are lucky with the calibre of international expertise in our community," she says.

GRAPE TREE ESTATE WINES INC
308 Mersea Road 3, Leamington, ON, N8H 3V5.
Tel: 519 322 2081; Website: www.grapetreewines.com

Steven Brook's journey to wine is a classic Canadian story. Born in Windsor in 1963, he grew up in a household with no interest in wine. "I didn't realize I liked wine until 1979 or 1980, when a friend dropped off a bottle of German wine," he recalls. Curiousity aroused, Brook took in a German wine tasting, joined the German wine society in Windsor, and cemented his infatuation with a trip to Germany in 1983 where he went on an "Auslese rampage". By the end of that decade, he was giving wine appreciation courses and had become a product consultant with the Liquor Control Board of Ontario, where he worked for twelve years.

Brook began growing grapes in 1991 and now has two vineyards totalling seven hectares. Fascinated with sweet wines, he began making small lots of Icewine in 1995, five years before opening Grape Tree, where Icewine has been a feature. In the 2002 vintage, he made five different Icewines, including what is believed to be the first in Ontario made from red French hybrid Chambourcin. The wine could not be labelled as Icewine because the Vintners Quality Alliance has not yet accepted Chambourcin as an authorized Icewine grape.

Brook believes he was one of the first growers in Essex County to plant Chambourcin. The variety now figures in a number of Grape Tree wines, including a fruity Nouveau in 2004 that combined Chambourcin and Gamay, and a Rosé of Chambourcin and Ortega. He also was one of the earliest to grow Shiraz in the county and has produced it as a varietal as well as component in Hexagon, the winery's premium red blend, so named because it is made up of six varieties. Grape Tree's sparkling white wine is also called Hexagon. Unfortunately, the frosts in the winters of 2002 and 2003 killed many buds and set back his Shiraz production. Other wines from Grape Tree include Pinot Noir and Chardonnay.

MASTRONARDI ESTATE WINERY (Range not tasted.)
1193 Concession Road 3 East, Kingsville, ON, N9Y 2E5.
Website: www.mastronardiestatewinery.com

In 2002, the Mastronardi brothers bought a forty-hectare vineyard from the Colio winery, intending to replace the vines with greenhouses. Tony, born in Leamington in 1966, and Rino, born in 1973, grow tomatoes and peppers under 28,800 square metres (310,000 square feet) of glass. They needed land for expansion. Colio sold the vineyard to replace it with a lakefront vineyard less susceptible to frost. Then Tony heard about frost protection with wind machines. He was so impressed by their effectiveness that he became a distributor.

The winemaker at the winery, which should open in 2006, is Lyse LeBlanc. The Mastronardi brothers continue to sell most of the grapes – a dozen different varieties including the three major Bordeaux reds, Chardonnay, Riesling, Gewürztraminer, and Pinot Gris. Shiraz has recently been added, and there is also Vidal: the winery's offerings when it opens will include Icewine, a wine with which LeBlanc showed particular skill at her own winery, LeBlanc Estate Winery, now sold. In time, Tony plans to erect another of those destination wineries that are springing up in Essex County. "When I do it, I am going to do it right," he promises.

MUSCEDERE VINEYARDS (Range not tasted.)

7457 County Road 18, RR 4, Harrow, ON, N0R 1G0.

Tel: 519 796 9007; Website: www.muscederevineyards.com

Fabbio and Roberto Muscedere – pronounced "moosh-eh-dairy" – are returning to their Italian roots with this winery, scheduled to open in 2006. Beginning in 2003, they have planted five hectares of vines on a sixty-six-hectare estate which their parents purchased in 1986 for a retirement home. There are seven varieties in the vineyard: Cabernet Sauvignon, Cabernet Franc, Merlot, Pinot Noir, Chardonnay, Pinot Grigio, and Vidal. Roberto would like to develop Cabernet Sauvignon into a signature variety, having been impressed by examples made by his mentor, Salvatore D'Angelo, even though the hard 1994 winter wiped out all the Cabernet Sauvignon in the nearby D'Angelo vineyard. The Muscedere brothers have installed a wind machine, primarily to reduce the frost risk but also to temper summer's heat spikes so that the grapes ripen evenly. As the business grows, Roberto will also look for a vineyard site beside Lake Erie, where the lake effect creates significantly different growing conditions.

The styles proposed for this winery include bold reds from the Bordeaux varieties with a distinctive light red from Pinot Noir (Roberto's models include Pinots from Sonoma's Russian River.) The Chardonnay will be crisp and fresh. The Pinot Grigio and Vidal table wines are likely to be finished with a touch of residual sugar. One thing the brothers have learned from operating a wine tour business is that Michigan consumers, their likely market, prefer a hint of sweetness in white wines.

PELEE ISLAND WINERY ****

455 Seacliff Drive, Kingsville, ON, N9Y 2K5.

Tel: 519 733 6551; Website: www.peleeisland.com

Like the phoenix, the Pelee Island Winery rose in 1982 from the ruins of Canada's first estate winery. With a production today of 275,000 cases a year, Pelee Island is the largest winery in southwestern Ontario. Its 222.5 hectares of vineyards are all on Pelee Island, so far south that it is at approximately the same latitude, 41.5 degrees north, as Rome. The grapes here get fully ripe, and the winery includes late harvest wines in its extensive portfolio.

The largest of several low-lying islands in Lake Erie, Pelee Island is about ninety minutes by ferry from Kingsville, where the modern-day winery is located. Vin Villa, the original estate winery, was built on the island in 1866. It closed during the general decline of wine production in southwestern Ontario just prior to World War I. In the late 1970s, winemaker Walter Strehn, whose family owned a winery in Austria, was looking for farmland in Canada. Discovering that land was inexpensive on Pelee Island and that grapes had grown there formerly, Strehn developed new vineyards not far from the Vin Villa ruins. The first wines were made in a barn at the edge of Kingsville, on the mainland. The winery was completed there in 1984 so that customers would have easier access. During the summer a pavilion on the island provides hospitality for those who make the day trip from the mainland.

The vineyard soil is clay over limestone which drains well even though the island's elevation rises only a few metres above the lake. Sixteen varieties grow in the winery's vineyards, including mainstream vinifera. "Chardonnay is our bread-and-butter white," says president Walter Schmoranz. He came to Pelee Island in 1986 from Rüdesheim in Germany, when Strehn returned to his family's winery in Austria. His winemaking colleague is Martin Janz, who grew up in Germany's Rheingau.

Pelee Island's wines cover the majority of tastes. It makes an unoaked Chardonnay, a subtly-oaked Premium Select Chardonnay, and a full-bodied Barrique Chardonnay, aged in French and Hungarian casks. Several off-dry white blends are made for those who want a hint of sweetness; those who want more are offered Gewürztraminer or late harvest Vidal. The winery grows more red varieties than whites. "We have always been relatively large in Pinot Noir," Schmoranz notes. The winery's premium reds include Cabernet Sauvignon, Merlot, Cabernet Franc, and an exceptional Meritage. These wines are not called reserves but are released under the "Vinedressers" label, with reproductions of photographs from the Vin Villa era.

Most of the wines are released under labels featuring Pelee Island wildlife, from pheasants and flying squirrels to tree swallows, herons, owls, and Monarch butterflies. Indeed, the profusion of wildlife on the island is surprising, considering how intensive agriculture here used to be. (The island was once an important supplier of soybeans.) Pelee Island Winery uses natural pest control and in 2004 made a commitment to growing grapes according to the World Wildlife Federation's strict guidelines for sustainable vineyard practice. Andrew von Teichman, one of the winery's owners, says the objective is growing "Canada's finest natural premium wines and to make Pelee Island the greenest community in North America."

While the summers are warm, this shallow end of Lake Erie can become ice-covered during winter. Pelee Island made one of Canada's first Icewines in 1983 and remains a significant producer. The island location of the vineyards presents a challenge. The ferry linking Pelee Island to the Canadian mainland operates, depending on ice, only from mid-March to mid-December. Usually the ferry has stopped running by the time the Icewine freeze arrives. The winery then charters light aircraft to fly its pickers in (a ten-minute flight). The grapes are crushed on the island; the juice, lightly sulphured, remains there in tank until the ferry begins running in March. Then it is transported to the winery at Kingsville. Pelee Island is believed to have made Canada's first red Icewines and continues this tradition by making sumptuous Cabernet Franc Icewine with perfect balance.

QUAI DU VIN ESTATE WINERY (Range not tasted.)
45811 Fruitridge Line, RR 5, St Thomas, ON, N5P 3S9.
Tel: 519 775 2216; Website: www.quaiduvin.com

This low-key winery opened in 1990, based on a vineyard planted by Roberto Quai twenty years earlier. In 2002 it celebrated the production of its millionth bottle of wine. Because of the age of the vineyard, the winery vinifies what are now considered heritage varieties in Ontario. The whites are made with such grapes as Niagara, Dutchess, Elvira, and Seyval Blanc, as well as Vidal, Chardonnay, and Gewürztraminer. Reds include Concord and De Chaunac as well as Cabernet Sauvignon and Pinot Noir. Quai's fruit vines also sometimes include grapes. Examples include Cranberry Elvira, Watermelon Vidal, and Concord Ripple. Dessert wines include a Vidal Icewine and a sweet Maple wine.

SANSON ESTATE WINERY ****
9238 Walker Rd, RR 1, McGregor, ON, N0R 1J0.
Tel: 519 726 9609; Website: www.sansonestatewinery.com

Professional chef Dennis Sanson opened his winery in 2002 with partner Maureen Jack, another food industry veteran. "My life has been about the pursuit of flavour," he says. Now he explores flavours on a thirty-six-hectare farm and wood-lot not far from Windsor, raising beef and growing three hectares of grapes planted in 1997.

His vineyard is primarily growing Vidal and Baco Noir. From Vidal, Sanson produces amiably refreshing whites and elegant Icewine. From

Baco Noir he makes powerful reds. His reserve Baco Noir, from low-cropped vines, is intensely ripe, tasting of plums, spice, and chocolate. Sanson also buys from other growers in Essex County, producing well made Chardonnay, Sauvignon Blanc, Cabernet, Sauvignon, Shiraz, and Merlot. He tends to produce wines in small lots, seldom more than 300 cases of any variety. Current production is about 3,500 cases and the winery has the capacity to triple that volume.

SPRUCEWOOD SHORES ESTATE WINERY (Range not tasted.)
7258 Heritage Road, County Road 50 W, RR 5, Harrow, ON. NOR 1G0.
Tel: 519 738 9253; Email: sprucewoodshores@systematics.ca

Planned to open in 2006, the eye-catching Sprucewood Shores winery is built in a fourteen-hectare vineyard that Gordon Mitchell planted in 1990. "I've never gotten away from agriculture," he says. Mitchell was born in 1945 at Woodslee, not far from the vineyard, and still owns a farm with his brother. He almost joined a tractor manufacturer when he graduated from the University of Windsor. Instead, he joined Chrysler, spending half of his thirty-year career there as a plant manager.

"I fell in love with vineyards as a small kid," says Mitchell . He has happy memories of purloining grapes from the many small backyard vineyards in Essex Country when he was growing up. "When I got older and looked around for opportunities in agriculture, I settled on grapes." In his vineyard not far from Lake Erie, Mitchell grows vinifera including Merlot, Cabernet Sauvignon, Pinot Noir, Chardonnay, and a little Vidal.

Sprucewood Shores, designed to produce as many as 10,000 cases a year, is a project involving the entire Mitchell family. Hannah, Gordon's Lebanese-born wife, is a software designer. Daughter Tanya, a recent graduate in chemical engineering from McMaster, is the winemaker. Her siblings, Stephan, Marlaina, and Jacob, will carve out roles here as well. The winery – consisting of two substantial structures connected by an underground cellar – is designed to be another of Essex County's new destination wineries.

VIEWPOINTE ESTATE WINERY ****
151 County Road 50 East, Harrow, ON, NOR 1G0.
Tel: 519 738 4718; Website: www.viewpointewinery.com

An emerging wine region needs a showman. Essex County has John Fancsy and Viewpointe, the winery he has opened with his brother, Steve, and his sister-in-law, Jean. The winery is a baronial structure with a large cellar and a panoramic view over Lake Erie. "We are a vineyard area that needs a destination to visit," maintains Fancsy. "We have an untapped market. Six million people live within 100 kilometres (sixty-two miles) – and the Essex County wineries are the only wineries." Even before his winery opened in 2005, Fancsy was running the local winery association and coordinating the development of a wine touring route.

Born in Windsor in 1958, Fancsy is an electrical engineer who also happens to be passionate about wine. He and his brother began planting grapes in 1999, the same year in which they sold their automotive business. Now they operate three vineyards on the Erie shore, totalling seventeen hectares, and have the property to double that. They also have a fifty per cent share in a vine nursery in California.

The lakeside vineyard in which the winery is located was originally planted by Salvatore D'Angelo (*see* page 117). When D'Angelo needed capital to develop a second winery in British Columbia's Okanagan Valley, he sold his property to the Fancsy brothers. He also agreed to be consulting winemaker at Viewpointe, producing wines from 2001 that could be sold under the D'Angelo licence until Viewpointe opened.

The vineyards, which are managed by Steve Fancsy, contain an astonishing seventeen varieties, almost all mainstream vinifera such as Cabernet Franc, Cabernet Sauvignon, Merlot, Syrah, and Chardonnay. Viewpointe also has plots of Tempranillo and Sangiovese, varieties rarely seen in Canada. Often the same varieties are planted in all of the vineyards. "The wines are a lot better if you mix vineyards," John argues. "You limit yourself by growing a variety only in one vineyard."

The winery was launched with a production of about 10,000 cases and has the capacity to triple that. One of Viewpointe's strengths is its Cabernet Franc. "You are not competing with California wines if you have Cabernet Franc," says John. Six different clones are grown in two of the three vineyards. The resulting wines are rich, showing the ripeness than can be achieved in this corner of Ontario.

10

Prince Edward County

Prince Edward County is the most controversial wine region in Ontario. Its vineyard owners compare it to Burgundy, because of the underlying limestone in the western half. Many have planted Chardonnay and Pinot Noir. But when other Ontario growers speak of the county's challenging winters, one would think they were talking about Siberia. Currently, about 200 hectares of grapes have been planted in about three dozen vineyards. Ten wineries, several remarkably grand, have been established. The size of the investment in most of the wineries is astonishing for a region whose wine-growing potential remains to be proven. Because land prices are much lower than Niagara, some predict that the area under vines will double by the end of the current decade. During the next five to ten years, the county aims to emerge as a hot new Ontario appellation.

"I see no reason why we couldn't add another ten wineries in the next five years," Dan Taylor, the county's economic development officer, said in 2004. One of those will be Domaine Calcaire, which Taylor himself intends to open. He is one reason why there is so much interest in wine-growing here. A former marketing executive who once operated a wine tour business in Toronto, Taylor was looking for vineyard property in the Niagara Peninsula in 1996 until he learned that property was cheaper in Prince Edward County. At the time, the county had a mere eight hectares of vines. As he was planting his own vineyard, Taylor was hired as development officer and was charged with reviving this backwater where employment was declining. He identified wine-growing potential and, to make it happen, engaged Geoff Heinricks, a fellow emerging vintner, to write a manual on viticulture that the development commission gives to aspiring growers.

About a two-and-a-half hour drive east of Toronto, the county, 1,010 square kilometres (390 square miles) in area, is almost an island in Lake Ontario, only attached to the mainland by a narrow neck of land at the western end (*see* map on page 34). It was first settled by Europeans in the late eighteenth century after the American War of Independence, when those loyal to the British Crown (the United Empire Loyalists) moved north to what is now Canada. The charming architecture reflects these beginnings. Several wineries are located in restored Loyalist buildings and one winery even has a Loyalist cemetery on the property.

The early farmers grew barley and hops, shipping them across Lake Ontario to American customers until the Americans imposed prohibitive tariffs. Farmers then switched to dairy and vegetable production. According to a history of the county, "By 1902 an estimated one third of canned fruits and vegetables produced in Canada came from Prince Edward."[1] By the 1950s, forty-one canneries operated in the county, which proudly called itself the "Garden County" of Canada. Then the industry went into a long decline, unable to compete with lower-cost canneries elsewhere. The last cannery closed in 1996.

There is a precedent for county grape-growing. A farmer named Dorland Noxon – one of many Quakers who moved to the area to escape religious persecution in the United States – grew grapes at a vineyard in what is now Hillier Township. Whether by luck or by shrewdness, Noxon had chosen to plant on those soils that latter-day growers like to compare to those of Burgundy. Perhaps because of the terroir, he made wine good enough to win a medal at the 1876 International Exposition in Philadelphia. Noxon and a handful of other grape-growers were shut down when the Temperance movement arrived in the county. Ontario's second chapter of the Women's Christian Temperance Union was formed in 1874 in Picton; in the following year, the county went dry entirely.[2]

There were few references to grape-growing in the county until the autumn of 1991, when a local magazine profiled farmer Phil Mathewson, who had been experimenting with grapes for a decade and made plans

1. *Historic Prince Edward: An Historical Guide to Prince Edward County, Ontario*; Millennium Edition; Prince Edward Historical Society, Picton, ON, p 4.

2. Heinricks, Geoff: *Starting a Vineyard in Prince Edward County: A Viticultural Primer for Investors and Growers*, Prince Edward County Economic Development Office, Picton, ON, 2001, p 12.

(never completed) for a winery and cidery. "His research shows that the County bears many similarities to Burgundy," the article suggested.

LIMESTONE RIDGES

The soil is one reason why references to Burgundy persist. Heinricks, a freelance journalist as well as one of the county's emerging winemakers at his property, Domaine La Reine, explained the terrain in his manual on county viticulture, published in 2001.[3] "Basically, the county is a rolling limestone table, with a slight northeast to southwest tilt, and numerous long, east-west gentle ridges." In Hillier, where Noxon grew his grapes and where many of the modern vineyards have been planted, "there is a lot of limestone rubble on the soil surface." This is well-drained, mineral-rich soil of a type in which Pinot Noir grows successfully elsewhere in the world. There are between 600 and 800 hectares of so-called Hillier clay loam. This region, on the western end of the county, with good exposure to Lake Ontario, has the highest number of degree days anywhere in the peninsula.

Why the dismissive references to Siberia? Even Heinricks uses that phrase when referring to the northwest shore of the county, bordering the Bay of Quinte. This is the least propitious area in which to plant vines – but other parts of the county might also prove challenging. Heinrick's handbook is quite candid. "Winters are much harder – brutal, actually – than Niagara," he writes. "Most winters can get near –30°C (–22°F) for at least a few hours every season. Good winter survival strategies and field practices are a must." The prevailing winter winds sweep down the length of Lake Ontario. The shallow eastern parts of the lake surrounding the county will freeze. Very occasionally, almost the entire lake will freeze during a severe winter. Heinricks noted such events in the winters of 1933-4 (which decimated orchards), 1978–9, 1980–1, and 1993–4. "The result was widespread death and terrible injuries in vineyards and orchards all around the Lake," he wrote.

The individuals planting grapes in the county choose to see the winters as a challenge to be managed, not a deterrent. Some bury the vines, as is done in Québec, while others rely on pruning only sparingly until they can judge the rate of winter survival. In several vineyards,

3. Ibid.

winter-hardy hybrids such as Seyval Blanc have been planted, although no one seriously considers growing the extremely hardy Minnesota hybrids that are now common in Québec. For the most part, the wine-growers of Prince Edward County intend to rise or fall with premium vinifera grapes.

There is logic to steering away, at least to a degree, from hybrids. Heinricks notes that, with consumers unwilling to pay much for wines from hybrids, "it is now quite difficult to make a good living growing Vidal and Seyval Blanc." But then he adds this cautious advice: "A very conservative strategy ... would be to plant a portion of the vineyard to the very best, most interesting hybrid varieties, to help buffer the risk of vine and crop loss." However, it is clear where his heart lies:

> I persist in believing that Pinot Noir (OK, Chardonnay too) is probably the variety most suited to Prince Edward County, given our climate, our soil, and the world market. There just isn't enough good Pinot Noir on earth ... If we can get it right (and we've been dealt a pretty decent hand), then there is a market, a very lucrative, passionate market.

In his own vineyard, Heinricks grows about thirty different clones of Pinot Noir in an effort to identify the best. Other vineyards are testing clones of Chardonnay for the same reason.

Many of the county's growers share Heinricks' view. Norman Hardie, the much-travelled winemaker at Carmela Estates, says: "This is the closest to Burgundy Pinot soils that I have seen around the world." Hardie made Pinot Noir in France, New Zealand, Oregon, and California before coming to the county. In addition to managing Carmela's ten hectares, he has planted three hectares nearby, most of it to Pinot Noir. He calls the property, destined to be a winery, Prince Edward County Pinot. Other vinifera vines are also planted in the county, including Pinot Gris, Gewürztraminer, St Laurent (an early ripening Austrian red), and some of the Bordeaux varieties.

The danger is always the winter. Vinifera vines in particular can be damaged or killed by temperatures below –20°C (–4°F). Such winters do not occur every year, just often enough to require the growers to take precautions. Vines may also be damaged or killed if, in late winter, the temperatures fluctuate sharply. "I believe a prudent business plan would expect to have three good to great harvests every five years, with the other two expected to be disasters," Heinricks warns. "And statistically, quite probably once in a lifetime, there will be a vineyard loss or near-loss."

Accordingly, the growers take precautions, including covering vines with straw or earth where the soil permits; the rock-laden Hilliard soil is difficult to plough over the vines and the rocks can be almost as damaging as frost. Pruning techniques also have been developed to improve the ability of vineyards to make it through winter. Most county vintners also hedge their bets by buying grapes from Niagara vineyards. Says Carmela's Hardie:

> *The long-term goal is to supply this winery entirely from the county. But I think that's a pipe dream from a risk management perspective. It is important that we do not keep all our eggs in one basket.*

11

Wineries of Prince Edward County

BLACK PRINCE WINERY **
13370 Loyalist Parkway, Picton, ON, K0K 2T0.
Tel: 613 476 4888; Website: www.blackprincewinery.com
This winery opened in June 2004 with two days of medieval jousting, a spectacle never before seen in the quiet town of Picton. The winery, located at the edge of the town, is named for the fourteenth-century English Prince Edward, the Black Prince, who established his court in Bordeaux, then ruled by the English Crown.

The single largest shareholder here is The Opimian Society, a national wine club formed in Canada in 1973 which now has about 10,000 members. For a number of years in the 1980s and 1990s, the society controlled the William Hill winery in California. When that interest was sold, some of the cash was reinvested in 2000 to develop a vineyard and winery in Prince Edward County. Having access to wine consumers across Canada gave Black Prince a running start. Even before the winery opened its tasting room, Opimian members had ordered 2,500 cases.

The tasting room, beside one of the county's busiest roads, occupies a large property formerly used as a riding stable. The 3.5-hectare vineyard has been planted on a sandy slope behind the winery. Geoffrey Webb, the general manager, was not prepared to bet the farm, so to speak, on just Pinot Noir. The other varieties planted include Chardonnay, Riesling, Cabernet Franc, Auxerrois, Maréchal Foch, and a dark red hybrid, Chambourcin, that Webb argues is useful for blending. Black Prince also buys from independent growers; one of these growers supplied the grapes for the winery's début 2002 Baco Noir. Niagara grapes were used for another of the winery's first releases, a 2002 Cabernet Franc. Icewine was made from Lake Erie juice. The winery also imports California grape juice, producing Cabernet Sauvignon and Chardonnay that is sold to Opimian members outside Ontario. The consulting winemaker is Californian Michael Fallow, one of the original winemakers at William Hill. "We see him once a month," Webb says. "Michael has been brutally vigilant in attention to detail."

This is an ambitious project. The winery is designed to grow to production of about 20,000 cases, using its own and purchased grapes. A subsidiary business installs on-premises winemaking for restaurants in Ontario and Webb is considering producing wine kits. "We're all about being a working winery and being in the wine business," Webb says.

CARMELA ESTATES WINERY ****
1186 Greer Road, RR 1, Wellington, ON, K0K 3L0.
Tel: 613 399 3939; Website: www.carmelaestates.com
In 1999, a partnership headed by Michael Peddlesden began planting what has become a twelve-hectare vineyard on Hillier township farmland. The winery opened three years later, operating as Peddlesden Wines for a year until it was acquired by Bob and Sherry Tompkins, business-people from nearby Belleville. Now it is named after Sherry's mother.

The winery has the capacity to make 10,000 cases a year. The well-equipped production area and cellars are partly, sometimes entirely, below ground, surmounted by a wine shop and restaurant designed to mirror the local Loyalist-era architecture. The restaurant affords sweeping views over the vineyards. Lake Ontario is only two kilometres (1.2 miles) away, and the moderating influence of the lake extends the growing season. However, there is enough risk of frost at either end of the season for wind machines to be installed in the vineyards.

To manage the vineyard and make the wine, the Tompkins engaged Norman Hardie, who has had a remarkable amount of experience in two hemispheres, doing four vintages at South Africa's Bouchard Finlayson, three in Burgundy, and then two each in New Zealand and California. It shows in the polished elegance of Carmela wines, which include a crisp, estate-grown Chardonnay aged in new French oak. "I believe in firmness in wines and in expressing minerality," he says.

The Carmela vineyard is being grown organically, with varieties including Riesling, Pinot Gris, Chardonnay, and Cabernet Franc. However, forty per cent of Carmela's vineyard is Pinot Noir, and it is the potential of Pinot Noir that draws Hardie to Prince Edward County. Nearly all of Hardie's own three hectares are also planted to Pinot Noir. "I am always a firm believer that wine is grown in the soil," Hardie says. "Having spent so much time in Burgundy, I understand this concept of terroir. "

BY CHADSEY'S CAIRNS WINERY AND VINEYARD **
17432 Loyalist Parkway, Wellington, ON, K0K 3L0.
Tel: 613 399 2992; Website: www.bychadseyscairns.com

Richard Johnston's options were limited in 1995 when he and Vida Zalnieriunas, his wife, were figuring out how to earn a living from the 200-year-old farm they had just bought in Prince Edward County. The area's typical cash crops did not pay. "We decided to practise intensive farming," he recounts. "It was either grapes or asparagus. Grapes make better wine." They started by planting Riesling. They now have eight hectares, and the winery opened in 2003. On one of the county's historic farms, it is named for Ira Chadsey (1828–1905), an independent-minded figure who listed himself in census records as an atheist – a surprising designation in a county settled by Quakers, Methodists, and Anglicans. Fourteen stone cairns line up like a fence at the back of the property. Johnston's explanation is that Chadsey, despite claiming he was an atheist, believed he would be reincarnated and return on a white horse, guided to his property by the cairns. When the Johnstons bought a dapple grey horse, some neighbouring farmers had a moment or two of concern.

The Johnstons are city folk with acute sensitivity for their adopted rural community. The house and the barns have been restored. Particular care was taken to preserve the Quaker meeting hall – a building that dates from 1840 and is now the wine shop. The cemetery on the farm (the oldest headstone is dated 1805) is available for viewing by history-conscious wine tourists.

The vineyard is at the western end of Hillier Township, on a slope close to Wellington Bay on Lake Ontario. Proximity to the lake extends the growing season in autumn while delaying bud-break when there still is a risk of spring frost. For winter protection, Johnston places the next year's fruiting canes on the ground each fall and covers them with earth. It is time-consuming but necessary, given the cold winters. Johnston calculates that a Prince Edward County vineyard could suffer crop loss fifty per cent of the time if prudent measures were not taken. "What you need to do is reduce the bad years to one or two out of ten," he says. The Johnstons expect the winery's maximum production to be about 5,500 cases a year. Niagara grapes play a role in some of the wines but most will be estate-grown. The three largest plantings are Riesling, Chardonnay, and St Laurent. There also are smaller quantities of Chenin Blanc, Gewürztraminer, Pinot Noir and Muscat Ottonel.

CLOSSON CHASE VINEYARD & WINERY (Range not tasted.)
629 Closson Road, Hillier, ON, K0K 2J0.
Tel: 613 399 1418

The germ of the idea that became Closson Chase began in the late 1990s when Geoff Heinricks, then developing his own small vineyard, asked Deborah Paskus for cuttings of Pinot Meunier from the Thirty Bench vineyard near Beamsville (see page 105), where she was then vineyard manager. Curiosity spurred, Paskus did her own research on Prince Edward County, reaching the conclusion that outstanding Burgundian varieties could be grown there. A seven-hectare vineyard was begun in 1998 and is now planted to Chardonnay (eighty per cent) and Pinot Noir.

Born in 1952, Paskus grew up in a blue collar Hamilton home with no exposure to wine. She became interested in viticulture while travelling in California and studied for a master's degree in oenology at the University of Guelph. After working at Cave Spring winery and Thirty Bench, Paskus teamed up with Toronto writer Steve Temkin to produce a benchmark Ontario Chardonnay from grapes cropped well below the average yield for Niagara. Those fully ripe grapes allowed Paskus to sculpt intensely rich Chardonnay and she was acclaimed as a master of the variety.

Fans of the Chardonnay included Toronto film-maker Seaton McLean and his wife Sonja Smits, who had acquired a former diary farm near Hillier, on the west side of Prince Edward Count. They offered to back Paskus in a wine-growing project, which resulted in the opening of Closson Chase winery in 2004. The winery's objective, at full production, is to make between 2,000 and 4,000 cases of premium Chardonnay and Pinot Noir. "We are going to be small and we are going to stay small," Paskus says. "It is meant to reflect our philosophy as growers and winemakers. If you want to put your hands on everything, then it has to be small."

Initial vintages, beginning with 2001, have all been made with grapes purchased from Niagara. There are two reasons for this. First, Paskus believes that grapes from older, well-established vines deliver better quality fruit. Second, she has found that it takes an extra year or so for vines to establish themselves in Prince Edward County's limestone soils. There have been other challenges for Paskus; the 2002 vintage was consumed by birds and the 2003 eaten by raccoons. However this rocky start has not dimmed her confidence in the region's potential for growing exceptional Chardonnay and Pinot Noir. "The soils are magnificent," Paskus says, adding that the county has "all the things that are the magic of Burgundy: south-facing slopes, well-drained slopes, shallow, fractured, limestone-based soils. It is going to be a lot of hard work, but I know the county will work."

COUNTY CIDER COMPANY ESTATE WINERY *
County Road 8, RR 4, Waupoos, ON, K0K 2T0.
Tel: 613 476 1022; Website: www.countycider.com
The revival of cider- and winemaking in Prince Edward County began when Grant Howes opened the County Cider Company in 1995 and then began selling wine in 1997, using Niagara grapes while developing two vineyards planted to Pinot Noir, Chardonnay, Gamay, and white Geisenheim hybrids. Born in 1956, Howes, who has degrees in business administration, biology, and economics, was working as a business consultant in western Canada in 1991 when he acquired the taste for cider after touring Vancouver Island's Merridale Cider Works (now Merridale Estate Cidery). It led to his decision to open a cidery on his family's historic orchard and extract more value from the apples. This winery and cidery has one of the most dramatic settings in the county. It is perched on a ridge with a panoramic view over Lake Ontario. The tasting room is one of the county's oldest structures, a stone barn built about 1820. The house on the property was built in 1837 and the barn, where cider and wine are made, dates from 1862.

LE DOMAINE DU CERVIN (Range not tasted.)
13845 Gibeault, Chesterville, ON, K0C 1H0.
Tel: 613 448 2245; Email: cervin@primus.ca
This winery, midway between Ottawa and Cornwall, operated by Swiss-born cheese-maker and deer-farmer Samuel Gutknecht, is so far off the beaten path that it does not fit into any established Ontario region. Prince Edward County is nearest but the winery, which opened in 2003, more closely resembles a Québec winery. His peers consider Gutknecht the most accomplished of the determined new breed of vintners in eastern Ontario.

THE GRANGE OF PRINCE EDWARD INC. ESTATE WINERY ***

990 Closson Road, Hillier, ON, K0K 2J0.

Tel: 613 399 1048; Website: www.thegrangewines.com

Opened in 2004 this winery has meticulously restored farm buildings, including a barn built about 1830 by some of the earliest of Loyalist settlers in Prince Edward County's Hillier Township. The tasting room, with a floor-to-ceiling fireplace made from field stones, is in the former loft. The bottling room was the stable and the barrel cellar, with room for 170 barrels, was the milking parlour.

Robert Granger, a retired Toronto lawyer, bought the property in the 1970s and raised livestock until his daughter, Caroline, persuaded him to plant grapes and join her in a winery. The 20-hectare vineyard was planted over four years. "We should have been finished last year but our Gamay fell in the ocean," said Caroline in early 2004. The vines were being shipped from France, but were washed overboard during a mid-ocean storm. The nursery replaced the order the following year.

About half the vineyard is planted to Pinot Noir; the remainder is Chardonnay, Pinot Gris, Riesling, Cabernet Franc, and Gamay. "Our focus is primarily Burgundian," Caroline explains. "We have wonderful gravel soil over fractured limestone." On its website, the winery observes that Hillier Township is on the same parallel, 44 degrees north, as Burgundy. To underline the focus, she recruited a consulting winemaker from Burgundy, who works with Jeff Innes, the full-time winemaker at Grange. Innes is responsible for making the wines from Niagara grapes, released under the Trumpour's Mill label. The winery has a capacity of 25,000 cases a year. "We are trying to create a business rather than a hobby," she says.It opened with 1,600 cases from the 2003 vintage, including well-crafted examples of Riesling, Gamay and Cabernet Franc, some made from Niagara grapes.

HUFF ESTATES WINERY ***

1527 Highway 62 at County Road 1, Bloomfield, ON, K0K 1G0.

Tel: 613 393 5802; Website: www.huffestates.com

The Huff winery may be the only one in Canada with its own helicopter landing pad. It would be fair to describe it as modestly extravagant for a start-up winery. Open since 2004, it is set on one of the highest points in Prince Edward County, near an intersection once known as Huff's Corner. The slope of the hill is harnessed for gravity-flow production in the winery.

Barrel cellars are partly below ground; the barrels are all French oak. The fermentation room gleams with polished stainless steel, including double-jacketed tanks and a new French wine press. Owner Lanny Huff, whose ancestors arrived here in 1825 as United Empire Loyalists, was a successful plastics manufacturer. He has built a splendid winery with a capacity of 15,000 cases a year. He could have built it in any region, but chose the county where he grew up and which, to him, is a special place.

Unlike most other county wineries, Huff has opted for Bordeaux varieties in its 45 hectares of vineyards. Currently, it is the only winery in the county to grow Merlot. The initial county wine was a 2002 blend of Cabernet Sauvignon, Cabernet Franc, and Merlot, from two-year-old vines in Huff's South Bay vineyard. The winery has vineyards in three locations. The coolest site is on the slope around the winery and the warmest, according to vineyard manager Michael Traynor, is South Bay, in the southern part of the county, close to Lake Ontario. The soils can be compared to Pomerol. Huff also subscribes to the county's Burgundy mantra, having planted Chardonnay and Pinot Gris. The normal protection is taken against winter's cold. "We've had to adapt our viticulture," Traynor says. "What we bury, we keep."

Having built an enviably-equipped winery, Huff installed a well-trained team. French Frédéric Picard is the winemaker; the cellarmaster is Alex Hunter. When the winery opened, most wines were made with Niagara grapes. They included Riesling, Gamay, Chardonnay, and a particularly impressive red blend of Cabernet Franc and Cabernet Sauvignon. Niagara fruit will play a role at least until 2007, when Huff expects to be growing all the grapes it needs in Prince Edward County. The Huff vineyards in the county are expected to produce about 8,500 cases a year.

LONG DOG VINEYARDS & WINERY ****
104 Brewers Road, South Marysburgh, RR 1, Milford, ON, K0K 2P0.
Tel: 613 476 4140; Email: james@longdog.ca

The objective of Toronto film-maker James Lahti, who opened this winery in 2004, is the production of Pinot Noir and Chardonnay wines that will fetch $50 a bottle. "I really believe it is not out of the question," he says. A tasting of barrel samples of his 2003 vintage left no doubt that the wines have that potential. Lahti was born in Sudbury in 1951, into a family that he describes as "peasant dairy farmers." However, his father was an amateur winemaker and an amateur film-maker and passed both interests on. "When

I was nineteen, I bought a motorcycle, went to Europe and travelled all over," Lahti says. Wineries were always included in those travels. In his successful film career, Lahti has always managed to visit wineries when working abroad. He did not have a vineyard in mind in 1997 when he bought his 121-hectare farm in Prince Edward County. Weary of the urban pace in Toronto, he was looking for a weekend retreat. Within a few years, he had moved here permanently and had turned a century-old barn into a film-editing studio.

When he analyzed the Burgundian nature of his terroir, he began planting a vineyard in 1999. "To grow great Chardonnay and great Pinot Noir, you need to be located between the 43rd parallel and the 45th, and you need hot days, cool nights, and limestone," he says. "I thought I would plant 1,000 vines." He increased that to 5,000 vines and just kept going. Today, the eight-hectare vineyard contains about 20,000 vines, half of which are Pinot Noir. Chardonnay accounts for a third, with Pinot Gris and Gamay in the rest of the vineyard. All are densely planted to encourage the low yields necessary to make the kind of wines Lahti has in mind.

The first wines were made in 2002. "It was really encouraging," Lahti says. "They are very Burgundian in style, very mineral-based." Long Dog opened with 1,000 cases and such a waiting list that Lahti immediately limited the number of bottles for each buyer. Within five years, he hopes to be producing about 4,000 cases a year. Lahti believes the winery has the potential to make more: the vineyard area could be quadrupled.

SUGARBUSH VINEYARDS (Range not tasted.)
1286 Wilson Road, RR 1, Hillier, ON, K0K 2J0.
Tel: 613 849 0521; Website: www.sugarbushvineyards.ca

Robert Peck and his wife, Sally, were drawn to the wine-grower's lifestyle while touring Okanagan wineries in 1997, but the price of vineyard land there deterred them. Finding Prince Edward County much more affordable, the Pecks purchased a nineteen-hectare farm and began planting vines in 2002. Currently, they have 3.4 hectares planted, with plenty of scope for more. The major varieties are Chardonnay, Gewürztraminer, Riesling, Pinot Noir, and Gamay. When the Pecks open their winery in 2006, they intend to model it after the family-owned Okanagan wineries. "We want to be the people meeting the public," says Robert. "It is a lot nicer for customers if they are talking to the owners."

THIRTY THREE VINES (Range not tasted.)

9261 Highway 33, The Loyalist Parkway, Conway, ON, K0K 2T0.

Tel: 613 373 1133; Website: www.pec.on.ca/33vines

Telecommunications consultant Paul Minaker grew up in Prince Edward County. His interest in wine began in 1997–8, when he spent a year as a project manager in the Napa Valley for an international technology firm. "Vineyards and wineries get under your skin," he discovered. "I went to Napa a beer drinker and returned home a wine drinker." In 2004, he planted vines on a two-hectare property beside Highway 33, which connects Picton and Kingston. He has also acquired another nine hectares in Cherry Valley, close to Lake Ontario in the county's southwestern corner. In developing these vineyards, Minaker intends to plant only vinifera, notably Chardonnay, Riesling, Pinot Noir, Merlot, and Cabernet Franc.

WAUPOOS ESTATES WINERY *

3016 County Road 8, Waupoos, ON, K0K 2T0.

Tel: 613 476 8338; Website: www.waupooswinery.com

Named after the nearby village, this was Prince Edward County's first winery exclusively based on grapes, when it opened in 2001. Or as crusty co-owner Ed Neuser puts it: "We were the fools who started it." His forty-hectare lakefront property was formerly planted entirely to apples. With the apple business in decline, he and his wife Rita Kaimins planted grapes in 1993. But before he made that decision, Neuser sought the advice of close friend Klaus Reif (*see* page 92). "What have you got to lose?" Reif asked.

The vineyard at Waupoos is now eight hectares in size. Neuser believes that the cool site is best suited to white varieties, so red grapes are purchased from the Reif vineyard in Niagara. Winemaker Jason MacDonald is another link to Reif. A Prince Edward County native, he came to Waupoos as a casual employee. When he showed an interest in wines, Neuser sent him to work a vintage with Reif. MacDonald has developed a light touch and is someone who knows when to use oak and when to avoid it. One of the winery's recent successes was an unoaked Chardonnay. Currently, Waupoos makes at least twenty different wines, ranging from a full-bodied Baco Noir from county grapes, to an off-dry liebfraumilch-style called Honeysuckle; and Winter Wine, which is similar to Vidal Icewine. "Next year," Kaimins sighed in 2004, "we have to make a decision and pare down what we make."

12

British Columbia: The Okanagan and Similkameen Valleys

The Okanagan Valley is an enigma. Most of British Columbia's vineyards and wineries are found in this valley, stretching 160 kilometres (100 miles) north to south, and spilling across the border into the USA. It encompasses microclimates resembling a variety of conditions from the Rhine to the Rhône. Grape varieties that are planted hundreds of kilometres apart in Europe often grow grow side by side in the Okanagan. For example, a fence separates the vineyards of Wild Goose and Stag's Hollow wineries near Okanagan Falls. Wild Goose grows acclaimed Gewürztraminer and Riesling, while Stag's Hollow grows excellent Pinot Noir, Chardonnay, and Merlot. This is the paradox of the Okanagan. Is it a blessed valley where everything can be grown everywhere? Or does the terroir still need to be figured out?

The answer is that British Columbia's wine-growers are now starting to unravel the terroir, a process that has taken generations elsewhere. Wine grapes have been grown in British Columbia for just three generations, with trial and error (mostly the latter) during the first two. The wine industry in British Columbia is young and small, with 2,185 hectares of vineyards, most of them planted or replanted with European grapes only since 1990. As the vines mature, wines of internationally competitive quality are being made from about fifty different varieties. The most widely planted red grape is Merlot; the most widely planted white is Chardonnay. Both produce excellent wines. In 2002, CedarCreek Estate Winery, one of the Okanagan's leading producers, entered both a reserve and a regular bottling of Chardonnay in the Los Angeles County Fair, the

ii. *British Columbia*

oldest wine competition in the USA. Six gold medals were awarded in the Chardonnay class and CedarCreek took two of them, an impressive performance against some of California's best Chardonnays.

There are over 125 wineries already open or being developed in British Columbia, including fruit wineries. Two thirds are in the Okanagan. A small number now operate in the Similkameen Valley, adjacent to the south Okanagan. The rest (excepting a few well off any beaten wine path) are either near Vancouver or on the islands between Vancouver and the Pacific Ocean. Most of the coastal wineries buy Okanagan grapes; a few make only estate-grown wines, even though it is more challenging to ripen wine grapes in the cool coastal vineyards than in the Okanagan, which is 480 kilometres (300 miles) inland from the coast and tucked behind mountain ranges.

British Columbia is vast and most of it is mountainous, with modest areas of arable land. The climate of southern British Columbia, especially at Vancouver and Vancouver Island, is among the most temperate in Canada. There is a long history of fruit-growing (peaches, apricots, apples, pears, and cherries). Many of those orchards have now become vineyards because the emerging wine industry has made it much more profitable to grow grapes than tree fruits.

FROM LOGANBERRIES TO GRAPES

There were no vineyards of consequence before 1928. The first commercial wines in British Columbia were made a few years earlier from loganberries. Farmers on the fertile Saanich Peninsula, just north of Victoria on Vancouver Island, organized the Growers' Wine Company in 1922 as an outlet for surplus loganberries. A second producer, Victoria Wineries (British Columbia) Ltd, opened five years later, to process a further berry surplus. The wines were sweet and fortified, like inexpensive ruby port. It proved easier to make the wine than to sell it. "We have manufactured this year nearly four times the quantity sold," the secretary of Victoria Wineries informed the shareholders in November 1931. "Our sales must therefore increase very considerably in the next six months, or it will be necessary to curtail our manufacture next year." The struggling winery merged the next year with Growers'. Loganberry wine remained in the Growers' portfolio into the 1960s, when disease wiped out most of the loganberry bushes. But by that time, consumers preferred grape wines to fruit wines.

The Okanagan's first vineyards for wine grapes were developed near Kelowna, beginning in 1928, by a horticulturist named J W Hughes, with Growers' negotiating the first grape purchase contract in 1932. It had been recognized for some time that grapes could be grown in the Okanagan, a valley where the summers are hot and dry and the winters are tempered by a chain of deep lakes.

A French Oblate priest, Charles Pandosy, established a mission to the aboriginal people in 1859 at what is now Kelowna. He was one of the earliest Europeans to live in the Okanagan. He may also have planted the first grapes. He described the mission site in a letter to his Oblate colleagues:

> It is a great valley situated on the left bank of the great Lake Okanagan and rather near the middle of the Lake.... The cultivable land is immense and I myself believe that if Friar Blanchet [a fellow Oblate in Oregon] is able to send us next year, some vine cuttings we shall be able to start a plantation, for when Bro. Surel arrives, if he accepts my plans, we shall elevate our little demesne to the middle of the plain, against a little hill very well exposed....

On the strength of that, Father Pandosy is sometimes called the father of the British Columbia wine industry. The claim is entirely fanciful. If the mission fathers ever made wine, there is no evidence that any was sold. The mission site now is a modern church, not far from vineyards that were started chiefly by J W Hughes.

Hughes and other early growers started with *Vitis labrusca* varieties. The prevailing view was that *Vitis vinifera* would not survive Okanagan winters. The federal government's research station at Summerland launched the first of its intermittent trials of grape varieties in 1928. "This planting consisted of the old standbys – Niagara, Campbell Early, Warden, Concord, etc," wrote Donald Fisher, a former superintendent of the station, in 1981. The station imported vines from around the world and, by 1936, had close to 150 under test. Vinifera grapes were dropped first, due to a perceived lack of winter hardiness. The programme was finally ended in 1948 due to what Fisher called "lack of interest in the industry". That was hardly surprising since the only significant wineries in British Columbia at the time were Growers' in Victoria and Calona Wines, which was launched in 1932 to make apple wine, switching to grapes when the Hughes vineyards came into production. Calona, which was financed largely by Italian immigrants, sustained its business for years by making sacramental wine for the Roman Catholic diocese. That suggests that the Pandosy mission had not continued making wine, if it ever did.

The winemaker at Growers' at the time was Hungarian-trained Dr Eugene Rittich. In 1941, he and his brother, Virgil, published the first book on Okanagan viticulture: *European Grape Growing in Cooler Districts where Winter Protection is Necessary*. It related what they had learned about growing vinifera in the Okanagan. Virgil said in a paper he wrote at the time the book was printed,

> *After ten years of experimenting with my brother, I have found that the Okanagan valley is not only perfectly suitable for European grape-growing, but its climate is in many respects superior to most vine-growing countries in Middle Europe. It seems to me that the early growers neglected chiefly two things: (1) They did not secure varieties which were suitable to our northern climate and, (2) they did not develop a training method which makes it possible to produce high quality grapes. With my brother I imported about fifty different varieties and planted them on our trial plot.*

Their only precaution against winter was to plough a protective layer of earth around the base of the vines each fall. The prescient Rittich brothers, whose vineyard also was at a poor site near Kelowna, had so much difficulty ripening vinifera grapes that the general manager of Growers' dismissed their fruit as "miserable European varieties". The vineyard was replanted to French hybrids in the 1960s.

The Summerland research station resumed its grape trials in 1957, this time avoiding vinifera in favour of the hybrids that in 1947 had been imported from France by Ontario's Horticultural Research Institute. The varieties, then bearing just the breeder's name, had been developed by plant scientists such as Albert Seibel, François Baco and Eugene Kuhlmann. At Summerland, Donald Fisher wrote,

> *We planted twelve of the most promising Seibel hybrids, plus other varieties gleaned from the breeding programmes of many European countries as well as from the USA and Ontario. Out of this programme came the recommendation in 1975 to plant Seibel 9549 …*

Somewhat academically, Fisher persisted in using the grape's breeder name even though Ontario had renamed it De Chaunac in 1972, after Adhemar de Chaunac, the influential technical director at the Brights winery. In the Okanagan, De Chaunac quickly displaced Bath, an American labrusca hybrid, as the most widely planted red. The most common white was Okanagan Riesling, a variety of uncertain origin but believed to have been a labrusca hybrid, either accidental or of Hungarian origin. The hybrids were hardy, prodigious producers but the wines were mediocre.

The grape trials at Summerland had been resumed because two new wineries were opened in British Columbia by a pair of Ontarians. In 1959, Chum Torno, who operated Danforth Wines in Toronto with two brothers and the Bronfman distilling family, opened Pacific Western Wines in New Westminster, a Vancouver suburb. Never a winery of significance, it was absorbed in 1973 by Jordan & Ste-Michelle Cellars (the successor to Growers').

A more important figure in British Columbia was Andrew Peller, who established Andrés Wines in 1961 in Port Moody, a Vancouver suburb. Formerly, he had operated a brewery in Hamilton. Ontario would not give him a license on reasonable terms because he had flaunted the government's ban against advertising his Peller's beer. (He had formed an ice company and taunted the regulators by advertising Peller's Ice instead.)

British Columbia allowed him to import California grapes on the condition that he plant grapes here. A few years later, Andrés imported the vines to launch Inkameep Vineyards. Owned by the Osoyoos Indian Band, it was the first extensive planting of vinifera in the Okanagan. The vines, flown in from Europe, were Riesling, Scheurebe and Ehrenfelser. Ironically, Andrés grew into one of Canada's largest wineries on the profits of a sparkling wine called Baby Duck, introduced in 1971 and for a time the single largest-selling Canadian wine (*see* page 10).

GROWTH IN THE SIXTIES AND SEVENTIES

In 1966, two more wineries opened: Casabello on Main Street in Penticton, and Mission Hill in a California-mission-styled winery with a breathtaking view from the top of Mount Boucherie, just south of Kelowna. At the time, British Columbia allowed neither tours nor tastings at wineries. Mission Hill's sales were so slow that it nearly went bankrupt.

Tours and tastings were not permitted for another decade. Casabello opened its tasting room in the summer of 1977.

The new wineries, along with rapid growth of wine sales by Calona and Growers', stimulated vineyards in the Okanagan. Annual wine grape production averaged 925 tons in the 1950s, 2,358 tons in the 1960s, and 11,254 tons in the 1970s. None of the large wineries owned vineyards (though Calona was a part-owner of a large vineyard for a few years). Wineries bought grapes from growers through a marketing board that was empowered to require wineries to buy all the fruit, with little reference to quality standards. It showed in the mediocrity of the wines. Soon, imported wines were outselling British Columbia wines. In the belief that winemakers would grow better wines from their own vineyards, the provincial government in 1978 was persuaded to create the new estate winery licence. The model was California where new estate wineries were amazing the world with their wines. Each Okanagan estate winery was required to own or control a minimum of eight hectares of vineyard.

The original five estate wineries were a mixed lot. Gray Monk and Sumac Ridge succeeded while the others stumbled (two failed). The big difference was the grapes. Gray Monk and Sumac Ridge made wines primarily from vinifera. As wineries began offering premiums for vinifera grapes, some growers began replacing hybrids. The industry as a whole began an eight-year-long trial of premium European grapes in consultation with the late Dr. Helmut Becker, the renowned director of oenology at Germany's Geisenheim Institute. The Becker Project wound up in 1986, providing valuable assessments on suitable varieties for the Okanagan.

The harvest of 1988, totalling 18,397 tons, was the largest since the first recorded harvest in the Okanagan. However, that year is remembered as the blackest for the British Columbia wine industry. In 1988 the Canadian government, under a new free trade agreement with the USA, stripped away the protections that had given Canadian wines a competitive edge. (The protections had included lower prices and preferred listings in liquor stores). Without their protected status, domestic wines not of international quality seemed doomed.

The wineries and the grape-growers were stunned that the effective adjustment period was only two years. In British Columbia (as in Ontario), they negotiated compensation so that growers could pull out grapes no longer wanted by wineries. Two-thirds of the vineyards, chiefly those growing hybrid grapes, were pulled out after the 1988 vintage. In 1989, the remaining 115 vineyards, comprising only 461 hectares, produced a mere 3,840 tons of grapes, mostly vinifera.

TOWARDS RESCUE

The next two steps were critical to rescuing the industry from the brink of irrelevance. Firstly, growers with vineyards that were too small to support their own estate wineries talked the government into establishing the farm winery licence, with a vineyard minimum of only 2.2 hectares. In effect, this was simply a small estate winery. Half a dozen farm wineries opened in quick succession, giving the lie to the pessimism that the wine industry was dying.

Secondly, the wineries adopted from Ontario the Vintners Quality Alliance (VQA) concept. Since 1990, most wines made exclusively from British Columbia grapes have been screened by a professional tasting panel. Those that pass are sold with the VQA seal on each bottle. Consumers have accepted these as honestly made wines, generally superior to the wines of earlier decades. Wine sales rose and the wineries and the remaining growers were justified in their view that British Columbia could compete in a free trade world.

Since that epochal year, the wine industry in British Columbia has re-invented itself, expanding rapidly in the process. First, new grape varieties were imported, primarily from nurseries in Europe, and the area under vine increased steadily. The ten most widely planted varieties are no longer hybrids; they are, in order, Merlot, Chardonnay, Pinot Noir, Pinot Gris, Pinot Blanc, Cabernet Sauvignon, Gewürztraminer, Cabernet Franc, Riesling, and Gamay.

If the Rittich brothers were correct about the Okanagan's potential, why were they only able to produce "miserable" fruit? Although they understood proper viticultural techniques, they had a poor site. Many of their peers lacked the skill to grow European grapes successfully. Most let the vigorous hybrid vines produce as much tonnage as possible, especially since the commercial wineries had to accept grapes of even marginal maturity. Today, the shoe is on the other foot: wineries will reject grapes that do not reach acceptable winemaking standards. Indifferent growers have been eliminated from the industry. Professional viticulturists now manage the large vineyards and consult to many smaller growers. There is an understanding of how to grow the European grape varieties that was sorely lacking two decades ago.

VALLEY VITICULTURE

Far from being unsuitable for these varieties, the Okanagan Valley and Similkameen Valleys have some advantages for growing high quality wine grapes. The Okanagan is hemmed in on both sides by mountains. In the growing season, little rain gets across those mountains to the vineyards, which are all irrigated. This dry climate is ideal for healthy grapes. It amazed winemaker Pascal Madevon, who had worked a dozen years in Bordeaux, when he arrived to handle the 2001 crush for the new Osoyoos Larose winery (*see* page 181), the Okanagan's first joint venture winery with a major French winery (Château Gruaud-Larose):

> *The advantage here is that you have no disease – no mildew, no oïdium, no botrytis. You can wait a very long time [while grapes ripen to perfection]. In France, you can't do that. Here, I pick the grapes when they are [at their] the best.*

Because of the position of the sun over the northern hemisphere in summer, the days are long, the light is intense, and July and August, when the grapes develop, are hot months. The grapes can, and often do, achieve ripeness similar to California's coastal vineyards. The skies are frequently cloudless, meaning that night temperatures are sharply lower. These cool nights nurture the piquant acidity and the vivid flavours that set the wines of British Columbia apart. "Here – this is very important – there is a big variation between the day and the night because there is a continental climate," Madevon found.

The changes in the wineries since 1990 have been as fundamental as those in the vineyards. In former years, the winemaking technology was primitive. The wine storage vessels at Growers' in Victoria included large redwood vats purchased during Prohibition from the Christian Brothers winery in California. Before 1980, when barrels were used they were usually old bourbon barrels. The supplier was Sweeney Cooperage, which operated in Victoria and Vancouver from 1889 to 1980 and which once claimed to be the biggest barrel maker in the British Empire. (Most of the customers were in the fruit and fishing industries.) Because bourbon is aged only in new American oak, the American distillers sold year-old barrels cheaply by the box car and Sweeney resold some to wineries at bargain prices.

Today, almost every winery owns French and American oak barrels. That transformation happened in a surprisingly short period. One of the first really sizeable orders for new barrels was placed by Mission Hill in 1992. John Simes, who had been chief winemaker at Montana, New Zealand's largest winery, arrived that September to take charge of Mission Hill's cellars. He was surprised at the quality of the Chardonnay in the Okanagan and appalled that the winery owned no new oak barrels. He promptly talked it into ordering a hundred American oak barrels. It was money well spent. The barrel-fermented wine he made won a major award, the Avery Trophy at the 1994 International Wine and Spirits Competition in London and was cleverly promoted by the winery as the world's best Chardonnay. It put the Okanagan wine region on the map.

Professionally-trained individuals like Simes now can today be found in many of British Columbia's wineries. The area's winemakers include graduates of Australia's Roseworthy; New Zealand's Lincoln University; South Africa's Stellenbosch University; Germany's Geisenheim and Weinsburg Institutes; oenology faculties at Bordeaux and Montpellier Universities; the University of California Davis and Fresno State College. Recently, Ontario's Brock University and Okanagan University College have begun to graduate winemakers and cellar technicians. In addition, several of top wineries are run by talented self-taught winemakers.

As the wineries have flourished, the industry has been able to attract the skilled individuals who would never have considered British Columbia a generation earlier. It is seen today as a place where a good winemaker, supported by a good vineyard, can make a name for himself.

13

Wineries of the Okanagan
and Similkameen Valleys

ADORA ESTATE WINERY ✳✳✳

6807 Highway 97, Summerland, BC, V0H 1Z0.

Tel: 250 404 4200; Website: www.adorawines.com

It helps to understand Latin at Adora. The signature blended wines are Decorus (a white) and Maximum (a red), both with vintage dates in Roman numerals, all signalling that things are done differently here. The winemaker partner at Adora is Geisenheim-educated Eric von Krosigk, a native of the Okanagan Valley and once the busiest consulting vintner in British Columbia. But here at his own winery, which opened in 2003, "there are a lot of styles that I can do that I can't do elsewhere," he says. Decorus and a companion wine, Elements No 8, are blends that seem to be inspired by Conundrum, the multi-varietal blend from California's Caymus Vineyards. All of the wines, red, white or sparkling – von Krosigk is a fanatic about bubbles – are matured slowly, to be ready to drink when released. Invariably, they are big and bold.

D'ANGELO VINEYARDS (Range not tasted.)

947 Lochore Road, Penticton, BC, V2A 8V1

Tel: 250 493 1364; Website: dangelowinery.com

Vintner Salvatore D'Angelo, who still runs the winery he opened near Windsor in 1989 (*see* page 117), will open a second winery in 2006 on a picturesque lake-view property on the Naramata Bench. D'Angelo spent more than a decade looking for a vineyard site in the Okanagan Valley, partly because he finds the hot, dry climate better for his health and in part because he can make the big reds here that he admires. On the eleven-hectare former orchard, D'Angelo has planted five Bordeaux red varieties as well as the Okanagan's first planting of Tempranillo. He also grows Viognier, Gewürztraminer, and Chardonnay. The winery is gravity-flow, taking advantage of a deep ravine separating the two halves of his vineyard.

ARROWLEAF CELLARS ***
1574 Camp Road, Lake Country, BC, V4V 1K1.
Tel: 250 766 2992; Website: www.arrowleafcellars.com

Arrowleaf Cellars takes its name from a common plant whose brilliant golden blossoms brighten the Okanagan each spring. Everything else about Arrowleaf, from the neat vineyard to the polished wines, reflects meticulous Swiss attention to detail. The owners, Josef and Margrit Zuppiger and winemaker son Manuel, came to Canada in 1986 as dairy farmers; ten years later they bought an Okanagan vineyard. Judging that the 6.5-hectare property was too small to support them as grape-growers, they added a winery in 2003. It is set among the vines, on a steep south-western slope that catches the reflected light and heat from nearby Lake Okanagan. The vineyard is located approximately on the fiftieth parallel, usually the northernmost limit of wine-growing. However, the immense lake has a depth of 300 metres (800 feet), moderating both the heat of summer and the cold of winter. This is one reason why Arrowleaf can mature varieties like Merlot. The tranquil lake vista also adds to the allure of Arrowleaf's wine shop and picnic area.

Manuel Zuppiger was trained in oenology at Wädenswil University in Switzerland, supplementing that by doing a vintage in Australia with Grant Burge. His experience shows in the reliable quality of the Arrowleaf wines. The winery's Gewürztraminer, from Alsace clones, is one of British Columbia's best. The other whites include Pinot Gris, Bacchus, Auxerrois, and a blend called Barrique that is the winery's offering to those who like oak-aged Chardonnay. In addition to Merlot, reds include Zweigelt and Pinot Noir.

BELLA VISTA VINEYARDS
3111 Agnew Road, Vernon, BC, V1H 1A1.
Tel: 250 558 0770; Website: www.bellavistawinery.ca

The party-time attitude at this winery began during its construction in the summer of 1994. The original partners, about a dozen professionals, spent the summer days erecting a three-storey winery on one of Vernon's best view lots. Then they pitched in on everything else, from the vineyard to the bottling – and the sampling. It was not the best of business plans. The partnership dissolved but founder Larry Passmore has kept the winery going. It is still a place for partying, however. This has become one of the Okanagan's busiest wedding venues.

BENCHLAND VINEYARDS ***
170 Upper Bench Road South, Penticton, BC, V2A 8T1.
Tel: 250 770 1733; Website: www.benchlandwines.com

Klaus Stadler, the founder of Benchland, was a Bavarian brewer before emigrating to Canada in 1997, where he acquired and redeveloped a nine-acre orchard. He was the first in British Columbia to plant Zweigelt, the red grape of Austria. It happened by chance: the Ontario nursery supplying his vines ran short of Pinot Noir vines and substituted Zweigelt. Stadler was delighted, having admired the wines in Europe. In addition to releasing a Zweigelt varietal, Stadler also uses it as a component with Cabernet Sauvignon and Lemberger in a premium Austrian-modelled blend called Mephisto.

In 2004 Stadler decided to return to Germany; he sold the winery to Keith and Lynn Holman, who own a substantial orchard nearby and who had opened their Spiller's Estate fruit winery in 2003. As winemaker, the Holmans recruited Craig Larson. Larson is every bit as meticulous as Stadler had been. "I do all the cellar work myself," he says. "Everything has to be sanitized and sterilized." However, he does not share Stadler's aversion to barrels. That portends an improved texture in Benchland's red wines which previously were matured only in stainless steel.

BLACK HILLS ESTATE WINERY *****
30880 71st Street (Black Sage Road), Oliver, BC, V0H 1T0.
Tel: 250 498 0666; Website: www.blackhillswinery.com

This winery recalls the old saying that you should not judge a book by its cover. The building itself is a large Quonset hut (similar to a Nissen hut) that might be a machinery shed at a mine. It came with the fallow fourteen-hectare vineyard, when it was purchased in 1996 by the two business couples who own the winery. Peter McCarrell and Bob Tennant had both been in the construction business. They measured the shed and concluded it was just fine as a winery and barrel cellar. "We're trying to put our money in our product," explains Tennant, whose wife, Senka, is the winemaker. The money went first into the vineyard: they planted 36,000 vines imported from nurseries in Europe. When they were ready to make wine, Senka struck a mentoring agreement for the first three vintages with Rusty Figgins, a Washington State winemaker who specializes in reds.

The result was instant acclaim for Black Hills when it released Nota Bene, its well-crafted Bordeaux blend. This focused little winery (production is 2,500 cases) makes only two other wines, a late-harvest Sauvignon Blanc called Sequentia and a crisp Sauvignon Blanc/Sémillon called Alibi, first released in 2004.

BLASTED CHURCH WINERY ***
378 Parsons Road, Okanagan Falls, BC, V0H 1R0.
Tel: 250 497 1125; Website: www.blastedchurch.com

Chris and Evelyn Campbell renamed this winery after buying it in 2002, choosing a name that refutes the canard that accountants are colourless. The winery was opened in 1998 by a grape-grower of Croatian origin named Dan Prpich, who called it Prpich Hills. The Campbells, who were Vancouver accountants before this career switch, found an excellent local story when searching for a new name. In the nearby village of Okanagan Falls, there is a church that in 1929 was moved from its original site, an abandoned mining town. For the move, the demolition crew loosened the heavy nails in the interior timbers with a dynamite explosion. The reassembled structure came to be known as the blasted church. The wines here are released under an ever-changing series of collector-quality labels, caricatures inspired by that tale.

Blasted Church has had unusual misfortune with winemakers. Frank Supernak, a veteran Okanagan winemaker hired soon after the Campbells took over the winery, died in an accident in November 2002. Several winemakers from other Okanagan wineries volunteered to finish the vintage for Blasted Church. In a gesture of gratitude, the winery put their portraits on its Pinot Noir label. Recruiting internationally, the Campbells then hired Willem Grobbelaar, a young South African, in 2003. He had to return to South Africa the following year when his Canadian work visa was not extended. So a few months before the 2004 vintage, the Campbells again had to hustle for a new winemaker. This time they hired an Australian, Marcus Ansems, with previous experience at Ontario's Creekside winery. He is a master of Syrah, one of the varieties in the seventeen-hectare vineyard.

With the changes in winemakers, the signature of the Blasted Church wines is still emerging. The whites, including a fragrant Chardonnay Musqué, show luscious fruit flavours. The reds, including Merlot, show a concentration reflecting the improvements that have been made in the vineyard. To best preserve these flavours, in 2004 Blasted Church was the first Okanagan winery to bottle most of its wines under screwcap closures.

BLUE MOUNTAIN VINEYARDS AND CELLARS *****
RR1, S3, C4, Okanagan Falls, BC, V0H 1R0.
Tel: 250 497 8244; Website: www.bluemountainwinery.com

In the 1970s, Ian and Jane Mavety prospered with the Maréchal Foch and other hybrids then growing in their picture-postcard vineyard in the south Okanagan. But like many other successful growers, they preferred wines quite different to the norm. In that era, Okanagan whites were often sweet and reds were light. Ian explains that before they converted their twenty-five-hectare vineyard entirely to Burgundy and Alsace grapes, they looked to Europe for the model:

> Jane and I actually packed our bags and went to Europe. We didn't really drink sweet wines, as such. After going to Europe, we realized that we did not have to make sweet wines. We decided that we were no different from others out there not being served by the BC wines at that time. That was basically it.

When he began ordering vines in the mid-1980s, Ian was told that Pinot Noir would fail at his site. He is nothing if not hard-headed. He believed his undulating site, with its fine southern exposure, had a lot in common with Burgundy. Besides, his favourite wine was red burgundy. "I couldn't afford it, so it would have to be made." From that determination, Blue Mountain, which opened in 1992, has come to make some of the best Canadian examples of Burgundy varietals. This disciplined 9,000-case winery produces only Pinot Noir, Gamay, Chardonnay, Pinot Gris, and Pinot Blanc, several of which are incorporated in Blue Mountain's bottle-fermented sparkling wines.

Ian also did trials with other vinifera, including Gewürztraminer and

Riesling, when he began converting the vineyard from hybrid varieties. He got rid of them when he decided the wines did not reach his stringent standards – even after the experimental wines, sold to another winery, won medals in competition.

A self-taught winemaker, Ian launched Blue Mountain with help from French-born Rafael Brisbois, a Champagne specialist working in California. Brisbois continued his association with Blue Mountain for years, with an increasingly light touch after Mavety's son, Matt, who was born in 1975, returned from New Zealand's Lincoln University a qualified winemaker. Matt brought back the concept of biodynamic farming. The Mavetys have since researched biodynamic vineyards in France and have been adopting these practices slowly in their Okanagan property. Chemicals have been replaced with natural nutrients and natural methods of pest control. This is not just responsible agriculture. Ian believes it is the way to make wines that reflect the vineyard:

> The best wines will be the best expression of your site, resulting from the least amount of intervention. You are trying to peel back all of these other things you are adding that are not organic, that are not pieces of the earth and pieces of the vine. That's how you are going to get to this expression of site. I would hope I would live to see that day when we can line up five, six, seven vintages, and be able to say: this is the site.

BURROWING OWL ESTATE WINERY *****
100 Burrowing Owl Place, RR 1, Site 52, Comp 20, Oliver, BC, V0H 1T0.
Tel: 250 498 0620; Website: www.bovwine.ca

As a novice to wine-growing, real estate developer Jim Wyse deliberately hired experts to help launch this winery, which opened in 1998. The vineyard was planted and managed by Richard Cleave, a thirty-year veteran of Okanagan grape-growing. Californian Bill Dyer, the former winemaker at Sterling Vineyards, made the wines through the first seven vintages. "We were not going to try to make the wine ourselves," says Wyse, whose son Stephen manages the cellar and mentored with Dyer. "We wanted to have a first-class person, with great experience and a great reputation." Dyer concluded his contract in 2004 after imprinting a distinctive style on the wines. "We are keeping his recipes," Jim says.

The ultra-premium strategy has succeeded. The winery now makes

24,000 cases of wine a year, all of it allocated to a clamouring market. Production is limited to varietals from the three major Bordeaux reds (plus a Meritage blend available only at the winery's Sonora Room restaurant), Syrah and Pinot Noir; and two elegantly-made whites, Chardonnay and Pinot Gris. Both the white wines express brilliantly clean fruit, with exceptionally subtle use of oak. The reds are bold, fruity, and concentrated. Says Jim:

> The Okanagan is infamous for its thin reds. Well, I wanted to be the opposite of that. To me, that's the name of the game – to get everything out of those grapes that's in there.

CALLIOPE VINTNERS ***
PO Box 995, Summerland, BC, V0H 1Z0.
Tel: 250 494 7213; Website: www.calliopewines.com
Named after an Okanagan hummingbird, the Calliope winery has flitted from one location to another after opening in 2001, finally declaring itself a "virtual" winery. It is all about running a winery without being encumbered with heavy investment. It is owned by four partners: Ross and Cherie Mirko, both winemakers, along with consulting viticulturalist Valerie Tait and her husband, Garth Purdie.

British Columbia allows a winery to operate under another winery's licence. The Calliope partners took advantage of this, operating initially at the Thornhaven winery near Summerland, and then at Poplar Grove on the Naramata Bench. In 2004, they stopped selling through Poplar Grove's crowded tasting room and limited Calliope largely to mail order and internet sales (but still under the Poplar Grove licence). The winery's explanation: "Free of the confines of bricks and mortars, Calliope has the freedom to pursue perfection." Pursuing that ideal involves tapping Tait's knowledge of where the best grapes are in the Okanagan. She is one of the valley's busiest vineyard consultants. Ross Mirko has plenty of contacts as well: he has consulted to a number of British Columbia wineries and is currently the winemaker at Lang Vineyards.

Calliope has seldom produced more than 1,000 cases a year. The winery has shown particular strength with red Bordeaux styles, often vineyard-designated. These include a succession of Merlots from Kaleden grower Chris Scott's Oak Knoll Vineyard. Calliope's 2002 Cabernet

Sauvignon bore the South Okanagan designation since grapes came from several of Tait's contacts. A gold-medal wine with astonishing concentration, it sold out quickly after release.

CALONA VINEYARDS ***
1125 Richter Street, Kelowna, BC, V1Y 2K6.
Tel: 250 762 3332; Website: www.calonavineyards.ca

In 1991, Calona began featuring the paintings of paraplegic artist Robb Dunfield on wine labels. That proved so effective that Calona now engages a number of British Columbia artists to create labels. The strategy not only sells the wines but has raised the profiles of all the artists. The formerly athletic Dunfield, who learned to paint with a brush in his teeth after breaking his vertebrae in an accident, now commands considerably better prices for his art.

Founded in 1932, Calona is British Columbia's oldest continually operating winery, and Howard Soon, who has been there since 1980, is the longest tenured winemaker of any in the Okanagan. Soon is also the winemaker for Sandhill, Calona's sister winery (*see* page 188). He juggles his work with the help of associate winemakers Kelly Moss, who joined Calona in 1999, and Stephanie Leinemann.

At the start, Calona made apple wines, switching to grapes after a few years. Launched by church-going Italians, Calona for some years made sacramental wines for the Roman Catholic Church in British Columbia. In the 1960s, the winery made hugely popular berry-flavoured fortified wines, switching to table wines in the 1970s as consumer tastes changed. Calona today produces cleanly-made, affordable wines from Okanagan grapes. The wines include Pinot Blanc, Gewürztraminer, Merlot, and Cabernet Franc, as well as Icewine from Ehrenfelser and Pinot Noir. The star of its Artist Series wines is a crisply fresh Pinot Gris. One varietal exclusive to Calona is a spicy white Sovereign Opal, a grape developed in British Columbia and grown only by a Calona grower. The winery, which operates from a sprawling complex in downtown Kelowna, also imports bulk wines from around the world, repackaging them for sale in Canada.

CARRIAGE HOUSE WINES *
32764 Black Sage Road, Oliver, BC,V0H 1T0.
Tel: 250 498 8818; Website: www.carriagehousewines.ca

There is a special passion here for wines made from Kerner, even though the largest part of the 3.4-hectare vineyard is in Bordeaux red varieties. Winemaker and co-proprietor Dave Wagner believes that the Okanagan's Black Sage Road area is one of the best places in Canada for growing the big Merlot, Cabernet Sauvignon, and Pinot Noir wines that he makes.

But then there is Kerner. Wagner came to winemaking as a member of an amateur winemaking club in British Columbia's Fraser Valley. He learned by making fruit wines. In 1985, he made Kerner for the first time and was hooked. In the Okanagan, Kerner can yield wines with citrus aromas and mouth-filling fruit.

CEDARCREEK ESTATE WINERY *****
5445 Lakeshore Road, Kelowna, BC, V1W 4S5.
Tel: 250 764 8866; Website: www.cedarcreek.bc.ca
GREATA RANCH VINEYARDS ****
697 Highway 97, Peachland, BC, V0H 1Z0.
Tel: 250 767 2605; Website: www.cedarcreek.bc.ca/greataranch.htm

A 25,000-case winery, CedarCreek has won a reputation as one of Canada's premium producers of Pinot Noir and Chardonnay, with a rising profile for Bordeaux reds. Established in 1980, it was acquired in 1986 by Ross Fitzpatrick, who is now a member of the Canadian Senate. Fitzpatrick grew up in the Okanagan and, while succeeding in mining, oil and gas, and aircraft parts, nurtured a romantic desire to own an apple orchard. When he bought CedarCreek, it was a struggling vineyard that also grew apples. Fitzpatrick was soon more intrigued with the grapes.

Active management of the winery was taken over in 1996 by his son Gordon. Then a producer of middling quality, CedarCreek has moved to the top ranks among Canadian wineries after major improvements in its vineyards, building a modern winery, and hiring experienced winemakers with University of California degrees. Tom DiBello, the current winemaker, started making wine at Napa's Stag's Leap Wine Cellars in 1983. Subsequently, he made wine in Australia, Arizona, Virginia, and Washington State before coming to CedarCreek in 2000.

Two of CedarCreek's three vineyards are located in the cooler north Okanagan – one at the winery and the other across the lake at Greata Ranch (pronounced "Gretta"). These grow prize-winning Chardonnay, Pinot Gris, and Pinot Noir. "I love Pinot Noir," says DiBello, who achieves sensual, velvet-textured wines with this grape. "It is such a challenging variety." He maintains that the Okanagan, if the sites are selected carefully for the right soil and climate, should produce exceptional Pinot Noir. "I look at it this way: if the Okanagan had been making wine first, all the Burgundians would be trying to imitate what we were doing."

CedarCreek's third vineyard, acquired in 2001, is at the southern end of the valley. Because this is the hottest part of the Okanagan, the winery grows most of its Cabernet Sauvignon and Merlot here. With these grapes, DiBello produces big, bold reds.

Since 2003, the sixteen-hectare vineyard at Greata Ranch has supplied CedarCreek's subsidiary winery, Greata Ranch Vineyards. This picturesque property was acquired in 1896 by an immigrant from the UK, George H Greata, who began an apple orchard. Fruit growing ended when the severe 1969 winter killed many of the trees. The ranch was utterly derelict by 1994, when Fitzpatrick bought it and began planting vines. The varieties planted include Pinot Noir, Merlot, Pinot Blanc, Gewürztraminer, and Chardonnay. Greata Ranch, whose wines are offered at lower prices than CedarCreek, also uses purchased grapes, including Ehrenfelser.

COLUMBIA GARDENS VINEYARD AND WINERY **
9340 Station Road, RR1, S11, C61, Trail, BC, V1R 4W6.
Tel: 250 367 7493; Website: www.cgwinery.com

Well off the beaten path, Columbia Gardens opened in 2001 near Trail, a historic smelter city in British Columbia's southeastern interior. Tom Bryden and Lawrence Wallace, his son-in-law, have 2.4 hectares of grapes growing in a former hayfield. "We got tired of the haying end of it," says Bryden, whose family has owned the farm since the 1930s. The property, on a bench overlooking the Columbia River, is in a sun-drenched valley with more than enough heat to ripen grapes. Bryden and Wallace planted early-ripening varieties, including Maréchal Foch, to protect against autumn frost. This first winery in the region has stirred an interest among others to plant vines. It has had particular success with its unoaked Chardonnay, its Gewürztraminer and a late-harvest Pinot Noir. The object at first had been to make a Pinot Noir Icewine in 2002 but Wallace and Bryden settled on the less risky option of picking before the frost.

CROWSNEST VINEYARDS **
Surprise Drive, RR 1, S18, C 18, Cawston, BC, V0X 1C0
Tel: 250 499 5129; Website: www.crowsnestvineyards.com

The Similkameen Valley still has to fully develop its apparent potential for vineyards and wineries. But a growing number of tourists have found it worthwhile to stop at this winery and its bistro since Olaf Heinecke and his family took over Crowsnest in 1998. Opened in 1995, it was making only 500 cases of wine a year. Heinecke has increased that twelvefold.

Born in Leipzig, Heinecke and his wife, Sabina, vacationed in British Columbia in 1995 after selling a successful real estate firm in Germany. Attracted by the beauty and the grape vines, he invested in a vineyard and then purchased Crowsnest. This is largely a family-run winery. Daughter Ann makes the wine with Todd Moore, a consulting winemaker, and son Sascha, trained in hotel management, handles sales. Crowsnest was making only white wines in its initial years but the Heinecke family has added Merlot, Pinot Noir, and Maréchal Foch. And it is the only winery in British Columbia (perhaps in North America) to release a varietal red from an old German grape, a Meunier mutation called Samtrot. The name improves with translation: it means "red velvet".

DESERT HILLS ESTATE WINERY ***
30480 71st Street (Black Sage Road), Oliver, BC, V0H 1T0.
Tel: 250 498 1040; Website: www.deserthills.ca

Twin brothers Randy and Jesse Toor, born in 1964 in India, spent summers working in Okanagan vineyards after coming to Canada. With this taste of the land, they bought a ten-hectare apple orchard in 1988 on Black Sage Road, one of the Okanagan's best vineyard areas. Seven years later they converted to grapes, mostly the Bordeaux reds and Syrah. They continue to sell most of the fruit to the Domaine de Chaberton winery at Langley but in 2003, they launched their own 1,500 case winery. "It was a little dream, to start a small winery," Randy says. "We love the industry. We love the taste of wine." The Syrah from this vineyard is distinctive for intense nutmeg spice in both the aroma and the taste.

DOMAINE COMBRET ESTATE WINERY ***
32057 13 Road, PO Box 1170, Oliver, BC, V0H 1T0.
Tel: 250 498 6966; Website: www.combretwine.com

The Combret family arrived in British Columbia from France in 1992, bringing their knowledge of ten generations of wine growing in Provence. In the early 1990s, good vineyard land still was available throughout the valley. Robert Combret bought one of the best sites in the south Okanagan's

Golden Mile. Then his son, Olivier, a twenty-one-year-old graduate from the wine school at Montpellier, designed Canada's first gravity-flow winery. A decade later, it remains a textbook model of efficiency. The property had a small planting of Riesling, Chardonnay, and Cabernet Franc. Today, the fourteen-hectare vineyard is planted eighty per cent to red varieties, including Merlot, Cabernet Sauvignon, and Pinot Noir.

The approach to winemaking is traditional. Olivier Combret's singular Riesling is bone dry. His Chardonnay is crisply reminiscent of Chablis. (In 1995, this was the first Canadian winery to win an award at the Chardonnay du Monde competition in Burgundy.) The winery's reds, notably the Cabernet Franc, are built to be cellared. It is Olivier's view that a winery should hold back some wines and let them gain maturity before releasing them. "We have to be able to offer the consumers old whites and old reds," he maintains. In 2004 he released 900 cases of ten-year-old Riesling, and followed that with the release of a 1995 Riesling.

FAIRVIEW CELLARS ESTATE WINERY ****
13147 334th Avenue (Old Golf Course Road), Oliver, BC, V0H 1T0.
Tel: 250 498 2211; Website: www.winegrowers.bc.ca

On a 2.4-hectare plateau overlooking the first tee of one of the Okanagan's most challenging golf courses, Bill Eggert has planted the major red Bordeaux varieties. There are no whites at all. "I have some of the best land for supporting reds and I honestly didn't want to waste any of my land on whites," he says. "It boils down to the site. We're in the hottest grape-growing area in Canada." There is a highly regarded Meritage blend, Merlot, Cabernet Franc, Cabernet Sauvignon, and blends incorporating two of those three. The Fairview Cellars winery opened in 2000 and now produces about 1,500 cases annually of robust reds.

FIRST ESTATE CELLARS (Range not tasted.)
5031 Cousins Road, Peachland, BC, V0H 1X2.
Tel: 250 767 2299

This was the first of British Columbia's cottage wineries, opened in 1979 as Chateau Jonn de Trepanier. Through a succession of owners and receiverships over the next two decades, the winery changed its name three times. Frank Silvestri, a Calgary trucking company executive, acquired First Estate, which was then closed, in 2001. He reopened the winery three years later after redeveloping the neglected seven-hectare vineyard. The best wine is an Old Vines Foch, made from a surviving block of mature vines in this mountainside property. Currently, Focus wines are being marketed as a premium brand of Pinot Reach Cellars (*see* page 184).

FOCUS OKANAGAN VALLEY ***
1670 Dehart Road, Kelowna, BC, V1W 4N6.
Tel: 250 764 0078

The only grape that Roger Wong works with for this label is Riesling because he believes it to be the ideal variety for the Okanagan Valley. He launched Focus in 2003 with a single wine, 3,200 bottles of a refined dry Riesling, and he released the wines in heavy Champagne-style bottles because they could be sealed with crown caps. "I have been having problems with corks for many years," he explains. Born in Vancouver in 1965 and a university geography graduate, Wong, after several years of home winemaking, became so enamoured with wine that he left a civil service job to volunteer to help with the 1995 crush at the Okanagan's Tinhorn Creek winery. In 1998, he became the chief winemaker at Pinot Reach Cellars in Kelowna where the Riesling infatuation began with that vineyard's 25-year-old vines. Wong's dream is to replicate the Focus concept in other wine regions with whatever he considers are the signature varieties in those regions.

GEHRINGER BROTHERS ESTATE WINERY ****
Highway 97 at Road 8, Oliver, BC, V0H 1T0.
Tel: 250 498 3537

Gehringer Brothers has been an enduringly popular Okanagan winery since opening in 1986. The wines are charmingly understated and, arguably, underpriced for their quality. In its first decade, the winery released whites almost exclusively, notably Riesling in a light, fruity, and off-dry German style. In the second decade, the winery added French varietals to its bread-and-butter whites.

The German style comes naturally. Walter and Gordon Gehringer were born in the Okanagan to a family of German immigrants; their father was a Mercedes Benz dealer. While the brothers were enrolled in German wine schools, their parents and an uncle acquired a vineyard in the south Okanagan in 1981, converting it from hybrid varieties to Riesling, Ehrenfelser, Auxerrois and Schönburger. When an adjoining property was acquired in 1995, the brothers added Chardonnay, Sauvignon Blanc,

Cabernet Sauvignon, and Cabernet Franc. As a result, there has been what Walter describes as

> ... *a definite change in direction from where we initially were, allowing us to round out our winemaking style, rather than just making Germanic whites. I can pretty well boast a wine for anybody's palate.*

The white wines are pristinely faultless. The reds emphasize fruit; the brothers, after once eschewing oak altogether, have a light touch with it.

Gehringer Brothers has become one of British Columbia's five best Icewine producers, an achievement that comes from being alert and prepared. They first made Icewine in 1991, catching an unusually early October 31 opportunity when Walter, walking through the vineyard, detected that the temperature was falling sharply. That cold spell persisted for three days, allowing them to make three different Icewines. Some years later, another October 31 freeze lasted only hours. The Gehringers were ready for it; no one else in the Okanagan managed to make Icewine until the next frost came in the new year.

GERSIGHEL WINEBERG
29690 Highway 97, Oliver, BC, V0H 1T0.
Tel: 250 495 3319

Everything about this roadside winery is informal, from the rudely hand-lettered sign proclaiming the "wonderful wines of British Columbia" to owner Dirk de Gussem's shirtless presence in the tasting room during the Okanagan's blistering summer. Born in 1946 on a Belgium potato farm, he worked the vineyards of Europe and South Africa for years before coming to British Columbia. He opened this winery in the south Okanagan in 1995, based on a small vineyard crowded with many varieties including Pinot Noir. Like so many other vintners, he has a love-hate relationship with the variety. "Pinot Noir is a difficult grape to grow," he says. "You have to net the grapes; and you have to pick them twice." Then, tossing off one of his typically obscure aphorisms, he adds: "You have to look after them like a chicken on a bed."

GOLDEN MILE CELLARS ***
13140 316A Avenue, Road 13, Oliver, BC, V0H 1T0.
Tel: 250 498 8330; Website: www.goldenmilecellars.com

Golden Mile, which opened in 1998, is an architectural oddity among

Okanagan wineries: it looks like a small Bavarian castle. It was designed by the original owners, European-born Peter and Helga Serwo, who have been growing grapes in British Columbia since 1980. When they sold the winery in December 2003, they spent almost a year screening potential buyers before settling on Mick and Pam Luckhurst. Mick, who was born in Port Alberni in 1950, previously owned a building supply business on Vancouver Island and built houses in Edmonton. He appreciated Serwo's workmanship in the castle. Pam, who is British, privately says it is draughty.

The entrepreneurial Luckhursts have put their life savings into the winery. Under the Serwo ownership, Golden Mile was producing perhaps 1,000 cases of value-priced wine annually. The Luckhursts are pushing that to 6,000 cases of premium wines. Within a month of taking over, they recruited Californian Lawrence Herder, who was working at nearby Jackson-Triggs winery, as winemaker. They substantially upgraded the Okanagan winery, on Herder's recommendations, adding sophisticated winemaking equipment and 130 barrels, most of them new. When Herder left after the 2004 vintage to focus on his own winery, he was succeeded by Michael Bartier, the author of prize-winning Chardonnays at several Okanagan wineries.

Because no wine had been made for Golden Mile in the 2003 vintage (the grapes were sold to other wineries), the Luckhursts bought wines from other wineries. The impressive blends that were assembled from these sustained Golden Mile until the winery could release its 2004 vintages. The 8.5 hectares of vineyard includes mature Riesling, Chardonnay, Chenin Blanc, Merlot, and smaller blocks of Pinot Noir, Syrah, and Viognier.

GRANITE CREEK ESTATE WINERY (Range not tasted.)
2302 Skimikin Road, Tappen, BC, V0E 2X0.
Tel: 250 835 0049; Website: www.granitecreek.ca
Granite Creek, which opened in 2004, is the most recent addition to the small group of producers in British Columbia's most northerly wine region. Salmon Arm, the small city anchoring this region, is a ninety-minute drive north of Kelowna, the Okanagan's biggest city. While the northern wineries like Granite Creek are off the usual wine tour routes, they tap the busy seasonal tourist traffic on the TransCanada Highway.

The vineyard has been planted on a farm operated since 1959 by Gary Kennedy and his wife, Heather, who are agricultural professionals. The initial vineyard, planted in 2003, is four hectares including Maréchal Foch, Gewürztraminer, Kerner, and test plots of Pinot Noir. The winery is operated by their son, Doug and his wife, Mayka. Both are keen amateur winemakers and now work with veteran consultant Gary Strachan. The winery's initial releases, which included Ehrenfelser, Chardonnay, Pinot Gris, Merlot, and Maréchal Foch, were all made from grapes purchased from Okanagan growers.

GRAY MONK ESTATE WINERY *****
1055 Camp Road, Okanagan Centre, BC, V4V 2H4.
Tel: 250 766 3168; Website: www.graymonk.com

One of the Okanagan's most attractively situated wineries, the family-operated Gray Monk is perched amid a steeply sloping vineyard. The view from the winery restaurant includes expansive Okanagan Lake and brilliant sunsets behind the mountains on the far side. Austrian-born George Heiss and his German-born wife, Trudy, were successful hair stylists who changed careers in 1972 to grow grapes and make wine.

Trudy's father, Hugo Peter, already had a small vineyard but the Heisses knew nothing about viticulture when they arrived in the Okanagan. They learned quickly. After correcting a few planting mistakes (the result of bad advice from wineries), they imported Auxerrois, Pinot Gris, and Gewürztraminer from Alsace. By 1978, the vineyard was looking so good that Professor Helmut Becker of the Geisenheim Institute in Germany offered them a large selection of Geisenheim's vine material. George and Trudy involved the entire Okanagan in the most thorough trial of vinifera grapes in British Columbia to that time. The results provided the impetus to replace the mediocre hybrids that dominated the vineyards.

The Heiss family opened Gray Monk in 1982. They hired a consultant to make the initial vintages while son George Jr, born in 1962, did his winemaking studies in Germany. His younger brother, Steven, handles much of the winery's marketing. The third brother, Bob, born in 1957 and trained as a meteorologist, joined the family's winery in 2004.

Gray Monk's wines have great consistency, most notably the Alsace Clone Gewürztraminer, the winery's signature Pinot Gris and the juicy-flavoured Auxerrois. The grapes from the old, deep-rooted vines that the Heiss family planted a quarter century ago now produce complex wines released under the winery's reserve label, Odyssey. An adept blender,

George Jr created the winery's fruity, German-style white, Latitude 50, whose huge success helped boost Gray Monk production to 60,000 cases a year. The brand is so named because the winery is almost on the fiftieth parallel. In the late 1990s, Bordeaux-trained consulting winemaker Christine Leroux joined the cellar team, bringing particular expertise in red production.

Gray Monk has one of the most extensive portfolios (currently twenty-six wines) of any premium winery in British Columbia. It seems that the Heiss family seldom drops a wine when it establishes a following. The winery's intensely fruity Siegerrebe is a personal favourite with Trudy Heiss. And the winery's dry rosé is unique, made from North America's only planting of the obscure Rotberger grape from Germany.

HAINLE VINEYARDS AND DEEP CREEK WINE ESTATE ***
5355 Trepanier Bench Road, Peachland, BC, V0H 1X2.
Tel: 250 767 2525; Website: www.hainle.com

This winery is recognized as the home of Canada's first Icewine, made by Walter Hainle. A German immigrant who settled his family in Canada, Hainle (rhymes with "finely") dabbled in home winemaking with grapes from a friend's vineyard. When an unusually early frost snapped across the vineyard in 1973, Hainle opportunistically made Icewine. It was five years before he made a commercial quantity; that 1978 Icewine was among the products in the tasting room when the Hainle winery opened in 1988. By then, the Hainle family operated its own vineyard, and to very demanding standards. In 1995 Hainle became Canada's first winery certified as an organic producer.

Walter, who died in 1995, was content in the vineyard and left winery management to his son Tilman, born in 1958. The latter is a technically-gifted German-trained winemaker who has carved out an idiosyncratic style, producing austerely dry wines crafted to develop slowly. On one occasion, he even made a dry Icewine. Tilman's style has become more conventional in recent years, especially since 2002 when the winery was purchased by Walter Huber. The well-financed Huber has expanded the winery, increased its grape supply contracts and enabled his winemaker to spend the Okanagan winters doing crushes in Australia and South Africa.

The Hainle winery has worked hard to popularize wines from the Zweigelt grape. Not widely grown in Canada, but a workhorse in

Austrian vineyards, Zweigelt yields a robustly fruity wine. Shelley Huber, Walter's wife, recognized that the acceptance of Zweigelt was held back because it is perceived to be hard to pronounce. Her solution was simple: the wine was re-badged as Z. Now Hainle has developed an entire range of Z wines that include Zweigelt in the blend.

HAWTHORNE MOUNTAIN VINEYARDS ****
Green Lake Road, Box 480, Okanagan Falls, BC, V0H 1R0.
Tel: 250 497 8267; Website: www.hmvineyard.com

Hawthorne Mountain's vineyard boasts the highest elevation in the Okanagan: its long slope, which paradoxically has a northeastern exposure, rises to 536 metres (1,759 feet). A cool site in a warm region, it grows some of the Okanagan's best Gewürztraminer and Riesling, along with excellent Pinot Blanc, Pinot Gris, and Pinot Noir. This property, now owned by Vincor International, has a colourful history. A former homestead, it was acquired after World War I by a returning veteran, Major Hugh Fraser. Legend has it that he brought an English bride. She was so distressed by the rural location that she returned to England, scrawling "see ya later" on a note, and never came back. The winery recently revived the story by releasing reserve-quality wines under the See Ya Later label.

Fraser continued to farm in the company of a succession of Border Collie dogs. Whenever a dog died, it was buried under a headstone. Today, twelve headstones have been gathered together in the shade of a tree in front of Hawthorne Mountain's tasting room. Fraser is believed to have planted the first vines on the property in 1961, shortly before he sold it. A subsequent owner, Albert LeComte, opened a winery in 1986. It operated as LeComte Estate Winery until it changed owners and name in 1995. The signature wines include Riesling, Gewürztraminer, and HMV Brut, a crisply dry sparkling wine. The flagship wine, however, is the See Ya Later Chardonnay, a rich, buttery wine that wins awards vintage after vintage. An excellent red Meritage is labelled Ping, the name of one of Fraser's dogs.

HERDER WINERY AND VINEYARDS ***
716 Lowe Drive, Cawston, BC, V0X 1C0.
Tel: 250 499 5595; Website: www.herder.ca

Lawrence Herder is one of two British Columbia vintners (the other is Ken Winchester) who previously operated wineries in California. Born in

San Diego in 1967, Herder began as a home winemaker when he was fourteen. "I was quite popular as a teenager," he laughs. He sold his Paso Robles winery after one vintage to run a Vancouver printing company, only to learn he had wine in his blood, not printer's ink. He opened this winery in 2004 to make the big, premium quality reds that can be grown in the hot Similkameen. He supplements the Cabernet Sauvignon and Syrah grown on his three-hectare vineyard with purchased grapes, targeting a maximum annual production of about 2,000 cases.

HESTER CREEK ESTATE WINERY **
13163 326th Avenue, Oliver, BC, V0H 1T0
Tel: 250 498 4435; Website: www.hestercreek.com

Hester Creek is the only British Columbia winery producing a Trebbiano; and therein lies one of the many tales from this winery's tangled history. The twenty-eight-hectare vineyard was started in the arid south Okanagan in 1968 by Joe Busnardo, who had grown up on a farm near Treviso in northern Italy. He was advised to plant the French hybrids that everyone grew. Famously stubborn, he planted only vinifera vines, including Trebbiano and several other Italian varieties that he personally imported. When a nearby winery refused to pay him a premium for vinifera, Busnardo refused to sell any grapes. He earned his living in construction until his vineyard proved itself by surviving a particularly severe winter that savaged the hybrid plantings in other vineyards. In 1983 he launched what he called Divino Estate Winery. When he sold the property in 1996 (to relocate Divino to a smaller Vancouver Island vineyard, *see* page 204), the new owners renamed it Hester Creek. Many of the Italian varieties were pulled out to make room for more Cabernet Franc and Merlot, but the Trebbiano continued to be grown for both dry and dessert wines. The winery's other signature product came to be Pinot Blanc, the single largest variety in the vineyard.

Hester Creek fell under the control of Boltons Capital Corporation (later renamed Valterra), a company listed on a junior Canadian stock exchange. This helped Hester Creek borrow money for redevelopment; the winery's revenue from the sale of its wines was seldom directed at repaying debt. But the bank lost patience when that debt reached $5 million and they put the winery into receivership in 2004. It was sold to Curt Garland, a wealthy trucking-company owner from Prince George.

Garland had only intended to buy a small Okanagan vineyard. However, he recognized the potential of Hester Creek to grow great wine if properly managed. He quickly hired a new winemaker and began building a modern winery to be ready for the 2005 vintage. He also prepared to adjust the mix in the vineyard to increase the red varieties. Trebbiano, however, retains its unique status on the Hester Creek wine list.

HILLSIDE ESTATE WINERY ***
1350 Naramata Road, Penticton, BC, V2A 8T6.
Tel: 250 493 6274; Website: www.hillsideestate.com

The greatest concentration of wineries in the Okanagan (fifteen and rising) is along the scenic Naramata Road as its winds above the eastern shore of the lake. Hillside, which opened in 1990 in a tiny farmhouse on a postcard vineyard, was one of the first. Today, Hillside operates from an imposing winery at the road's edge, making a name for itself with Merlot and Bordeaux blends. The original winery was launched by two former employees of the Czechoslovakian (as it was then) state airline. In 1968, Vera and Bohumir Klokocka, under the cover of a vacation, came to Canada as political refugees. They bought a small orchard on Naramata Road in 1979, converting it to a vineyard five years later. The plantings include some of the first Cabernet Sauvignon in the Okanagan.

A self-taught winemaker, Vera was one of three small growers – Lang Vineyards and Wild Goose were the others – who opened farm wineries in 1990 after lobbying the provincial government for the appropriate regulatory framework. Legend has it that Vera's home-baked bread, which complemented Rieslings from the three producers, was especially persuasive during a tasting with politicians. She sold the winery in 1996 after her husband's death. The new owners, investors from Alberta, superimposed a large winery on Vera's farmhouse.

Now with several vineyards on the Naramata Bench and contracts with growers elsewhere, Hillside offers a much larger portfolio. The premium red, first made in 2002, is Mosaic, a complex Bordeaux blend crafted to be cellared for fifteen years. One of Hillside's signature wines remains a fragrant white made from Muscat Ottonel. Ironically, the original cuttings were misidentified and for several years, Vera sold it as Klevner, a synonym for Auxerrois. The correct identification was provided in 1992 by a visiting expert from France.

HOUSE OF ROSE VINEYARDS

2270 Garner Road, Kelowna, BC, V1P 1E2.

Tel: 250 765 0802; Email: arose@shuswap.net

Vern Rose, who retired from teaching in Alberta in 1982, long dreamed of travelling to New Zealand. He realized that dream in 1988 when he attended a viticulture conference there and volunteered his labour in a vineyard. Exhilarated by the experience, he returned to launch a winery in 1993. "It's been a great fling," he said in 2004 when a discouraging summer had him thinking of selling. Forest fires raging in the nearby mountains that August forced him to evacuate the winery twice and kept visitors away. It was unusual for visitors not to seek out this winery, for the enthusiastic Rose has a reputation for conducting one of the Okanagan's most entertaining winery tours. There is also something for every person in the tasting room, since he makes as many as twenty-six different wines a year. One of his coups in an industry known for Icewine was to register Winter Wine as the trade mark for his sweet wine.

HUNTING HAWK VINEYARDS *

4758 Gulch Road, Spallumcheen, BC, V0E 1B4

Tel: 250 546 2164; Website: www.huntinghawkvineyards.com

After growing up in a military household that constantly relocated, Russ Niles coveted stability. That is why he spent twenty years writing for and editing a small-town newspaper in Vernon; and why he and his wife built a home on quiet rural site nearby, in the north Okanagan. When the newspaper closed, Niles was inspired by a neighbour's small patch of vines to begin a 1.2-hectare vineyard and launch a winery in 2002. This is one of the most northerly vineyards in the Okanagan; prudently, Niles also buys from growers in the heart of the valley's vineyards to produce Merlot, Chardonnay, and Gewürztraminer. One of Hunting Hawk's successes came about when one grower sold him over-mature Pinot Blanc with high potential alcohol. Niles finished the wine in the style of white port.

INNISKILLIN OKANAGAN VINEYARDS *****

Road 11 West, Oliver, BC, V0H 1T0.

Tel: 250 498 6663; Website: www.inniskillin.com

Acquired in 1996 by Ontario's Inniskillin, this Okanagan winery has wine-growing conditions dramatically different from those of Ontario. It produces powerful wines from its nine-hectare Dark Horse Vineyard and from nearby vineyards in the south Okanagan. Among these was British Columbia's first Zinfandel, from the 2002 vintage.

The vineyard took some time to find its feet. The first winery that opened here in 1980, Vinitera, made rustic wines from mediocre grapes, failed and went through two changes in ownership. In 1988, now called Okanagan Vineyards, it accepted government compensation to pull out all its vines. Two years later, Hungarian-born winemaker Sandor Mayer, then newly arrived in Canada, replanted the vineyard almost entirely to vinifera, including some of the south Okanagan's first Cabernet Sauvignon. He says,

> Since we produced the first Cabernet Sauvignon in 1993, I don't remember a bad year. Cabernet loves this place and I love Cabernet Sauvignon. In 1990, nobody had experience in what varieties could grow here. I know what I would plant if it were bare land now.

Only half the vineyard was planted to reds (the Bordeaux varieties and Pinot Noir). The remainder was planted to whites, including Chardonnay, Riesling, and Gewürztraminer. While Mayer is not unhappy with those choices, he suggests that "it almost seems to be a waste of space if we can grow Cabernet Sauvignon". He also produces one of the Okanagan's best Meritage reds. Dark Horse grows grapes for two-thirds of Inniskillin's 25,000 cases of wine a year, with other fruit coming from nearby vineyards on the Osoyoos Lake Bench. "This vineyard is very significant," he says firmly. "This is the cream of all the wines we make."

JACKSON-TRIGGS VINTNERS *****
38691 Highway 97 North, Oliver, BC, V0H 1T0.
Tel: 250 498 4961; Website: www.jacksontriggswinery.com

In 2004, Bruce Nicholson, winemaker at the sprawling Jackson-Triggs winery, was the first Canadian to win the Winemaker of the Year trophy at the San Francisco International Wine Competition. When he accepted the award, he praised vineyard manager Mark Sheridan for growing prize-winning grapes. Jackson-Triggs controls 400 hectares of prime vineyard in the south Okanagan, more than any other producer. These sun-drenched sites, planted since 1997 to the mainstream varieties, give Nicholson a rich palette to work with.

Jackson-Triggs established its reputation with rich and supple Merlot.

Subsequently, Nicholson has included a juicy Shiraz, an intense Cabernet Sauvignon, and a full-bodied Meritage blend among the reds; and lively Viognier, elegant Chardonnay, and racy Riesling among the whites. Nicholson's Icewines dominate competitions.

Jackson-Triggs is Vincor International's major Canadian label, also used by the company's winery in Ontario. The Okanagan winery was established in 1981 by TG Bright (*see* page 15). By leasing the land and the building from the 350-member Osoyoos Indian Band, Brights established a critically important relationship that was in place when Vincor was formed in the 1990s. Moving to increase British Columbia wine production significantly, Vincor leased some of the best sites for vineyards on the undeveloped Osoyoos Reserve. (The relation was cemented further when Vincor became the partner in developing Nk'Mip Cellars, the Band's own winery, which opened in 2002.)

Vincor's style usually burnishes the corporate image rather than making stars of its individual winemakers. The premier label, for example, is named for the company's co-founders, vice-president Allan Jackson and chief executive Donald Triggs. However, Nicholson's many awards have made him one of Vincor's most prominent winemakers. He is also one of the most driven:

I keep setting the bar higher for myself. If the Wine Spectator *gives me 100 points on every wine, I'm going to look for 105. It may not be realistic but I am going to do that.*

KETTLE VALLEY WINERY *****
2988 Hayman Road, Naramata, BC, V0H 1N0.
Tel: 250 496 5898; Website: www.kettlevalleywinery.com

Schönburger is a minor, Muscat-flavoured German grape that is generally made into a pleasant summertime sipper. One year, Kettle Valley grower Dick Lancaster sold this variety to Bob Ferguson and Tim Watts, the winery's winemaking owners. The spectacular result was a serious wine: intensely fragrant, dry, and complex. Ferguson and Watts only make serious wine. They made bold wines from the start. "We set out to see how powerful a Pinot Noir we could produce," Watts says. The 1992 Pinot Noir remained alive a decade later, having developed in the bottle like good burgundy. The power of their wines, especially the reds, reflects both winemaking style and vineyard practices. Watts and Ferguson leave grapes hanging on the vines later in the season than most growers, squeezing the maximum flavour and sugar from the autumn sun. "Essentially, all the flavour we can get into those grapes comes out in the wine," Watts says. In a typical example, the Bordeaux red grapes in a vineyard called Old Main are often not picked until November. Of course, the Naramata Bench has one of the longest ripening seasons in the Okanagan: the vineyards share a gentle westward slope facing the lake, an immense, frost-deterring heat reservoir.

Initially, Kettle Valley's flagship wine was Pinot Noir. The range has since expanded to include Shiraz, Merlot, Cabernet Sauvignon, Cabernet Franc, a fine Bordeaux blend called Old Main Red, and Malbec. The white wines include Chardonnay, Pinot Gris, Gewürztraminer, and that singular Schönburger. Production is between 4,000 and 5,000 cases a year and the partners do not want to become larger.

We want to be hands-on. We want to be involved in the process. The whole idea of being involved in the wine business was to do it, not to give the good jobs to someone else while you turn out to be the management.

LA FRENZ WINERY ****
740 Naramata Road, Penticton, BC, V2A 8T5.
Tel: 250 492 6690; Website: www.lafrenzwinery.com
In 1998, after making five vintages in the Okanagan for Quails' Gate (*see* page 185), winemaker Jeff Martin returned to his native Australia to start a winery. Within months, he was back to open an Okanagan winery, having concluded it would be easier to make his mark in Canada rather than winery-fatigued Australia. La Frenz, which bears the surname of his maternal grandfather, opened in 2000. Martin and his wife Niva got a quick start with purchased grapes, selling La Frenz wines for several years at the nearby Poplar Grove winery until opening a shop of their own. They were initially successful with zesty Sémillon and rich, barrel-fermented Chardonnay. For their own winery, the Martins purchased an apple orchard at a busy corner on Naramata Road. Beginning in 2002, they planted a 2.5 hectare vineyard to Shiraz, Merlot, Viognier – and a bit of Schönburger. Martin incorporates this spicy variety into a wine called Alexandria that is inspired by Australia's Rutherglen Muscats.

LAKE BREEZE VINEYARDS ***

930 Sammet Road, Naramata, BC, V0H 1N0.

Tel: 250 496 5659; Website: www.lakebreezewinery.ca

It is no accident that Lake Breeze, with its white stucco buildings grouped around a shaded patio, recalls the small wineries of South Africa. The founding owner was Paul Moser, a business immigrant from South Africa. Not only did he bring Cape architecture; he also brought South African viticulture by planting the Okanagan's only Pinotage vines and by hiring a South African winemaker, Garron Elmes. Moser has since moved on: the new owners are two business couples from Alberta who went looking for a vineyard and were seduced by the beauty of Lake Breeze with its site overlooking the lake. Managing partner Gary Reynolds, a chartered accountant, was the financial chief of Edmonton's public school system. The other partners continue to work in banking and accounting while Reynolds is the winery's hands-on manager.

The original winery was so compact that Elmes, with insufficient space for all the barrels he needed, had to mature some reds in stainless steel. Reynolds and his colleagues built a substantial cellar and bought the required number of barrels. Elmes now brings the same polish to Pinotage, Pinot Noir, Merlot, and Cabernet Franc as he did earlier to Pinot Blanc, Gewürztraminer, Ehrenfelser, and tangy Sémillon. He has the great advantage that many of the vines in the Lake Breeze vineyard are now about twenty years old.

LANG VINEYARDS ***

2493 Gammon Road, Naramata, BC, V0H 1N0.

Tel: 250 496 5987; Website: www.langvineyards.com

Günther Lang, born in Stuttgart in 1951 and trained at Mercedes-Benz, brought marketing acumen to this winery which he opened in 1990. When he first made Icewine in 1992, he packaged it in cobalt blue bottles. They were such a hit that visitors to his wine shop bought empty bottles when the wine was sold out.

His greatest success was his idea in 1998 to blend maple syrup with wine. "I asked myself how we would serve the Asian markets in years when we could not make Icewine," he recalls. Lang's "Original Canadian Maple Wines" – a white, red, and sparkling version – now comprise half the sales of the winery. Lang Vineyards now makes a total of 8,000 cases a year. For customers with conventional wine palates, Lang produces a range that includes Pinot Noir, Pinot Meunier, Viognier, and excellent Rieslings. Since 2002, New Zealand-trained Ross Mirko has made the wines here and has broadened the range of Lang's wines by, among other techniques, barrel-ageing. One result was Lang's Burgundian-modelled 2003 Soaring Eagle Chardonnay, critically acclaimed upon its release.

LARCH HILLS VINEYARD AND WINERY ***
110 Timms Road, Salmon Arm, BC, V1E 2P8.
Tel: 250 832 0155; Website: www.larchhillswinery.com

At 700 meters (2,300 feet) above sea level, this is British Columbia's highest vineyard and one of the most northerly. Hans and Hazel Nevrkla – pronounced "never claw" – succeed because they grow the appropriate cool-climate vines on a steep slope with a warm southerly exposure. The signature varieties here are Ortega and Siegerrebe, two early-ripening whites. The major red variety is the robust Hungarian red, Agria. The area of this was expanded only recently after the Nevrklas monitored a test plot for several years.

Larch Hills, now producing between 2,000 and 2,500 cases a year, is off the beaten path but the cleanly-made wines attract a steady clientele to the wine shop. The business is compact enough for the owners to manage it themselves. "It makes us a living," says Hans. "We sell out virtually every year, so that marketing is not a major headache: 2,500 cases almost sell themselves."

LAUGHING STOCK VINEYARDS ***
1548 Naramata Road, Penticton, BC, V2A 8T7.
Tel: 250 493 8466; Website: www.laughingstock.ca

The name of this vineyard is something of an inside joke. Owners David and Cynthia Enns operate a successful consultancy to the mutual fund industry. They intend to make wine of a quality that their stockmarket peers will find anything but laughable. They came to wine as consumers with a broad and passionate interest. Believing he had to make wine for a complete understanding of it, David plunged into home winemaking in 2001 with enough Washington State Cabernet Sauvignon to fill a barrel. That led to the couple moving their business from Vancouver to a Naramata Road property in 2002 where they planted Merlot and Cabernet Sauvignon. Shrewdly, David struck a three-year agreement in

2003 to make Laughing Stock wines under the tutelage of Ian Sutherland at Poplar Grove. The winery is releasing its first wine in autumn 2005.

LITTLE STRAW VINEYARDS **
2815 Ourtoland Road, Kelowna, BC, V1Z 2H5.
Tel: 250 769 0404; Website: www.slamka.bc.ca
This winery opened in 1996 as Slamka Cellars. After the family spent eight years explaining that their Slovak name means "little straw," they simply renamed the winery. The Slamka family has grown grapes in the Okanagan since 1969, twenty-one years after machinist Joe Slamka came to Canada. He was one of the first to plant Auxerrois, a white variety from Alsace. Today, Old Vines Auxerrois, partially barrel-aged, is the signature wine for Little Straw. With its vineyard in the cooler north Okanagan, Little Straw has settled on Pinot Noir as its primary red wine.

Little Straw is a family winery operated by three brothers, led by winemaker Peter Slamka, who says:

I've learned to keep the wines as safe as possible. I don't have any razzle-dazzle formula. Winemaking's been around for thousands of years. I just keep it simple.

He also likes to take his turn in the winery's tasting room. "It's valuable experience. You get to know your customers and you see what they like."

MISSION HILL FAMILY ESTATE WINERY *****
1730 Mission Hill Road, Westbank, BC, V4T 2E4.
Tel: 250 768 7611; Website: www.missionhillwinery.com
A total reconstruction of this mountaintop winery since 1999 has turned Mission Hill into one of the most breathtaking wineries in western North America. Visitors begin tours in a room dominated by a tapestry by Marc Chagall. This is part of owner Anthony von Mandl's announced determination to elevate Mission Hill to nothing less than one of the world's "ten top wineries".

Von Mandl is a bold strategist but not the first visionary at Mission Hill. The original winery was conceived by a Kelowna businessman named Tiny Walrod (naturally, he was a large man). His design, inspired after touring in California, replicated a Spanish mission building. The location offers a dramatic vista of the Okanagan Valley. Walrod intended to build a business around vigorous wine tourism, just as wineries in the

Napa Valley were beginning to do, even though winery tours were still forbidden in British Columbia. However, Walrod died of a heart attack, at the age of fifty-seven, before the winery opened in 1966, Deprived of its dynamic leader, the business struggled. In the spring of 1970, it was almost bankrupt.

It was acquired that spring by Ben Ginter, one of the most outrageous individuals ever to enter the industry. He once offered to exchange shares in his business for bottle caps sent in by purchasers of his beer. When he added Mission Hill to his empire he changed its name to Uncle Ben's; eventually he called it Golden Valley. The most successful wines were Baby Duck clones that he called Hot Goose, Yellow Bird, and Fuddle Duck. The latter phrase was attributed to the Canadian prime minister of the day, Pierre Trudeau, who had mouthed an expletive during parliamentary debate in 1971 and claimed he had only said "fuddle duck".

The winery was in sorry shape in the summer of 1981 when von Mandl paid $4 million for it (and returned it to its original Mission Hill name). Some floors were earthen. Light bulbs were burned out. There were fruit flies throughout the building. Yet, not long after taking over the winery, von Mandl laid out a lyrical vision in a speech to the Kelowna Chamber of Commerce:

> When I look out over the valley, I see world-class vinifera vineyards winding their way down the valley: numerous estate wineries, each distinctively different ...

With thirteen wineries then in British Columbia, few of them very good, it must have struck the listeners as a pipe-dream.

Leveraged to the hilt, von Mandl and Nick Clark, his partner between 1981 and 1989, revived the winery's trade. They made up for the lack of vinifera in the Okanagan by importing Pinot Noir and Cabernet Sauvignon from Washington State, producing premium wines. Quick cash flow came from apple and pear ciders. They were quick to capitalize on wine fads. The Beaujolais Nouveau bubble swept across North America at this time; beginning in 1982, Mission Hill made a good nouveau-style wine for a number of years from Maréchal Foch grapes, which were readily available in the Okanagan. In 1983, spotting the global surplus of spirits, Mission Hill imported bulk spirits, bottled them and sold them at a discount to the major brands.

Daniel Lagnaz, a Swiss winemaker who had been working at Lindemans in Australia, was hired in 1982. Versatile and technically adept, he had a hand in making everything from table wines to eau-de-vie from Okanagan fruit (which were very good but hard to sell). Later he made arguably his greatest contribution to Mission Hill by completing the development of Mike's Hard Lemonade. The enormous profits from Mike's funded the rebuilding and expansion of the winery.

The lean and laconic John Simes is now the winemaker. Born in 1950, he was chief winemaker at Montana, then New Zealand's largest winery, when he moved to Canada in 1992. He found Chardonnay grapes in several of Mission Hill's contracted vineyards so fine that they demanded barrel fermentation. Unfortunately, Mission Hill had a sketchy barrel inventory. Simes had 100 new oak barrels rushed to the winery from California. With them, he made 2,980 cases of Mission Hill's remarkable breakthrough wine, the 1992 Grand Reserve Barrel Select Chardonnay.

The wine was a winner as soon as it was released: gold in the major Okanagan competition in 1993; wine of the year a few months later at the All-Canadian Wine Championships; and Avery's Trophy in London in June, 1994 as the best of the 260 Chardonnays in the competition. Helpfully, the chairman of the competition referred to it as "the best Chardonnay world-wide" in his report. In Mission Hill's publicity, that became the "best Chardonnay in the world". A little hyperbole never hurts.

By November, Mission Hill's sales of all its top wines had tripled; half its 1993 Grand Reserve Barrel Select Chardonnay was sold prior to release. Subsequent vintages of this wine have brought home medals with metronomic regularity. The London award gave von Mandl the confidence to turn Mission Hill into the winery that coincided with his vision for the Okanagan Valley. For the first time in its history, in 1994 Mission Hill began buying its own vineyards. Within less than a decade, the winery owned or leased close to 364 hectares, or about sixteen per cent of all the Okanagan's vineyards.

The design of a grand new winery in the footprint of the original began in 1996. Said von Mandl later:

I really have always looked to Robert Mondavi as a mentor. I studied carefully what Bob did in 1966. At a time when not only California but Napa was unknown and certainly not recognized for quality at all, he

> *built that landmark showcase winery. It was clear to me that a landmark*
> *showcase winery was absolutely essential to the future of the Okanagan.*

That had also been Tiny Walrod's vision a generation earlier but a destination winery was impossible because tours were forbidden until the mid 1970s. The totally rebuilt winery was unveiled in 2003. Today, about 150,000 people visit each year.

Von Mandl believes that the winery's classic design (by Seattle architect Tom Kundig) will be relevant for at least a few hundred years. Seen in the late afternoon sunlight, the winery's sand-tinted concrete glows warmly on the volcanic shoulder of Mount Boucherie, above the surface of the nearby Okanagan Lake. The structures include Greek arches, Roman colonnades, and a slender bell tower rising above a plaza. There is also a seventeenth-century stone fountain that von Mandl found in Austria and had shipped to Canada. No expense was spared. In the arid Okanagan, where plants grow slowly, hundreds of mature trees were transplanted. One barrel cellar excavated from the rock under the winery has the size and ambience of a small cathedral. Taken together, the cellars contain at least 6,500 barrels. It's a far cry from what Simes found on his arrival in 1992, but he is crafting wines to match. He still makes the Grand Reserve Chardonnay is a style comparable to the 1992 classic, made with purchased fruit. But now Mission Hill gets most of its grapes from its own vineyards, primarily in the southernmost part of the Okanagan. One vineyard runs right up to the border with the USA, producing grapes so fine that Simes looks enviously at the mundane apple orchard on the American side. The estate wines that come from Mission Hill's vineyards, such as the winery's fruit-driven Estate Chardonnay, show additional polish and finesse. When von Mandl was scouting the Okanagan for Josef Milz, he believed that fine white wines could be grown there. "We did not know at the time that we could be so successful with Bordeaux reds and with Syrah," he says. "That has been one of the most exciting discoveries."

Since 1997, Mission Hill's signature red has been a Bordeaux blend called Oculus, based on but not dominated by Merlot. Curiously, Oculus has not been the Okanagan's most expensive red table wine; it was released at $35 a bottle while a competitor's Bordeaux-style red was launched at $50. "I truly believe the wine is underpriced," von Mandl says. However, it is probable that when the Okanagan's first $100 red table wine is released, it will come from Mission Hill. "I would think it's in the offing," says von Mandl.

MT BOUCHERIE ESTATE WINERY ***
829 Douglas Road, Kelowna, BC, V1Z 1N9.
Tel: 250 769 8803; Website: www.mtboucherie.bc.ca

After he brought his family to Canada in 1958 from India, Mehtad Gidda invested his savings in Okanagan orchards. He switched to grapes in 1975. Today his sons Sarwan, Nirmal, and Kaldep operate seventy-one hectares of vineyards in the Okanagan and Similkameen Valleys. They opened their own winery in 2001 but they continue to supply grapes to a number of other wineries. Sarwan says candidly that:

> I didn't like wine at the beginning. But the winemakers would come by at Christmas. We'd get all this wine and we'd start drinking it. Then we'd start tasting tank samples and they'd tell us why this wine is better than that wine. I'm a wine drinker now. I'd rather drink wine than anything else, but it took time.

Mt Boucherie's vineyards, strategically located in three different terroirs, grow all of British Columbia's mainstream varieties. The best wines so far are Gewürztraminer, Pinot Gris, Pinot Noir, and a Bordeaux blend called Summit Reserve. Syrah plantings began producing in 2002. Winemaker Graham Pierce also makes Riesling, Pinot Noir, and Merlot Icewines.

NICHOL VINEYARD & FARM WINERY ****
RR1, S14, C13, 1285 Smethurst Road, Naramata, BC, V0H 1N0.
Tel: 250 496 5962; Website: www.nicholvineyard.com

In 1991, Alex and Kathleen Nichol were the first in the Okanagan to plant Syrah, importing 1,350 vines from a Rhône nursery. Syrah made Nichol Vineyard's reputation well before it became the fifth most planted variety in the Okanagan. Nichol's Syrah has perhaps even overshadowed the solid Cabernet Franc and idiosyncratic Pinot Gris that emerges from this 1.8-hectare vineyard. The winery produces about 1,200 cases a year.

Formerly a double bass player in the Vancouver Symphony, Nichol's interest in wine was fired when he took a Wine & Spirits Education Trust course concurrently with a music sabbatical in the UK. He researched the British Columbia industry by self-publishing a book on Okanagan vineyards and wineries in 1983. He and Kathleen moved to the Okanagan in 1989, converting a Naramata orchard to grapes. The winery opened in 1993.

Nichol's muscular, pink Pinot Gris achieves as much as fifteen degrees of alcohol. Maxine's, a voluptuous rosé incorporating Pinot Gris, Syrah and Cabernet Franc, is almost as powerful. One of the biggest wines he makes (he promises it will "knock your socks off") is called Impromptu, a barrel-aged blend of full-blooded Michurinetz[1] tempered with twenty-five per cent Syrah.

NK'MIP CELLARS ****
1400 Rancher Creek Road, Osoyoos, BC, V0H 1V0.
Tel: 250 495 2985; Website: www.nkmipcellars.com

North America's first aboriginal-owned winery, Nk'Mip Cellars (which is pronounced "Inkameep") was launched in 2002 by the Osoyoos Indian Band, which consists of about 370 people occupying a 12,950-hectare reserve in the south Okanagan. The band operates nine other commercial ventures. Its first, established in 1968, is Inkameep Vineyards which now produces about 850 short tons of grapes annually and sells them to many wineries. Vincor International's Jackson-Triggs winery at Oliver and about 400 hectares of Vincor vineyard are on land leased from the band.

The 16,000-case Nk'Mip winery emerged when the band sought to anchor a resort project with a casino. When the government turned down the casino, the application was redrafted for a winery. Vincor was enlisted as a forty-nine-per-cent partner. The Santa Fe-style building, surrounded by vineyards, is on a hillside near the US border, with a fine view over Osoyoos Lake. Winemaker Randy Picton gets some of the best grapes from Inkameep vineyards; it is a point of pride for the band that its winery should produce top quality table wine. Nk'Mip focuses on eight mainstream varietals: Syrah, Cabernet Sauvignon, Merlot, Pinot Noir, Pinot Gris, Chardonnay, Riesling, and Pinot Blanc. The reserve-grade wines are identified as QWAM QWMT (pronounced "kw-em kw-empt"), an Okanagan language phrase that means "achieving excellence". The winery quickly has accumulated the awards in competition to show it is reaching its objective.

1. Michurinetz is a vinifera x labrusca hybrid from Eastern Europe.

OROFINO VINEYARDS (Range not tasted.)
2152 Barcello Road, Cawston, BC, V0X 1C0.
Tel: 250 499 0068; Website: www.orofinovineyards.com

Former Saskatchewan teacher John Weber and his wife Virginia, a nurse, began learning about wine during 1991 travels in Bordeaux and Burgundy. Deciding on a change in careers, they took over a 2.4-hectare producing vineyard in British Columbia's hot Similkameen Valley. "I guess there is a certain amount of romance in growing grapes," says Weber. "That's maybe before you sit on the tractor for hours and hours, and do all your pruning."

With the help of a consulting winemaker, Weber opened Orofino in 2005 in an unusual winery built with bales of straw. The vineyard provides many options and the varieties grown include Pinot Noir, Merlot, Cabernet Franc, Pinot Blanc, Chardonnay, Riesling, three different varieties of Muscat, and small numbers of other vines under trial.

OSOYOOS LAROSE *****
Jackson-Triggs Winery, Oliver, BC, V0N 1T0.
Tel: 250 498 4981; Website: www.jacksontriggswinery.com

This joint-venture winery – the partners are Canada's Vincor and Bordeaux's Groupe Taillan – created a sensation in 2004 when it released its first wine, a Bordeaux blend of exceptional quality. It was remarkable that the 2001 Osoyoos Larose, as the wine was called, showed such richness and elegance, considering that the grapes were from a three-year-old vineyard. Paris-born winemaker Pascal Madevon (*see* page 147) notes that no classed growth in France, least of all Taillan's Gruaud Larose, would consider releasing wines from young vines under the main label. The French partners at Osoyoos Larose intended, in fact, to release the first several vintages under a second label, in the French tradition. However, as Madevon explains:

> ... the wine is so good, we decided to put Osoyoos Larose on the 2001 label and we put ninety-five per cent of the 2001 wine into the blend. Incredible. I am very surprised by the quality of the wine here because it is a very young industry.

This provides a clue to the rapid improvement in Okanagan wine in less than a decade. The majority of the south Okanagan's 1,238 hectares of vineyard has been planted or replanted with vinifera since 1992; and about half the total was planted only since 1997. The terroir seems capable of producing remarkable fruit, even from young vines.

Vincor sought wine with a French pedigree. While the two companies are equal partners in the venture, the French chose the vineyard site, selected the vines, designed the vineyard, sent in the processing equipment, and hired the winemaker. "We just went to school," Vincor chief executive Donald Triggs says modestly.

The twenty-four hectares of vineyard, with complex soils of sand, gravel, and clay, are on a southeastern slope above Osoyoos Lake. Planting started in 1999. About two-thirds of the vineyard grows Merlot; just under a quarter is Cabernet Sauvignon. The remaining acreage is planted evenly to Cabernet Franc, Malbec, and Petit Verdot. The close spacing of the vines and their training mimics Bordeaux practices. The first release, a full-bodied, ripe wine with good ageing potential, was 2,200 cases. When the vineyard is in full production, Osoyoos Larose will release up to 25,000 cases annually of a classic Bordeaux-style red. Currently, the wines are made in a dedicated section of Vincor's Jackson-Triggs winery near Oliver. But space has been set aside on the Osoyoos Larose vineyard for a winery, tentatively scheduled to open in 2010.

PARADISE RANCH WINES ***
901-525 Seymour Street, Vancouver, BC, V6B 3H7.
Tel: 604 683-6040; Website: www.icewines.com

Paradise Ranch is the only winery in the Okanagan (and one of just two in Canada) producing exclusively Icewine and late-harvest wine. Its grapes originally came from the Paradise Ranch vineyard near Naramata, which used to be a cattle ranch. Vines were first planted on its lakeside plateaus in 1979. In 1986, a Penticton doctor, Jeff Harries, took over and managed the vineyard until 2003 when he sold it to Mission Hill Family Estate. Icewine production had been launched by Harries in partnership with Jim Stewart, a Vancouver businessman. When the vineyard was sold, Stewart purchased the winery assets and has continued to operate, buying grapes elsewhere in the Okanagan. There are tentative plans to construct a dedicated winery and perhaps expand production to include table wines. One of Canada's larger Icewine producers, Paradise Ranch makes tasty Icewine (Chardonnay, Riesling, and Merlot) presented in frosted Italian bottles printed with a reproduction, based on a real incident, of a black bear gorging itself on Icewine grapes on a moonlit night.

PELLER ESTATES ***

2120 Vintner Street, Port Moody, BC, V3H 1W8.

Tel: 604 937 3411; Website: www.andreswines.com

Now overshadowed by the baronial Peller Estates winery at Niagara-on-the-Lake, this winery in suburban Vancouver is where Andrew Peller founded Andrés Wines in 1961 (*see* page 86). The Hungarian-born Peller had applied first for a winery licence in Ontario, where he lived and had operated a successful brewery. The restrictive conditions proposed by Ontario drove Peller to British Columbia and to Port Moody, where the development-minded city practically gave him a winery site. Andrés had wineries across Canada by 1974.

John Peller, the grandson of Andrew (who died in 1994) runs the business now. The premium wines appear under the Peller name. Perhaps the Peller family's greatest impact in British Columbia was on grape-growing in the Okanagan. Andrew Peller enlisted the Osoyoos Indian Band to develop the Inkameep Vineyards (not the same as Nk'Mip, q.v.) near Oliver in 1968. "We would supply the technical knowledge, and the Indians would contribute the land and their labour," Peller wrote in his autobiography. This was the first extensive vinifera planting in the south Okanagan, with Andrés providing Riesling, Ehrenfelser, and Scheurebe vines since there was a greater demand for white wines than for reds at the time. Today, the majority of the vineyard's ninety-three hectares grows red grapes; Andrés still buys some of the grapes.

The company diversified its grape source in 1998 when it launched its twenty-six-hectare Rocky Ridge Vineyards in the Similkameen Valley. In a joint venture with landowner Roger Hol, Peller spent about $1 million to turn an alfalfa farm into vineyard, planting vines imported from French nurseries. With an ample selection of red varieties, Peller Estates has an increasing strong portfolio, notably Merlot and Cabernet Franc.

Because the venerable Port Moody winery no longer provides regular wine tours and tastings, Peller intends ultimately to build a destination winery closer to vineyard country, likely in the Okanagan Valley.

PENTAGE WINERY ***

4400 Lakeside Road, Penticton, BC, V2A 8W3.

Tel: 250 493 4008; Website: www.pentage.com

Pentâge Winery's vineyard, on a plateau overlooking Skaha Lake just south of Penticton, is one of the Okanagan's most picturesque sites. That led Paul Gardner and Julie Rennie to buy it in 1996 when it was still a tangled former orchard. They decided to plant vines and establish a winery only after purchasing their country getaway. Rennie is a corporate executive assistant in Vancouver. Gardner is a marine engineer. On nine hectares, they planted Sauvignon Blanc, Gewürztraminer, and five reds: Syrah, Gamay, Merlot, Cabernet Sauvignon, and Cabernet Franc. These inspired the winery's name, and go into the Pentâge red blend. The winery opened in 2003 with wines, which won immediate acclaim, notably Sauvignon Blanc and Syrah. The winery also offers a Pinot Gris. In full production the winery expects to make 6,000 cases a year.

PINOT REACH CELLARS ***
1670 Dehart Road, Kelowna, BC, V1W 4N6.
Tel: 250 764 0078

This site, one of the Okanagan's first commercial vineyards, has grown grapes since about 1930. The Dulik family, who operated the property for more than seventy years, replaced labrusca vines with vinifera in the 1970s. Susan Dulik, of the third generation, opened a small winery in 1997, with the pick of the grapes grown by her father, Den. She and her winemaker, Roger Wong, scored their greatest success with the vineyard's mature Riesling (planted in 1978). The winery's Old Vines Riesling has consistently won awards. In 2004, the Duliks sold the vineyard and winery to Eric Savics, a Vancouver stockbroker, and Eira Thomas, a geologist. They invested substantially to expand the winery and to create a shop. And they told Wong to keep on making that remarkable Riesling. "We think the strength [of the property] is these old vines that we have," Thomas says.

POPLAR GROVE WINERY *****
1060 Poplar Grove Road, Penticton, BC, V2A 8T6.
Tel: 250 492 4575; Website: www.poplargrove.ca

The only thing that winemaking, cheese production, and the boiler-maker's trade have in common is Ian Sutherland. He has done all three well. The latter gave him the cash to open one of the best small wineries in the Okanagan – and the only one that also makes cheese. Sutherland is a self-taught winemaker with so much natural talent that Poplar Grove won gold and silver medals with its first two red wines when the winery opened in 1997. Credit for the winery's consistently good wines is shared with his wife, Gitta, a Danish-born nurse who grows the superb grapes in Poplar Grove's vineyard (and still works as a nurse).

Sutherland augmented his winemaking skill by working several vintages at wineries in Australia and New Zealand. "I'll work for nothing," he says. "I'll work for food." He got the idea of making cheese during one vintage in Australia. Fascinated by a cheese factory near the winery, he plied the owner with wine while figuring out how cheese is made. "It's all in the quality of the industrial espionage," he says. Back in Canada, Sutherland and a partner began making artisanal blue and double-cream cheeses in a winery annex, selling them in the wine shop. The cheese pairs easily with the winery's complex Bordeaux reds and its aromatic whites (Gewürztraminer, Pinot Gris, and Viognier).

Poplar Grove's production, about 2,000 cases annually, is snapped up by restaurants and by the winery's mail-order customers. Sutherland shares his winery and wine shop with other small producers. Some are still building their own wineries; others have been budding winemakers with a mentorship arrangement, perhaps counting on industrial espionage of their own to acquire Sutherland's winemaking touch.

QUAILS' GATE ESTATE WINERY *****
3303 Boucherie Road, Kelowna, BC, V1Z 2H3.
Tel: 250 769 4451; Website: www.quailsgate.com

Ben and Tony Stewart, the brothers who own Quails' Gate, are members of a family that pioneered horticulture in the Okanagan; their grandfather arrived from Ireland in 1906. Their father, Richard, was a partner in planting one of the first vineyards on Black Sage Road in south Okanagan. In 1961, he began planting the north Okanagan vineyard in which Quails' Gate now grows, among others, some of the Okanagan's best Pinot Noir and Chardonnay.

Now making about 40,000 cases a year, Quails' Gate started out humbly in 1989 as a small farm winery. The brothers were feeling their way into the business. Together, they have turned Quails' Gate into a leading winery. They have refined the vineyard continually, in particular planting a broad selection of the best clones of several varieties.

Their recruitment of winemakers from Australia and New Zealand has stamped a consistent style on the winery. First to arrive, in 1994, was Jeff Martin, previously with McWilliams. His style is bold fruit unabashedly aged in or fermented in oak. His boldest wine, the Old Vines Foch, is now a cult favourite. Martin spotted the twenty-five-year-old Maréchal Foch vines, the oldest reds in the vineyard, and turned the dark, intensely flavoured grapes into a rich, plummy wine in the style of Australian Shiraz.

When Martin left in 1998, another Australian was recruited; and when he died after less than a year on the job, Quails' Gate hired its third Australian in 2000, a self-confident rugby player named Ashley Hooper. It was good that he had confidence for, while he had made wine with most varieties, he had no experience with Pinot Noir, arguably the flagship at Quails' Gate. His solution was simple. He spent three days with Oregon winemakers to pick up technique and then he proceeded to make excellent Pinot Noir in the 2000 vintage.

Hooper returned to Australia in 2003. His successor is Grant Stanley, who was born in Vancouver in 1967 and drifted into wine through the hotel and restaurant trade. He learned winemaking in New Zealand, where he made six vintages at Ata Rangi, one of that country's top Pinot Noir producers. He says,

Canada is not yet in the higher echelons of winemaking countries in the world. I know we're good. But how good can we be? I wouldn't be here if I didn't think we can be right up there with some of the great producers.

The least expensive wine is the Allison Ranch range, named after the Allison family who homesteaded the property before the Stewarts bought it. The mid-range is Limited Release, which includes one of the winery's most popular budget whites, a Chasselas/Pinot Blanc blend. Chasselas, the leading white of Switzerland, was planted by chance here as early as 1961. A labrusca hybrid had been ordered but the nursery erred, shipping the vinifera instead. The Stewarts never regretted the error. The top range is Family Reserve, which was initiated in the 1994 vintage with Chardonnay and Pinot Noir. It now extends to Riesling, Chenin Blanc, Sauvignon Blanc, Merlot, and Gamay.

RECLINE RIDGE VINEYARDS AND WINERY **
2640 Skimikin Road, Tappen, BC, V0E 2X0.
Tel: 250 835 2212; Website: www.recline-ridge.bc.ca
One of British Columbia's northernmost wineries, Recline Ridge is located in a sun-drenched valley a short drive west of Salmon Arm. The

winery is a few hours north of the Okanagan, where wine touring is well established. Fortunately for Recline Ridge, the nearby highway is the TransCanada. During the summer, that highway delivers many tourists to the modern log cabin that serves at the wine shop here.

The winery is owned by Michael and Susan Smith, who initially purchased the property as a home in the country with a pasture for horses. Vineyard planting began in 1998 and the winery opened with Michael, a veteran award-winning amateur vintner, making the wine from purchased grapes. Recline Ridge continues to buy Pinot Noir, Chancellor and Merlot from Okanagan vineyards. Its own vineyard primarily produces Maréchal Foch, Siegerrebe, Ortega, and Madeleine Sylvaner.

RED ROOSTER WINERY ***

891 Naramata Road, Penticton, BC, V2A 8T5.

Tel: 250 492 2424; Website: www.redroosterwinery.com

Beat and Prudence Mahrer seem able to succeed at whatever they put their hands to. In their native Switzerland they prospered as owners of a Basle fitness club. Coming to Canada in 1990, they bought an apple orchard near Naramata. Even though the market for apples was still healthy (it has weakened since), they decided to convert the property to grapes. Once they had learned how to grow grapes, they opened a small winery in 1996. Eight years later, they moved into a new winery six times the size of the original one (the new tasting room alone is as large as the former winery). While building the business, the Mahrers even found time to learn to fly the float-equipped Cessna plane that is moored on Okanagan Lake.

The Red Rooster name came about because the Mahrers had always kept chickens as pets, if only because these undemanding birds fit their busy lifestyles. The winery's roosters are named Prince Charles and Prince Edward. Guests were attracted to the original winery's grand opening with the announcement that Prince Charles would be attending. Buckingham Palace's Prince Charles politely declined his invitation but his stand-in strutted proudly in his hut beside the winery's driveway. Continuing the theme, the winery's super-premium Bordeaux-style red is called The Golden Egg and its easy-drinking blended white is Bantam. Others include a broad selection of table wines, sparkling wine, and perhaps the only dessert wine in the Okanagan made in the style of an Italian Vin Santo.

SANDHILL WINES *****

1125 Richter Street, Kelowna, BC, V1Y 2K6.

Tel: 250 762 9144; Website: www.sandhillwines.ca

Vineyard manager Richard Cleave co-signs bottles of Sandhill wines with Howard Soon, the winemaker. Cleave, a British agriculturalist, has managed vineyards on the south Okanagan's Black Sage Road since 1975. Originally the vineyards grew hybrid varieties that, in Cleave's judgment, made such mediocre wine that he did not drink it. But since the early 1990s, Black Sage Road, including Sandhill's Burrowing Owl Vineyard, has grown vinifera. Cleave is so proud of the results that he signs, cellars, and drinks the results.

Now producing about 20,000 cases of wine annually, Sandhill was established in 1999 by Cascadia Brands, also the parent of Calona Vineyards, which had already been buying Burrowing Owl grapes. The 116.5-hectare vineyard was planted over several years, starting in 1993, by real estate developer James Wyse, who hired Cleave as vineyard manager. Cascadia then invested in building Wyse's Burrowing Owl Winery, which opened in 1998. When the partnership with Wyse dissolved five years later, Cascadia retained seventy hectares of vineyard and a site for a planned Sandhill winery. Until that winery opens, the wine continues to be made in the vast Calona facility in Kelowna.

Sandhill produces only single-vineyard wines. In addition to Burrowing Owl grapes, it also gets grapes (notably Pinot Gris) from the King Family vineyard on the Naramata Bench and from Cleave's own Phantom Creek vineyard (Syrah, Petit Verdot, and Malbec) on Black Sage Road. Winemaker Soon, a twenty-five year Calona veteran, has the full range of premium varieties to work with. Some of Sandhill's most complex wines are released under its Small Lots programme. These include the Okanagan's first Sangiovese, its first Barbera, and three blended reds simply called One, Two, and Three. Production of the Small Lots wine is limited. For example, only 398 cases were released of the 2001 Sandhill Three, a blend of fifty per cent Sangiovese, thirty per cent Barbera, and ten per cent each of Merlot and Cabernet Sauvignon.

SCHERZINGER VINEYARDS **

7311 Fiske Street, Summerland, BC, V0H 1Z2.

Tel: 250 494 8815; Website: www.scherzingervineyards.com

Edgar Scherzinger was a wood-carver from Bavaria who, after living in Vancouver for thirteen years, purchased a cherry orchard in 1974 on a peaceful road at the edge of Summerland. In 1978 he converted it to a three-hectare vineyard when he discovered he could not make a living with cherries. Ignoring the advice he got from wineries of the day, Scherzinger planted primarily vinifera, notably Pinot Noir, Chardonnay, and Gewürztraminer. Since the winery opened in 1995, the flagship wines have been made with Gewürztraminer. The most consistent award-winner is an off-dry blend of Gewürztraminer and Merlot called Sweet Caroline, named for a Scherzinger daughter who died in a car accident. When Scherzinger retired in 2001, he sold the winery to Ron and Cher Watkins, who have maintained the popular styles of the wines. Putting their stamp on the winery included changing the name in 2005 to Dirty Laundry Vineyard. The reference is to an early 1900s Summerland laundry that fronted for a bordello.

SILVER SAGE WINERY ***
32032 87th Avenue, Oliver, BC, V0H 1T0.
Tel: 250 498 0310; website: www.silversagewinery.com
This winery is named for the sage that had overgrown much of this property, an abandoned south Okanagan vineyard, by the time Victor and Anna Manola bought it in 1996. They brought the winery back to life by planting nine hectares of grapes and by building a baronial winery beside the Okanagan River. Some sage remained, however, and they hit on the idea of infusing Gewürztraminer with some herbs to create a wine called Grand Sage Reserve. There are other original wines here, including Flame (an Icewine with a red pepper in the bottle) and excellent fruit wines.

However, there is also a tragic history here. In 1975 Victor smuggled himself out of Romania, when he was twenty. Once he had established himself in Canada he arranged for Anna, his childhood sweetheart, to join him. They purchased the Okanagan property because they found the valley's beauty alluring. Anna, a former mathematics teacher with a poetic bent, insists that the first three letters of the postal code stand for Valley of Heaven. Both had grown up in Romania's wine industry; Anna learned to make fruit wines with her winemaker father. Their backgrounds led them to plant vines in 1997 and begin selling wine in 2001. Sadly, at the end of the 2002 vintage, both Victor and consulting winemaker Frank Supernak died when they were overcome by carbon dioxide in a fermentation tank. The winery closes every November 10 in their memory.

SONORAN ESTATE WINERY **

21606 Highway 97 North, Summerland, BC, V0H 1Z0.

Tel: 250 494 9323

Sonoran Estate was opened in the summer of 2004 by Arjan and Ada Smits and their son, Adrian. Immigrants from Holland in 1981, the Smits family grew flowers both in Ontario and in British Columbia's Fraser Valley until moving to the Okanagan in 2000. After opening a roadside bed-and-breakfast, they switched the lake-view side of the property from apple trees to vines. The 2.2-hectare vineyard is planted to Merlot, Pinot Noir, Chardonnay, Riesling, and Gewürztraminer.

ST HUBERTUS ESTATE WINERY ***

5225 Lakeshore Road, Kelowna, BC, V1W 4J1.

Tel: 250 764 7888; Website: www.st-hubertus.bc.ca

St Hubertus has the unfortunate distinction of being the only Canadian winery destroyed by a forest fire. Because the owners, Leo and Andy Gebert, are superbly organized, a new tasting room and new winemaking facilities opened within ten days of that disaster, just before the 2003 vintage. The fire also claimed Leo Gebert's 1932 vintage home, which was next to the winery. However, the only wine lost was 2,000 litres of port-style. The brothers had bottled the rest of the 2002 vintage earlier in the season, storing it in a warehouse that was not destroyed.

In gratitude to the firefighters, the winery created two special labels – Firemen's Red (Gamay) and Glowing Amber (Chardonnay/Pinot Blanc). Proceeds from the sales of these wines are donated to a fire relief fund. The fire ruined all the grapes in their vineyard (Andy said that even the birds refused to eat the smoke-drenched fruit). Vineyards throughout the Okanagan provided the grapes they needed for the 2003 vintage, including rare Chasselas, an obvious variety for the winery since the brothers and their wives (who are sisters) are Swiss.

Born in 1958 at Rapperswil, Leo became a banker but really wanted to be a farmer. The price of Swiss farmland being out of reach, he settled in 1984 on this Okanagan vineyard, where grapes have grown since 1928. The vineyard has been replanted several times and now includes Pinot Blanc and one of the oldest Riesling blocks in the valley. Andy, born in 1965, spent some years as a yacht captain in the Caribbean before coming to Canada in 1990. Four years later, he joined his brother as a partner in the winery. St. Hubertus bottles its wines under its own label and under the Oak Bay label; the name is taken from Andy's vineyard. Signature wines include Oak Bay Gewürztraminer, Oak Bay Maréchal Foch, and St Hubertus Icewines, made from Pinot Noir and Pinot Blanc.

ST LASZLO VINEYARDS
2605 Highway 3 E, Keremeos, BC, V0X 1N0
Tel: 250 499 2856

Wine tourists turning off the highway to visit this rustic winery's tasting room will find a bewildering array of wines, from heritage grape varieties to fruit wines and, occasionally, a spicy confection made with rose petals. Joe Ritlop, who was born in 1933 in Slovenia, began growing grapes in this Similkameen Valley vineyard in 1976. Concerned about the cold winters, he planted some of the hardiest vines he could find, including such old American hybrids as Clinton and Interlaken. St Laszlo is almost certainly the only Canadian winery making varietal wines with these grapes.

Joe Ritlop Jr has added some mainstream vinifera since taking over the winemaking. Nevertheless, he has retained his father's basic, no-chemicals style of winemaking. "We are from the old school of thought," he says. The winery, which opened in 1984, has never received credit for being the first Canadian winery to market Icewine. (Hainle Vineyards is considered the first because, on opening in 1988, it offered a 1978 Icewine.) St Laszlo's Icewine was made after an early winter froze unpicked grapes. Proudly, the winery tried to enter it in a major British Columbia competition in 1985, but was refused because there was no Icewine category.

STAG'S HOLLOW WINERY ★★★★
2237 Sun Valley Way, Okanagan Falls, BC, V0H 1R0.
Tel: 250 497 6162; Website: www.stagshollowwinery.com

The term "reserve" has been devalued by being attached far too often to everyday wines. Linda Pruegger and Larry Gerelus, the couple who opened this winery in 1996, avoid it when they identify tiers of quality among the 1,500 to 2,000 cases of wine they make each year. Chardonnay, Pinot Noir, and Merlot that achieve the owners' general expectation of quality are labelled "Simply", while wines above that level are labelled as unadorned varietals. The "something special" wines, however, get the Renaissance label – Renaissance Merlot is one of the best wines here. The winery also releases well-made Renaissance Chardonnay and Renaissance Pinot Noir.

Born in Winnipeg in 1952, the boyish-looking Gerelus was a financial consultant in Calgary when he was seized by the desire to grow wine. In 1992, he and Pruegger, who was working in an oil company marketing department, bought four hectares near Okanagan Falls, replacing the Chasselas and most of the Vidal they found with the three varieties that have become Stag's Hollow's signatures. They retained a little Vidal; now, they call the table wine Tragically Vidal because so little of this grape remains in the Okanagan.

SUMAC RIDGE ESTATE WINERY *****
17403 Highway 97 N, Summerland, BC, V0H 1Z0
Tel: 250 494 0451; Website: www.sumacridge.com

Harry McWatters and his first partner, viticulturist Lloyd Schmidt, hit upon an original way to launch a winery on a shoestring when they started Sumac Ridge in 1979. They bought a nine-hole golf course beside the Okanagan's busiest highway and relocated some fairways to make room for Riesling and Gewürztraminer. But they continued to run the golf course for its cash flow. Sumac Ridge's tasting room opened in the clubhouse and the restaurant continued to operate. In effect, Sumac Ridge had the only winery restaurant in the Okanagan for fifteen years until 1995, when the government formally allowed winery restaurants. Today, the golf club operates independently with its own clubhouse. The old clubhouse was absorbed into Sumac Ridge's hospitality centre and vastly expanded winery. Vincor International bought the winery in 2000 but the hard-driving McWatters remains Sumac Ridge's guiding force.

Very early in its history, Sumac Ridge made its mark with Gewürztraminer; the winery's flagship Private Reserve Gewürztraminer is the brand leader among Okanagan wines from this variety. The winery pioneered bottle-fermented sparkling wines in the Okanagan, beginning winemaking trials in 1985 and releasing its premier brand, Steller's Jay Brut, in 1989. The wine, named for British Columbia's provincial bird, is a cuvée based on Pinot Blanc, Chardonnay, and Pinot Noir.

In its second decade, the winery emerged as a leading red producer. In 1993, when large-scale vinifera plantings still seemed a gamble in the Okanagan, McWatters planted forty-six hectares on sun-baked Black Sage Road primarily to Bordeaux varieties. Sumac Ridge's first Merlot from this planting, the 1995 vintage, went on to be named Canada's red wine of the year in a national competition. Sumac Ridge was the first Canadian winery to which California's Meritage Association has given permission to use the term (*see* pages 13–4). The White Meritage, a barrel-aged blend of Sauvignon Blanc and Sémillon, is one of the finest whites made in the Okanagan.

When a non-Bordeaux grape joins the blend, however, a proprietary name is used. The premium red Pinnacle includes some Syrah, as well as Merlot, Cabernet Sauvignon, and Cabernet Franc. Pinnacle is made only in exceptional vintages and production is limited to 500 cases a year. At $50 a bottle, it was British Columbia's most expensive table wine when the 1997 vintage was released in 2000.

SUMMERHILL PYRAMID WINERY ***
4870 Chute Lake Road, Kelowna, BC, V1W 4M3.
Tel: 250 764 8000; Website: www.summerhill.bc.ca

Stephen Cipes (rhymes with pipes), the elfin former New York property developer who opened the Summerhill winery in 1992, is an original. Many of his wines are aged in a gleaming white pyramid, a scale model of the Great Pyramid of Egypt. It was built in 1997 after several years of trials with a much smaller pyramid. The trials, Cipes maintains, proved that pyramid-aged wines taste better. He points out that many of Europe's classical wineries have long cellared wines in structures whose arches share the geometry of pyramids. "There is a definite correlation between liquids and perfect geometry," Cipes maintains. A firm believer in the positive energy inside pyramids, Cipes frequently welcomes winery visitors into the candlelit pyramid during winery tours.

Cipes brings personal idealism to the wine business. He was attracted to the Okanagan in 1987 by its clean environment. He bought a rambling house overlooking Okanagan Lake with twenty-six hectares, much of it planted to vines, and quickly adopted organic growing practices. Today, most of the vineyards supplying Summerhill follow similar practices. "Flawless sparkling wine can only be made from organic grapes," he says.

The winery opened after Cipes participated in a sparkling wine project initiated by California's Schramsberg Cellars. The Californians liked the Okanagan's crisp sparkling wines, but did not open a winery because in the late 1980s the grape supply was inadequate. So Cipes hired a winemaker and launched Cipes Brut, a crisp bubbly made with Riesling. The winery now offers a full range of wines, from the traditional sparkling wine cuvées to table wines and Icewines. Summerhill is notable especially for red Icewines, variously made from Pinot Noir and Zweigelt grapes.

SUMMERLAND CELLARS ESTATE WINERY (Range not tasted.)
11612 Morrow Avenue, Summerland, BC, V0H 1Z0.
Tel: 250 494 5423

Winemaker Eric von Krosigk has been infatuated with sparkling wine since studying at Geisenheim and doing an apprenticeship with a German sekt producer. Returning to British Columbia after his studies, he had a hand in creating most of the sparkling wines now made by several wineries in that region. In 2005, he opened his own small winery at Summerland, producing only sparkling wine. "Bubbly is really about life," he says. "It's about subtleties. It's about elegance and whispers. It's one of those wines that always tastes like more. Try just eating only one peanut – or having only one glass of bubbly."

THORNHAVEN ESTATES WINERY ***
6816 Andrew Avenue, RR2, S68, C15, Summerland, BC, V0H 1Z0.
Tel: 250 494 7778; Website: www.thornhaven.com

In its design, this winery, which opened in 2001, echoes the serenity of a *pueblo* in New Mexico. The sand-hued winery perches on the toe of Giant's Head Mountain, with a view over a vineyard that falls away into a valley. The 3.6-hectare vineyard was planted in 1996 after proprietor Dennis Fraser sold a vast grain farm in northern British Columbia. He planted a few vines to keep busy, and it just grew until he had a winery. His son, Alex, a restaurant chef, helped run it for a few years. Fraser then retained a consulting winemaker, Canadian-born Christine Leroux. Thornhaven's soundly made wines are from Chardonnay, Pinot Noir, Pinot Meunier, Sauvignon Blanc, and Gewürztraminer.

TINHORN CREEK VINEYARDS ****
32830 Tinhorn Creek Road, Oliver, BC, V0H 1T0.
Tel: 250 498 3743; Website: www.tinhorn.com

A California style can be detected in several of Tinhorn Creek's wines, and for good reason. The husband and wife managers of this winery, Sandra and Kenn Oldfield, met while completing postgraduate degrees at the University of California Davis. Winemaker Sandra learned her craft after getting a taste for the wine industry while working in the tasting room of Sonoma's Rodney Strong winery. Kenn, who was born in Orillia in 1955, was a chemical engineer in Alberta until 1992 when he became partners with Alberta oilman Bob Shaunessy, a wine-loving friend, to develop Tinhorn Creek.

They joined the Okanagan wine industry just as it began to recover from the trauma of the free trade agreement with the USA, which stripped away British Columbia wine's historic protections. After the 1988 vintage, two-thirds of the Okanagan's vineyards were uprooted as the industry tore out mediocre hybrid vines. In the spring of 1993, Shaunessy bought fifty-three hectares of vineyard land on Black Sage Road that had been fallow for five years. At the same time, he bought twelve hectares across the valley, on what is called the Golden Mile. This was a producing vineyard on a plateau high above the valley.

The Tinhorn Creek winery perches on the nose of the plateau. Sitting 100 metres (328 feet) above the valley floor, it offers views from the tasting room that few other wineries can match. The winery takes its name from both a creek and a nineteenth-century gold mine, some of whose ruins are still visible in the hillside beyond the Gewürztraminer.

Unlike many Okanagan wineries, Tinhorn Creek limits itself to a disciplined number of varieties. There are three reds: Merlot (which was already growing in the Golden Mile vineyard), Cabernet Franc (because it ripens earlier than Cabernet Sauvignon), and Pinot Noir. For whites, the winery picked Chardonnay, Pinot Gris, and Gewürztraminer. There was already Kerner in the Golden Mile vineyard; this variety is used exclusively for Icewine and late-harvest.

Sandra considers Merlot to be Tinhorn Creek's signature wine. The début vintage, 1994, was made from Golden Mile grapes and won the winery its first silver medal. The Black Sage Road vineyard began producing in 1998 and the winery's big, rich Merlot from that vintage, a gold medallist, was named red wine of the year at a subsequent Canadian Wine Awards competition. The winery's first reserve wine was a 2001 Merlot, released in 2004 under the Oldfield's Collection label.

TOWNSHIP 7 VINEYARDS AND WINERY ****
21152 16th Avenue, Langley, BC, V2Z 1K3
Tel: 604 532 1766; Website: www.township7.com

SECOND WINERY: 1450 McMillan Ave, Penticton, BC, V2A 8T4.

Tel: 250 770 1743; Website: www.township7.com

Gwen and Corey Coleman operate two wineries under the Township 7 banner. Their original boutique winery at Langley, a suburb of Vancouver, opened in 2001. They opened the second in 2004 in the Okanagan by investing in a vineyard and winery project on the Naramata Bench initiated by Michael Bartier, their former winemaker. The grapes for both wineries come almost entirely from Okanagan vineyards. The postage-stamp-sized Langley vineyard's grapes are used primarily in Township 7's sparkling wine, called Seven Stars.

Commerce graduates from the University of Saskatchewan, the Colemans pursued commercial careers until a Napa Valley wine tour in 1989 introduced them to the vintner's lifestyle. They arrived in the Okanagan in 1995 from Montréal and just knocked on winery doors, looking for work. Gwen ended up with a marketing job at Sumac Ridge while Corey, after handing out twenty-three résumés, joined the crew planting Tinhorn Creek's vineyards. From there, he moved into the cellars at Hawthorne Mountain Vineyards. Here, he learned the fundamentals of winemaking, working with Bartier, and laid plans for Township 7.

The original winery was placed on a farm near Vancouver because the Colemans wanted to be close to their customers, including restaurants, in the city. That strategy, along with very sound winemaking, vaulted Township 7's wines onto the lists of many of the best restaurants. The winery opened with excellent Chardonnay, Merlot, and Cabernet Sauvignon, expanding in subsequent vintages to include Syrah and Sauvignon Blanc. Most of the winery's production is done in the Okanagan, at the Naramata Bench winery.

WILD GOOSE VINEYARDS AND WINERY ****

2145 Sun Valley Way, Okanagan Falls, BC, V0H 1R0.

Tel: 250 497 8919; Website: www.wildgoosewinery.com

There are so many rocks among the vines in the rugged four-hectare Wild Goose vineyard that some visitors think they were put there deliberately. "You could plant no other crop here," says Roland Kruger. He and his winemaker brother, Hagen, helped their father, Adolf, plant in 1983. With the surface almost impervious to shovels, they sank holes for the vines with high-pressure water jets. The sun-baked rubble, however, is producing some of British Columbia's best Riesling and Gewürztraminer.

Adolf Kruger, who was born in Germany in 1931 and came to Canada at the age of twenty, bought this property when a downturn in the consulting business threatened his engineering career. The farm winery that he opened in 1990 was named for the flock of geese that Kruger had frightened into the sky when he walked the property for the first time. He expected Wild Goose to make a few thousand bottles of wine each year and continue to sell most of its grapes to other wineries. The winery has been considerably more successful. It now produces about 5,000 cases a year, has a second small vineyard and buys grapes as well.

The success of Wild Goose is based not only on the well-made, reasonably-priced wines, but also on the Kruger family welcome in the wine shop. A member of the family almost always presides at the tasting bar. The tradition should continue. Hagen's teenage son, Nicholas, has shown an interest in winemaking, to the family's conspicuous delight.

14

British Columbia's West Coast

The 143 hectares of vines growing in British Columbia's coastal viticultural area make up a mere 6.5 per cent of the province's total. Yet about twenty per cent of British Columbia's wineries are based here. Many supplement the output of their vineyards by buying from the Okanagan those varieties, such as Merlot and Syrah, that do not ripen well on the coast. Several wineries are purely estate producers, arguing that the wines should express the distinctive regional terroir only. Giordano Venturi, co-owner of Venturi-Schulze on Vancouver Island, maintains that,

> You can't get this wine anywhere else. I would really like to develop this area as a destination – that people would come here to get wines they cannot get anywhere else.

The coastal region is defined as including the Fraser Valley east of Vancouver, Vancouver Island, and the Gulf Islands in the Strait of Georgia between the mainland and Vancouver Island. Most British Columbians live here, in Greater Vancouver, the province's commercial centre, and in Victoria, the provincial capital (see map on page 142). Both cities are important tourist destinations as well as population centres. Several producers, notably Domaine de Chaberton and Township 7 in the Fraser Valley, and Victoria Estate Winery near Victoria, deliberately chose to be near population centres, concluding that it is easier to transport grapes than to attract people to distant vineyards.

The largest cluster of seasoned wineries is in the Cowichan Valley, not far from the city of Duncan. The soils, climate and exposures combine to create the conditions for grape-growing, with potential for expansion. The valley's largest landowner is the Cowichan Indian Band, with a

2,400-hectare reserve. Looking to create jobs for its 3,700 members, the band has identified about 120 hectares suitable for vines which, if planted, would double Vancouver Island's vineyards. In 2004, in order to learn the wine business before diving in with additional vineyards, the band purchased a ten-year-old winery, Cherry Point Vineyards.

The coastal viticultural conditions stand in sharp contrast with the hot, arid Okanagan where most vineyards are. The maritime climate is more temperate, with virtually no risk of mid-winter vine-killing cold. The frost-free growing season generally lasts from mid-April to mid-October. Precipitation is substantial but seasonal; the summers, while cooler than in the Okanagan, are long and dry enough for selected varieties to mature. Vancouver Island's high spine of mountains also deflects the Pacific storms, creating microclimates here and on the Gulf Islands, which can be so dry in summer that many vineyards have installed irrigation.

COMMERCIAL BEGINNINGS
Vancouver Island's first modern commercial vineyard, now twelve hectares in size, began in 1970 with an experimental planting by Dennis Zanatta, on a former dairy farm just south of Duncan. A wine-loving immigrant from northern Italy, he was confident that wine grapes could grow in the sheltered Cowichan Valley, where the season is long and dry. Zanatta's trials caught the attention of the provincial government, which used his vineyard to assess about 100 different vines. The Duncan Project, as this test was called, ran from 1983 to 1990, and had identified Ortega, Auxerrois, and Pinot Gris as especially promising. The Duncan Project's funding ran out prematurely, long before reliable conclusions were reached. The final report on the project observed that it would take twenty to thirty years to determine whether a region is suitable for growing wine grapes. Numerous vineyards today have trial plots of promising new cool-climate hybrids recently developed in Switzerland by plant breeder Valentin Blattner. Many vineyards grow Ortega, a cool-climate variety from Germany that matures early and makes bread-and-butter whites.

The first significant commercial vineyard in the Fraser Valley, and still the largest, was planted in 1981 by Claude and Inge Violet, who went on to open the Domaine de Chaberton winery a decade later. The Violets planted sixteen hectares of white varieties, including Ortega, Bacchus, Madeleine Angevine, and Madeleine Sylvaner.[1] In the course of two decades, the Violets have proved the viability of growing grapes in the Fraser Valley. Several other small vineyards, some with wineries, have followed. The barrier to development is the cost of farmland: it would be difficult to build a profitable winery on just those varieties that ripen reliably here. The reds that Domaine de Chaberton makes from Okanagan grapes (Syrah, Merlot, and Cabernet Sauvignon) command much higher prices than the winery's excellent Bacchus.

Coastal wineries also grow more commercially acceptable varieties than can be matured in cooler climates. These include Pinot Noir, Gamay, Pinot Gris, Gewürztraminer, and Chardonnay. In general, the coastal reds are lighter in body while the coastal whites are crisper and fruitier than similar varieties from the Okanagan. Increasingly, coastal grape growers erect plastic tents over vines in the spring, for greater ripeness. Venturi-Schulze and Alderlea Vineyards, both near Duncan, use this technique for producing full-bodied Pinot Noir.

The opening of Domaine de Chaberton and Vigneti Zanatta helped create the interest in wine in the local communities that encouraged other wineries. Five vineyard-based coastal wineries were operating by 1995. Momentum has been increasing since then, and particularly since 2000, driven partly by rising wine tourism on Vancouver Island and by the energetic proselytizing of the Wine Islands Growers Association. This group was formed in 1997 as the Vancouver Island Grape Growers Association and now has 100 members. Founder Fraser Smith, a financial consultant and hobby grape-grower, confidently projects fifty wineries on Vancouver Island and the Gulf Islands. In 2005, thirty wineries were operating or being developed in the coastal region, with two meaderies, one cidery, and seven fruit wineries also open or under development. New wineries have opened at such a rate that they have outpaced the viticultural and winemaking skills on the coast. In recognition of this, Okanagan University College began offering courses in 2004 at a satellite campus in Victoria Estate Winery.

---

1. Early-ripening white varieties, Madeleine Angevine and Madeleine Sylvaner were crosses developed around 1850 by a Loire nursery called Moreau-Robert. They are also grown in UK vineyards.

15

Wineries of Coastal British Columbia

ALDERLEA VINEYARDS ****
1751 Stamps Road, Duncan, BC, V9L 5W2.
Tel: 250 746 7122
Perfectionist Roger Dosman and his wife, Nancy, opened this tiny estate winery in 1998 after running an automobile body repair shop for two decades. He has learned that healthy vines lightly cropped are the way to produce intense and ripe wine on cool Vancouver Island. He even gets some ripe enough to make a creditable port-style wine called Hearth. Dosman buys no Okanagan grapes:

> My commitment is to use only estate-grown fruit. That's pretty firm. It costs more to grow it here but that's what I want to do. Quite frankly, I think I make some very distinct wines.

Alderlea's production of 1,200 to 1,600 cases a year is all sold from the wine shop. The signature whites are Bacchus and Auxerrois; in warm years, a Viognier is made. The signature reds are Pinot Noir and a rich Maréchal Foch called Clarinet. "It was too good to be called just Foch," Dosman explains.

AVERILL CREEK VINEYARDS (Range not tasted.)
6552 North Road, Duncan, BC, V9L 6K9.
Tel: 250 715 7379; Website: www.averillcreek
Andy Johnston's tutelage as a winemaker began in 1998 when he helped with the crush at a small winery in Tuscany. Born in the UK in 1947, he had practised medicine, mostly in Canada, since 1973 while dreaming of making wine. In 2002, he planted Pinot Gris, Gewürztraminer, and Pinot

Noir on a mountainside slope on Vancouver Island. "I knew a long time ago that I had only so much doctoring in me," he said after thirty-two years in medicine. "I planned an exit strategy, which is Averill Creek winery." After Tuscany, he continued his hands-on training as a volunteer at wineries in Bordeaux, Australia, New Zealand, and in recent years at the nearby Alderlea Vineyards on the island. A serious wine *aficionado* with a taste for old Bordeaux, Johnston intends to open this winery in 2005 with premium wines. "If I can't get into the $15 to $25 range, then I shouldn't be in business," he says. "It's an expensive place to start a vineyard, the Cowichan Valley." Johnston took advantage of the natural contours of his mountain property to build Vancouver Island's first gravity-flow winery, for the gentlest possible treatment of delicate Pinot Noir.

BLUE GROUSE ESTATE WINERY ****

4365 Blue Grouse Road, Duncan, BC, V9L 6M3.
Tel: 250 743 3834; Website: www.bluegrousevineyards.com

No one in the British Columbia wine industry has as much scientific education as Hans Kiltz, a former veterinarian who opened this winery in 1993. Born in Berlin in 1938, he has degrees in veterinary medicine, tropical veterinary medicine, and fish pathology, topped off by a doctorate in microbiology. As a result, the wines at Blue Grouse all show a clean, technical precision, from the floral Bacchus and crisp Pinot Gris to his aromatic, oak-aged Black Muscat. This exotic red is rare because no one else grows it in British Columbia and Kiltz isn't giving away cuttings. He is one of a small group of Vancouver Island vintners making wine only with fruit grown on the island. His son Richard, who has a winemaking diploma from Germany, has joined his father on the 12.5-hectare farm.

CHALET ESTATE VINEYARD ***

11195 Chalet Road, North Saanich, BC, V8L 5M1.
Tel: 250 656 2552; Website: www.chaletestatevineyard.ca

On following Michael Betts around his winery's compact cellar, one marvels at his ease in negotiating tight spaces until hearing about his life before wine. Betts was a submarine officer in the Royal Navy until he emigrated to Vancouver Island in 1967. In the 1980s, Betts and Linda Plimley, his wife, bought a quiet property on the Saanich Peninsula, a broad finger of well-treed farmland north of Victoria. After dismissing trout farming and walnut farming, he started a 1.2-hectare vineyard in

1998. Saanich is far removed from traditional British Columbia vineyards. However, Betts chose appropriate varieties for his cool site: Ortega, Bacchus, and Pinot Gris.

Realistic about what cannot be grown here, Betts purchases most of the red grapes he needs from vineyards in the Okanagan. When the winery opened in 2001, he and Plimley had the best of both worlds: vividly fruity white wines from their vineyard, and ripe Merlot and Syrah from the Okanagan. Chalet Estate produces between 1,500 and 2,000 cases a year.

CHASE AND WARREN ESTATE WINERY
6253 Drinkwater Road, Port Alberni, BC, V9Y 8H9.
Tel: 250 724 4906

Located in the heart of Vancouver Island, this is the westernmost vineyard-based winery in Canada. Port Alberni is better known for its pulp mill and its superb salmon fishing. Vaughan Chase opened this small winery in 2003 ("Warren" is an obscure literary allusion that Chase felt would lend the winery name more weight). Chase, a schoolteacher, planted a few Gewürztraminer vines in 1991 on the slope below his home at the edge of Port Alberni. Now he and his brother-in-law Ron Crema have planted a number of varieties, including Siegerrebe, Bacchus, Pinot Noir, Oraniensteiner, and Müller-Thurgau. The wines, made to complement the region's seafood, are a local novelty and are rarely seen ouside the area.

CHATEAU WOLFF
2534 Maxey Road, Nanaimo, BC V9S 5V6.
Tel: 250 753 4613; Email: chateauwolff@shaw.ca

Harry von Wolff, a native of Latvia who came to Canada in 1953, became passionate about the wines of Burgundy when he worked as a hotel food and beverage manager. He has planted primarily Pinot Noir and Chardonnay in the two hectares of vineyards he has developed since 1987. Von Wolff makes some of the darkest, most extracted Pinot Noir in British Columbia. The wine is designed to age. "I know Pinot Noirs can handle thirty years," he says.

CHERRY POINT VINEYARDS ***
840 Cherry Point Road, RR 3, Cobble Hill, BC,VOR 1L0.
Tel: 250 743 1272; Website: www.cherrypointvineyards.com

Cherry Point is Canada's second winery owned by an aboriginal band. The Cowichan Indian Band, having identified potential vineyard land on its 2,400-hectare reserve in the Cowichan Valley, purchased Cherry Point in 2004, vaulting into the wine business with an established producer (founded in 1990 by Wayne and Helena Ulrich).

The winery currently has a ten-hectare vineyard in production. The varieties include Pinot Gris, Gewürztraminer, and Ortega. One of the curiosities here is a red variety called Agria. Developed by a Hungarian plant breeder, it is an early ripening vine capable of yielding deeply coloured, tannic wines with a gamey, rustic quality. At Cherry Point, Agria is tamed by blending with some Pinot Noir. A cult product is a sweet dessert wine made from locally grown wild blackberries.

DIVINO ESTATE WINERY
1500 Freeman Road, Cobble Hill, BC, V0R 1L0.
Tel: 250 743 2311

This winery is unique for having transferred its operations from one of British Columbia's viticultural areas, the Okanagan, to another, Vancouver Island. Owner Joe Busnardo explains that he had tired of the Okanagan's hot climate. The Okanagan winery was renamed Hester Creek in 1996 after Busnardo sold it (*see* page 169). He bought a vineyard half the size at Cobble Hill in the Cowichan Valley. Busnardo took along many vine cuttings from the Okanagan for the new vineyard, including the Italian whites.

DOMAINE DE CHABERTON ESTATE WINERY ****
1064-216th Street, Langley, BC, V2Z 1R3.
Tel: 604 530 1736; Website: www.domainedechaberton.com

Claude Violet's wine tradition dates back to 1644; his family came from Perpignan. He returned to his heritage after a brief detour into banking. Coming to Canada, in 1981 he planted the first major vineyard in British Columbia's Fraser Valley. Nine years later, he and Inge, his German-born wife, opened the first winery in the valley, naming it for the Violet family farm in France. Because the Fraser Valley is cool, the Violets planted white grapes, including Bacchus, Madeleine Angevine, Madeleine Sylvaner[1], and Chardonnay, plus a little Pinot Noir. Almost none of the whites are mainstream varieties but the wines were so sound as to become flagships for Domaine de Chaberton.

By the mid-1990s, however, the demand for red wines began to out-pace the demand for whites. The Violets were unable to buy enough red varieties in the Okanagan and, after flirting with importing bulk wines, they sponsored a grower to convert an apple orchard on Black Sage Road to a vineyard. Beginning in 2000, Domaine de Chaberton added such wines as Syrah, Merlot, and Cabernet Sauvignon. In March, 2005, when Claude reached seventy and the couple decided to retire, the winery was purchased by a group of wine afficionados led Eugene Kwan, a Vancouver lawyer. The Violets, legendary for their welcoming presence in the tasting room, remain as consultants.

ECHO VALLEY VINEYARDS *

4651 Waters Road, PO Box 816, Duncan, BC, V9L 3Y2.

Tel: 250 748 1470; Website: www.echovalley-vineyards.com

Echo Valley is the project of Albert and Edward Brennink, a father and son team who were both born in Holland. The elder Brennink is an architect who had maintained a practice in Switzerland for eighteen years before deciding to retire to Canada in 1979. He settled his family on a sixty-five-hectare farm in a quiet valley. In 1999, they cleared ten hectares on a sun-baked slope of gravely soil and planned a vineyard. Cautiously, the Brenninks started with a test block of twenty varieties, including Ortega – a variety already proven on the island – and Chasselas. Planting of the vineyard began in earnest in 2003. Meanwhile, the winery opened in that year with Chardonnay, Pinot Gris, and Gamay, all made at an Okanagan winery.

GARRY OAKS VINEYARD ****

1880 Fulford-Ganges Road, Salt Spring Island, BC, V8K 2A5.

Tel: 250 653 4687; Website: www.saltspringwine.com

When Elaine Kozak and Marcel Mercier opened this winery in 2003, it marked a dramatic career switch: she is an economist and he is an environmental consultant with a talent for growing things. The vineyard, which is currently about three hectares in size, is planted to Pinot Noir, Gewürztraminer, Pinot Gris, Zweigelt, and Léon Millot (a hybrid similar to Maréchal Foch). Nearly all the vines are grafted to early-ripening rootstock. As warm as the Garry Oaks slope is, the island's growing season is a little shorter than that of the Okanagan, although nearly as dry because the mountains on nearby Vancouver Island deflect the Pacific rains. Mercier's capable viticulture delivers high quality grapes to the winery.

Okanagan consultant Ross Mirko supervises the winemaking and

Garry Oaks has been notably successful with estate-grown Pinot Gris and Pinot Noir as well as two proprietary reds made with Okanagan grapes: Labyrinth is made with Blaufränkisch and Fetish is a blend of Merlot, Cabernet Sauvignon, and Cabernet Franc.

GLENTERRA VINEYARDS ***

3897 Cobble Hill Road, Cobble Hill, BC, V0R 1L0.

Tel: 250 743 2330

Scot John Kelly and his partner, Ruth Luxton, bought a small vineyard called Ayle Moselle in 1998, where John Harper, a pioneer grower, had made plant trials. Kelly found about forty varieties in Harper's overgrown 0.4-hectare block. He has since planted 2.5 hectares to mainstream varieties (Pinots Gris, Blanc, and Noir, Merlot, and Gewürztraminer). But rather than discard the fruit from Harper's eclectic collection, he uses them in two excellent blends: Vivace is a Muscat-based white wine and Brio is a robust red. The first red grown here, a 2000 Pinot Noir, won a silver medal in competition. Kelly also purchases Okanagan grapes for barrel-fermented Chardonnay and full-bodied reds. His benchmark Bordeaux wine is Château Pichon-Lalande, and he has shown adeptness at blending his own red Meritage.

GLENUGIE WINERY ***

3033 232nd Street, Langley, BC, V2Z 3A8.

Tel: 604 539 9463; Website: www.glenugiewinery.com

Born in Edmonton in 1939 but still proud of his Scottish roots, Gary Tayler puts the Campbell of Argyle tartan on the labels of his wines and displays his family's other clan crests in his tasting room. The winery itself is named after a family farm in Scotland and not, as might be assumed, after a defunct distillery. Pinot Noir is Tayler's passion. Once an Okanagan grape-grower and then a builder, Tayler decided to plant a few vines on his farm when he retired. When the hobby grew to 8,700 vines, the Tayler family launched Glenugie in 2002. The winery's production is supplemented with Pinot Noir, Chardonnay, Pinot Blanc, and Gamay purchased from the Okanagan.

GODFREY-BROWNELL VINEYARDS **

4911 Marshall Road, Duncan, BC, V9L 6T3.

Tel: 250 715 0504; Website: www.gbvineyards.com

David Godfrey's eight-hectare vineyard in the Cowichan Valley was established in 1999. The one-time English professor and internet consultant avows a particular taste for big reds. The red varieties in the Vancouver Island vineyard include Maréchal Foch, Agria, Lemberger, and Dunkelfelder, all capable of making robust wines. The vineyard also grows Pinot Noir and Gamay, along with such whites as Chardonnay and Pinot Gris. One of Godfrey's sentimental favourites is late-ripening Cabernet Sauvignon. However, the winery is more likely to purchase its late-ripening varieties from the Okanagan. Godfrey-Brownell has also dabbled in fruit wines made from the tasty wild blackberries that grow all over Vancouver Island.

LOTUSLAND VINEYARDS **
28450 King Road, Abbotsford, BC,V4X 1B1.
Tel: 604 857 4188; Website: www.lotuslandvineyards.com
David and Liz Avery opened this winery in 2002 and coyly dubbed it A'Very Fine Winery. When they tired of explaining the pun, they turned to Vancouver marketing consultant Bernie Hadley-Beauregard and changed the name to Lotusland, Canada's colloquial term for the easy-going Vancouver lifestyle. The new name was matched with catchy labels to get consumers talking: the Merlot has photographs of twenty-one prominent Vancouver citizens, turning the bottle into a conversation piece.

MALAHAT ESTATE VINEYARD (Range not tasted.)
1197 Aspen Road, Malahat, BC, V0R 2L0.
Tel: 250 474 5129
Twenty minutes north of Victoria, Vancouver Island's main highway climbs through a low mountain pass called The Malahat. Lorne Tomalty's steeply terraced two-hectare vineyard is near the summit. Tomalty was born in Ottawa in 1923. He only began planting vines in 1995, a decade after retiring as a senior personnel executive in the British Columbia government. His site certainly qualifies as cool climate and the vineyard choices reflect that: Ortega, Pinot Noir, and Pinot Gris.

MARSHWOOD ESTATE WINERY (Range not tasted.)
548 Jade Road, Heriot Bay, Quadra Island, BC, V0P 1H0.
Tel: 250 285 2068
Some go to established wine country to open wineries and others do it where they live. Martina and Kerry Kowalchuck happen to live on Quadra, one of the northernmost of the Gulf Islands on the British

Columbia coast. The only wineries further north on the Pacific Coast are the three in Alaska. Marshwood, which opened in 2004, offers fruit and grape wines, with some of the grapes coming from its own vineyard which grows Ortega, Pinot Gris, Dornfelder, Agria and Pinot Noir. Fruit wines are sparkling strawberry and sparkling cranberry.

MORNING BAY FARM (Range not tasted.)
6621 Harbour Hill Road, North Pender Island, BC, V0N 2M1.
Tel: 250 629 8351

The artists, writers, and musicians who favour British Columbia's scenic Gulf Islands should be a receptive milieu for a growing number of boutique wineries. Pender Island's Morning Bay was launched in 2005 by award-winning broadcast journalist Keith Watt. He now has two hectares of grapes on a terraced hillside and contracts with Okanagan growers for those varieties, such as Cabernet Sauvignon and Merlot, not suited to the cooler island climate. The Morning Bay vineyard has primarily Pinot Noir, Maréchal Foch, Pinot Gris, and Gewürztraminer.

NEWTON RIDGE VINEYARDS ****
1595 Newton Heights Road, Saanichton, BC, V8M 1T6.
Tel: 250 652 1644

Undoubtedly, this is Canada's smallest commercial grape winery, making about 250 cases of wine annually from a 1.2-hectare vineyard situated on a mountain slope north of Victoria. The steep southern exposure catches the sun, allowing the vineyard to mature Pinot Noir, Pinot Blanc, Pinot Gris and Ortega. The winery has now had three owners in succession, all of them with the wealth and the pride to keep the winery operating. Consulting winemaker Todd Moore and resident cellarman Bob Bentham hand-craft wines that are as good as they are rare. The Ortega from this vineyard is British Columbia's best: a crisp white with a fruit intensity approaching New Zealand Sauvignon Blanc.

PEMBERTON VALLEY VINEYARD AND INN *
1427 Collins Road, Pemberton, BC, V0N 2L0.
Tel: 604 894 5857; Website: www.whistlerwine.com

In real estate, location is everything. When amateur winemaker Patrick Bradner decided to plant a vineyard, he did so at Pemberton, a village half an hour's drive north of Whistler, one of North America's leading ski resorts. He has developed a small country inn beside his 1.2-hectare vineyard. Pemberton Valley has a hot growing season that suits Maréchal Foch and Pinot Gris but, as Bradner discovered, is not long enough for Chardonnay. He also makes wine from Okanagan grapes.

SALT SPRING VINEYARDS ****
151 Lee Road at the 1700 Block, Fulford-Ganges Road, Salt Spring Island, BC, V8K 2A5.
Tel: 250 653 9463; Website: www.saltspringvineyards.com

Bill and Jan Harkley – he is a former Air Canada pilot and she is an accountant and executive coach – opened this winery, which also offers bed and breakfast accommodation, in 2003. It is based on a 1.2-hectare vineyard planted on former orchard land to varieties that include Léon Millot, Pinot Gris, and Pinot Noir. Because the vineyard was only planted in 2001, the winery opened with wines made with grapes purchased in the Okanagan. This temporary measure became permanent after it found a particularly good Okanagan supplier of Merlot grapes. The flagship wines here include Oliver-grown Bin 537 Merlot, island-grown Pinot Gris, and an oak-aged port-style wine made from wild blackberries.

SATURNA ISLAND VINEYARDS *
8 Quarry Road, Saturna Island, BC, V0N 2Y0.
Tel: 250 539 5139; Website: www.saturnavineyards.com

When it opened in 1998, Saturna Island Vineyards was the first winery to be established on the Gulf Islands. Today, there are half a dozen island wineries and more are under development. It is possible to grow grapes and other fruits in this maritime climate because nearby mountains deflect the Pacific storms, leaving the islands hot and dry in summer. Saturna is the second largest of the the Gulf Islands.

The vineyard grew from a real estate development scheme. Between 1995 and 2000, twenty-four hectares of vines were planted, making it the largest of the island vineyards. Because only about 200 people live on Saturna throughout the year, the vineyard manager uses mechanical harvesting to deal with a perennial labour shortage. One of the most striking features of the island's geography is the majestic granite cliff. Facing southwest, the cliff retains the sun's heat and reflects it across the vines. The varieties grown here include Chardonnay, Gewürztraminer, Riesling, Muscat, Pinot Noir, Pinot Meunier, Merlot, and an experimental row of Cabernet Sauvignon. Nearly a quarter of the vineyard is planted to Pinot Gris.

Wine tourists arrive at this attractive winery with their own boats or with the ferry that serves the islands. Overnight visitors often stay at Saturna Island Lodge, a small inn on the other side of the island and also owned by Page. Through a curious quirk of British Columbia regulation, the lodge, which has a good wine list in its dining room, is prohibited from selling Saturna Island Vineyards wines.

ST URBAN WINERY (Range not tasted.)
47189 Bailey Road, Chilliwack, BC, V2R 4S8.
Tel: 604 858 7652.

In 2001, civil engineer Paul Kompauer and his wife, Kathy, took over a small neglected vineyard at the eastern end of the Fraser Valley. He has rehabilitated the vines, which included Ortega and Siegerrebe, and as well as planting Zweigelt, Pinot Noir, and Gamay Noir. Kompauer plans to open a winery in the future, naming it for the patron saint who is said to protect vines from frost in Slovakia. "I am a seventh-generation winemaker," he says. "I made my first wine when I was twelve or thirteen years old – independently. And it was drinkable, too."

THETIS ISLAND VINEYARDS **
90 Pilkey Point Road, Thetis Island, BC, V0R 2Y0.
Tel: 250 246 2258; Website: www.cedar-beach.com

Heavily forested Thetis Island, with a population of 300, seems an unlikely site for a vineyard and winery. However, it is a charming island and that is what drew Colin and Carola Sparkes. He is British, she is German, and they met in Heidelberg while working at a German software company. They came to Canada to pursue adventure tourism. The winery opened in 2004, based on a 1.6-hectare vineyard. The varieties include Pinot Noir, Pinot Gris, Gewürztraminer, Chardonnay, Agria, and Merlot, chosen for the most part with an eye to the cool island terroir. Sparkes has one of only two plantings of Pinotage in British Columbia.

VENTURI-SCHULZE VINEYARDS *****
4235 Trans Canada Highway, RR 1, Cobble Hill, BC, V0R 1L0.
Tel: 250 743 5630; Website: www.venturischulze.com

Some of Vancouver Island's best wines, and certainly the most individual, come from Venturi-Schulze Vineyards. There is a a crisp and fragrant white called Millefiori ("thousand flowers") made by fermenting Ortega and Siegerrebe together. The winery's best-selling white, it is one of several wines whose proprietary names (Brandenburg No 3, Primavera, Mille Miglia) underline the thoroughly original wine-growing at this gem among Canadian boutique wineries.

Giordano Venturi and Marilyn Schulze opened the business in 1993 and built a new winery in 1999. Venturi was born in 1941 near Modena, the centre of balsamic vinegar production in Italy. He came to Canada as a teenager and became an electronics teacher, but remained true to his heritage, so that today the winery is also known for its excellent balsamic vinegar. Venturi makes about 2,000 bottles each year using traditional methods. When Venturi-Schulze gives tours (only by appointment), the fragrant vinegary is a highlight.

Schulze, also a former teacher, is an Australian-born microbiologist. She shares Venturi's commendable fanaticism about growing top quality grapes in their 6.5-hectare vineyard. This was one of the first on Vancouver Island to undertake extensive tenting of the vines each spring. By accelerating the plants' development, they are able to produce dark, full-bodied Pinot Noir, which sells for more than any other British Columbia Pinot. It is becoming the flagship. However, Venturi treats all of his wines, including the well-regarded sparkling wines, as flagships and conducts tastings with theatrical passion. Almost all Venturi-Schulze wines are released in bottles sealed with crown caps, assuring that no cork-tainted wines leave the winery.

VICTORIA ESTATE WINERY ***
1445 Benvenuto Avenue, Box 160, Brentwood Bay, BC, V8M 1R3.
Tel: 250 652 2671; Website: www.victoriaestatewinery.com
Vancouver Island's largest winery, Victoria Estate opened in 2003 in a location near several established tourist destinations. The winery, with its restaurant, expansive tasting room, and excellent tour programme, has become a destination itself. Financed by private investors, it was conceived by financial consultant Fraser Smith. The former owner of a hobby vineyard nearby, Smith has been a driving force in encouraging vineyards on Vancouver Island. Victoria Estate's substantial demand for grapes is creating a market for burgeoning vineyards.

However, Victoria Estate has relied on Okanagan grapes and initially released a plethora of ordinary wines, reflecting the grapes it could buy. In 2004, the new winemaker, California-trained Ken Winchester (*see* below), imposed discipline on an improved portfolio. The flagship red varietal is Merlot, including a reserve that Winchester describes as "unapologetically full-bodied". The whites include Chardonnay, Sauvignon Blanc, Pinot Gris, and Ortega. The estate vineyard has Kerner, Schönburger, Gewürztraminer, Pinot Noir, and Dunkelfelder, a German teinturier.

VIGNETI ZANATTA WINERY AND VINEYARDS ***
5039 Marshall Road, RR 3, Duncan, BC, V9L 6S3.
Tel: 250 748 2338; Website: www.zanatta.ca

The twelve-hectare vineyard at Zanatta, with some vines planted twenty years ago, is the largest on Vancouver Island. It is also one of the most important, for it was here that government-sponsored viticulture trials took place in the early 1980s. The vineyard was started by Italian-born Dennis Zanatta. The main varieties are Ortega, Auxerrois, Pinot Gris, Pinot Noir, Madeleine Sylvaner, and Cayuga; but there also are small plantings of about thirty other varieties. Before the family opened the winery in 1992, Loretta, one of Zanatta's daughters, completed her winemaking training in Italy, specializing in sparkling wines, which now account for about a third of the winery's production. The best-selling example is the winery's Glenora Fantasia Brut. A fruity, even exotic, wine, it is made with Cayuga grapes, a hybrid developed in New York in 1945 and only grown in British Columbia by Zanatta. The other bubblies include Fatima Brut 1994 (Cayuga and Pinot Gris), Allegria Brut Rosé (Pinot Noir and Auxerrois), and Taglio Rosso (Cabernet Sauvignon and Castel).[2]

WINCHESTER CELLARS ***
6170 Old West Saanich Road, Victoria, BC, V8V 1NZ.
Tel: 250 544 8218; Website: www.winchestercellars.com

Born in New York in 1952, Ken Winchester started making wine at home in 1980, not long before he set up a publishing house in Montréal. In 1993 he took a job as editorial director of a Californian magazine, though his real reason for moving to the West Coast was to take winemaking courses at the University of California, Davis. By 1996, he had a vineyard in the Paso Robles district and began releasing wines three years later. In 2002 Winchester returned to Canada, this time to Victoria. His sabbatical from winemaking lasted only a year: he began making Pinot Noir and Pinot Gris in 2003 for Winchester Cellars, opening the boutique winery the following year. He also is the winemaker for Victoria Estate Winery (*see* above).

2. Castel 19637 is a late-ripening red French hybrid with good sugar levels but with high acidity. It also is planted in Nova Scotia and in some UK vineyards.

16

Québec

It would be hard to find *vignerons* more challenged and courageous than those of Québec. Most of the vineyards are found at latitudes between 45 and 47 North, in regions without the moderating influences of the large lakes that enable vineyards in Ontario and British Columbia to get through winter. In Québec, winter temperatures can frequently reach −30°C (−22°F), occasionally even lower. *Vitis vinifera* vines do not tolerate temperatures much below −20°C (−4°F); as a result, few Québec vineyards grow vinifera. The vintners have had to create an industry

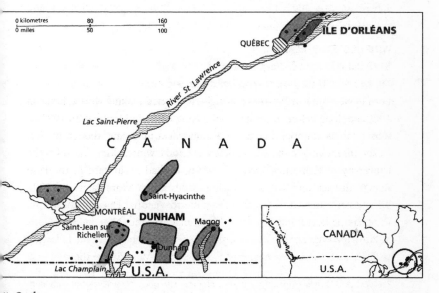

ii. *Québec*

based either on hybrid vines seldom in fashion elsewhere in Canada, or on the winter-hardy Minnesota hybrids that are unfamiliar to consumers. Controversially, Pierre Rousseau, co-owner of Le Moulin du Petit Pré near Québec City, says: "We don't have the pretension that there is great wine in Québec. There is interesting wine."

Wine tourism is just being developed in Québec, and the wineries as yet have only a miniscule share of the market. In a market that prefers red wines to whites, the best wines of Québec are invariably white. "Why don't we concentrate on making crisp, clean whites?" asks Michael Marler, who makes one of Québec's rare Chardonnays at Les Pervenches. "The whites we make are of a more international standard. The reds are tourist wines." Ripening grapes to reduce excessive acidity requires lower yields than is the norm in vineyards elsewhere. "In France the yield might be four bottles of wine per vine," says Jacqueline Dubé, one of the owners of Vignobles Les Blancs Coteaux. "Here, the yield is one bottle to a vine. We have to work very hard – it's a passion."

Most of the three dozen operating wineries are small and of tenuous viability. "Making wine in Québec is a little bit crazy," says artist-turned-winemaker Irénée Belley. During one brutal winter at his Vignoble de la Sablière, he lost half the vines, having forgotten to cover them with a protective blanket of earth. The failure rate or the ownership turnover among under-financed wineries is comparatively high for a small industry. "One year, you will make money," says Gilles Benoit of Vignoble des Pins, "the next year, you will be living off your wife's salary. Here, you need passionate people, people who are willing to go where others have never gone." Against the odds, individuals continue to develop vineyards and wineries. The industry participants forecast that the number of operating wineries will double by the end of this decade.

The majority of Québec's wineries are located an hour or two by car south or east of Montréal, although three wineries operate near Oka, on Montréal's north shore, forty minutes from the city centre. A string of wineries is beaded loosely along the Richelieu River, east of Montréal. The greatest cluster is around the village of Dunham, in the heart of what is known as the Eastern Townships. The vineyard-based wineries began in 1980 with the development of two vineyards close to each other, just outside Dunham. In both cases, the proponents were French immigrants who had grown up amid vineyards. This rural corner of Québec, now an emerging wine route, was once an enclave of English-speaking farmers who came from New England after the American War of Independence. Today, the first language of the region's bilingual inhabitants is French, but the wine towns retain their historic names: Brigham, Bedford, Cowansville, Farnham, and so on.

Remarkably, there are five wineries north of Québec City, and they are among the most northerly wineries in Canada. However, there is a history of vine-growing here. The French explorer Jacques Cartier landed in 1535 on a large island in the St Lawrence north of what is now Québec City and found wild vines. He proposed calling it Île de Bacchus until the need arose to curry the favour of his royal sponsors. The island was called Île d'Orléans. The original name has been revived for the winery – one of two on the island – that Donald Bouchard, a retired Québec government lawyer, established in 1988.

The grape wineries are only part of the picture. A dozen wineries have arisen making products with fermented honey, for example. Cider producers can also be found throughout the province; farm ciders, made by unlicensed producers for home consumption and for informal sale, have a long history in Québec. When the province began to license and tax cideries in 1971, nearly all small producers shut down. Even though ciders could be sold in corner grocery stores, farm producers could not compete with the large beer companies, nor with the provincial liquor monopoly's offerings of cheap imported wines. Cider producers began reappearing in the 1990s, succeeding now in a market that is more interested in quality artisanal products (craft beers and farm cheeses are other examples) than was the case in the 1970s. Many cideries remain small, making cider only for local sale. A handful have emerged internationally with remarkable ice ciders, made by fermenting apple juice that has been concentrated by freezing. Domaine Pinnacle and La Face Cachée de la Pomme, both south of Dunham near the Vermont border, are leading ice cider producers.

SACRAMENTAL BEGINNINGS

The existence of wild grapes has frequently been cited to give a dubious antiquity to the Québec wine industry. There are, after all, numerous references to winemaking in the seventeenth-century writings of the Jesuits. It seems the mission fathers, needing a supply of sacramental wine, fermented the native grapes when the supply from France ran out.

Father Lejeune also wrote that a few of his colleagues made some wine "*par curiosité*". Without vineyards, a wine culture could not develop in the colony of New France. Historian Craig Heron writes:

> *In the early years of French settlement, the habitants of New France, like the French peasantry, could not afford alcohol every day. Indeed, when the Swedish botanist Peter Kalm visited the colony in 1749 he noted that most settlers could not afford wine.*[1]

A decade later, the British took over the colony, severing the links to France and closing to door to French wine traditions. Along with other Canadians of the day, Quebeckers consumed beer, homemade cider, and distilled products and became adept at their production. Heron recounts that, in 1868, thirty illegal stills were seized in Montréal alone.

According to information gathered by Vignoble de l'Orpailleur, one of Québec's modern wineries, sporadic vineyard trials in the province were conducted between 1860 and 1880 before the winters ended the plantings. It is not clear why; one of the proponents was a French count who had more success with subsequent plantings near Toronto. A familiar pattern emerges, however: it is usually someone from France who launches new efforts in viticulture. In 1935, French biologist Georges Masson began testing vines at Oka, where he was teaching in the agriculture school. He explained:

> *The reason for importing grapevines to Oka was pure curiosity. Vineyards were then almost non-existent in the province of Québec.* [The total, according to one report, was two hectares.] *Since French hybrids had been doing very well in the cold region of Lorraine in France, I wondered whether they would survive in Canada. My father sent me about six cuttings – three Baco Noir and three De Chaunac – which we planted on the south slope of a gully.*

The vines did well; however, Masson wrote later:

> *Since the experiment was interrupted by my departure from the school six years later, one cannot predict what would have happened over a longer period of time.*[2]

1. Heron, Craig, *Booze: A Distilled History*, Between the Lines, Toronto, 2003, p. 30.

2. Correspondence with author, May 10, 1983. The grape referred to as De Chaunac was only named in 1972 and previously bore the breeder's name and number, Seibel 9549.

Masson retired to the Niagara Peninsula where he grew grapes and wrote wine books. At the time of Masson's Oka experiment, the only winery in Québec had been opened in 1935 by TG Bright of Niagara Falls to blend and store Ontario-made fortified wines.

THE FIRST WINERIES

It was primarily Italians who launched the small postwar boom of Québec wineries, usually starting with the importation of California grapes for home winemakers. The first one was Vincent Geloso. An immigrant from Naples, he started importing California grapes for home winemakers in 1961. Five years later, he got the province's first licence for making wine. An innovative man, he tried to import fresh Italian wine grapes in refrigerated shipboard containers; when that proved impractical, he switched to muted must, dosed with sulphur to prevent fermentation during transport. At the winery, the sulphur was vaporized by heating the juice, which was then fermented. All this handling, however, did not make for good wines. In 1970, Geloso helped sponsor a viticulture trial at Macdonald College in suburban Montréal. Neither the Italian vinifera vines nor the French hybrids planted by the college flourished on what was a very cool site. About the same time, a winery called Les Vignobles Chantecler supported a trial planting near Rougemont, before running into financial troubles.

The wineries of the 1970s, however, were anomalies. By the end of the decade, eleven had been licensed, none of them with vineyards. Often, they were the creations of public policy. First, the Québec and federal governments began offering industrial development grants. In a typical example, Calona Wines from British Columbia received $275,000 in government grants to build a million-gallon winery at St-Hyacinthe. (A money-loser, it was sold a few years later to a competitor.) Second, the provincial government allowed these wineries to sell some of their wines through the vast network of corner grocers. These wines were generally mediocre since wineries were required to ferment seventy per cent of the product in Québec, and were limited to poor raw materials. A few, such as Les Entreprises Verdi which made Kosher wines, imported fresh grapes but most did not.

The wines improved after 1978, when wineries were allowed to bring in bulk wine and bottle it in Québec. This is what the province's own liquor retailer had been doing for years. North America's first state liquor retailing monopoly, the Société des Alcools du Québec (SAQ), became one of the largest wine buyers in the world. It continues to operate a large bottling plant. However, nearly all of the 1970-era wineries have either closed or been merged into a handful of large commercial producers, like Vincor International, that bottle generic brands.

GETTING TO GRIPS WITH GRAPES

One of those wineries did try to grow grapes. Les Vignobles du Québec was established at Hemmingford in 1974. The driving force was Michael Croix, a French wine-grower who believed that *Vitis vinifera* grapes could succeed. On a 1.2-hectare site, he planted Chardonnay, Gamay, Cabernet Sauvignon, and De Chaunac. He was fortunate to have several mild winters in a row, harvesting enough fruit to make a modest quantity of wine. The next two winters, however, wiped out the vines. The winery was taken over a Toronto grape importer and Croix quit.

By this time, there were enough small vineyards in Quebec for the growers to form L'Association des Viticulteurs du Québec in 1979. There was also encouragement from professionals. In 1947, at Laval University in Québec City, a geneticist named J O Vandal began making vine crosses; he is said to have tested 12,000 crosses before he died in the late 1980s. His research was disbursed to several quarters and some of it was carried on by Mario Cliche at a provincial government agriculture station near St-Hyacinthe. The one important variety to emerge from that work, so far at least, is an extremely winter-hardy white called Vandal-Cliche, now grown increasingly in Québec's more northern vineyards.

The foundation for modern wine-growing in Québec was laid by two individuals from the south of France. Christian Barthomeuf, who had arrived as a tourist in 1974, began planting vines five years later on a hillside a short drive west of Dunham. This vineyard now supports the Domaine des Côtes d'Ardoise winery. Charles-Henri de Coussergues, another tourist who settled in Canada, began with several partners to plant a large vineyard just down the road in 1982, the base today for Vignoble de l'Orpailleur.

These individuals identified several varieties that would mature in the Québec terroir, but notably Seyval Blanc. It was an inspired choice, taking growers beyond the dead-end of vinifera. Today, Seyval Blanc is the workhorse white of Québec wine-growing – to the point where some growers think too much is grown. Barthomeuf also tried several vinifera, including Pinot Noir, Chardonnay, Auxerrois, and Gamay; only Gamay remains at Côtes d'Ardoise.

These two early wineries succeeded because the owners figured out how to deal with Québec's severe, vine-killing winters. Burying the vines with earth is the most widely practised method. Using custom-designed ploughs, workers push earth from the middle of each row around the base of the vines, depositing a protective blanket at least two feet thick. This is done in late October or early November, sometimes requiring a powerful tractor if the vineyard has become soggy with late-season rains. Early the following May, the vines are uncovered, allowing them to grow again. Vine burial is laborious and may be impossible in vineyards which are stony or terraced. Consequently, several growers cover the vines with heavy fabric or even straw and hope for an additional protective blanket of snow.

In recent years, vineyards in which vine burial is impractical or not desired have begun to plant extremely winter-hardy vines that survive without being covered. Vandal's plant breeding was directed to this end. As well, he recommended the hybrids that were emerging from a Wisconsin plant breeder named Elmer Swenson, whose work is now being carried on at the University of Minnesota. Swenson, who died in 2004 aged ninety, was a self-taught horticulturalist who began crossing grape varieties in 1943 on his farm in Osceola, Wisconsin. There and at a University of Minnesota research farm where he worked for a decade, Swenson (and a few colleagues) generated many new varieties.

The merits of several are being proven in Québec, where there are extensive plantings of red varieties such as Frontenac, Sainte-Croix, and Sabrevois, and white varieties such as Éona, St Pepin, Kay Gray, and Louise Swenson. Also widely planted now is the Québec-developed white, Vandal-Cliche. Many other varieties, often still bearing only the breeder's number, are also being tested, perhaps more widely in Québec than anywhere else in North America. Whether the wineries of Québec can win a significant piece of their own wine market with these varieties remains to be proven. The wines are promising and they are certainly better and more interesting than the Québec wines of the 1970s. "I think we can make honest wines," says Guy Tardif of Les Clos Saint-Denis winery.

17

Wineries of Québec

VIGNOBLE ANGELL (Range not tasted.)
134 Rang St-Georges, St-Bernard-de-Lacolle, QC, JOJ 1V0.
Tel: 450 246 4219
One of the earliest winery owners to test viticulture in Québec, Jean-Guy Angell planted 200 vines in 1978. He learned that his location, south of Montréal and close to the US border, actually has one of the longest growing seasons in the province, long enough even to plant vinifera vines. Today, there are more than 34,000 vines growing here. Grape varieties include Vidal, Seyval Blanc, Chardonnay, De Chaunac, Merlot, and Pinot Noir. The winery opened in 1985, with the owner's son, Guy, as the winemaker.

VIGNOBLE ARTISANS DU TERROIR (Range not tasted.)
1150 Rang de la Montagne, St-Paul-d'Abbotsford, QC, JOE 1A0.
Tel: 450 379 5353; Website: www.vignerons-du-quebec.com
South of Montréal, near Mount Yamaska, Céline and Réjean Guertin, along with daughter Annie and son David, have developed a substantial family-owned fruit and wine enterprise. The couple started with 20,000 apple trees, subsequently adding a remarkable array of fruits and berries to the property. Annie and David both followed their father's footsteps, studying horticulture and food sciences at the technical institute in St-Hyacinthe.

Since 1997, four hectares of vines have been planted here, with the first wines made in 1999. "Viticulture is hard work but it is another beautiful challenge," Céline told a local journalist after a few years experience with the vineyard. The wines are sold in a farm shop, along with preserves and fruit syrups. The grape varieties include the familiar winter-hardy varieties: Seyval Blanc, Cayuga, Kuhlmann, Maréchal Foch, and Chancellor.

VIGNOBLE DE LA BAUGE ★★★★
155 Rue des Érables, Brigham, QC, J2K 4E1.
Tel: 450 266 2149; Website: www.labauge.com

In the 2002 vintage, winemaker Simon Naud created an apéritif by infusing white wine with lemon and orange peels. The result, whimsically called Folies du Vigneron ("Winemaker's Madness"), is rather like sipping a tangy Scottish marmalade. Its popularity in the tasting room has Naud determined to produce a "surprise of the year" regularly.

The object is to lure wine tourists. The Naud family has become good at attracting customers to the farm, about an hour's drive east of Montréal, since planting grapes in 1987. Naud's father, Alcide, acquired the 142-hectare farm in 1951, keeping a herd of dairy cattle until he retired in 1984. Three years later, the owners of a Dunham winery rented what Naud calls "a good hill" on the farm and planted about 5,000 Seyval Blanc vines. The Nauds took over the vineyard the following year and, when the vines bore fruit, retained a consultant to make wines in the former dairy barn.

Naud took over the winemaking in 1997 after four years of being mentored. In addition to making wine, he carries on an active programme of evaluating new grape varieties for Québec. Early experiments in the five-hectare vineyard included trials with Bacchus and Ortega. The varieties ripened early, as they should, but like so many vinifera, they were not productive after being buried over winter. "The buds rotted under the soil," Naud explains. The vineyard now has both French and Minnesota hybrids, including Sabrevois, Sainte-Croix and Prairie Star. The flagship red wine, Les Patriarches, is made with Chancellor.

Naud is conducting trials with vines from various breeders, including Switzerland's Valentin Blattner. The vineyard at La Bauge can easily be expanded as wine sales grow. With his "surprise of the year" philosophy, Naud has his eyes open for interesting new varieties. "I don't want to plant more Seyval Blanc," he says, referring to Québec's most widely-grown white. Even so, the variety serves him well. Naud singles out his lightly oak-aged Seyval Blanc, a crisply refreshing wine called Solitaire, as one of his best.

VIGNOBLE LES BLANCS COTEAUX **

1046 Bruce, Route 202, Dunham, QC, J0E 1M0.

Tel: 450 295 3503; Website: www.vignoblelesblancscoteaux.com

This winery is described as a retirement project by the Dubé family – two sisters and two brothers – who now own it. Some retirement. The vineyard covers eleven hectares, grows about 24,000 vines, and planting is not complete. That involves a great deal of work. Jacqueline Dubé, a former nurse who now makes the wines (with a consultant), has learned that "taking care of a vine is like taking care of people".

Begun in 1986 in a former orchard, this is one of the earlier vineyards in the Dunham area. The winery was launched in 1989 by Pierre Genesse and Marie Claude Lysotte, a young couple who decided to sell in 2002 to concentrate on their other careers and their children. The Dubé clan, after a lifetime in city jobs, wanted to retire to farming. "We were not ready to sit in a rocking chair," Claire Dubé explains. "We still have lots of energy." They took over a well-equipped and well-scrubbed winery that is only a few years old. The primary grapes in the vineyard are Seyval Blanc, Frontenac, and Sabrevois. Red grapes are also purchased. In order to raise red wine production, recent plantings have been mostly Frontenac. The flagship oak-aged red is La Vieille Grange.

There are still apple orchards in the area. The winery's name, in fact, was inspired because in springtime the hillsides are white with apple blossom. The winery's products include a brandy-fortified ice apple beverage, made in the winter with frozen apples.

VIGNOBLE BOURG ROYAL (Range not tasted.)

1910 Rue des Érables, Charlesbourg, QC, G2L 1R8.

Tel: 418 681 9119; Website: www.vignoblebourgroyal.com

Real estate developers very nearly snapped up this vineyard several years ago when, as a bankrupt former cooperative winery, it lay in neglect. The property is in a suburb of Québec City, surrounded by houses and shopping malls. It was revived after being acquired by Cidrerie de la Capitale, a cider company operated by Jorj Radu, a Romanian-born oenologist. The grateful neighbours even proposed changing the name of the street to "rue des Vignobles".

The vineyard dates from 1980. It was developed by a group of keen amateurs with the help of Gilles Rondeau, an assistant to the Laval

University grape breeder, J O Vandal. Many of Vandal's experimental crossings remain under trial in this vineyard. Naturally, the vines grown here include one hectare of Vandal-Cliche, the best wine grape so far to emerge from Vandal's work (see page 220).

Radu and his partners have restored the once-desolate vineyard and Bourg Royal resumed making a range of table wines that include an award-winning rosé. Radu not only folded his ciders into Bourg Royal's product range; he added a sparkling cranberry wine and a claimed world first, an ice cranberry wine. He called it L'Âme de Dracula.

Winemaking in climate-challenged Québec has had its surprises for him. "In Romania, it is possible to make twenty bottles from a single vine," he says. Now, he is pleased if each vine gives him four bottles. "It is necessary to love the vine, to caress it, to speak to it," he adds.

VIGNOBLE CAPPABIANCA (Range not tasted.)
586 St-Jean-Baptiste, Mercier, QC, J6R 2A7.
Tel: 450 691 1515; Email: paulal@sympatico.ca

Italian-born winemaker Francesco Lapenna's family has a long history of wine-growing in Italy. The winery is based on a 3.2-hectare vineyard very near Montréal. Lapenna began planting vines in 1993. Varieties grown include Seyval Blanc, Maréchal Foch, Kuhlmann, Seyval Noir, and Pinot Noir. The winery has been open since 2002 and produces more white wine than red. Lapenna also makes Icewine.

VIGNOBLE CARONE (Range not tasted.)
75 Roy Street, Lanoraie, QC, J0K 1E0.
Tel: 514 240 4220/514 630 4146; Website: www.canadavintage.com

Wine enthusiast Anthony Carone began planting his vineyard in 1999 at Lanoraie, on the north shore of the St Lawrence forty kilometres (twenty-five miles) northeast of Montréal. He started with 300 vines in a test plot and has been expanding carefully, based on results. He has discovered that snowfall is so abundant each winter that burying vines is not required. Two hectares are now planted, with another six available. The winery is projected to open in 2005, and will start with a red table wine:

Lanoraie, our medium-bodied red, is produced from a field blend of Cabernet Severnyi, Frontenac, and Landot. It is full of dark, ripe, black-fruit flavours with lots of smoky oak, liquorice, and vanilla.

Carone shares his viticulture experience freely, even posting comments on the internet, such as: "Frontenac, developed at the University of Minnesota to be winter hardy to –35°C (–31°F), ripens by the middle of September, but needs to be fully ripe before its teeth-rattling acidity declines." One of Carone's favourites is Geisenheim 311, a white variety bred to mimic Riesling, but with greater winter hardiness. Carone has found that good snow cover is adequate protection. "I like this plant very much," he wrote in one of his reports. He also is a supporter of Vandal-Cliche, more winter-hardy than Geisenheim and an excellent white variety. On the other hand, Sainte-Croix, a red grown widely in Québec, is "overrated", in his opinion.

VIGNOBLE LE CEP D'ARGENT ***
1257 Chemin de la Rivière, Magog, QC, J1X 3W5.
Tel: 819 864 4441; Website: www.cepdargent.com

Denis Drouin, the president of Le Cep d'Argent, can speak of the sacrifices that go into building a winery. During the first three years after he and the other five original partners planted vines in 1985, they also grew vegetables to cover their costs. Most of the partners had jobs fifteen minutes away, in Sherbrooke. When the vegetables were ready, they left home at 5am to pick up the produce and deliver it to a wholesale grocer before going to their day jobs. "We worked eighteen- and twenty-hour days," remembers Drouin. "It was worth it." He once had an ultimatum from his former wife: it was her or the vineyard. "I chose the vineyard," Drouin admits. "There is a thirty-six-hole golf course next door to the winery but, in more than twenty years here, I have never had the time to play," he adds.

The group that started Le Cep d'Argent, now one of Québec's larger wineries with a production of about 120,000 bottles a year, jumped into grape-growing only a few years after the first Dunham vineyards had been planted. Their property, a former beef farm, is on a gentle, southwest slope beside Lac Magog, which extends the vineyard's ripening period and which, because of the low temperatures of its water in spring, retards vine growth until the risk of major frost is over. Early in the vineyard's development, Drouin was standing on the slope as the setting sun created a silver sheen on the lake. That inspired the winery name: silver vines. The location is a popular tour stop and, with a large dining pavilion, the winery caters to as many as 50,000 tourists a year. Drouin believes the winery can double its sales by the end of the current decade.

There are now about forty-five hectares of vineyard. The first variety planted, and still the major one, was Seyval Blanc. It remains the backbone of the wines. There are two Seyval Blanc table wines – one with oak ageing, one without – and a third late-harvest wine in which a little Seyval Blanc is blended with Geisenheim. It is the variety that French winemaker Jean-Pierre Bonville, who comes from Champagne, uses for a traditional bottled-fermented wine, La Sélection des Mousquetaires. Seyval Blanc is used to make Mistral, a fortified apéritif; and it is also used for Fleur de Lys, a light apéritif blended with blackcurrant juice. That creative winemaking also extends to the reds in the portfolio. One of the winery's most singular products, L'Archer, is a brandy-fortified dessert wine flavoured with maple syrup.

The sparkling wine has the ability to age. The other wines, Drouin suggests, should be consumed within a few years of being released because wines from hybrid gapes do not age like vinifera wines. "We don't pretend to produce long-keeping wine," he says. "We have honest wines that are very good." The influence of Champagne in this winery began in 1991 when some of Drouin's original partners sold their interests to two brothers from the French wine region. Today, the vineyard manager as well as the winemaker at Le Cep d'Argent have been trained in Champagne. Drouin, who was born in Ontario in 1944, is content to deal with the winery's substantial business affairs. "I can still grow grapes, but I can't make wine," he admits. "My mother always made some at home. I tried, but I didn't like the result."

VIGNOBLE LES CHANTS DE VIGNES **
459 Chemin de la Rivière, Canton de Magog, QC, J0E 1M0.
Tel: 819 847 8467

Original partners in Le Cep d'Argent (see above), Marc Daniel and his father Jacques established a smaller winery down the road after selling their interest. According to Marc, Le Cep had become too large. The Les Chants de Vignes vineyard, at four hectares, is a tenth the size. Marc, who was born in Sherbrooke in 1963, works the vineyard with his father, makes the wine, and even cooks for the winery's catered dinners. "I'm in charge of flavours and aromas here," he laughs. "I do the wine and I do the cooking.'

The vineyard was begun in 1996, and planted primarily with Seyval Blanc. Subsequent plantings have focused on winter-hardy varieties, including Sainte-Croix and Vandal-Cliche, that need not be buried during the winter. Marc complains that it is a "pain in the butt" to clear the earth from the vines each spring. However, it is a chore to which he has had to reconcile himself. In 2004, Les Chants de Vignes acquired the vineyard of an unsuccessful Dunham winery, Les Arpents de Neige. The vineyard, which is the same size as that at Les Chants, is planted to varieties that must be covered each autumn, including Ortega, Cayuga, and Maréchal Foch.

Les Chants made an impression on the wine world with its first vintage in 1997, winning a silver medal in a national competition for an apéritif wine called L'Opéra. It was made by fortifying the juice from two old Geisenheim 318 vines, an inspired winemaking trick to compensate for the immaturity of the fruit that year. Now this is one of the signature wines. Picking up on the winery name, every one of the eight wines has a musical name including Le Kyrie, Le Boléro, and Le Jazz.

VIGNOBLE CHAPELLE STE AGNES ****
2565 Chemin Scenic, Sutton, QC, J0E 2K0.
Tel: 450 538 0303; Website: www.vindeglace.com

There is no vineyard in Québec with a setting more beautiful than Chapelle Ste Agnès. The vineyard straddles the aptly-named Chemin Scenic, which winds through the low, forested mountains of southern Québec, just north of the Vermont border. The 7,000 vines have been planted on eighteen terraces, in a south-facing amphitheatre with a 30 degree slope. The winery and the cellars have been dug thirteen metres (forty-two feet) into the bedrock, with a tunnel connecting the winery to the vineyard.

Chapelle Ste Agnès is the creation of a devout Montréal antique dealer, Henrietta Antony. The private chapel, only large enough for two dozen people, honours a saint from her own birthplace in what is today the Czech Republic. It is furnished with religious items collected by Antony, including doors that once hung at the Hospices de Dieu in Beaune. Interior columns are from an Italian abbey ruined by wartime bombs.

The vineyard was planted in 1997 under the direction of Christian Barthomeuf, formerly the founder of Domaine des Côtes d'Ardoise, and now consulting winemaker at several properties. The vines are packed closely on a painstakingly prepared site; rock for the terraces came from the neighbourhood's abandoned stone fences. Tons of gravel were laid along the terraces, creating excellent soil for the vines. The vineyard, now managed by John Antony, the owner's son, is planted primarily with Vidal, and with some Riesling, Muscat Ottonel, and Gewürztraminer. The most recent plantings have been winter-hardy Geisenheim 322, which Antony believes is the "better" of the Geisenheim white hybrids. This is a comparatively warm vineyard where grapes ripen well because the exposure catches the sun and the rocks retain the heat. The geometry of the vineyard makes it impossible to cover the vines with earth for winter protection. Instead, a heavy piece of fabric is wrapped around the base of each vine. The vines get additional protection from the same abundant snow cover that covers nearby ski hills in Vermont.

With Barthomeuf as the consulting winemaker, Chapelle Ste Agnès made its first vintage in 2001. The winery produces one white table wine but the focus is sweet wine. The 2001 wines, released two years later, were a late-harvest wine from Geisenheim, Icewine, and *vin de paille* (from air-dried grapes) from Vidal. In the 2002 vintage, the winery also began making Gewürztraminer Icewine. More recently, Barthomeuf has produced ice cider, one of his specialties.

VIGNOBLE DU CLOS BAILLIE (Range not tasted.)
490 Baillie, Gatineau (Aylmer) QC, J9J 3R5.
Tel: 819 827 3220; Website: www.quebecvino.com

This tiny vineyard, now with about 3,100 vines, is in the Gatineau Hills, close to Ottawa. The vineyard is named after a Scottish family that once lived on the land. Owner Raymond Huneault began planting in 1998, on a south-facing slope ending at a six-hectare lake formed when an old quarry flooded. He credits his ability to grow wine grapes to this lake, along with the exposure of the site, the protection of the Gatineau Hills to the north and the heat radiating from Ottawa. The vines are those that survive winter in Québec vineyards without being buried: Vandal-Cliche, Sainte-Croix, Seyval, Swenson, Frontenac, and Sabrevois. In 2001 Huneault planted a second small vineyard near Montebello. As well, he rents another nearby vineyard from a friend. The winery is scheduled to open in September 2005. The wines are being made by an experienced vintner, Jean-Marc Major, who also has a vineyard in suburban Ottawa called Le Domaine des Chouettes.

VIGNOBLE CLOS DE LA MONTAGNE ***

330 De la Montagne, Mont-Saint-Grégoire, QC, J0J 1K0.

Tel: 450 358 4868; Website: www.closdelamontagne.com

Rare among Québec wineries, Clos de la Montagne, which produces about 20,000 bottles a year in total, makes twice as much red wine as white. Owner Aristide Pigeon and his consulting winemaker, Jean Paul Martin, set out to raise the bar in 2004 with the release of a robust De Chaunac red that had been aged in oak for three years. At $18 a bottle, it is one of the top-priced Québec reds. "That's a fair price," Pigeon insists. "Maybe next year, it should be $20."

Robust winemaking mirrors Pigeon's personality. A keen boat racer for many years, he has now bought touring motorcycles, and with son Yannick looking after the winery, he has set off on bike tours that span half the continent. In 2004, he and his wife wheeled off to California. "I am sixty-six," he says. "The only thing I want from now on is time to travel."

Both wines and ciders are made at Clos de la Montagne. The vineyard, with 11,000 vines, is planted primarily to French hybrids, notably De Chaunac, Maréchal Foch, Kuhlmann, and Chancellor. Vidal, for Icewine, has replaced Minnesota hybrid red grapes, which Pigeon pulled out because, in his view, the resulting wines are too acidic. Unlike many neighbouring growers, Pigeon does not cover the vines with earth for winter protection. He has found that a straw covering is effective and easier to handle (it attracts mice but poison keeps them in check). Pigeon also propagates vines for other growers, imports barrels for a number of Québec wineries and raises llamas. Indeed, he even ran a stained-glass studio in the winery's baronial tasting room until closing it in 2002. "You can't do everything," he sighs.

VIGNOBLE CLOS SAINT-DENIS ***

1150 Chemin des Patriotes, Saint-Denis-sur-Richelieu, QC, J0H 1K0.

Tel: 450 787 3766; Website: www.clos-saint-denis.qc.ca

Guy Tardif, born in Montréal in 1935, is a man of many successful careers: he was in the Royal Canadian Mounted Police, then a university professor until he was elected to the National Assembly in 1976, becoming a minister in René Lévesque's sovereignist[1] government.

1. The sovereignist politicians seek to convert Québec from a province of Canada into an independent nation.

Out of office, Tardif bought a farm overlooking the Richelieu River, as well as a cornfield and abandoned, century-old farm buildings across the road. "We were not farmers," he says. "We lived in Montréal." François, one of his sons, had become an agrologist, specializing in fruit, and the farm was to be where he would practice his profession after volunteering in Africa for several years. A meeting with plant breeder Mario Cliche triggered the decision in 1990 to plant vines, starting with 200 from Cliche's vineyard. Today, the 7.5-hectare vineyard grows Vandal-Cliche, Québec's indigenous white variety. Ever the nationalist, Tardif labels the wine Vin de Mon Pays. The other two varieties are Éona and Sainte-Croix. Like Vandal-Cliche, they are hardy and need not be buried in winter. Cuttings from Tardif's vineyard have helped develop two nearby vineyards.

In 1997 Clos Saint-Denis created one of Québec's first ice ciders. Called Pomme de Glace, it accounts for seventy-five per cent of the winery's sales and many of its gold medals in competition.

VIGNOBLE DOMAINE DE L'ARDENNAIS **
158 Ridge, Standbridge East, QC, J0J 2H0.
Tel: 450 248 0597; Website: www.vignobledelardennais.com

The vineyard, now with 15,500 vines over 4.5 hectares, was planted initially in 1994 by François Samray. He sold the winery in 2002 but has continued to provide winemaking counsel to the new owner, Gary Skinner. Most of the vines are French hybrids, with a significant number of reds to satisfy rising consumer taste. The winery also produces a number of popular fruit wines, using concentrates from France. These are as bold in name as in style: the fortified raspberry wine is La Flamboyante.

VIGNOBLE DOMAINE DES COTES D'ARDOISE *****
879 Rue Bruce, (Route 202), Dunham, QC, J0E 1M0.
Tel: 450 295 2020; Website: www.cotesdardoise.com

By his own admission, Christian Barthomeuf was considered "the town crazy" in 1980 when he planted the first 2,300 vines in this vineyard and organized the first wine festival in nearby Dunham. Barthomeuf has since moved on to consult for other Québec wine and cider producers but Côtes d'Ardoise remains one of the best Québec estate wineries.

Barthomeuf had become convinced that viticulture in Québec was feasible, providing that the vines were covered with earth during winter. That conclusion was confirmed for him in the spring of 1981 when he discovered that De Chaunac, Seyval Blanc, and Maréchal Foch had survived. He planted more Seyval Blanc and organized Dunham's second wine festival. Late that year, one of the founding partners of Vignoble de l'Orpailleur spent a few weeks poring over Barthomeuf's experience and then decided to launch the area's second vineyard.

Barthomeuf had shrewdly located one of Québec's best sites for grapes. Weather monitoring since the winery opened shows that these vineyards get as many degree days as Niagara and average about 180 frost-free days a year. By 1983, about 40,000 vines had been planted near Dunham. Today, the 7.5-hectare vineyard at Côtes d'Ardoise alone contains more than 30,000 vines. The theme of Dunham's third wine festival in the fall of 1982 was "wine capital of Québec".

The first vintage at Domaine Côtes d'Ardoise, in 1982, yielded all of thirty-eight bottles of wine. But with this miniscule production and the enthusiasm of Barthomeuf and his friends, the modern Quebec wine industry was on its way. Barthomeuf's initial wines, sold without a licence, were early-drinking "nouveau" style wines. This provided not only quick cash but also early notice in the wine press. In 1984 the winery got a licence and its finances improved when it was acquired by Jacques Papillon, a successful Montréal plastic surgeon.

As well as planting hybrid grapes, Barthomeuf put in many trial plots of vinifera, fully expecting that one day he would release premium-priced noble varietals. But the only vinifera with which the winery has had prolonged success is Gamay. The grapes are blended with Maréchal Foch to make an oak-aged red called Côtes d'Ardoise. At $16 a bottle in the province's liquor retailer, it is one of the top-priced reds made in Québec and, in the view of many critics, it is the province's best red wine. Today, half of the winery's annual production, which ranges from 15,000 to 25,000 bottles a year, is red.

The other vinifera of significance here is Riesling, used for both table wine and, along with Vidal, for Icewine. The winery attempted Icewine early in the 1990s. However, systematic production began in 1998 when Vera Klokocka and John Fletcher, winemakers from British Columbia, were retained to make the wines. They found that making Icewine in Québec required a different approach. The problem was that the vines had to be buried for the winter before it froze hard enough for Icewine. Their solution involved picking grapes just before the vines were buried, and storing the fruit on trays until it was cold enough to freeze them naturally. Since 2001, when Fletcher and Klokocka returned to British Columbia, the winemaker at Côtes d'Ardoise has been David Cottineaux, a young French-trained oenologist. He is broadening the range, which now includes crisply fresh whites, an excellent dry rosé, and even a pair of light fortified dessert wines.

VIGNOBLE DOMAINE DU RIDGE (Range not tasted.)
205 Chemin Ridge, Saint-Armand, QC, J0J 1T0.

Tel: 450 248 3987

Opened in 1999, Domaine du Ridge takes its name from the prominent ridge that runs through this area. The vineyard produces 20,000 bottles a year, many of which are sold through the winery's wine boutique.

DOMAINE FELIBRE *
740 Chemin Bean, Stanstead, QC, J0B 3E0.

Tel: 819 876 7900; Website: www.domainefelibre.com

Catherine Hébert sums up the remoteness of this site when she says: "We are the last winery in Québec." Domaine Félibre is tucked away in the quiet countryside of southeastern Québec, far off the wine route. Hébert and her winemaking husband, Gilles Desjardins, both Montréalers, bought this 100 hectare farm in 1991 because they wanted a quiet rural life. The decision to make wine came the next year when they planted two hectares of Éona, a winter-hardy Minnesota hybrid. Desjardins complains that it is hard to make a wine that does not show some of Éona's labrusca roots; but somehow he succeeds. The wine, labelled Cru des Vallons, is a crisp and fresh white that has earned awards for the winery. With a good deal more land available, Desjardins now intends to plant a red variety.

Fruit wines make up the majority of Domaine Félibre's production. From its own orchard, purchased apples, and local wild apples, the winery makes hard cider,[2] fruit-flavoured cider coolers, and an ice cider. The latter, called Givré ("covered in frost"), is made with apples picked and pressed after a big frost. The juice is further concentrated by being frozen naturally a second time before being fermented, producing a tart dessert wine. Hébert says that five kilograms (eleven pounds) of apples are required to produce each 375 millilitre bottle of Givré, a wine that has

2. Hard cider is alcoholic cider, as differentiated from soft, or non-alcoholic cider.

made it onto wine lists in Paris. Using wild cherries, Desjardins has created Vice Caché, a richly fruity liqueur, marinating the cherries in alcohol with the pits to extract an almond flavour. Currently, he is making trial lots of wine from maple syrup.

VIGNOBLE DOMAINE DE L'ILE RONDE (Range not tasted.)
Île Ronde, St-Sulpice, QC, J5W 4L9.
Tel: 514 609 7223; Website: www.domainedelileronde.com

When a 1995 planting of 100 vines thrived, Jocelyn Lafortune increased the vineyard cautiously for several years and then made the big plunge in 1999, planting 20,000 vines. He added another 10,000 Sainte-Croix vines in 2001. Currently, the vineyard is eight hectares in size, about eighty per cent planted to red varieties. In addition to Sainte-Croix, these include Maréchal Foch, Kuhlmann, Sabrevois, and De Chaunac. The whites are Vandal-Cliche and New York Muscat. Lafortune began producing wines in 2000. Typically, the winery releases proprietary blends rather than varietally-named wines.

DOMAINE LEDUC-PIEDIMONTE (Range not tasted.)
30 Chemin de Marieville, Rougemont, QC, J0L 1M0.
Tel: 450 469 1469; Website: www.leduc-piedimonte.com

This focused winery with its own vineyard on the south slope of Mont St-Hilaire has chosen to specialize in dry white wine made from Pinot Gris and a red blend of Maréchal Foch and Frontenac. With a large apple orchard, it also recently added ice cider and sparkling apple cider to its range. Proprietor Robert McKeown lets his customers sponsor vines – even one single vine. When the vines are producing, sponsors will collect, at no charge for ten years, a bottle for each vine sponsored. In the longer term, his "Friends of the Vineyard" also qualify for discounted wine purchases.

VIGNOBLE LE DOMAINE ROYARNOIS ***
146 Chemin du Cap-Tourmente, Saint-Joachim, QC, G0A 3X0.
Tel: 418 827 4465; Website: www.royarnois.com

Forty kilometres (twenty-five miles) north of Québec City, Le Domaine Royarnois is able to call itself the "northernmost vineyard in North America". The vineyard is an extension of owner Roland Harnois' hobby of planting trees. He has planted thousands of trees during the past forty years. Recently, he began plantations of oaks from which he hopes that his grandchildren might be able to make wine barrels. Born in 1927 at Trois-Rivières, friendly, silver-haired Harnois is a mechanical engineer who built many of Québec's largest industrial plants. Retiring in 1990, he bought a former 273-hectare dairy farm both for trees and for his new hobby, a vineyard.

Harnois needed a few years to figure out how to keep his vines alive when he first planted in 1992. During the first two years, most vines died during winter, even though he grows the extremely hardy Vandal-Cliche. Winter survival in this twelve-hectare vineyard improved substantially after grass was grown between the rows to retain the region's abundant snowfalls. Harnois and his wife Camille Roy now have 15,000 vines. The land slopes gently with a southeastern exposure toward the moderating influence of the St Lawrence River. This region long served as the garden of Québec City.

The white wines made since the first vintage in 1996 are invariably crisp and fresh. In addition to Vandal-Cliche, Harnois grows Sainte-Croix; "a very good grape". "I wish we had planted more," he adds. He has had less success with Frontenac, another Minnesota red hybrid, but he has trial plots of four Minnesota hybrids that have yet to be named.

VIGNOBLE ISLE DE BACCHUS **
1071 Chemin Royal, Saint-Pierre, Île d'Orléans, QC, G0A 4E0.
Tel: 418 828 9562; Website: www.isledebacchus.com

North of Québec City, the Île d'Orléans splits the St Lawrence, a location which gives the island, with its population of 7,000, a comparatively Mediterranean climate. The explorer Jacques Cartier found native vines growing here in 1535 and referred to it as the island of Bacchus. The name now lives on in this winery, opened in 1988 by retired lawyer Donald Bouchard and based on the vineyard he planted in 1982.

The flagship white among the 16,000 bottles made each year is called Le 1535. The vines grow on a terraced slope with a southwestern exposure towards the river. On his island vineyard, now expanded to three hectares, Bouchard grows primarily white varieties (Vandal-Cliche, Éona, and Geisenheim), but he has been expanding the vineyard's reds (Maréchal Foch, Sainte-Croix, and Michurinetz) to respond to growing demand for reds.

VIGNOBLE DE LAVOIE POITEVIN **

311 Route 112, Rougemont, QC, JOL 1M0.

Tel: 450 469 3894; Website: www.de-lavoie.com

The vineyard, now about five hectares in size, has been developed since 1996 on a plain on the south side of Rougemont mountain. Robert Poitevin, one of the partners, is an architect, and designed the winery which opened in 2000. It is set in the middle of the vineyard, not far from the foot of the mountain. Co-owner Francis Lavoie believes this is one of the best microclimates for grapes in Québec. The red varieties include Maréchal Foch, Baco Noir, Kuhlmann, and De Chaunac, producing two dry blends, Rouge Mont Rouge and La Tourelle. The major white varieties are Seyval Blanc, Cayuga, and Geisenheim. Located in the heart of Québec's apple production region, the winery also makes several ciders, including an ice cider.

VIGNOBLE DU MARATHONIEN ****

318 Route 202, Havelock, QC, J0S 2C0.

Tel: 450 826 0522; Website: www.marathonien.qc.ca

Previously a keen home winemaker, electrical engineer Jean Joly bought this apple orchard with his father-in-law in 1989 and added the vineyard in the following year for a home-grown source of grapes. The property is an hour's drive south of Montréal, an easy weekend commute for this pair who, like so many small Québec vintners, support their passion for wine with jobs in the city. They stay on top of their 6,000 vines by being energetic weekend farmers and by having a resident vineyard manager through the summer. They open the wine shop in the front porch of their rustic, metal-clad farm house. Except for some restaurant sales, Joly sells his entire annual production – about 7,000 bottles of table wine and 1,500 half bottles of Icewine – from the winery.

The primary varieties grown here are Seyval Blanc, Cayuga, Geisenheim 318, Vidal, Maréchal Foch, and De Chaunac. Joly has two small plots of Merlot and Cabernet Franc, nurtured through Québec's hard winters, like the rest of the vineyard, by covering the vines with earth each fall. Vinifera buds, however, do not survive as well when buried as do buds on hybrid vines. He keeps the Merlot and Cabernet just to show it can be done, turning the grapes into a quaffable fruity summer wine. Joly also buys red grapes from nearby vineyards.

The "jewel of the house" is the Icewine that Joly has made since 1994. In the 2003 harvest, the Vidal grapes for Icewine were picked at −20°C (−4°F). Joly has devised a clever way to reconcile leaving grapes exposed for Icewine while burying the canes needed for next year's grapes. The vines are trained with fruit-bearing canes on both upper and lower wires. In autumn, the canes on the upper wires are netted to protect the grapes from birds. After the leaves fall and just before the lower canes are buried, the bunches are picked and tucked into netting above to await the Icewine freeze. As a result, all the grapes are naturally frozen. While the exposed parts of the vines are often killed during winter, the next year's production comes from the live canes uncovered the following spring. "It is the only way to have a good quantity of Icewine," Joly says.

VIGNOBLE LA MISSION ***
1044 Pierre Laporte (Route 241), Brigham, QC, J2K 4R3.
Tel: 450 263 1524; Website: www.vignoble-lamission.com
Built in a style vaguely recalling Mexico's Spanish-style missions, this winery is owned by Alejandro Guerrero, who was born in Mexico City in 1960, and his Québec-born wife Marie-Josée Clusiau. Guerrero, who has a master's degree in civil engineering and worked with provincial electrical utility Hydro-Québec, had long wanted to farm. In 1997 they bought a twenty-hectare former beef farm. Guerrero immediately planted 250 vines to get the feel of growing grapes. In 1998, finding he liked viticulture, he planted another 5,000. Since then, he has added about 2,000 more vines each year, bringing the vineyard to three hectares.

The major variety in the vineyard is Vidal for Icewine. With the help of consulting winemakers, he also produces red and white table wines and a port-style fortified. He believes that the majority of tourists visiting Québec wineries still are casual wine drinkers that find sweet wines appealing. He plans to add more red table wines, but at a cautious pace.

VIGNOBLE MOROU ***
238 Route 221, Napierville, QC, J0J 1L0.
Tel: 450 245 7569; Website: www3.sympatico.ca/morou/
Yvon Roy recalls his first crush as the new owner of Vignoble Morou in 2003 with tangible excitement. "It was quite an experience, to see the movement in the fermenting juice and the power." He had been a home winemaker since his student days at the University of Sherbrooke, when

he started with raisins. But it was the real thing to work alongside Morou founder Étienne Héroux, who had agreed to mentor him. An accountant and former department store marketing executive, Roy decided to retire to the country and chose a winery for a good reason. "It is prestigious to be a vineyard owner. We are highly respected."

Morou is a tiny winery with about 6,000 vines and a house that is 250 years old. Héroux had started the vineyard in 1987 and opened the winery four years later. From eighteen varieties in the early plantings, the vineyard has come to focus on such winter-hardy vines as Seyval Blanc, Vidal, Cayuga, Geisenheim, Maréchal Foch, De Chaunac, and Chancellor. Gamay makes up the largest vinifera planting and may also be the most difficult variety to grow, Roy has discovered. He has maintained the tight focus that Héroux established by making only five wines – three whites, one red wine and Le Rose de Vents, an attractive rosé made from Gamay.

VIGNOBLE LE MOULIN DU PETIT PRE ***
707 Avenue Royale, Château-Richer, QC, G0A 1N0.
Tel: 418 824 4411/418.824.7007; Website: www.moulin-petitpre.com

This young winery north of Québec City, operates within North America's oldest commercial flour mill. Built in 1695, Le Moulin du Petit Pré has now been restored as a functioning mill after a tumultuous history in which it was twice razed by fire. During its recent history, the mill was owned by the Québec government who converted it to office space. That is why today a modern elevator links the main floor to the winery cellar.

In 1995, a partnership headed by beekeeper turned winemaker Pierre Rousseau purchased the mill from the government. Rousseau was a biochemist and had learned winemaking from one of his professors, making several honey wines. When he and his partners considered how to turn the flour mill into a tourist attraction, winemaking was a logical step. Since 1997, 4.5 hectares of vines have been planted on a hillside above the mill. The partners also planted several berry plots, including Saskatoon berries, blackberries, and currants.[3] "To think of planting grapes here in 1996 was crazy," Rousseau admits. Since both the vines and the berries flourished, Le Moulin now offers grape and fruit wines, with raspberry

---

3. The Saskatoon berry (*Amelanchier alnifolia*) is a shrub belonging to the rose family (*Rosaceae*). The fruit, resembling a small blueberry, is also called Juneberry, serviceberry or shadbush. The name Saskatoon is restricted mostly to western Canada, where the berry grows in wild abundance.

liqueur being one of its most popular. The locally-developed Vandal-Cliche grape is the major variety. Rousseau is assessing about eighty trial varieties at Le Moulin, hoping to find a successful red. He is not convinced that the red hybrids from Minnesota, grown elsewhere in Québec, are suitable this far north. "Minnesota is a little warmer than here," he notes.

VIGNOBLE DES NEGONDOS (Range not tasted.)

7100 Rang Saint-Vincent, Saint-Benoît de Mirabel, QC, J7N 3N1.

Tel: 450 437 9621

One of Quebec's first organic vineyards, Négondos was developed from rough waste land from which vast quantities of rocks were first removed, leaving behind three hectares of well-drained slopes with good exposure. Owners Carole Desrochers and Mario Plante planted all the hybrids common to Québec. The first vintage was 1996.

VIGNOBLE LE NORDET (Range not tasted.)

991 Chemin des Îles, Pintendre, Lévis, QC, G6C 1B5.

Tel: 418 833 7183

Proprietor Carl Bourget began planting vines in 1997 and made wine from his first harvest two years later. The varieties in the vineyard include the hardy vines capable of surviving winter this far north: Delisle, Prairie Star, St-Pépin, Sabrevois, and Sainte-Croix. Bourget offers both red and white table wines, along with a white apéritif, Icewine, and ice cider.

VIGNOBLE DE L'ORPAILLEUR *****

1086 Rue Bruce (Route 202), Dunham, QC, J0E 1M0.

Tel: 450 295 2763; Website: www.orpailleur.ca

Of Québec's first five vineyard-based wineries licensed in 1985, l'Orpailleur is the only one still run by the original owners. The nearby Domaine des Côtes d'Ardoise changed ownership and the other three failed. Now a solid success, l'Orpailleur – the name means "gold seeker" – did not become profitable until 1996. "I wouldn't have come to Québec if growing wine here was easy," says Charles-Henri de Coussergues, a French oenologist and one of the original partners.

A native of Avignon, de Coussergues was enticed to plant a vineyard near Dunham in 1982 by his friend, Hervé Durand, another oenologist from the south of France. They enlisted two other partners: lawyer Pierre Rodrique and Montréal entertainment agent Frank Furtado. Of the four, de Coussergues has the day-to-day management of the winery. Durand now also manages his family's château in France. De Coussergues remains a leading figure in Quebec wine-growing, having been a founder of several industry associations.

Arguably, the Dunham area, with its light soils and abundant slopes with southern or western exposures, is the best vineyard terroir in Québec. But it gets the same hard winters as the rest of the province. De Coussergues and Durand are credited with perfecting the technique – *buttage*, hilling an insulating layer of earth around the base of the vines in late October – for winter protection of vines. The exposed parts of the vines are usually killed by frost but the protected fruiting canes survive and are uncovered the following May. Québec *vignerons* cannot relax, however, until the unquestionable arrival of summer. On June 2 1986, l'Orpailleur lost most of its crop when a late spring frost killed the buds. Since then, de Coussergues has deployed oil-burning heaters around the vineyard and has saved at least three crops.

This has become one of the largest vineyards in the province, with about 65,000 vines on its gently rolling thirteen hectares. It also buys grapes from six other vineyards, and operates a modern winery staffed by some of the best-trained professionals in Québec. Since 2002, the winemaker has been Mathilde Morel, a young oenology graduate from Montpellier who previously worked at wineries in Australia and China. The marketing is as savvy as the winemaking: the winery attracts tourists with a restaurant and a wine museum as well as with a product range extending from sparkling wine to *vin de glace*, or Icewine. The winery began making Icewine with Vidal in 1997 and the owners believe Québec Icewines have a strong future.

Seyval Blanc was one of the first varieties planted here and it still dominates the vineyard. It is used to make a variety of styles from a fruity light white through to an oak-aged version, a late-harvest, a fortified white port-style, and a classically-made sparkling wine. One of the more unusual is La Part des Anges ("the angels' share"), first made in 1993. It is made with the ripest Seyval Blanc, fortified with eau-de-vie and then aged for six years in oak barrels and glass demijohns exposed to the sun. As much as thirty per cent of the volume evaporates before it is bottled. The result is a complex, golden wine tasting richly of caramel, nuts, and butter.

Continually experimenting, l'Orpailleur has done trials with more than sixty grape varieties. One objective has been identifying suitable reds; currently, it is assessing varieties from eastern Europe. Initially, the partners figured that the Québec terroir was best for white wines. Since then, the winery has had considerable success with Maréchal Foch and other red hybrids, and recently has added Sainte-Croix, a Minnesota hybrid. The winery's red, a blend of Foch, Chancellor, De Chaunac, and Seyval Noir, was first produced in 1998.

VIGNOBLE LES PERVENCHES *****
150 Chemin Boulais, Farnham, QC, J2P 2P9.
Tel: 450 293 8311; Website: www.lespervenches.com

This winery is Québec's only producer of Chardonnay. Yves Monachon, who started planting this two-hectare vineyard in 1991, imported Chardonnay vines the following year from his native France. Michael Marler, who bought the winery in 2000 just as wine sales commenced, now has about half a hectare of painstakingly-nurtured Chardonnay. The vines are brought through the winter, along with the others in the vineyard, by having the fruiting canes covered with earth. Where other wine-growers have given up on vinifera varieties, Marler has mastered techniques for sustaining them.

Marler was born in Montréal in 1972 and with farming in his blood, he studied agriculture at community college, then at McGill, and finally as an exchange student in France, where most of the courses involved wine-growing. "A winery is much more interesting than a conventional farm," Marler believes. "A conventional farm is about reducing your costs until you make a profit. Here, you make a profit by making better wine and selling it for more." His barrel-fermented Chardonnay makes the point. Approaching $20 a bottle, it is one of Québec's most expensive table wines, and one of the best.

Marler extends the limited quantity of Chardonnay in the vineyard with Chardonnay grapes purchased in Ontario (all Quebec wineries are allowed to use up to fifteen per cent Ontario fruit in their wines). Then he blends the result with an equal quantity of Seyval Blanc, a chameleon variety that takes on the character of Chardonnay. Both varieties appear on the label. Marler's restaurant clients – most of the wines are sold directly to restaurants – also press him to make a 100 per cent Chardonnay.

Les Pervenches currently offers only two other wines. Its other white is made primarily with Seyval Blanc, in a fresh and fruity style that distinguishes it from the oaked Chardonnay. A small quantity of red is made with Maréchal Foch and is sold as Cuvée de Montmollin. A wine from Baco Noir is under development. This tiny winery produces only 10,000 bottles a year but that is a full-time job for Marler. He has no immediate plan to expand quickly, in part because grape-growing is risky in Québec and in part because he enjoys hands-on agriculture. "It is my dream lifestyle," he says. "Even in the winter, I dream about walking up and down the vineyard rows."

VIGNOBLE DES PINS *****
136 Grand Sabrevois, Sabrevois, QC, J0J 2G0.
Tel: 450 347 1073

Gilles Benoit is one of Québec's most idealistic and uncompromising wine growers. Since 1986, he has replanted his Richelieu Valley vineyard approximately three times, continually replacing varieties that have not made it through winter, or varieties not in tune with his winemaking philosophy. He has pulled out Seyval Blanc, one of his first plantings and a proven workhorse of Quebec vineyards, saying: "I felt uninspired making the wine. It lacked personality. I am not a bland person and my wines should have more personality." He prefers to use Cayuga.

Benoit, who owns the winery with his wife Laurie, was born in Montréal in 1958 and grew up on the military bases in Europe to which his father was posted. "That's where I got the wine bug," he says. He obtained a degree in wildlife management and became a quality control technician in a laboratory, acquiring skills that have served him well in his modest winery. A desire for a country home led to the purchase of this small farm. "The vineyard came later," he says. Benoit juggled a full-time job with his vineyard for many years before dedicating himself entirely to the winery with an annual production of between 200 and 1,000 cases.

Benoit has been more willing than most to test the new varietals, many of which were released under just the plant breeder's number, hardly suitable for wine labels. With one of those numbered red varieties, Benoit several years ago made a wine so good that the breeding committee called the vine Sabrevois after the village down the road from his vineyard. The variety has been picked up by a number of other growers. Currently, he is evaluating two Minnesota white hybrids, Prairie Star and Louise Swenson. The challenge of the Minnesota hybrids, he believes, is producing good wines with grapes that are sometimes (not always) high in acid and low in sugar. Benoit often uses carbonic maceration to bring out the fruitiness, yeast strains that reduce acidity, and artful blending. The best white here, Pin Blanc, is a fragrant, lime-flavoured Cayuga fermented at a cool temperature and left on the lees all winter.

Benoit continues to test various vinifera vines as well. He manages to bring Zweigelt and Cabernet Franc, about 1,000 vines in total, through winter, incorporating them in blends. Lemberger, however, was pulled out when the vines went into decline at only three years. "Like many vineyard owners, we are on a mission to see what can be done," he says. "For us, it has to be more than a money-making operation."

VIGNOBLE DE LA RIVIERE DU CHENE (Range not tasted.)
807, Rivière Nord, St-Eustache, QC, J7R 4K3.
Tel: 450 491 3997; Website: www.vignobledelarivièreduchene.qc.ca

Vignoble de la Rivière du Chêne was opened in 2000 by Daniel Lalande and Isabelle Gonthier, and now has an eight-hectare vineyard planted to a wide range of winter-hardy varieties. For its white wines, the winery employs Vandal-Cliche, St-Pépin, Key-Grey, and Geisenheim. The varieties for reds include Maréchal Foch, Lucie Kuhlmann, Seyval Noir, Sabrevois, De Chaunac, Frontenac, Baco Noir and Sainte-Croix. The winery also makes late-harvest wines and Icewine with Vidal grapes. Lalande grew up on a Québec farm that produces maple syrup and has carried some of that heritage into the winery, producing several maple-flavoured wines including l'Adélard, which has a white wine base, and fortified L'Éraportéros.

VIGNOBLE LA ROCHE DES BRISES ****
2007 Rue Principale, St-Joseph-du-Lac, QC, J0N 1M0.
Tel: 450 472 2722; Website: www.rochedesbrises.com

Established in 1993, this was the first winery on Montréal's north shore. Before Jean-Pierre Bélisle and his wife, Gina Pratt, planted vines, they researched the weather records, discovering that the climate during the growing season can be warmer here than in the Eastern Townships, where most vineyards are situated. The explanation, Bélisle says, is the proximity of the city. "Montréal is a big furnace," he says. Two other wineries have opened in the region since La Roche des Brises. Only the high cost of land, Bélisle believes, has slowed the conversion of farms, mostly apple orchards, to vineyards.

Vigorous and forceful, Bélisle is the president of Les Vignerons du Québec, and is prodding the provincial government to provide financial support to the wine industry. A lawyer who was born in Montréal in 1948, he spent almost a decade as a Liberal member of the National Assembly, where he was deputy house leader until retiring from politics in 1994. By then, he and Pratt had purchased this farm and started to turn it into an country resort, with a restaurant, inn, spa, and winery.

"I learned my first lesson in grape-growing in 1993," Bélisle laughs. At the time the varieties planted included Gamay, Seyval Blanc, Vidal, and Maréchal Foch. For winter protection, he intended to plough earth around the lower parts of the vines. However, La Roche was named for the rocks in the vineyard which made hilling the vines impossible. Most of the unprotected vines, except for Foch, died that winter. Now, most of the 30,000 vines are the extremely hardy varieties that survive without being covered, including Sainte-Croix and Vandal-Cliche. Recently, Frontenac has been planted as well.

Bélisle takes his turn on the tractor but, with a busy law practice in the city, he leaves the winery to Jean-Paul Martin, a consulting winemaker for several Quebec wineries. Inside the winery, prominently displayed, is a strict protocol of operations. "It is taped on the wall and the employees know they have to follow it," Bélisle says. One example from this protocol: grapes are not to be picked unless the ripeness is at least twenty-two Brix. This helped the winery to make a remarkable Alsace-style Vendange Tardive white, fermented almost fully dry with fifteen degrees of alcohol in 2001.

La Roche, which also buys grapes from nearby vineyards, produces about 50,000 bottles a year, with planned vineyard expansions that will almost double production. That could be doubled again if Bélisle had the capital for a high-speed bottling line. One of his demands to the government is for grants that would help wineries such as his to upgrade their equipment. Unlike most Québec wineries, La Roche produces more red than white. One of its leading reds, Mariabriand, is a full-bodied blend of Maréchal Foch and Kuhlmann. Sainte-Croix is released as a varietal, a lively red with a tart edge. The winery produces two fortified dessert wines, a white and a red.

VIGNOBLE LE ROYER ST-PIERRE ****

182 Route 221, St-Cyprien de Napierville, QC, J0J 1L0.

Tel: 450 245 0208; Website: www.vignobleleroyer.com

After finishing college in 1972, Robert Le Royer, who was born in 1952, set out to see America and soon found himself in California, working at a winery. A few years after returning to Québec in 1976, he started testing vines at farm at Mirabel just north of Montréal, owned by his father-in-law. The more successful varieties were transplanted when Le Royer and his wife, wanting to live in the country, bought this twenty-four-hectare farm near Napierville on an impulse. Located in the Richelieu Valley southeast of Montréal, it is near five or six other wineries. This cluster suggested to Le Royer that this was a better place for vines than Mirabel. He now has seven hectares in production. He is also a professor with the recently-formed École de viticulture et de vinification du Québec.

Some varieties, like Maréchal Foch, have remained in his vineyard from the start. Gradually, however, Le Royer has shifted the varietal mix from French hybrids like Seyval Blanc and De Chaunac to the hardier Minnesota hybrids, such as Sainte-Croix, Frontenac, and Louise Swensen. He wants to reduce the need for burying the vines each autumn, a job that requires a powerful tractor, a big plough, and a tolerance for bad weather. "I have buried my vines during a snow storm," he says. He believes that Sainte-Croix can survive −30°C (−4°F) without having to be buried. The flagship wines are full-bodied, barrel-aged reds, notably Le Lambertois Carte Noire, a blend of Foch, Sainte-Croix, and Cabernet Franc aged for three years before its release. There is also a lively Beaujolais-like red, Givre Noir.

VIGNOBLE DE LA SABLIERE ***

1050 Chemin Dutch, Saint-Armand, QC, J0J 1T0.

Tel: 450 248 2634

Sometimes Irénée Belley of Vignoble de la Sablière can be found clad in paint-spattered trousers as he works in the stone barn that serves as winery and tasting room for Sablière. Born in the Gaspé in 1951, Belley is an artist and, for many years, a painter of sets for movies. He and his wife bought this farm in 1992, in the peaceful countryside of southern Québec, and then debated what to produce. Encouraged by a winemaking friend, they planted grapes, learned to make wine, and released his first wines a few years later.

About 10,000 vines grow in the organic vineyard, whose sandy soils prompted Belley to call his winery Sablière, or "sand box". His flagship wine is a crisp light white made from Seyval Blanc, with about 8.5 degrees of alcohol. The majority of the vineyard is dedicated to white varieties. Belley has small plantings of Maréchal Foch and Sainte-Croix. Most of the wines, about 5,000 bottles a year, are sold from the tasting room. Sablière's well-made rosé, Folichon, also sells through the province's liquor stores.

VIGNOBLE DE SAINTE-PETRONILLE (Range not tasted.)
1A Chemin du Bout de l'Île, Sainte-Pétronille, QC, G0A 4C0.
Tel: 418 828 9554; Website: www.vignobleorleans.com
In 1648, the first French settlement on Île d'Orléans was established at the southern end of the island, at what is now Sainte-Pétronille. It is renowned as one Québec's most beautiful villages, with views towards Québec City and the majestic Montmorency Falls. Sharing that view is this 4.5-hectare vineyard with 11,000 vines, planted in 1989, primarily with Vandal-Cliche and Sainte-Croix. Wine production began in 1992.

VIGNOBLE LES TROIS CLOCHERS **
341 Chemin Bruce (Route 202), Dunham, QC, J0E 1M0.
Tel: 450 295 2034
"The tractor," says Robert Brisebois as he dismounts from it, "is my vocation." A geologist who works for the provincial government, he gives his spare time to this vineyard and winery that he bought in 1997 with his schoolteacher wife Nadège Marion. The winery is perched on a hilltop overlooking the four hectares of vines, some planted as early as 1986. The winery began production in 1992 and was sold to Brisebois when the original owners dissolved their partnership. Born in Montréal in 1961, Brisebois had long been a home winemaker. "When I heard a vineyard was for sale, I just changed the scale," he says.

Brisebois has "been planting ever since" and the vineyard has doubled in size to 13,000 vines, with production of over 10,000 bottles a year. Wines include a dry Seyval Blanc, a fortified Seyval Blanc, and a blended red made from Maréchal Foch and Chancellor. In 2003, the winery made its first Icewine. "With that wine, we'll be at a financial turning point, if we don't have a bad year," says Brisebois. "The vines have to suffer to make good wine but I don't know why the *vigneron* has to suffer as much as his vines."

18

Atlantic Canada

The cornerstone for Atlantic Canada's wine industry was laid in 1972 when Roger Dial planted in Nova Scotia cuttings of a vine then known only as V.53261. It was a hardy white variety created in 1953 at the Horticultural Research Institute of Ontario. For subsequent trials, cuttings were sent to the federal government's research station at Kentville in Nova Scotia's Annapolis Valley. The station gave some to Dial, who was testing many varieties in a nearby vineyard. The vines, which did not do well in Ontario vineyards, flourished in the cooler climate of Nova Scotia. Dial made an attractive wine, with a crispness and freshness that recalled Sauvignon Blanc, and he recognized that it could be the leading white for Grand Pré, the winery that he established (with partners) in 1977 (*see* page 252). Obviously, the wine would not be a commercial success if released with the grape breeder's number on the label. So Dial christened the grape L'Acadie, the historic French name for Nova Scotia and New Brunswick. Today, L'Acadie (also called L'Acadie Blanc), the most successful wine grape ever developed in Canada, is grown more widely in Atlantic Canada than any other vine. Nearly every winery offers L'Acadie wine, both in Dial's original style and in barrel-aged versions that offer an alternative to Chardonnay, which seldom succeeds in Atlantic vineyards.

The research station at Kentville began grape trials almost as soon as it opened in 1913, primarily to assess table grapes for a region already growing tree fruits. It stopped testing vines when the scientist in charge, Dr. Donald Craig, retired in 1983. Atlantic Canada had no wine culture; in fact, it had a vigorous prohibitionist tradition. New Brunswick prohibited the sale of alcohol in 1855, successfully defending its Temperance Act all the way to the Privy Council in London. Prince Edward Island banned the sale

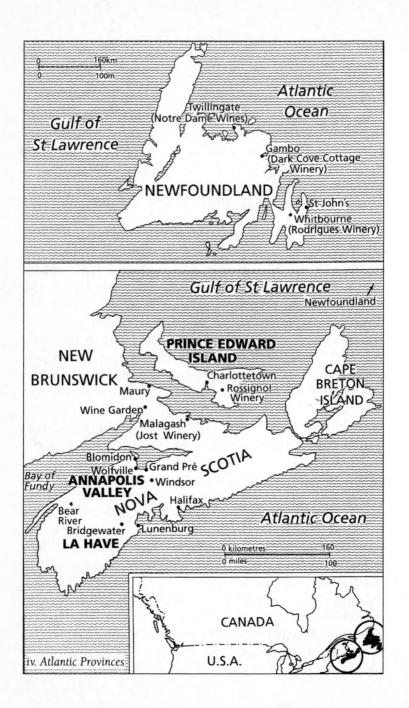

Atlantic
Ocean

Gulf of
St Lawrence

160km
100m

Twillingate
(Notre Dame Wines)

Gambo
(Dark Cove Cottage
Winery)

NEWFOUNDLAND

St John's

Whitbourne
(Rodrigues Winery)

Gulf of St Lawrence

Newfoundland

NEW
BRUNSWICK

PRINCE EDWARD
ISLAND

CAPE
BRETON
ISLAND

Charlottetown

Maury

Rossignol
Winery

Wine Garden

Malagash
(Jost Winery)

Blomidon

Wolfville

Grand Pré

SCOTIA

Bay of
Fundy

ANNAPOLIS
VALLEY

Windsor

Halifax

NOVA

Bear
River

Bridgewater

LA HAVE

Lunenburg

Atlantic Ocean

0 kilometres   160
0 miles   100

CANADA

U.S.A.

iv. Atlantic Provinces

of alcohol from 1901 to 1948. Remnants of that ban had to be expunged in 1993 so that John Rossignol could build the island province's first winery the following year. Even then, it took him a few more years to have the province remove a ban on exporting wine to the mainland.

The first commercial winery in the Atlantic region was a fruit winery, Chipman Wines. The winery started in the 1930s near Kentville to make a hard apple cider, sold under the Golden Glow brand. It was only a year or two before closing in 1983 that Chipman expanded into grape wines by bottling imported bulk wines. The Chipman brands were acquired by Ontario-headquartered Andrés Wines which, in 1965, had opened Abbey Wines in Truro, primarily to bottle wine imported from Ontario.

GRAND DESIGNS

Roger Dial arrived in Nova Scotia in 1969 to teach at Dalhousie University in Halifax. Born in California, he had financed his way through college while working for the Davis Bynum winery in Berkeley. Norman Morse, an economist at Dalhousie, had just begun to grow table grapes and a few wine grapes near Grand Pré, a hamlet in the Annapolis Valley about an hour's drive west of Halifax. After Dial made wine from the Morse grapes, the pair launched the Grand Pré winery, which began selling wine in 1980. The first red was made with Maréchal Foch, still a mainstay in many Atlantic vineyards. Dial had tested some of the vinifera vines he knew from California. However, most were too tender to make it through an Atlantic winter and needed a longer growing season. From Kentville's sister research station in British Columbia, Dial obtained cuttings of Russian vines, including Michurinetz and Severnyi, two winter-hardy varieties that produce rustic reds. Few vineyards now grow these varieties because growers, wineries, and consumers prefer the French hybrids, including Foch, Kuhlmann and, in particular, Léon Millot.

Twenty years ago, Dial created a sensation by making a robust Michurinetz at Grand Pré that he called Cuvée d'Amour. In a tasting of Canadian reds to be used in Canadian embassies, his 1983 vintage was selected as Canada's best red. Not all assessments were that generous. In 1984, Chablis producer Jean-Jacques Moreau visited Grand Pré. He made a face when he tasted a Michurinetz wine and a journalist in earshot quoted Moreau's devastating critique: "This is hostile to my tongue." It is not surprising that the wine has fallen from favour. It is almost black in colour, and coarse compared with vinifera reds. And the name is ill-suited to labels, as Dial had recognized from the start. Moreover, his winemaking style – robustly dry reds – was not in step with the Nova Scotia palate at that time.

The Grand Pré winery collapsed under its debt in 1987. (It was revived for a few years by a Halifax car leasing company and then closed again. It was put on its feet solidly as Domaine de Grand Pré in 1994 when Swiss banker Hanspeter Stutz bought it.) But by the time the Dial winery failed, viticulture had taken hold in Nova Scotia. Hans Wilhelm Jost, who had left behind a winery in Germany to take over a 280-hectare farm in the province, was in 1978 persuaded to plant a few vines. Within five years, the Jost family was back in the wine business. Suzanne Corkum, who had grown up in Oregon, planted grapes in 1979 and, with husband Doug, opened the Sainte-Famille winery in 1990.

The pace of new vineyards and new wineries has picked up. In 2004 Nova Scotia had six grape wineries and three fruit wineries operating; at least three other grape wineries were under development. Some predict that as many as twenty will be open by 2020. "We need more wineries and we need more acreage, to create the stability that is needed to create a true industry," says Hans Christian Jost, son of Hans Wilhelm, whose 40,000-case Jost Vineyards is now the largest winery in Atlantic Canada. "I see quite a few more small wineries coming along. But for this province to move ahead, it needs another winery of our size, or more."

Nova Scotia's momentum is now influencing developments elsewhere in the region, with one winery in Prince Edward Island, two and perhaps three in Newfoundland, at least five in New Brunswick and evidence of further interest, both in grape and in fruit wineries. The challenge is whether wine consumption will rise quickly enough to support the ambitious new vintners. The per capita consumption of wine in the Atlantic provinces is about two-thirds the national average for Canada. Naturally, the optimists see potential growth in such a ratio. "If I can just convert the rum drinkers to become wine drinkers," Jost says wistfully.

The vineyard area in production in Nova Scotia has risen from thirty-six hectares in 1994 to more than 100 hectares. Most of the vineyards are in the Annapolis Valley or in two contiguous valleys, the Gaspereau and the Avon. The defining feature is a very long ridge called North Mountain, which creates excellent south-facing slopes and shields the vines from cold northern winds. The tides in the nearby Bay of Fundy, the highest in the world, create vigorous air movements that reduce frost risks at the start and the end of a fairly short growing season. "The North Mountain ridge could easily supply all of Atlantic Canada with wine, several times over," says Jost.

Vines have been planted in many other areas of the province. At LaHave, south of Lunenburg, the maritime climate gives growers a season long enough to ripen Pinot Noir. One commercial four-hectare vineyard has been developed on Cape Breton Island by John Pratt, called "Johnny Grape" by his neighbours. This vineyard boasts one of the province's longest growing seasons because it is on a sheltered, south-facing slope above a large lake.

The original Jost vineyard is near the Nova Scotia coast along the Northumberland Strait, a shallow body of water that warms to swimming-pool tepidity by late summer, and acts as a heat sink to extend the growing season to late October. This is why Jost can grow grapes successfully on property that slopes slightly toward the north. Hans Christian Jost maintains that there is more potential vineyard land on the Northumberland coast than in Ontario's Niagara Peninsula (which, coincidentally, also slopes toward the north and is warmed by Lake Ontario). Clearly, Nova Scotia will not be held back by a lack of vineyard sites.

On the Prince Edward Island side of the strait, John Rossignol's south-facing vineyard, planted on a plateau high above the ocean, also benefits from the warm water. There is potential vineyard property about ten kilo-metres (six miles) inland from the Rossignol winery, on the former tobacco farms with the island's warmest microclimate. Vineyard development is held back only by the modest size of the local wine market in a province with only 140,000 people and a short, even if significant, tourist season.

In New Brunswick and Newfoundland, wineries, often making fruit wines, have become established only recently. There are, however, a number of individuals doing vine trials with wine production as the ultimate goal. One example is Glenda Baker of Gambo in Newfoundland, who intends to open the Dark Cove Cottage Winery in about 2006. In 2003 she planted about 200 vines, including Pinot Noir, and in 2004 she planted another 600, the majority again being Pinot Noir, with some Pinot Gris, Auxerrois, and Gewürztraminer. Baker also is testing a wide range of French and Minnesota hybrids.

19

Wineries of Atlantic Canada

L'ACADIE VINEYARDS (Range not tasted.)
310 Slayter Road, RR 1, Wolfville, NS, B4P 2R1
Tel: 902 542 3034; Website: www.lacadievineyards.ca
Winemaker Bruce Ewert is exploring the potential of the L'Acadie grape from this winery's five-hectare vineyard in the sunny Gaspereau Valley. When he opens the winery in 2008, he expects to offer sparkling wines, several styles of table wine, and perhaps even a L'Acadie Icewine. Ewert is a British Columbian (born in 1963 in Prince George), who has made wine at Sumac Ridge, Hawthorne Mountain Vineyards, and Summerhill, as well as in Australia. The desire to open a winery of his own in Nova Scotia arose when Andrés Wines, where he started his career in 1986, posted him for two years to its large winery in Truro, NS.

BEAR RIVER VINEYARDS (Range not tasted.)
133 Chute Road, Bear River, NS, B0S 1B0.
Tel: 902 467 4156; Website: www.bearrivervineyards.com
This may be Atlantic Canada's most picturesque vineyard. The vines cling to a south-facing incline. The pretty village of Bear River is in the valley bottom, its houses on stilts above the tides. The village is not far off the main Nova Scotia highway to the tourist destination of Annapolis Royal, yet it is quiet and somewhat remote. "It is at the nether end of nether," admits Christopher Hawes, who owns the 1.2-hectare vineyard and plans to open a winery, converting a sturdy old barn built into the side of a hill.

A lot of history attaches to Bear River. It is recorded that French colonists planted vines along the river in 1611, making this Nova Scotia's earliest vineyard site. Nothing much came of this planting; the next vineyard in the area was a test site established in 1963 by the Kentville Research Station. That site is approximately where Hawes grows grapes today. The varieties grown here include Pinot Noir, Chardonnay, Riesling, Seyval Blanc, Maréchal Foch, Baco Noir, and one of the white Geisenheim crosses. Hawes also has small plots of Auxerrois and Pinot Gris. As well as making his own wines, he has kept the area's home winemakers supplied with fresh grape juice. His property is large enough to triple the vineyard, should enough tourists leave the main highway to explore the charm of Bear River.

BLOMIDON ESTATE WINERY ***
10318 Highway 221, Canning, NS, B0P 1H0.
Tel: 902 582 7565; Website: creeksideestatewinery.com

Currently producing about 1,600 cases of wine a year from a winery with a lot more capacity, Blomidon Estate describes itself as "Canada's tidal winery". Its nine-hectare vineyard is on a slope undulating down almost to the shore of the Bay of Fundy's Minas Basin, renowned for the world's highest tides. Beginning in 1986, the property, which is across the basin from Wolfville, was planted primarily with the varieties then in vogue in Nova Scotia: L'Acadie, Seyval Blanc, and Michurinetz, along with a little Chardonnay. The grapes were sold to wineries until 1996, when the winery, initially called Habitant Vineyards, opened. The original name came from a neighbouring hamlet. The winery's current name is taken from the nearby ridge, an extension of North Mountain, that shields the vineyard from northerly winds.

The winery was launched by Peter Jensen and his wife, Laura McCain, who now also operate Creekside Estate Winery in Ontario (see page 53). Habitant started tentatively with low-priced bulk wines before refocusing on premium varietals. The wines include estate-grown Chardonnay, L'Acadie, and Baco Noir. The winery's L'Acadie, packed with fresh peach flavours, is one of Nova Scotia's best, and sells for more than the Chardonnay. Michurinetz has been removed from the vineyard while Seyval Blanc is retained for making off-dry white.

In 2004, a young Ontarian, Wes Lowery, took over as the winemaker and general manager. When he arrived to prune the vines, Lowery discovered some Pinot Noir growing in the vineyard as well. It has given him an idea for extending the modest range of wines. "The potential for making a sparkling wine is here," he says.

DARK COVE COTTAGE FARM AND WINERY (Range not tasted.)

220 JR Smallwood Boulevard, Gambo, NF, A0G 1T0.

Tel: 709 674 4545; Website: www.dccw.ca

Glenda Baker was born in Toronto, but spent many of her childhood summers in Newfoundland and became determined to live in what she calls "the greenest place I ever saw". That ambition was realized when her husband, John Bickerton, an officer (now retired) in the Royal Canadian Mounted Police, was posted to Newfoundland. During that tour of duty, the couple purchased a small farm at Gambo, a community on the province's northeastern coast, on the TransCanada Highway about forty kilometres southwest of Gander. Baker knew the original owners of her property and had even shopped in their little corner store, the building now destined to become a winery.

The farm had once produced cabbages and chickens but had gone wild, with stinging nettles growing in profusion. While researching for advice on how to deal with the nettles, she found a recipe for nettle wine on the internet and made some on a whim. "My wine actually was a success," she says. "Almost everyone who tried it loved it." This country wine, which she still makes each year, led Baker, a former nurse, into making fruit wines and red wines with concentrates. While looking for a source of fresh juice for home winemaking, she found information on cool climate grape varieties. She realized that grapes might actually grow in Gambo. The community, roughly at the same latitude as Paris, is at the end of a long fjord. The summers are warm; there are enough frost-free days to accommodate many vinifera vines and most hybrids. February temperatures are cold enough to kill vinifera, however a heavy blanket of snow – as much as three metres (nine feet) – is adequate insulation.

"The more research I did, the more it looked like this spot was ideal," Baker says. In 2003, about 200 vines were planted, including Pinot Noir. In 2004, another 600 were planted, the majority again being Pinot Noir, with some Pinot Gris, Auxerrois, and Gewürztraminer. She is also testing a wide range of French and Minnesota hybrid grape wines. "I have to see for myself what will and will not work here," she explains. Baker and Bickerton only have two hectares, but are already considering leasing nearby land for additional vineyards. They hope to have the winery completed in 2006. "It will be small to start with and we don't plan on getting too big. We aren't in a hurry and we are enjoying every minute of what we are doing."

DOMAINE DE GRAND PRE ****

11611 Highway 1, Grand Pré, NS, B0P 1M0.

Tel: 902 542 1753; Website: www.grandprewines.ns.ca

The land on which Domaine de Grand Pré is located was settled and dyked in the seventeenth century by the French, who gave the name of L'Acadie (Acadia) to Atlantic Canada. During the subsequent wars for North America, the British won Atlantic Canada. The Acadians declared themselves neutral but this was not good enough for the British who, from about 1750, deported 10,000 of them (some as far as the Falkland Islands), very nearly destroying the Acadian culture. This deportation is remembered with a national park and a memorial church built in the 1920s, near the Grand Pré winery.

The first Nova Scotia winery (*see* page 247), Grand Pré had slipped into financial distress for a second time when Hanspeter Stutz, a Swiss banker, bought it in 1994. He took another six years to reopen it but it was time well spent. Neglected vineyards were replanted. Jürg Stutz, the owner's son, who had also been working in a bank, returned to school, learning to grow grapes and make wine. The winery was renovated. Additional buildings, one of them a restaurant, went up in the serenely beautiful style of the original 1828 house. The winery overlooks the dyke-protected farmlands of Grand Pré. Under the management of the Stutz family, underperforming varieties were pulled out, including Pinot Noir, Chardonnay, Siegerrebe, and Ehrenfelser. At least twenty different varieties have been planted; in fact, the search for better ones never ends. The winery recently put in a trial planting of Cabernet Foch, a red hybrid from the stable of Swiss breeder Valentin Blattner.

The primary wine varieties at Grand Pré are Maréchal Foch and Léon Millot for red wines, New York Muscat and L'Acadie for whites, and Vidal and New York Muscat for Icewines. When the winery reopened in 2000, it was only able to offer a Foch table wine and Vidal Icewine, both from the 1999 vintage. As other vines began yielding fruit, production has climbed to about 6,000 cases a year. There is room to grow by a few more thousand cases, although the winery's current underground cellar already seems jammed to capacity. To use every available inch, the winery is equipped with square stainless steel tanks, custom-designed in Switzerland.

Like other winemakers in Atlantic Canada, Jürg Stutz describes L'Acadie as "the perfect grape" for the region – and perhaps particularly so for Grand

Pré, since the hybrid was christened by the winery's founder Roger Dial. The vine is winter-hardy, it has easily-managed upright growth, it resists the common plant diseases and it ripens early. At harvest, the grapes are sweet enough to yield wines with eleven to twelve degrees of alcohol, with crisp, but not excessive acidity. It has become the flagship variety at Grand Pré, where two styles are made – a moderately oak-aged white and a delicately fresh version aged only in stainless steel.

Perhaps the most versatile grape here is the New York Muscat, a white hybrid developed in New York State precisely for cool climates like Nova Scotia. Grand Pré's table wine displays exotic rose petal and spice aromas and flavours. The winery's New York Muscat Icewine – the grapes are from contract grower John Warner – is an extraordinary example, a barrel-fermented wine with a dramatic aroma and a core of intense, mango-flavoured fruit. Grand Pré's apple ciders should not be overlooked. The dry cider, slightly carbonated, is crisply refreshing. The winery's Pomme d'Or is an ice cider where the candied spice flavours of the apples is cleanly balanced with bracing acidity.

LA FERME MAURY – LES VINS DE L'ACADIE (Range not tasted.)
2021 Route 475, St-Édouard-de-Kent, NB, E4S 4W2.
Tel: 506 743 5347

Fewer than half a dozen red hybrids – including Baco Noir, Kuhlmann, and Maréchal Foch – grow on sixty-one hectares here. By 2004, the vineyard had 2,400 vines, with plans in place to add L'Acadie for white wine. Initially both the grape wines and fruit wines were vinified at Winegarden Estate Winery, a cooperative arrangement allowed by New Brunswick's enlightened liquor regulations (which enable wineries to open without huge investments). However, fermentation equipment was installed in 2004. The Maury range includes dry table wines but much of the annual production of 12,000 bottles consists of off-dry fruit wines.

GASPEREAU VINEYARDS **
2239 White Rock Road, Gaspereau, NS, B4P 2R1.
Tel: 902 542 1455; Website: www.nswine.ca

Only a few kilometres southeast of the Annapolis Valley community of Wolfville, the Gaspereau River defines an attractive valley with a number of sun-bathed vineyards on southern slopes. The thirteen-hectare vineyard that supports this 2,000-case winery was planted, beginning in 1996, by

Hans Christian Jost, owner of the Jost Vineyards winery at Malagash in northern Nova Scotia (see page 256). His initial motive was to spread his risk across several regions.

In August 2004, Jost opened this winery in the Gaspereau in order to take advantage of the growing wine tourism of the Annapolis Valley. Other wineries are expected to follow. Halifax mining executive Gerald McConnell has developed a nearby vineyard for his proposed Benjamin Bridge winery, likely to open about 2006, specializing in sparkling wines. Nearby, L'Acadie Vineyards (see page 248), another sparkling wine producer, is under development.

At Gaspereau, Jost planted Chardonnay, Riesling, Ortega, and Vidal on the warmer upper part and varieties such as De Chaunac, L'Acadie, New York Muscat, and Kuhlmann further down what is a fairly continual slope. "Chardonnay always makes it through the winter and it produces a decent wine," Jost says. "But I like L'Acadie." In the Gaspereau site, the variety yields a wine that the wine shop staff describe as "dangerously drinkable". The wine shows sweet, zesty citrus flavours with a dry finish.

GILLIS OF BELLEISLE WINERY (Range not tasted.)
1826 Route 124, Belleisle Valley, Springfield, NB, E5T 2K2.
Tel: 506 485 8846

This winery started innocently. Lawyer Rod Gillis began planting a few grapevines in 1995 on the hobby farm he and his wife, Judy, own in the pastoral valley overlooking Belleisle Bay. The Gillis family needed a crop to compete with the native alder trees that were taking over the property. Says Gillis, "a small vineyard got a little larger, then larger still." Ultimately, he had three hectares of vines. He opened a winery in 2003, producing about 1,000 cases a year. The capacity is about five times that. Gillis intends to plant another hectare or two, as well as buy grapes from many of the new vineyards just being planted in New Brunswick. The winery offers table wines from Baco Noir, L'Acadie, and Cayuga. The vineyard also has Frontenac,which handles New Brunswick winters well. The winery also has been developing sweeter wines from apples, raspberries, and cranberries. Buyers in China, impressed by the Cranberry Celebration wine, offered to order large amounts of it – more than the winery's total capacity. "I said no," recounts Gillis. "I think I will just stick with the cottage winery, enjoy life and stay reasonably small."

JOST VINEYARDS ****

48 Vintage Lane, Malagash, NS, B0K 1E0.

Tel: 902 257 2636; Website: www.jostwine.com

With an annual production of 40,000 cases, Jost Vineyards is Atlantic Canada's largest vineyard-based winery. It is driving vineyard expansion by purchasing half the region's grapes. Yet when it was launched in 1983, the odds were long that it would succeed. Hans Christian Jost, the current owner, was just twenty-one when his father, Hans Wilhelm, applied for a winery licence in the same month that he was diagnosed with cancer and given five years to live. The burden of moving ahead with the winery landed on Jost's shoulders.

In the winery's first year it had over 10,000 visitors. Those numbers have quadrupled since then, requiring Jost to build a much larger wine shop and to expand the underground cellars. One reason for visiting has always been Jost's award-winning Icewine. Atlantic Canada's first Icewine (and one of the first in Canada) was made in 1985 by Hans Wilhelm, using Kerner and Bacchus then being grown in the vineyard. The winery has made Icewine almost every year since then, now using both Vidal and New York Muscat. Jost's 1999 Vidal Icewine was selected as wine of the year in one Canadian wine competition; it was the first time that that any Nova Scotian wine had won that accolade.

The Icewine grapes come from a vineyard in the Annapolis Valley owned by grower John Warner. Also a supplier to Domaine de Grand Pré, Warner presses the frozen grapes right at the vineyard and ships the juice to the wineries. Jost, who buys from many growers, makes a point of not submerging superlative fruit in generic blends. "We do a lot of individual wine batches from individual vineyards," he says. "It's like destroying a friend when you blend wine batches together." Jost's vineyard-designated wines highlight the diversity of Nova Scotia's terroir. One such remarkable vineyard, about four hectares in size, is owned by John Pratt. It is on a steep, sun-bathed slope overlooking the Bras d'Or Lakes in Cape Breton. Several Jost wines, including a white from Cayuga (*see* page 212) and a reserve red from Maréchal Foch, are labelled Côtes de Bras d'Or.

The Jost wines are made primarily with red hybrid varieties such as Foch, Baco Noir, Léon Millot and Severnyi; and with white hybrids such as L'Acadie, New York Muscat, Cayuga, and one of the Geisenheim crosses that Jost has renamed Avondale (a local geographic designation). The vinifera wines include Pinot Noir, Chardonnay, and Ortega. The wine styles range from dry table wines to Icewines and even a dessert-style wine.

The Jost portfolio extends beyond grapes to include an ice apple wine called Pomme Glacé, a raspberry wine, and a Canadian curiosity, a maple wine. Maple syrup is produced in abundance in this corner of Nova Scotia. The winemaking is straightforward: the syrup is diluted to about thirty-five Brix from an initial concentration of nearly sixty-seven Brix. Then it is fermented much like Icewine, resulting in an off-dry beverage with pure maple flavours. "This wine has been a surprise hit," Hans Christian says.

PETITE RIVIERE VINEYARDS AND WINERY ***
1300 Italy Cross Road, Crousetown, NS, B0J 1V0.
Tel: 902 688 2295

One of Canada's earliest vineyards is believed to have been planted in 1633 in the French colony at LaHave, not far from modern-day Lunenburg. Like every other early planting of vinifera in North America at the time, it failed. Now that viticulture is being mastered in the LaHave River Valley, growers have begun to demarcate the region with the language of an appellation: Côtes de LaHave. Petite Riviere Vineyards, which opened in the spring of 2004, is the region's first winery. One winery alone does not make an appellation, but Petite Riviere's superbly crafted wines set a high standard.

This emerging viticultural area, about a ninety-minute drive southwest from Halifax, is in rolling terrain, often well-treed, just far enough inland from the ocean to escape fog during the day. The maritime climate provides long, frost-free seasons and the terrain offers many southern slopes. Some of the soils are a little too rich. But the vineyard of Petite Riviere has so much rock that the owners, Philip Wamboldt and Carol Slack-Wamboldt, were able to sell excess stones by the truckload for harbour construction.

They bought their first Côtes de LaHave vineyard property in 1994 and a second one, where the winery is located, in 2000. Within sight of each other, the properties total about six hectares of vineyard. There are modest plantings of Pinot Noir, Pinot Meunier, Chardonnay, and Zweigelt. However, the Wamboldts prudently devoted the majority of their vineyards to hybrids that already have proven themselves in Nova Scotia. These include Seyval Blanc, L'Acadie, Léon Millot, Kuhlmann, Baco Noir, and Triomphe d'Alsace. The latter red hybrid, Wamboldt notes, is one of the most widely planted varieties in English vineyards. "For a hybrid, it is pretty good," he maintains. He has another red hybrid, Maréchal Joffre, whose only fame is that it is planted in Belgium. Perhaps Wamboldt has been overly cautious. Most of the other new vineyards in the LeHave area are more heavily committed to Pinot Noir and Chardonnay.

The wines show considerable polish. The Côtes de LaHave White Sur Lie is a blend of Seyval Blanc and L'Acadie, matured on its lees. The Chardonnay, from purchased LaHave grapes, has the minerality of Chablis. The reds, almost all of which are barrel-aged, are blends often anchored on Léon Millot, Philip's preferred red hybrid. Invariably, the reds have power. "We personally like big, bold, oaky reds," Slack-Wamboldt explains.

ROSSIGNOL ESTATE WINERY **
RR 4, Murray River, PEI, COA 1W0.
Tel: 902 962 4193; Website: www.rossignolwinery.com

Winemaking was illegal in Prince Edward Island when John Rossignol began experimental plantings of vines in 1992. It had never occurred to the government that anyone would ever grow wine on this quiet, pastoral island renowned for potatoes. Alcohol had been prohibited for the first half of the twentieth century, the longest stretch of prohibition of any Canadian province. It took Rossignol a year to get the law changed. After the winery opened in 1994, he had another struggle before the province removed an old ban against shipping alcoholic products off the island. Today, however, the Rossignol Estate Winery's products are found not only in the island's restaurants but as far afield as Alberta and Ontario.

Rossignol planted test plots of vines, prudently not making a major commitment until winemaking became legal. Most of his vineyard, about four hectares in total, is well back from the ocean; he has found that the vines must be at least 152 metres (500 feet) back from the cliff to protect them from salt spray.

Initially, he made wines with purchased fruit while the vineyard was being developed. For his fruit wines, Rossignol employs blueberries, raspberries, strawberries, rhubarb, cranberries, and apples. He makes a mead with blackberries and honey, and a tasty apple cider enriched with maple syrup. The wines, sweetened naturally with fruit juice, make up about half the winery's sales.

The major grape varieties in the vineyard are Maréchal Foch and Seyval Blanc. In 2004, Rossignol was planning to add L'Acadie. For a number of years, he was also producing excellent wines from vinifera grapes grown for him in greenhouses: varieties such as Pinot Noir, Cabernet Franc, Baco Noir,

Merlot, Chardonnay, and Ortega. To the best of his knowledge, his was the only winery in Canada growing wine grapes this way. "We ran that experiment for five years," he says. "We had interesting wines for a while, but it was not very practical and we pulled them out."

SAINTE-FAMILLE WINES **
RR 2 Dudley Park Lane, Falmouth, NS, B0P 1L0.
Tel: 902 798 8311; Website: www.st-famille.com

This property, like Grand Pré, was once part of the former French colony of Acadia (see page 252). The Corkum vineyard was in La Paroisse ("the parish of") Sainte-Famille and that inspired the winery's name. Suzanne and Douglas Corkum, the owners of Sainte-Famille, began growing grapes in 1979 as suppliers for Roger Dial's Grand Pré winery, which had just opened about twenty minutes down the highway. They opened their own winery a decade later after Grand Pré went into receivership. They have nurtured their business to an annual production of 6,000 cases, with an ultimate target of 10,000 cases.

The vineyard, now twelve hectares, was planted originally to the varieties that Dial espoused, including L'Acadie, Michurinetz, Seyval Blanc, Maréchal Foch, and Chardonnay. They struggled with the latter variety and finally removed it after several cold winters killed many of the vines, replacing it with an expanded planting of reliable L'Acadie. The Corkums have not given up on Chardonnay, which is to be replanted on a warmer site in the vineyard. Recently, they also have planted Baco Noir, Siegfried, Cabernet Franc, and Pollux. The latter is a white German cross of Riesling and Müller-Thurgau that makes delicate wines.

As the winemaker, Suzanne has worked hard to master Michurinetz. The initial Nova Scotia style of wine from this grape was defined at Grand Pré, where Dial was handling it like a California vinifera to make big, rustic reds. Suzanne eventually took a fresh approach to the grape. She reduced tonnage per vine. In the winery, she cut back on the length of maceration. Treated this way, Michurinetz produces cleaner berry flavours and is ready to drink when young. Sainte-Famille's most successful wine with the grape is, in fact, a charming, fast-selling rosé. The grape is also a component in several blended reds, including Pheasant Run, the winery's popular barrel-aged red.

20

Fruit wines, cider, and mead

Fruit wines in Canada moved out of mother's pantry and into commercial production in the 1990s. Now, more than 100 fruit wineries operate across the country, including the members of the Fruit Wines of Canada, formed in 2000 to promote quality standards. Modelled on the grape wineries' Vintners Quality Alliance standards, the Quality Certified programme is meant to identify the best fruit wines to consumers. Bill Redelmeier, the owner of Southbrook Farms winery and the founding chair of Fruit Wines of Canada, says: "While our industry is small in comparison to the grape wine sector, we are equally passionate about what we do."

There is a long history of country wines in Canada. In regions with no vineyards, hobby vintners turned to the local berries and fruits to make alcoholic beverages they could afford. "If you wanted wine, you had to make it yourself," says Winston Jennings, the owner of a Newfoundland fruit winery. In Québec, the Sulpician priests in 1650 planted apple trees and built a cider press on the slopes of Mount Royal, the mountain in the middle of modern-day Montréal. They sold cider surplus to their needs. According to the Association des Cidriculteurs Artisans du Québec, several producers in the Montréal area were successful enough by 1850 to export cider as far as the Caribbean. Through an apparent drafting oversight, cider production was not covered when Québec established its liquor regulatory framework in 1921. Québec's farmers simply continued to make country ciders for themselves, selling it to their neighbours on the grey market. In 1971, the province began licensing cider producers in a way that favoured large commercial production and shut down most farm cideries. The commercial ciders were mediocre and by 1980 the market had shrivelled.

The current golden age for ciders began in the 1990s. The Association puts the start of the revival at 1998 when the government created a licence for so-called artisanal cider. The beverages have been well-received; the new and uniquely Canadian ice ciders bid to rival Icewine. According to the Beverage Testing Institute of Chicago: "The finest ciders in North America may well emanate from the province of Québec, which has an established artisanal cider industry with historical ties to Normandy cider."

Some consumers and producers regard fruit wines as introductory wines, easier for novice palates because they are often sweeter and less complicated than grape wines. "Not everybody loves a dry burgundy," argues Hilary Rodrigues, whose Rodrigues winery in Newfoundland is Canada's largest. "The average person likes a semi-sweet wine." Most producers cover all markets by making dry fruit wines but off-dry and dessert styles seem to predominate. "We do not want to compete with grape wines," Rodrigues says. "We are different and unique."

FRUIT WINES IN BC

The British Columbia wine industry started in the 1920s with fruit wines, before any significant vineyards were planted. The first commercial wineries processed loganberries. Believed to be a cross of raspberry and blackberry, the plant was named after Judge J H Logan, because it was first found in his Santa Cruz garden in California in 1881. Within a generation, it was grown so extensively on salubrious Vancouver Island that the farmers turned to wine production to relieve surpluses. Loganberry wines, typically sweet, remained on the market for about forty years. When disease wiped out most of the bushes, wineries turned to such fruits as blueberries. More often, the new fruit wines that appeared in the 1960s, and were briefly popular, were just flavoured beverages fortified with alcohol. They were not sophisticated and were not designed to be. The largest Canadian wineries still make fruit-flavoured refreshment beverages, such as Mike's Hard Lemonade (see page 177), continuing the lucrative tradition that has introduced so many consumers to alcoholic beverages.

For some early fruit wineries, the business was challenging. Consider the struggles of Nova Scotia's Chipman Wines. Believed to have been the province's first winery, Chipman was founded in the 1930s at Kentville in the apple-growing Annapolis Valley. Founder Lewis D Chipman operated from his home until he erected a purpose-built winery in 1941. Its major product was Golden Glow, a hard apple cider. When fire destroyed the winery in 1953, Chipman sold the business to a group of local investors. A number of new products were introduced, including apple, blueberry, and cranberry wines. The new owners even acquired a cranberry farm, the losses from which drained Chipman's treasury. By the early 1980s, the winery, with its dirt floors and leaking wood vats, looked as tired as the brands. In 1984, the brands were sold to a national winery and Chipman closed.

Two years later, Michael and Cledwyn Lewis opened Lewis Brothers Winery in Grande Prairie, Alberta, calling it the most northerly winery in the world. (At the time, it may have been so.) It remained in business only until the early 1990s. It did leave a legacy, however. For most of its existence, Lewis Brothers employed a winemaker named Todd Moore, a former bicycle racer who went on to make wine in the Okanagan. When Columbia Classsics, British Columbia's first modern fruit winery, opened in 1998, its novice winemaker, Dominic Rivard, tapped Moore's knowledge. Rivard went on to become western Canada's leading fruit winemaker before leaving in 2004 to consult to wineries in China.

Since 1985, the Canadian wine industry has enjoyed remarkable growth. The new grape wineries laid down a foundation for a wine culture. That environment spurred fruit growers and winemakers to explore fruit wines. One of the the strongest proponents of fruit wines was Jim Warren, who founded Stoney Ridge winery in Ontario in 1985 (see page 98). In 1998, Warren was a founder and is the executive director of Fruit Wines of Ontario, whose fifteen members are Ontario's leading exclusive fruit wine producers. A number of the grape wineries also make fruit wines.

Fruit Wines of Canada was formed in 2000, with about fifty members, overlaping the Ontario group and including two of Canada's largest producers, Rodrigues Winery in Newfoundland and The Fort Wine Company in British Columbia. The national association has endeavoured to develop standards designed to raise the quality of all fruit wines, developing a programme called Quality Certified (QC) to reassure consumers. "People don't associate high quality with fruit wines," Hilary Rodrigues admits. The QC programme specifies that the wines must be made from "authorized" fruits. "Grape wines are not authorized," Fruit Wines of Canada stated in one document, probably reacting against grape wines flavoured with fruit. While the QC seal still has not achieved the profile of the Vintners Quality Alliance VQA seal, it is a useful start.

ICE CIDER

There is a parallel effort to establish standards for ice cider. This luxurious Canadian beverage is inspired by Icewine. The leading producers in volume, and perhaps also in quality, are in Québec. There, ice cider is taken so seriously that in 2001, the association of cider makers crafted a legal definition and Québec's state liquor retailer has agreed to sell in its stores only ciders made in conformity with the standard. It reads:

> Ice cider (Apple Ice Wine) is obtained by the alcoholic fermentation of apple juice, which must have a level of sugar concentration before fermentation – produced solely through direct exposure to natural cold either before or after the apple harvest – of at least 310 grams per litre. Residual sugar content must be at least 150 grams per litre. Product labelling and advertising must specify which technique was used to produce the beverage in question (i.e. whether the exposure to natural cold occurred before or after harvest). Alcoholic content must be at least nine per cent and no greater than thirteen per cent per volume. It is forbidden to artificially refrigerate the apples, apple juice, must or cider at a temperature lower than –6°C, or to use industrially concentrated juice at any stage of the production of apple ice wine.

Credit for creating ice cider usually is given to Christian Barthomeuf, a seminal individual in both Québec's wine industry and in ice cider. Self-taught as a winemaker, he was a founder of Domaine des Côtes d'Ardoise, one of the first vineyards planted at Dunham (see page 229). He started working on the ice cider technique in 1989. Once perfected, he began making it at Québec's two largest ice cider producers, La Face Cachée de la Pomme and Domaine Pinnacle. Now that ice cider production has grown to significant volumes, Barthomeuf makes cider exclusively at Pinnacle.

This is a growing category in Québec. Currently, twenty-two producers make ice cider according to the industry's exacting standard, triple the number doing so in the late 1990s. La Face Cachée's François Pouliot explains: "We can make good Icewine here, but volume-wise, you could never compete with what they do in Ontario and BC. I wanted to make a product that I could sell all over the world. So when I saw what I could do with apples, I said, 'There I have something that is of world standard. I can sell this in France. I can compete with any great wine in the world.'"

The growing popularity of fruit wines may be accelerated by the health claims now being made for many of the berries. Credible studies show that dark-coloured fruits, especially blueberries, cranberries, blackcurrants, and elderberries, are rich in antioxidants. (Of course, that is also true of red wines.) On its website, Rush Creek Wines states: "Nutritionally, the elderberry is way ahead even of that superb fruit which is always held to be ideal for winemakers – the grape." Proponents of berries lay out a long list of beneficial results from their consumption, ranging from improved eyesight and memory, to less vulnerability to cancer and limiting the effects of ageing. "Blueberries have the highest amount of antioxidants and they transfer into the wine," says Newfoundland's Hilary Rodrigues, a practising dentist as well as a winemaker. "We are targeting people who are more health conscious, not just those who want to go and have a glass of wine."

A University of Guelph study has found that most fruit wines are lower in histamines than grape wines. Some fruit wineries also use organic fruit or wild berries and avoid adding sulphites as preservatives. Rodrigues believes this purity of production also reduces the reactions among the increasing number of people with allergies. A few fruit wineries, among them Rodrigues, have taken the additional step of securing Kosher certification. To do that, the wines must be produced to very high standards of cleanliness, also implying a certain quality. For Rodrigues, the strategy has worked, generating a ten-fold increase in its sales in the big Ontario market.

N.B. No star ratings are given in this chapter.

CIDER PRODUCERS

AU PAVILLON DE LA POMME

1130 Boulevard Laurier, Mont-Saint-Hilaire, QC, J3G 4S6.

Tel: 450 464 2654; Website: www.pavillondelapomme.com

The Robert family, which has owned this property near Mont-Saint-Hilaire since 1779, has grown apples here since 1930. The cidery opened in 1993, making ciders according to old family recipes. The products include a still cider, a sparkling cider, and an apéritif cider to which a dash of cassis has been added. As at almost all Québec cider producers, dessert apple varieties such as McIntosh and Spartan are used.

BOURGEOIS FARMS AND BELLIVEAU ORCHARDS

Pré-d'en Haut, 1209 Principale Street, Memramcook, NB, E4K 2S6.

Tel: 506 758 2325; Website: www.fermebourgeoisfarms.ca

The orchard here was planted in 1932 and was acquired in 1955 by Father Azarias Massé, a well-loved local parish priest who, as the winery puts it, "confided its care" to the current owner, Louis Bourgeois. The winery's still apple wine is named Massé. Four sparkling apple wines made here, one is called Beliveau, the former name of the village of Pré-d'en Haut in which the orchard is located. One of the newest products is an ice cider. Wines also are made with blueberries, pears, and cherries.

BRUS' ORCHARDS AND WINERY

244263 Airport Road, Tillsonburg, ON, N4G 4H1.

Tel: 519 842 2262; Website: www.execulink.com/~brus

Hans Brus believes that his may be "the smallest winery in this country." Production is not much more than 1,000 bottles a year. He offers a dry Vidal late-harvest wine with purchased grapes, a cherry-flavoured apple wine and an ice cider made with apples left to freeze on the trees. "We have fourteen varieties of apples," he says. "But the best ciders are made with McIntosh and a small portion of either Golden Delicious or Royal Gala." He describes the cider as being "sweet with a touch of equatorial herbs".

CIDRERIE DE L'ABBAYE SAINT-BENOIT

Chemin de l'Abbaye, Saint-Benoit-du-Lac, QC, J0B 2M0.

Tel: 819 843 4080; Website: www.st-benoit-du-lac.com

The Benedictine monks at this abbey in the Eastern Townships have harnessed an old tradition to produce both hard and soft ciders. The fine bottle-fermented ciders are made with a technique similar to that involved in making Champagne.

CIDRERIE FLEURS DE POMMIERS

1047 Route 202, Dunham, QC, J0E 1M0

Tel: 450 295 2223

Established in 1992, this cidery benefits from its proximity with Québec's greatest concentration of wineries. The cider-maker here since 1996 is Marie-Andrée Tremblay, said to be Québec's only female in that role. Products include oak-aged dry ciders, a product called Cuvée de Noel in which raspberries, strawberries, blackcurrants, and blackberries are added, and a bottle-fermented sparkling cider.

CIDERY LA FACE CACHÉE DE LA POMME
617 Route 202, Hemmingford, QC, J0L 1H0.

Tel: 450 247 2899; Website: www.appleicewine.com

This cidery operates from a colonial stone house on a property just two kilometres (1.2 miles) from the US border. Owner François Pouliot, a Montréal-born filmmaker, bought it after meeting Christian Barthomeuf (*see* page 229). He bought the orchard to convert it to grapes but, familiar with Barthomeuf's trial ice ciders, changed his mind. "I thought why bother with Icewine when I can do something really, really great, that represents our terroir here," Pouliot recalls. He and Barthomeuf crushed their first apples in 1994 and set out to explore what Pouliot calls "the dark side of the moon – the hidden face of the apple [*la face cachée de la pomme*] that nobody had yet seen". Barthomeuf made the cider here as well as at Domaine Pinnacle, the other dominant ice cider producer in Québec, until 2004. Pouliot concluded that he needed his own full-time cider-maker and recruited French winemaker Loïc Chanut.

In 2000 Pouliot stopped making films (he had been a major producer of music videos) to focus entirely on the cider business. La Face Cachée had made only 2,500 bottles in 1999. Today, the cidery is one of Québec's leading producers, making about 200,000 bottles a year and distributing it around the world. One of Pouliot's proudest moments came when the French retailer, Galeries Lafayette, listed his La Neige brand ice cider and extravagantly compared it with Château d'Yquem. La Neige is made primarily with McIntosh and Spartan apples harvested at the normal time. Stored until the winter turns cold, usually around Christmas, the apples are frozen in the open air and then pressed. The juice is further concentrated in a second freeze cycle: the warehouse doors are left open to the elements when temperatures drop to –25°C (–13°F). Waiting for that hard natural freeze is a time of high risk. Says Pouliot:

> In 2003 I had over 300,000 litres of juice outside. In January 2002, it warmed up to 15°C (59°F) outside during the second week of January. I can tell you that we were freaking out. If it starts to ferment on its own, then it won't freeze again.

In that case, the juice might have to be diverted to the cidery's lower-value still cider, Dégel, which is usually made from the second pressings of frozen apples at warmer temperatures.

The cidery's Frimas brand (which aptly means "wintery weather") is made from apples left on the trees to freeze naturally during Québec's famously cold January. In his twenty-four hectares of orchards, Pouliot grows several varieties that cling to trees after the leaves have fallen, including Golden Russet, an old variety with a high sugar content. About fifty apples are crushed for each bottle of Frimas, of which total production averages 6,000 bottles a season. Of Québec's Icewine-like approach to making ice cider, he says:

> To me, it is very important that you keep it natural. When you put the apples in the freezer, they just freeze. When they stays outside for a month and a half, something happens. I can taste the difference.

CIDRERIE MICHEL JODOIN

1130 Petite Caroline, Rougemont, QC, J0L 1M0.

Tel: 450 469 2676; Website: www.cidrerie-michel-jodoin.qc.ca

According to Michel Jodoin, his cider story began on a Sunday afternoon in 1901 when his great grandfather bought a hundred apple trees at a churchyard auction. The orchard now has more than 8,000 trees in nine hectares on the south slope of Rougemont Mountain. Jodoin began selling a variety of ciders in 1988, including a dry, wood-aged cider from McIntosh apples, Blanc de Pépin Fort, which is fermented to twelve degrees like a wine. The sparkling ciders are bottle fermented. Jodoin's peers in Québec cider-making recognized his craftsmanship in 1995 by making him Knight of the Confrérie des Chevaliers du Cidre du Québec.

CIDRERIE DU MINOT

376 Covey-Hill Road, Hemmingford, QC, J0L 1H0.

Tel: 450 247 3111; Website: www.duminot.com

Owners Robert and Joëlle Demoy claim they were "born into the tradition of apple cultivation and cider-making" in their native Breton in France. Cidermaker Robert is a Bordeaux-educated oenologist who started his career in the French wine industry, before moving to Canada to work in the Québec wine and cider industries, and as a technical consultant. The fifty-two-hectare apple orchard grows a rich mix of varieties. Red-fleshed Geneva is used to make a pink-hued sparkling cider called Crémant de Pomme du Minot Rosé. The products range from a cider with almost no alcohol to a brandy-fortified apéritif and Du Minot des Glaces, a sparkling ice cider.

CIDRERIE VERGER BILODEAU

2200 Chemin Royal, Saint-Pierre, Île d'Orléans, QC, GOA 4EO.

Tel: 418 828 9316; Website: www.cidreriebilodeau.qc.ca

In 1982, Benoit Bilodeau and his wife, Micheline, established a farm on Île d'Orléans, planting 3,000 apple trees encompassing ten varieties. In 1997, two years after establishing a shop to sell apple-based confections, they opened the first cidery on the island, a popular tourist destination just north of Québec City. Bilodeau is an innovative cider-maker. The products include a maple-flavoured apéritif cider and a strawberry cider as well as conventional apple ciders, both still and sparkling. Bilodeau also makes ice cider, picking apples that have been frozen naturally at −15°C (5°F).

CIDRERIE-VERGER LEO BOUTIN

710 Rang de la Montagne, Mont-Saint-Grégoire, QC, JOJ 1KO.

Tel: 450 346 3326; Website: www.vergerboutin.com

The orchard was already thirty years old when Léo and Denise Boutin purchased it in 1980. They have diversified the production to include apple products from sauce to ciders. The ciders range from sparkling to ice cider. The Boutins compare the taste of Sieur de Monnoir, their oak-aged cider, to "oven-baked apples". Châteaulin, their bottle-fermented sparkling cider, has won several gold medals in competition.

DOMAINE PINNACLE

150 Chemin Richford, Frelighsburg, QC, JOJ 1CO.

Tel: 450 298 1222; Website: www.icecider.com

Domaine Pinnacle has become one of the leading Canadian producers of ice cider. In 2000, Charles Crawford and Susan Reid, his wife, bought an historic farm on Québec's Vermont border with 2,500 apples trees on its 160 hectares. The farm was purchased for its charm, not for the apple trees. However, a friend suggested that Crawford look at making cider, in particular ice cider, and the couple produced 1,500 cases in 2000. Now Domaine Pinnacle makes nearly 15,000 cases (twelve bottles of 375 millilitres) a year, selling them across Canada as well as in Asia and Europe. In Paris, the cider has even appeared on the wine list of the Hotel Crillon.

The cider-maker is Christian Barthomeuf (*see* page 229), who uses heritage apple varieties to produce the premium "Signature" ice cider with concentrated flavours and aromas reminiscent of crème brûlée. Barthomeuf signs every bottle personally, which means autographing somewhere between 1,000 and 5,000 bottles per vintage. Having created a new beverage category, Domaine Pinnacle and its peers are now extending it. In 2004, Domaine Pinnacle made what it claims is the world's first sparkling ice cider. "I have it with caviar," Crawford says.

DOMAINE STEINBACH

2205 Chemin Royal, Saint-Pierre de l'Île-d'Orléans, QC, G0A 4E0.

Tel: 418 828 0000; Website: www.domainesteinbach.com

Claire and Philippe Steinbach came to Québec from Belgium in 1995 on a sabbatical and, captivated by the Île d'Orléans, decided to stay. Two years later, they purchased a twelve-hectare farm and set about restoring both the old stone house and the neglected apple orchard. They practise organic agriculture, with some biodynamic methods. They produce a number of ciders, including an ice cider, as well as several cider vinegars.

EAST KELOWNA CIDER COMPANY

2960 McCulloch Road, Kelowna, BC, V1W 4A5.

Tel: 250 860 8118

At its picturesque setting beside Okanagan Lake, Kelowna has become one of the largest cities in the British Columbia interior. Yet the twenty-minute drive from the city into the foothills of East Kelowna is a step back in time. Orchards and vineyards still hold urban sprawl at bay. One of these farms is the 3.6-hectare apple orchard and cidery operated by David and Theressa Ross. They launched in 1997 with non-alcoholic cider. Perhaps the most challenging part of launching the business was the seven years of lobbying for the regulations that enabled them to begin selling hard cider in 2003. It should have been easy since British Columbia's first cidery, Merridale on Vancouver Island, had been licensed a decade earlier. The regulations, however, were designed around the use of English cider apples. The Rosses had to convince regulators that hard cider also can be made from the dessert apples they grow. They do not care for the taste of English cider. "Cider apples are very bitter, or tart," Theressa explains. "When you taste that in the apples, you are going to taste that in the beverage as well. If you can eat the apple and it tastes good, why would it not make a good drink?"

GAGETOWN CIDER COMPANY

16 Fox Road, Gagetown, NB, E5M 1W6.

Tel: 506 488 2147; Website: www.gagetown99.com/cider.html

The Gagetown Cider Company is an outgrowth of New Brunswick's largest apple orchard, located near the village of Gagetown on the banks of the Saint John River. The owners are Blair and Brenda Stirling. The product list is substantial, including non-alcoholic as well as hard ciders. The range of alcoholic ciders extends from light coolers to ice cider. There are also fruit wines from raspberry, strawberry, and cranberry, along with blends of berry fruits and apples. Stirling also has just under half a hectare of labrusca grapes and makes blends of apple and grape wine.

LA CIDRERIE DU VILLAGE

509 Rue Principale, Rougemont, QC, J0L 1M0.

Tel: 450 469 3945; Website: www.lacidrerieduvillage.qc.ca

This formerly operated as Les Vergers Bernard Dubé and members of the Dubé family made hard cider for twenty years until 1970, stopping when the provincial government began demanding that producers be licensed. The tradition resumed in 1996 when the family got a licence. The cider factory is on Rougemont's main street. The nearby orchard, with about 7,000 trees, grows twenty different varieties of apples. Products include a bottle-fermented sparking cider, a still cider and a brandy-fortified ice cider.

LES PETITS FRUITS LEGER

331 Chemin Brome, Fulford, Lac Brome, QC, J0E 1S0.

Tel: 450 534 2753; Website: www.petits-fruits-leger.com

A small producer in the Eastern Townships, Les Petits Fruits Léger makes five ciders that cover a remarkable range of styles. Kir Layral is an apéritif combining apples and blackcurrants; Mathildoise is a raspberry-flavoured cider; Le Blanc de Brome is a strong cider; Philoup is a fortified style with twenty-two degrees of alcohol; while Clos Léger is a refreshing light cider.

MERRIDALE ESTATE CIDERY

1230 Merridale Road, RR1, Cobble Hill, BC, V0R 1L0.

Tel: 250 743 4293; Website: www.merridalecider.com

Merridale is dedicated to making authentic European-style cider from a 5.6-hectare orchard of traditional English and French cider apples. Only an aficionado would recognize the varieties: Chisel Jersey, Dabinett, Frequin Rouge, Hauxapfel, Judaine, Julienne, Kermerien, Michelin, and Yarlington Mill. The orchard was originally planted by Albert Piggott, who was born in Scotland in 1925 and retired to southern Vancouver Island to pursue a lifelong dream of opening a cidery. He launched Merridale in 1992 but, after struggling with a market that did not understand his ciders, sold the business in 2000 to Victoria lawyer Rick Pipes and his wife Janet Docherty.

Pipes sought advice from English cider makers through the Internet and as a result has reformulated some of the ciders. Merridale's rustic Scrumpy is now made in a style more suited to his taste and has won him a gold medal at a subsequent US competition. Pipes has also added new products, including a sparkling cider, called Champagne-Style Somerset. After building a new tasting room in Merridale's manicured orchard, Pipes and Docherty have also turned the farm into a popular tour destination.

RAVEN RIDGE CIDERY CO
3002 Dunster Road, Kelowna, BC, V1W 4A6.
Tel: 250 763 9404; Website: www.k-l-o.com
Launched in 2003, Raven Ridge is yet another attraction for visitors to this hustling sixty-one-hectare destination farm operated by Richard Bullock and his family about twenty minutes from the heart of the city. Its first ice ciders were made after the Bullocks crushed frozen Fuji, Braemar, and Granny Smith apples. The varietal ciders were widely acclaimed upon release. Raven Ridge subsequently extended its range to include a blended ice cider appropriately called Ambrosia, a bottle-fermented sparkling cider and an apple wine.

VERGER CIDRERIE LARIVIERE
1188 Rang 8, Saint-Théodore d'Acton, QC, J0H 1Z0.
Tel: 450 546 3411; Website: www.clementlariviere.com
Apple growers since 1980, Clément and Monique Larivière only began producing cider in 1999. The cidery opened the following year, and they also planted a small vineyard. The products include two apéritifs – one a fortified cider with strawberries, the other made by adding alcohol to apples and other fruit. As well, there is a festive sparkling cider called La Fête au Village, and a dry still cider, La Ruée vers l'Or, which is recommended to accompany seafood.

VERGER ET VIGNOBLE CASA BRETON
270 Chemin Jean-Guérin, ouest, St-Henri-de-Lévis, QC, G0R 3E0.
Tel: 418 882 2929; Website: www.casabreton.com
Just thirty minutes east of Québec City, this business began in 1982 when the owners, Lisette Casabon and Jean-Paul Breton, began planting an orchard. It has now grown to 5,000 apple trees, along with some blueberries

and other small fruits. Wine production began in 1998 with a sparkling apple cider fermented in the bottle. Casa Breton added three fortified fruit digestifs in 1999 and an apéritif cider in 2000. The latter, a fruity rosé with fifteen degrees of alcohol called Le Jaseur, won a gold medal in an important Québec competition in 2001. Casa Breton continues to expand its range and now offers both ice cider and dry red table wines, available in its boutique and in its country restaurant.

VERGER HENRYVILLE
660 Route 133, Henryville, QC, J0J 1E0.
Tel: 450 299 2733; Website: www.vergerhenryville.com
The orchard dates from 1935 and was acquired in 1978 by the family of Éric Peeters. They now have 10,000 trees, comprising eight apple varieties. In 2000, Peeters began cider production, quickly winning several awards. The range includes a sparkling cider, a still cider, and two ice ciders.

VERGERS ET CIDRERIE DENIS CHARBONNEAU
575 Rang de la Montagne, Mont Saint-Grégoire, QC, J0J 1K0.
Tel: 450 347 9184; Website: www.vergersdc.qc.ca.
Apple growers in Mont Saint-Grégoire since 1981, Denis and Claudine Charbonneau began making cider in 1990. They also produce maple syrup and related products, and grow other tree and berry fruits. Both still and bottle-fermented sparkling ciders are made.

Other cider producers:

ABBAYE CISTERCIENNE
471 Rue Principale, Rougemont, QC, J0L 1M0.
Tel: 450 469 2880

CIDRERIE DR ALIX
169 Rang de la Montagne, Rougemont, QC, J0L 1M0.
Tel: 450 469 3004

CIDRERIE COTEAUX ST-JACQUES
995 Grand Rang St-Charles, Saint-Paul d'Abbotsford, QC, J0E 1A0.
Tel: 450 379 9732

CIDRERIE DU BOUT DE L'ÎLE
20 Chemin du Bout de l'île, Sainte-Pétronille, Île d'Orléans, QC, G0A 4C0.
Tel: 418 828 9603; Website: www.polycultureplante.com

CIDRERIE DU VERGER GASTON
1074 Chemin de la Montagne, Mont-Saint-Hilaire, Québec, J3G 4S6.
Tel: 450 464 3455

CIDRERIE LA POMME DU ST-LAURENT
505 Chemin Bellevue, ouest, Cap St-Ignace, G0R 1H0, QC.
Tel: 418 246 5957

CIDRERIE LA VIRGINIE
485 Route 277, Sainte-Germaine, QC, G0R 1S0.
Tel: 418 625 3456; Website: www.cidrerievirginie.qc.ca

CIDRERIE ST-NICOLAS
2068 Marie Victorin, St-Nicolas, Québec, G0S 2Z0.
Tel: 418 836 5505

CIDRERIES ET VERGERS SAINT-ANTOINE
3101 Route Marie-Victorin, Saint-Antoine-de-Tilly, QC, G0S 2C0.
Tel: 418 886 2375; Website: www.mediom.com/~emileaub

CIDRERIE VERGER LAMARCHE
175 Montée du Village, Saint-Joseph-du-Lac, QC, J0N 1M0.
Tel: 450 623 0695; Website: www.vergerlamarche.com

DOMAINE DE LA SOURCE A MARGUERITE
3788 Chemin Royal, Ste-Famille, Île d'Orléans, QC, G0A 3P0.
Tel: 418 952 6277

FERME HUBERT SAUVE
140 Rang du Milieu, Saint-Timothée, QC.
Tel: 450 373 2979

FERME QUINN
2495 Boulevard Perrot, Notre-Dame-de-l'Île-Perrot, J7V 8P4, QC.
Tel: 450 453 1510

LES VERGERS DE LA COLLINE
5 Route 137 Nord, Ste-Cécile-de-Milton, QC, J0E 2C0.
Tel: 450 777 2442; Website: www.lesvergersdelacolline.com

LES VERGERS LAFRANCE
1473 Chemin Principal, Saint-Joseph-du-Lac, QC, J0N 1M0.
Tel: 450 491 7859

LES VERGERS NICOLET
5760 Rue Principale, Grand Saint-Esprit, QC, JOG 1B0.
Tel: 819 289 2101

PEPINIERE ET VERGERS PEDNEAULT ET FRERES
45 Rue Royale Est, Ile-aux-Coudres, QC, G0A 3J0.
Tel: 418 438 2365

ST JACOB'S WINERY & CIDERY
40 Benjamin Road East, Waterloo, ON N2J 3Z4.
Tel: 519 747 2337

FRUIT AND BERRY WINERIES

APPLEWOOD FARM WINERY
12442 McCowan Road, Stouffville, ON, L4A 7X5.
Tel: 905 642 4720; Website: www.applewoodfarmwinery.com

Applewood Farm, which has been in the Passafiume family for almost thirty years, began as one of the first pick-your-own strawberry and apple farms in Stouffville, northeast of Toronto. Applewood Farm Winery opened in September 2000. The fruit wine and mead offering is extensive. Several products are based on honey: Meade (as the winery likes to spell it) which is rich, sweet, and has twenty degrees of alcohol; Mac Meade, a sparkling blend of honey and apple cider, which the winery suggests pairing with baked brie and roasted garlic; and Madrigal Meade, a sparkling blend of honey, apples, and spices. The estate-grown fruit wines are made with apples, blueberries, cherries, and strawberries, either on their own or in blends. One of the most popular wines is a refreshing summer sipper called Eloras Harvest, made by blending honey and five fruit wines. Applewood seeks to cater to red wine lovers with its Proprietors Reserve, a blend of blueberries and McIntosh apples aged fourteen months in American oak.

ARCHIBALD ORCHARDS AND ESTATE WINERY
6275 Liberty Street North, Bowmanville, ON, L1C 3K6.
Tel: 905 263 2396; Website: www.archibaldswinery.com

Fred Archibald has established such a reputation with his expressively clean wines that at least one wine writer has described him as the "king" of Ontario fruit wines. Archibald grows about twenty different apple varieties here and he produces only fruit wines. "I wasn't brave enough to grow grapes here and I still am not," he says. Fruits and berries not grown on the farm are purchased from nearby farms, if at all possible. "Close to home is our philosophy," says Archibald, who insists that his apples have the flavour of the terroir that distinguishes them from those grown elsewhere.

Apples figure most of the wines made here, which run in style from dry to intensely sweet. The Oak-Aged McIntosh or the Oak-Aged Ida Red apple wines stand comfortably on the dinner table alongside dry grape wines. Archibald's delicate apple-raspberry wine, with a trace of residual sweetness, appeals as an apéritif. Archibald's favourite is his apple-blackcurrant blend, with a hint of caramel toffee on the finish. His apple-peach blend is made in a plump, late-harvest style, oozing flavour. "The recipe is based on childhood memories of eating a peach right off the tree," he says.

The Archibalds also have created several striking dessert wines. The Spiced Winter Apple, made with frozen apples, is this winery's answer to Icewine; Canadian Maple is reminiscent of a tawny port. The latter wine is a blend of McIntosh apple juice and maple syrup sourced from a specific Ontario farm that produces the precise quality Archibald wants.

The recipe, as with most of Archibald's wines, is his secret. "I want to have my personal signature on every product," he says. "My tasting partner is my wife. Sandy and I developed every recipe." Whatever they are doing, it is working. Archibald swept the 2003 National Fruit Wineries of Canada Competition and was named winery of the year. The winery has grown from 1,500 cases a year to 3,500 cases, almost all sold at the farm gate.

ASPEN GROVE COTTAGE WINERY
PO Box 281, White City, SK, S0G 5B0.
Tel: 306 771 2921; Website: www.aspengrovewinery.com
This winery is based on the seven hectares of berry orchard operated by Graham Topp in a suburb just east of Regina, Saskatchewan. The fruits include apples, rhubarb, plums, strawberries, raspberries, pin cherries, saskatoon berries, and chokecherries (the abundant, succulent but mouth-puckering berries that grow across the Prairies).[1] Topp makes the wines in a versatile off-dry style.

1. The chokecherry is a small, savoury berry that grows wild but sometimes also is cultivated. Horticulturist Tom Ward of the University of Saskatchewan writes: "The chokecherry (*Prunus virginiana*) is a member of the plum family common to most of Canada and much of the USA."

BANACH WINERY

341 22nd Street West, Battleford, SK, S0M 0E0.

Tel: 306 445 9463

Most amateurs in Saskatchewan make wine at one time or another with chokecherries. Walter and Diane Banach started that way. Their wine, which they called Battle River Red after the river north of town, was so successful that they launched a winery with it in 1996. Subsequently, they have expanded to making wines from crab apples, raspberries, and strawberries.

BELLAMERE COUNTRY MARKET & WINERY

1260 Gainsborough Road, London, ON, N6H 5K8.

Tel: 519 473 2273; Website: www.bellamere.com

Fruit farmer Don Mader launched a farm market in 1984 in a strategic location at the edge of London. The winery opened in 1998. Since 2002, the winemaker has been Scott Douglas. He has brought a tighter focus to the range of products, cutting back from eighteen wines to about a dozen. Bellamere's iced pear wine is called Polar Pear and the dry pear wine is called Pear Naked, underlining the pristine purity of the fruit flavours.

BIRTCH FARMS & ESTATE WINERY

RR 7, Woodstock, ON, N4S 7W2.

Tel: 519 469 3040; Website: www.birtchfarms.com

The farm here has been in the Birtch family since 1946 and was a mixed cash crop farm with a small orchard until 1982, when Bob Birtch bought it from his grandfather. Birtch and his wife Dyann expanded the orchard to more than fourteen hectares and moved into value-added products when wholesale fruit prices deteriorated. "Bob had been making wines from apples for a number of years, so it seemed a natural progression to add a winery," Dyann explains. The winery opened in 2001 and now offers almost two dozen fruit wines, in styles running from dry to sweet. In particular, Birtch makes varietal wines from apples: oak-aged McIntosh, Northern Spy, Royal Gala blush, and Orchard Gold from Golden Delicious. Dyann adds:

> The winemaker's style is to create a very balanced wine that benefits from ageing at least one to two years. Many fruit wines in the past have been made to be consumed young, but Bob chose a different route. The wines are slightly acidic when young but mellow out very nicely with age.

The winery has plenty of awards to validate this approach.

BLOSSOM WINERY

5491 Minoru Boulevard, Richmond, BC, V6X 2B1.

Tel: 604 232 9839; Website: www.blossomwinery.com

The memory of his grandmother's farmhouse in Taiwan is one of the inspirations behind this winery opened by John Chang in 2001, two years after emigrating to Canada. He recalled his grandmother making fruit wines, in particular, a potent plum wine. With the help of consultants, Chang made trial wines with various fruits, settling on the abundant and full-flavoured blueberries and raspberries grown on farms near this Vancouver suburb. The Blossom fruit wines capture the flavours well. The winery also makes sound late-harvest Rieslings and dry red wines, including a tasty Meritage called Two Left Feet, with grapes grown in the Okanagan. Chang exports a substantial portion of his sweet wine production to Asia.

BLUE HERON FRUIT WINERY

18539 Dewdney Trunk Road, Pitt Meadows, BC, V3Y 2R9.

Tel: 604 465 5563; Website: www.blueheronwinery.ca

Born in 1919 in Saskatchewan, George Flynn is the most senior of Canada's winery owners. He launched Blue Heron in 2004 on a farm where he has grown blueberries for about fifty years and where, more recently, he added a cranberry bog. The wines are made for Blue Heron by Derrick Power, also winemaker for The Fort Wine Co. The flagship wines are cranberry, blueberry, and strawberry. Blue Heron also offers a range of dessert wines.

BONAPARTE BEND WINERY

Highway 97, Cache Creek, BC, V0K 1H0.

Tel: 250 457 6667

This small fruit winery, which opened in 1999, is just at the edge of a town that is one of the gateways to British Columbia ranch country. Winery owners JoAnn and Gary Armstrong produce more than a dozen wines with fruit from their own small orchard or with purchased fruit. The wines include apricot, apple, blueberry, chokecherry, blackcurrant, blackberry, cranberry, raspberry, rhubarb, and honey.

CAROLINIAN WINERY

4823 Dundas Street, Thorndale, ON, N0M 2P0.

Tel: 519 268 2000; Website: www.carolinianwinery.com

The winery derives its name from the fertile Carolinian forest belt in southwestern Ontario. James Corcoran, who opened the winery in 2001 and sold it in 2004, is a horticulturist specializing in trees. The new owners are winemaker Brian Foley and Anissa, his wife. Brian's debut, a dry strawberry wine, was so well received that the production was sold before the end of that summer. He followed that with Mistura, an off-dry blend of raspberry and strawberry with a touch of blackcurrant, all fruits grown on the farm. Its success encouraged the Foleys to experiment with other fruit blends. There is a precedent: Corcoran had success with a cranberry/Riesling blend. The winery also offers single variety fruit wines, including peach, elderberry and saskatoon, along with mead, purchased from another producer. Carolinian's 2003 Black Currant Wine was a gold medallist at a major Toronto competition in 2004, edging out one of Canada's most renowned fruit wines, Southbrook's Framboise. Foley makes both mead and grape wines as well. All of Carolinian's sales are at the cellar door.

CHATEAU BOURGET/PINE HILL ORCHARDS
1818 St Félix Road, Bourget, ON, K0A 1E0.
Tel: 613 487 2064; Website: www.lavoieagricole.ca
When they took over this lower Ottawa Valley orchard in 1995, Paul and Carole Doran had only 1,500 apples trees growing on twenty hectares. That has been increased to 7,000 apple trees and 7,000 grape vines. With Paul as winemaker, they launched both apple and grape wines in 2002. The range includes a oak-aged Baco Noir as well as wines made by blending grapes and fruit. L'Ancêtre is a blend of De Chaunac and apple wine while L'Espiègle ("rascal") is a blend of Baco Noir and crab apple wine.

COLUMBIA VALLEY CLASSICS WINERY
1385 Frost Road, Lindell Beach, BC, V2R 4X8.
Tel: 604 858 5233
This fruit winery, which opened in 1998, set off the modest wave of new fruit wineries in British Columbia. It is based on a sixteen-hectare fruit and nut farm near Cultus Lake, a popular summer resort in the Fraser Valley, about two hours east of Vancouver. At one time or another, all of the well-known berries were turned into wine or into confections here.

COX CREEK CELLARS
RR 5, Guelph Ontario, N1H 6J2.
Tel: 519 767 3253; Website: www.coxcreekcellars.on.ca
Emigrés in 1968 from Czechoslovakia, Kamil Trochta (pronounced Trok-ta)

and his wife, Jerry, established Kamil Juices in Guelph in 1981. The winery, which opened in 1998, was a natural extension of the juice business, which sells fresh grape must from Europe to home winemakers. Cox Creek Cellars, however, is licensed as a fruit winery and is thus limited by regulation to making no more than twenty per cent grape wine. The grapes are purchased from Niagara vineyards although the Trochta family is trying to develop a 1.5-hectare vineyard on their twenty-two-hectare farm near Guelph.

Apples and blackcurrants grown on the farm are primary components in the wines. "We make a dry wine we call Back Home from blackcurrants, barrel-aged in Limousin oak barrels," Jerry says. "It tastes like Cabernet Sauvignon. We also have a barrel-aged apple wine that tastes like a Chardonnay." For those who insist on the real thing, Cox Creek also makes a barrel-aged Chardonnay. Admirers of Beethoven symphonies, they produce several wines that are called country symphonies. No 6 is a blend of apple and raspberry and No 9, which the Trochta family calls its Ode to Joy, is Vidal Icewine touched up with seven per cent blackcurrant wine for acidity. In total the winery produces about 35,000 litres of wine a year. Other fruit wines include elderberry, raspberry, cherry, blackberry and a range of varietal apple wines.

D D LEOBARD WINERY
133 De Baets Street, Winnipeg, MB, R2J 3R9.
Tel: 204 661 9007; Website: www.ddleobardwinery.com
The proprietors of this winery had to fill out a brewery application when they applied for a licence in 2000 because the Manitoba Liquor Commission had not yet created any forms for licensing a winery. Prior to the opening of the two fruit wineries now operating in Manitoba, the closest the province got to a winery was a bottling plant twenty years earlier in the community of Gimli. Now producing about 4,000 cases a year, D D Leobard is the brainchild of two former home winemakers, Denis d'Eschambault and Leonard Streilein. They have done it on a shoestring because no financing was available; the winery is currently in a small industrial mall with no tasting room. When business warrants, the partners intend to open a shop.

Much of the winemaking is done by Streilein. D'Eschambault handles the winery's business. Using purchased fruit – both wild and cultivated – the winery makes three distinct lines of fruit wines. There are five light and refreshing blends where strawberry wine is the base, with the taste-tweaking addition of fruits such as rhubarb and raspberry. The off-dry premium wines include saskatoon berry, strawberry, wild blueberry, and birch sap, which is comparable to maple syrup. There are also two dessert wines – iced strawberry and a dessert-style wild blueberry wine, fermented naturally to fourteen degrees. "We are trying to show people that there is an alternative to grape wine," says d'Eschambault. "The grape is just another fruit."

DOMAINE ACER

145 Route du Vieux Moulin, Auclair, QC, GOL 1AO.

Tel: 418 899 2825;

Website: www.mrctemiscouata.qc.ca/pme/entreprises/EveilPri

Vallier Robert's description of himself as the "ambassador of maple" is fully justified, considering all of the maple syrup products he crafts here with partner Nathalie Decaigny. The establishment's name, Acer, is the Latin name for "maple". The maple syrup industry was launched in 1972 by Vallier's father, Charles-Aimé Robert. Looking for a way to revive the economy of this remote region of Québec, Charles began harvesting sap by tapping 200 trees in a maple grove. The sap is concentrated to syrup by boiling. By the time Vallier took over the business in 1996, the operation had expanded to 7,800 taps. The products sold today in Domaine Acer's café and museum range from pure maple syrup to chocolates and sugar. More than 5,000 tourists find Domaine Acer each year.

Vallier began experimenting in 1992 with fermented beverages using maple sap, supported by government grants and aided by scientists at the research station in Sainte-Hyacinthe. He launched his Collection Acer in 1997. Currently, four maple wines are made. The dry white, with twelve degrees of alcohol, is called Prémices d'Avril, or "first fruit of April", the month of the maple sap harvest. A light wine, it surprises with notes of green apple and citrus and only a subtle hint of maple. Mousse des Bois is a dry sparkling wine. Val Ambré is an oak-aged apéritif in the style of Pineau des Charentes, but sweeter and more mellow. Finally, there is a dessert style with 17.5 degrees of alcohol, named Charles-Aimé Robert.

DOWNEY'S ESTATE WINERY

13682 Heart Lake Road, Brampton, ON, LON 1KO.

Tel: 905 838 5395; Website: www.downeysfarm.on.ca

Owned by the Downey family since 1920, this eighty-seven-hectare farm's renovated dairy barn houses a farmer's market with an in-house bakery and estate winery. The business is run by John and Ruth Downey and their five children. Winemaker Brian Moreau produces such a long list of fruit and grape wines and mead (more than forty) that almost every palate is served. For the sweet tooth, there is a selection that includes Vidal Icewine and iced fruit wines, notably a gold medal ice cranberry. There are succulent dessert wines made with blackcurrants, raspberries, plums, blackberries, and cherries; the latter is called Cherries Jubilee.

ELEPHANT ISLAND ORCHARD WINES
2730 Aikens Loop, RR1, S5, C18, Naramata, BC, V0H 1N0.
Tel: 250 496 5522; Website: www.elephantislandwine.com

The majority of Elephant Island's fruit wines are dry. It is the strategy of this winery, which opened in 2001, to makes wines that are as friendly with food as grape wines. To that end, owners Del and Miranda Halliday retained a winemaker, Christine Leroux, whose training is entirely with grapes. Her approach yields fruit wines with clarity of aroma and flavour, and a crisp balance that gives them an easy place on the table. "A lot of people have a misconception that you cannot produce good dry fruit wines," says Del.

The winery's orchard occupies a lakefront property purchased years ago by Miranda's grandparents, Paul and Catherine Wisnicki. It became known within the family as Elephant Island because Paul dismissed the purchase, his architect wife's retirement investment, as a white elephant, adding that she had designed the house purely for the eye (hence, "elephant eye land"). Using primarily estate-grown fruit, Elephant Island makes its dry wines from pears, apples, cherries, blackcurrants and quince.

Excellent dessert wines also are made. These include an apricot wine made from the Goldrich variety, which is rarely grown because of its acidic skin. That tartness is a virtue for producing a zesty, well-balanced late-harvest wine. Elephant Island was the first to make an ice cider in British Columbia, using Fuji apples picked and crushed after being frozen naturally on the trees. One of the most intense wines made here is Stellaport, a wood-aged dessert style made with Stella cherries. Successive vintages of this wine are being held back to produce a five-vintage, solera-style wine.

THE FORT WINE COMPANY
26151 84th Avenue, Fort Langley, BC, V1M 3M6.
Tel: 604 857 1101; Website: www.thefortwineco.com

Now the largest fruit winery in western Canada, The Fort was launched when a collapse in fresh berry prices sent cranberry grower Wade Bauck looking for ways to add value to the crop from his eight-hectare farm. The winery opened in 2001, offering a medley that included wines from cranberry, blueberry, and raspberry. Subsequently, The Fort has added wines from peaches, strawberries, blackberries, and apples, in both dry and fortified dessert styles. The winery, now with a capacity to make 30,000 cases annually, considers its cranberry wines to be its flagship. Both red and white cranberry wines are made, as well as a fortified dessert wine called Cranberry Klondike. Happily for the wine business, the medical community has recently begun to tout the health benefits of the fruit. Perhaps this is a case of déjà vu: the berry is indigenous to North America and the aboriginals have been aware of its beneficial properties for a very long time. The Fort also produces fruit wines under contract for Blue Heron Winery at Pitt Meadows, on the north side of the Fraser, and for Wellbrook Winery in Delta, south of Vancouver.

HONEYMOON BAY WILD BLACKBERRY WINERY
Honeymoon Bay, BC, V0R 1Y0.
Tel: 250 749 4681

Five years in the planning, this winery opened on Cowichan Lake in the summer of 2004, operated by Ray Mogg. It was conceived by Merna and Walter Moffat, who had retired here in the early 1990s. They saw the winery as a modest economic development project in a community that formerly thrived on forestry and still is a tourist destination. Wines are produced from the succulent Himalayan blackberry, which grows in wild profusion on Vancouver Island.

HORNBY ISLAND WINERY
7000 Anderson Drive, Hornby Island, BC, V0R 1Z0.
Tel: 250 335 3019; Website: www.hornbywine.com

Primarily a producer of cranberry, currant, blackberry, and gooseberry wines, Hornby Island Winery is being launched in 2005 by yet another of those Renaissance personalities one finds in Canadian wine. John Grayson started as a classical musician, composer, and instrument maker. He discovered wine while studying in California, where he worked with Harry Partch, a giant of avant-garde American music. When the winery opens, Grayson intends to merge his two interests by staging concerts at the winery.

LA FRAMBOISIERE DES 3

17 Rue du Domaine, Saint-Pacôme, Comté de Kamouraska, QC, GOL 3X0.

Tel: 418 852 2159; Website: www.lepacomois.qc.ca

Véronique Gagné was in her sixties when she began taking winemaking courses. She and her husband, Pierre Ouellet, who died in 1993, had been raspberry growers since 1987. In 1994 she launched a raspberry-based apéritif called Le Pacômois. The range has now been expanded to include Le Pier-O, a sweet apéritif with raspberries and blueberries; La Différence, a dessert wine from strawberries, raspberries, and blueberries; Cap au Diable, a blueberry dessert wine, and Lune d'Hiver, an apple-based table wine.

LUNENBURG COUNTY WINERY

813 Walburne Road, RR3, Mahone Bay, Newburne, NS, B0J 2E0.

Tel: 902 644 2415; Website: www.canada-wine.com

This winery sells one of the most unusually-named fruit wines: Sambucus Canadensis (the Latin name for the American elderberry bush). The name owes something to the fact that Daniel and Heather Sanft, who operate this winery, make twenty-three other wines and are running out of names. Daniel grows most of the winery's fruit on this forty-hectare farm half an hour from Lunenburg. He planted the small vineyard in 1984, with varieties such as Baco Noir, New York Muscat, and Michurinetz. "Grapes are just one more fruit to us," he says. The winery opened in 1994. Daniel believes that blueberry and pear are the flagship wines. He also produces wines with honey, raspberry, strawberry, peach, apple, cranberry, blackcurrant, maple syrup, kiwi fruit, apricot, gooseberry, and grapes. Wines are sold through the provincial liquor stores and in export markets.

KAWARTHA COUNTRY WINES

2275 County Road 36, Buckhorn, ON, K0L 2J0.

Tel: 705 657 9916; Website: www.kawarthacountrywines.ca

John Rufa opened this winery after encouragement from friends who admired his fruit wines. He offers an astonishing array, including rhubarb, strawberry, peach, pear, and blends involving apples. Much of his raw material comes from the winery's nine hectares of fruit and berry trees. He also has a test plot of grape vines; in addition, he buys grapes from Niagara vineyards. Rufa makes wines in four styles – dry, off-dry, sweet, and dessert – for "every taste and wine occasion". A rich and sweet maple syrup wine is among the more original.

MARLEY FARM WINERY

1831D Mount Newton Cross Road, Saanichton, BC, V8M 1L1.

Tel: 250 652 8667; Website: www.marleyfarm.ca

Visitors to this winery in the hobby-farm countryside north of Victoria should expect an eclectic choice of fruit and grape wines. Michael Marley is a cousin of reggae musician Bob Marley. His wife Beverly had dabbled for years with fruit wines but when the family got serious enough about a winery to plant vines on their farm, they retaining consulting winemaker Eric von Krosigk. The winery opened in 2003 with fruit wines from kiwi, raspberry, blackberry, and loganberry, and grape wines from Pinot Gris and Pinot Noir.

MEADOW LANE WINERY

44892 Talbot Lane, St Thomas, ON, N5P 3S7.

Tel: 519 633 1933; Website: www.meadowlanewinery.com

Meadow Lane is another case of a hobby that has now been taken to the professional level by owners, Walter and Debbie Myszko (pronounced mish-ko). They purchased an eighteen-hectare farm on a busy highway just outside St Thomas, planted a variety of berries, and opened a winery in late 1998. Meadow Lane produces between 14,000 and 23,000 litres of wine annually. Its top-selling wine is blueberry, followed by cranberry and kiwi. The wines are finished in the medium-sweet style that Walter thinks best expresses the flavours of the fruits. "I would call them social wines," he says. In 2000, the couple also began developing a three-hectare vineyard. The first variety planted was Zweigelt. "I wanted to go with something different," explains Walter. He has added Cabernet Franc, Merlot, and Geisenheim 322, and will plant Seyval Blanc and Chardonnay in 2005. Vine damage from late winter frosts in several recent winters delayed the first harvest of Zweigelt to 2004.

MUSKOKA LAKES WINERY

Johnston's Cranberry Marsh, 1074 Cranberry Road, PO Box 24, Bala, ON, P0C 1A0.

Tel: 705 762 3203; Website: www.cranberry.ca

A seminal figure in the Canadian cranberry industry, Orville Johnston planted what is now the country's oldest commercial cranberry marsh in northern Ontario in 1952. In 1969, he was the consultant when a second one was developed on the Iroquois Nation's Gibson Reserve. Today, the Johnston marsh is run by Orville's son, Murray and his wife Wendy Hogarth. With the assistance of Niagara winemaker Jim Warren (*see* page 98), they launched the winery in 2001 with 600 cases of cranberry wine, which was all sold within weeks. Now, with cousin Steve Johnston making the wine, they are producing about 3,000 cases a year, most sold from the cellar door.

The best-selling wines are cranberry and a cranberry/blueberry blend; both are off-dry. The winery believes it was the first in Canada to release a white cranberry wine. This is made from berries that are fully ripe but have not been touched by the autumn frost that brings out the red pigmentation. The winery makes two dry wines from wild blueberries, one of them oak-aged, that compete on the table with grape wines. In 2004, the winery added a light, refreshing fruit wine spritzer, a successful blend of white cranberry and carbonated water, called Muskoka Moment.

NORFOLK ESTATE WINERY

488 West Quarter Line, RR 1, St Williams, ON, N0E 1P0.

Tel: 519 586 2237

When tobacco and apple grower George Benko switched from tobacco in 1984, he committed totally to apples, including many exotic new varieties. In 1995 he and Shirley, his wife, opened Ontario's first apple winery. Among those wines is Ice Apple Wine, a gold medal winner in various competitions, and a creative companion called Ice Apple Ginseng. There is a root of ginseng in each bottle.

NOTRE DAME WINES

29 Durrell Street, Twillingate, NL, A0G 1Y0.

Tel: 709 884 2707; Website: www3.nf.sympatico.ca/weilwinery

This fruit winery, which opened in 1998, emerged from what winemaker and co-proprietor Winston Jennings describes as a traditional era when money was hard to come by in Newfoundland. "If you wanted wine, you had to make it," he says. "I made my first bottle of wine when I was sixteen years old." Jennings makes a large selection of wines with wild and cultivated fruit. His favourite is raspberry, made both in a dry and a medium sweet style. There are wines here that one is unlikely to find anywhere else because they are made with native berries. There is, for example, a dogberry wine (Newfoundland's name for the mountain ash berry), recommended with wild game. There is a cloudberry wine made from a yellow marsh berry inexplicably called bakeapple in Newfoundland. Other unusual wines are partridgeberry (a cranberry cousin known elsewhere as lingonberry), and black crowberry, a round black fruit called blackberry in Newfoundland.

Jennings also makes blueberry wine. It is his theory that the Vikings, perhaps the first Europeans to land on Newfoundland, called the place Vineland because they mistook the native blueberries for grapes.

OCALA ORCHARDS FARM WINERY
971 High Point Road, Port Perry, ON, L9L 1B3.
Tel: 905 985 9924; Website: www.ocalawinery.com

The Smith family has lived on this forty-hectare property for three generations, since 1915. Irwin Smith and his wife Alissa took over the farm in 1991. The following year, he planted 300 vines in a test plot – Gamay and Chardonnay for personal winemaking and table grapes for market. When those vines thrived, Smith undertook a significant extension of the vineyard in 1994. Port Perry is a challenging new vineyard area about an hour north-east of Toronto. The varieties grown include some surprises for a vineyard this far away from the moderating influence of Lake Ontario. Smith says:

> It is recognized that, although the Ocala location is excellent for orchard fruits, winter temperatures (two times out of ten) are severe enough to damage the buds, and greatly limit next year's crop.

There are safe bets among other varieties here: Riesling, Chardonnay, Pinot Gris, Auxerrois, Muscat, Vidal, Seyval, Baco Noir, and Maréchal Foch. More recently, Smith has added several winter-hardy Minnesota varieties, such as Prairie Star and Frontenac. These will "secure house wine production in the event of a severe winter." The winery opened in 1995 in a renovated 100-year old dairy barn. Production now averages 30,000 bottles a year, with fruit wines comprising sixty per cent. The orchard includes apples, cherries, plums, and pears. The farm also produces blackcurrants, raspberries, elderberries, gooseberries, and hardy kiwis. "In all my wines, my effort is to make the taste of the fruit the primary component," Smith says.

Ocala also makes Icewine but the winery, some of whose wines are VQA certified, is forbidden by VQA to use that term because the winery is not in one of Ontario's designated viticultural areas. Smith simply labels the wine as Vin de Glace, the use of which term is not restricted. The irony, in his view, is that Ocala has better conditions for Icewine production than most Ontario wineries:

> We have been able to harvest Icewine grapes as early as the first week in December. New Year's Eve has been the latest. More moderate areas in Ontario have on occasion struggled into late January.

PERKINS MAPLERY

1825 Robinson Road, Dunham, QC, JOE 1M0.

Tel: 450 538 3607

Winemaker Neil Perkins is the sixth generation on this farm which his family settled in 1805. He claims the distinction of making Québec's first maple wine, called Ode Erable: the 1996 is described as a full-bodied, golden wine to be paired with game, Chinese food or cheese. His 1997 is semi-dry. In 2002, he produced a low-alcohol maple liqueur. These three are all made by fermenting maple syrup. In 2000, Perkins made a dry white wine by fermenting the maple sap itself. Organic practices are employed.

RIGBY ORCHARDS ESTATE WINERY

Killarney, MB, R0K 1G0. (No public tasting room.)

Tel: 204 523 8879

Licensed in 1999, this winery started life as a raspberry juice business developed by Grant Rigby. The farm has grown to 324 hectares and Rigby has been running it since 1978. In addition to canola and other speciality crops, he has 6.5 hectares of organically-grown Boyne raspberry, a quality variety developed in Manitoba. Rigby identifies the variety of berry on the labels: Boyne for raspberry, and Alder and Lomond for blackcurrants. The wines are made in two styles. The semi-dry wines are recommended as apéritifs or with food while the sweet wines are dessert wines. The wines are sold through liquor stores in Manitoba and private wine stores in Alberta. Rigby usually persuades store managers to display them with table wines, not fruit wines. "There is enough strength of colour and robustness to the wines that they belong with Canadian red wines," he says. "Nobody looks for a quality wine in the fruit wine section."

RODRIGUES WINERY

Whitbourne, NL, A0B 3K0.

Tel: 709 759 3003; Website: www.rodrigueswinery.com

Now Canada's largest fruit winery (annual production of 17,000 cases), Rodrigues Winery was Newfoundland's first when it opened in 1993. The force behind it is an entrepreneurial dentist, Hilary Rodrigues and his Burgundy-born wife, Marie-France. In 1986 he bought the Markland Cottage Hospital when its medical services moved to a new clinic, and converted it to a winery. Its first release was 300 cases of what has become the flagship, a product called Exotique Wild Semi-Sweet Blueberry wine.

There is now a whole range under the Exotique tag, including lingonberry, cloudberry, strawberry, raspberry, and plum. The cloudberry is a rare and comparatively costly dessert wine, made with wild Labrador berries that are somewhat like raspberries. Laboriously picked from bushes close to the ground, cloudberries at $5 a pound are the most expensive wild berry purchased by the winery. Rodrigues also has a distillery licence and can triple distil products with a European-made pot still. He is currently developing several unique vodkas.

The winery is one of the few in Canada fully certified to produce kosher wines – and to the strictest level, kosher for Passover. Great efforts have been taken to make wines free from chemical contaminants, even sulphur. Many of the fruits are picked in the wild or secured from organic farms:

> Since we make clean wines with no contaminants, we wanted to find a group that would appreciate them and that had a history of drinking fruit wines. The Jewish community fits the bill.

The next venture is a line of fruit products called nutraceuticals. These include fruit juices, power drinks, and related products aimed at the health market. "Niche markets for organic, kosher, and value-added foods exist all over the world," Rodrigues says. Because the juicing technology extracts almost all the colour in fruits and berries, it will also benefit the wines:

> I have always want to make health products. Our wines are clean, healthy, and they are good for you. But we are diversifying because we do not know how far we can go with fruit wines. Fruit wines will be a division where we will be selling around 20,000 cases; at the moment, that is our projection.

RUSH CREEK WINES

RR 2, Jamestown Line, Aylmer, ON, N5H 2R2.
Tel: 519 773 5432; Website: www.rushcreekwines.com

Opened in 1997 as an outlet for the products of a twenty-three-hectare orchard, this winery is operated by Kim Flintoft and his wife Wendy. Primarily using their own fruit, they produce more than two dozen wines, including iced strawberry, peach, gooseberry, an unusual wine called Watermelon Splash, and several meads and a maple-flavoured wine. Many are certified as kosher. In 2001, Rush Creek was recognized by its peers as the fruit winery of the year.

SCOTCH BLOCK WINERY

RR 5, 9365 10th Sideroad, Milton, ON, L9T 2X9.

Tel: 905 878 5807; Website: www.scotchblock.com

Bert and Lauraine Andrews converted this rundown forty-hectare property into a berry farm. Expanding since with leased land, they now farm 317 hectares. The Scotch Block winery opened in 1999, providing an additional outlet for substantial crops of strawberries, raspberries, blueberries, elderberries, apples, and blackcurrants. The recent planting of 3.2 hectares of vines has enabled them to add grape wines, building the list to about three dozen fruit and grape wines.

The legendary winemaker, Jim Warren, who founded both the Fruit Wines of Canada association and Stoney Ridge winery (*see* page 98), recommended Fred Bulbeck, one of his protegés, to make the wines at Scotch Block. Bulbeck started there in 2002 by making Black Currant Obsession, a dessert wine that caused a sensation in the winery tasting room. It is one of six blackcurrant wines made at Scotch Block. The best-seller and the driest is Regal Black Currant, a wine made to drink with food.

SPILLER ESTATE WINERY

475 Upper Bench Road North, Penticton, BC, V2A 8T4.

Tel: 250 490 4162; Website: www.spillerestates.com

Lynn and Keith Holman have been fruit growers for more than twenty-five years, with a substantial forty hectares of orchard. Helped by a professional winemaker, they offer wines crafted to capture vivid flavours. The Holmans in 2004 acquired the nearby Benchland Estates winery.

SUNNYBROOK FARM ESTATE WINERY

1425 Lakeshore Road, Niagara-on-the-Lake, ON, L0S 1J0.

Tel: 905 468 1122; Website: www.sunnybrookfarmwinery.com

Orchardists Gerald Goertz and his wife Vivien opened the 4.5-hectare Sunnybrook Farm, three kilometres (1.9 miles) from Niagara-on-the-Lake, in 1993, claiming it to be Ontario's first licensed fruit winery. Being the only fruit winery in the Niagara Peninsula was not easy. When resistance from established grape wineries threatened to frustrate his application, Goertz made 100 cases of grape wine, just enough to qualify for membership of the Wine Council of Ontario. Since that time, the production has been entirely "wine from trees", as he once termed it. Pointedly, he refers to a dictionary definition that says wine is "fermented juice of the grape, or other fruit". Goertz believes the Quality Certified programme (see page 260) has helped to bring credibility to fruit wines. "People used to think fruit wine was what

Uncle George made forty years ago and is still in the basement because nobody would drink it," Goertz says.

Goertz does not think that fruit wines should mimic grape wines, although Sunnybrook's Iced Peach had been compared to Vidal Icewine. "My philosophy is to make the wine taste as close to the fruit as possible," he explains. Consumers seldom eat wine grapes, he explains, and do not come to wines expecting them to taste like grapes; but because consumers eat fruit, they want the wines to reflect those familiar flavours. Most fruit wines are sweet, even if only slightly so, because the raw fruit that people eat always contains natural sugar. The only Sunnybrook wine that is completely dry is called Poire Sec, made with the juice of Bartlett and Bosc pears. Goertz recommends seafood with this wine. The winery's Bosc Pear wine, recommended with cheese, is slightly sweet. The winery's apple, plum, and cherry wines all have a barely perceptible sweetness, allowing them to be paired with many main course dishes. "I find that fruit wines are much more versatile for pairing with food than grape wines," Goertz maintains.

For those who prefer sweet wines, Goertz has been making iced fruit wines since 1995. These are made by freezing the fruit, crushing it, and then extracting that sugar-rich fraction of the juice that remains unfrozen. At first, Goertz encountered objections to the term "iced" from Icewine producers. He got around this by dubbing his first iced wine "Winter Pear". The Icewine producers stopped objecting after the fruit wineries launched their QC standards programme. In addition to Winter Pear, Goertz now makes Iced Apple, Iced Cherry, Iced Apricot, and Iced Peach wines.

TIERNEY POINT WINERY
5086 Route 1, Pennfield, NB, E5H 1Y5.
Tel: 506 755 6942
This fruit winery opened in 2001, based on a New Brunswick blueberry and cranberry farm. Ken Hawkins and his wife Serri make blueberry, cranberry, rhubarb, and strawberry wines.

TELDER BERRY FARM AND WINERY
1251 Enfield Road, Nine Mile River, NS, B3S 2T7.
Tel: 902 883 8433; Website: www.telderberrywines.com
This winery was opened in 1993, not far from Halifax International Airport, to exploit the excellent fruits that Robert and Barbera Telder had been

growing on the farm they established in 1975. Since 1997, the winery has been operated by the Telders' son and daughter-in-law, Brian and Lisa. The flagship blueberry wine now has been joined by wines from apples, pears, cranberries, raspberries and strawberries. For a change of pace, the winery also produces a citrus-flavoured sangria-style and a mulled apple wine.

TUDDENHAM FARMS
Route 1, Oak Bay, St Stephen, NB, E3L 2X1.

Tel: 506 466 1840

Todd Tuddenham opened this farm winery in 2001 to commercialize the successful blueberry wines that his mother, Janet, had been making as a hobby. The fruit comes from a large blueberry farm that has been in the family since 1923. The wine shop is just off the main highway near Oak Bay.

WAGNER ESTATE WINERY
1222 8th Concession, Maidstone, ON, N0R 1K0.

Tel: 519 723 4807

In 1984, Harold Wagner and his wife Janice bought this farm next to a busy expressway, about a thirty-minute drive from Windsor. The winery is a natural extension. "There is a certain romance to owning a winery," Wagner says. "I was in pig farming. There's no romance in pig farming." The winery opened with a crisply dry apple wine, labelled Saddle Notch – in keeping with the equestrian theme, his daughter's pony appears on labels. Wagner also offers wines from raspberries, strawberries, pears, and blueberries, including several iced wines. He is experimenting with other fruits, and is testing the market with two generic grape wines made at another winery.

WELLBROOK WINERY
4626 88th Street, Delta, BC, V4K 3N3.

Tel: 604 946 1868; Website: www.wellbrookwinery.com

Wellbrook offers a selection of fruit wines, notably blueberry and cranberry. The wine shop also sells the pure blueberry and cranberry juices that berry farmer Terry Bremner developed in 2000 and now distributes to gourmet food shops on the west coast.

WESTHAM ISLAND ESTATE WINERY
2170 Westham Island Road, Delta, BC, V4K 3N2.

Tel: 604 946 7471

Lorraine Bissett and her family have operated a fourteen-hectare fruit farm on Westham Island for more than twenty-five years. The farm, which also includes grape vines, provides the winery's raw material. Veteran winemaker Ron Taylor makes a broad and eclectic range here, including wines from peaches, pumpkins, blackberries, strawberries, raspberries, blackcurrants, and the rare tayberry (a cross of raspberry and blackberry). The winery's flagship is a dry gooseberry wine, aptly named SnoGoos for the vast flocks of snow geese that migrate through the island each autumn.

WILLIAMSDALE WINERY
1330 Collingwood Road, Williamsdale, NS, B0M 1E0.
Tel: 902 686 3117
Established in 1987, this producer specializes in making wines from the blueberries grown in northern Nova Scotia.

WINEGARDEN ESTATE
851 Route 970, Baie Verte, NB, E4M 1Z7.
Tel: 506 538 7405; Website: www.winegardenestate.com
It is because of Werner and Roswitha Rosswog that there now are half a dozen producers of wines and ciders in New Brunswick. They broke the ground by lobbying the government for the appropriate regulations and succeeded in getting one of the most flexible regulatory regimes in Atlantic Canada. One example is that producers are not limited to selling only their own products at their cellar door, and Winegarden stocks nearly all New Brunswick's wines and spirits. Making wine and distilled spirits seemed a natural idea to the Rosswogs, who made both wine and spirits in Germany before coming to Canada in 1983.

"Here in the Maritimes, I saw a lot of fruit falling to the ground, especially apples," Werner recalls. "I thought, why not apply for a distillery licence?" That was secured in 1991, followed in 1997 by the first fruit winery licence in New Brunswick. The Rosswogs then organized a winemaking cooperative so that several other producers could make fruit wines without immediately setting up independent operations. "We are quite proud to show the world that New Brunswick has more than Christmas trees," he laughs. Winegarden now has about fifty products spanning the alcoholic range, included a forty-degree schnapps named Johnny Ziegler, after Werner's grandfather, who was a distiller. The first wine, released in 1997, was a dry apple beverage called Dry Adam, with only seven degrees of alcohol. In between are table wines. In the vineyard Rosswog has planted Maréchal Foch, Éona, and L'Acadie. He also has wines made from Ontario grapes since the winery, before it planted grapes, had secured the right to use fruit from elsewhere.

LA VINERIE DU KILDARE

205 Rue Louis-Bazinet, Joliette, QC, J6E 7J5

Tel: 450 756 1525; Website: www.vinderable.com

Agronomist Janick Choquette and microbiologist Chantal Lemieux, whose primary business is the production of maple syrup and related products, began developing alcoholic maple beverages in 1995. They offer four products. Grand Esprit is fortified, L'Esprit d'Érable, is an organically-made dessert wine while Le Marie-Chantal is an apéritif. One of the more original products is La Désirable, which combines maple syrup and cream. It is "an artisanal product," the winery warns on its website. "One cannot always guarantee its stability perfectly."

MEAD HOUSES

INTERMIEL

10291 Rang de La Fresnière, Mirabel, Saint-Benoît, QC, J7N 3M3.

Tel: 450 258 2713; Website: www.intermiel.com

Intermiel was founded in 1976 by Christian and Viviane Macle, who have developed the business into one of Quebec's major honey farms, with about 2,000 hives. Honey wines were launched in 1991. Today, Intermiel is the largest of the dozen or so Québec honey producers who make mead. Its meads all show clean, delicate aromas and flavours of the underlying honey or fruit. Most are dry enough to be matched with various foods. Bouquet Printanier, almost dry, is comparable to a fresh and fruity white grape wine, has thirteen degrees of alcohol, and is served with seafood. There are two lighter, off-dry honey wines: Mélilot, made with clover honey, and Verge d'Or, made with golden rod honey. Benoîte, which has fourteen degrees of alcohol and a more unctuous finish, is both an apéritif and a dessert wine.

Winemaker André Abi Raad also blends fruit, including raspberries, blueberries and blackcurrants with honey in meads. Perhaps the most exotic of his meads is Rosée, a wine with twelve degrees of alcohol made by fermenting honey with a maceration of cranberries and rose petals. The rose petals contribute a spicy aroma while the cranberries provide crisp balance. Abi Raad believes his wines should be consumed when they are fresh.

"Mead is totally different when it is aged," he says. Abi Raad has also explored the vinous possibilities of maple syrup. He did not care for wines made from fermented maple sap. Instead, he crafted a richly-flavoured maple liquor, bronze in colour, with twenty-two degrees of alcohol. He recommends it with maple desserts "or even on the rocks as a digestif".

MIDDLE MOUNTAIN MEAD

3505 Euston Road, Hornby Island, BC, V0R 1Z0

Tel: 250 335 1392; Website: www.middlemountainmead.com

Mead maker Campbell Graham and his wife, Helen Grond launched their mead house in 2004. In addition to purchasing honey, they have deployed bee hives on their farm, where Grond has planted a substantial amount of lavender. "I expect that will make lovely mead," Graham says. "And we are sowing our meadow areas with fireweed; I know the fireweed honey will make great mead."

MUNRO HONEY AND MEADERY

3115 River Street, Alvinston, ON, N0N 1A0.

Tel: 519 847 5333; Website: www.munrohoney.com

Fourth generation beekeepers, brothers Davis and John Bryans took over this honey business from their parents in 1989. The brothers, leading members of the Ontario Beekeepers Association, manage 2,500 hives and process honey products in a large, modern plant in Alviston in southwest Ontario. For at least fifteen years, John has been refining old mead recipes to make products that he believes will appeal to wine enthusiasts. Mead sales were launched in 2000. Bryans claims that this is Ontario's only meadery, defining that as a business that makes honey wine from honey produced in its own hives. The six meads that Bryans offered in 2004 ranged in style from dry to sweet. John suggests that the dry mead, subtle in its flavour, often surprises consumers expecting a big punch of sweetness from honey products. He does make a sweet mead, designed to be an after-dinner drink. Between these two stylistic bookmarks, he produces meads flavoured with blueberry, cranberry, and raspberry. Others are under development. "I try to add a new flavour each year," he says.

TUGWELL CREEK HONEY FARM AND MEADERY

8750 West Coast Road, Sooke, BC, V0S 1N0.

Tel: 250 642 1956; Website: www.tugwellcreekfarm.com

Robert Liptrot and Dana LeComte opened British Columbia's first meadery in 2003, after a long apprenticeship with bees. "I have been keeping bees since I was seven years old," says Liptrot. Now he has about 100 hives in the alpine meadows of the island's mountains. Most of the honey produced is sold, but enough is retained to produce about 5,000 litres of mead annually. His range includes a dry oak-aged vintage mead, a dessert style, a spiced mead, and a berry-flavoured mead. In the ancient tradition of meads, these latter two are called Metheglin and Melomel.

Other mead producers

FERME APICOLE DESROCHERS
113 Rang 2 Gravel, Ferme-Neuve, QC, J0W 1CO.
Tel: 819 587 3471

HYDROMEL DE LA FEE
250 Rang Saint-Édouard, Saint-Philibert, QC.
Tel: 418 228 7525

HYDROMELERIE LES SAULES
1135 Rue Denisson Est, Granby, QC, J2G 8C7.
Tel: 450 372 3403; Website: www.hydromel.ca

HYDROMELLERIE LES VINS MUSTIER GERZER
3299 Route 209 Saint-Antoine-Abbé, QC, J0S 1E0.
Tel 450 826 4609

LES RUCHERS PROMIEL (MUSEE DE L'ABEILLE)
8862 Boulevard Sainte-Anne, Château-Richer, QC, G0A 1N0.
Tel: 418 824 4411

LE RUCHER BERNARD BEE BEC
152 Rue Principale, Beebe Plain, Stanstead, QC.
Tel: 819 876 2800

LE VIEUX MOULIN
141 Route de la Mer, Sainte-Flavie, QC, G0J 2L0.
Tel: 418 775 8383; Website: www.vieuxmoulin.qc.ca

Appendix
Vintage ratings

The following ratings should be read as indicative because the Canadian wine industry is in total flux. Vineyard development, vintner education, and the application of technology are ongoing.

	Ontario*			British Columbia**	
	White	Red		White	Red
2003	8	7	2004	7.5	9
2002	9	9.5	2003	8	9
2001	8.5	8.5	2002	9.5	9.5
2000	8.5	8	2001	9	7.5
1999	8.5	8.5	2000	9	9
1998	8.5	9	1999	7	6.5
1997	7	7	1998	7.5	8.5
1996	7	6	1997	8.5	8
1995	8	9	1996	6	5
1994	7.5	6.5	1995	7	7
1993	8.5	8	1994	8	9
1992	7.5	5	1993	7	7
			1992	8	8.5

	Nova Scotia***	
2004	6	6
2003	8	8
2002	7	7
2001	9	9
2000	8	8
1999	9	9

* *Adapted from ratings by the Wine Council of Ontario, Konrad Ejbich, and the Ontario Wine Society.*
** *Rated by the author.*
*** *Rated by Jürg Stutz of Domaine de Grand Pré.*

Index